# DEMOGRAPHIC APPLICATIONS OF
EVENT HISTORY ANALYSIS

The International Union for the Scientific Study of Population Problems was set up in 1928, with Dr Raymond Pearl as President. At that time the Union's main purpose was to promote international scientific co-operation to study the various aspects of population problems, through national committees and through its members themselves. In 1947 the International Union for the Scientific Study of Population (IUSSP) was reconstituted into its present form. It expanded its activities to:

- stimulate research on population
- develop interest in demographic matters among governments, national and international organizations, scientific bodies, and the general public
- foster relations between people involved in population studies
- disseminate scientific knowledge on population.

The principal ways through which the IUSSP currently achieves its aims are:

- organization of worldwide or regional conferences operations of Scientific Committees under the responsibility of the Council
- organization of training courses
- publication of conference proceedings and committee reports.

Demography can be defined by its field of study and its analytical methods. Accordingly, it can be regarded as the scientific study of human populations primarily with respect to their size, their structure, and their development. For reasons which are related to the history of the discipline, the demographic method is essentially inductive: progress in the knowledge results from the improvement of observation, the sophistication of measurement methods, the search for regularities and stable factors leading to the formulation of explanatory models. In conclusion, the three objectives of demographic analysis are to describe, measure, and analyse.

**International Studies in Demography** is the outcome of an agreement concluded by the IUSSP and the Oxford University Press. This joint series is expected to reflect the broad range of the Union's activities and, in the first instance, will be based on the seminars organized by the Union. The Editorial Board of the series is comprised of:

# Demographic Applications of Event History Analysis

Editors:

JAMES TRUSSELL
RICHARD HANKINSON
JUDITH TILTON

CLARENDON PRESS · OXFORD
1992

Oxford University Press, Walton Street, Oxford OX2 6DP

Oxford   New York   Toronto
Delhi   Bombay   Calcutta   Madras   Karachi
Petaling Jaya   Singapore   Hong Kong   Tokyo
Nairobi   Dar es Salaam   Cape Town
Melbourne   Auckland
and associated companies in
Berlin   Ibadan

Oxford is a trade mark of Oxford University Press

Published in the United States
by Oxford University Press, New York

British Library Cataloguing in Publication Data
Data available

Library of Congress Cataloging in Publication Data
Demographic applications of event history analysis/editors:
James Trussell, Richard Hankinson, Judith Tilton.
p.   cm.
Includes bibliographical references and index.
1. Event history analysis.   I. Trussell, James.   II. Hankinson,
Richard R. B.   III. Tilton, Judith.
H61.D3385 1992     304.6—dc20     91–30485
ISBN 0–19–828386–5

Typeset by
Pure Tech Corporation, Pondicherry, India
Printed in Great Britain by
Bookcraft (Bath) Ltd,
Midsomer Norton, Avon

# Acknowledgements

*Chapter 1*

The work of Drs Manton and Woodbury was supported by NIA Grants AG01159–07, AG03188–06, and AG07025. Dr Singer's work was supported by NIA Contract No. NO1-AG-02105.

*Chapter 2*

Work on this project was supported by NIH Grant No. RO1–HD11720–08 and by unsponsored research funds allocated by Princeton University. The authors are grateful to Statistics Sweden for permission to use the 1981 survey *Women in Sweden*, and to Jan Hoem for his patient answers to their many inquiries concerning both the data and life and love in Sweden.

*Chapter 3*

The authors are grateful to Mike Murphy and Tapani Valkonen for discussions and arguments that helped them formulate elements of their approach and the theoretical position of this chapter. R. Ingelhart and W. Jagodzinsky convinced the authors of the need to include some indicator of personal values in their investigations. Charles Westoff underlined the importance of including the planning status of each child during the preparations of the questionnaire for the 1981 Swedish Fertility Survey. Under the authors' direction, Pilkyun Shin-Lindström has competently carried out analyses of the dissolution of second unions. During part of the work with this chapter, the authors enjoyed the hospitality of the Center for Demography and Ecology in the University of Wisconsin at Madison. They wish to acknowledge partial support from the National Institute of Child Health and Human Development Center Grant No. HD 05876, and from the William and Flora Hewlett Foundation for Research and Training.

*Chapter 6*

Financial support from the Tercentenary Foundation of the Royal Bank of Sweden is gratefully acknowledged. Thanks are also due to Professor Jan Hoem and his colleagues at the Demography Section of the University of Stockholm for their hospitality and help, and to Statistics Sweden for use of their 1981 *Women in Sweden* survey.

*Chapter 7*

This research was supported by NIH Grant No. HD–19226 to NORC. The authors have benefited from the comments of Elja Arjas, Ricardo Barros, D. R. Cox, and James Trussell. This chapter forms part of a series of papers. Heckman and Walker (1990*b*) presents a succinct summary of the main economic results. Heckman and Walker (1990*a*) presents a more complete discussion of the statistical models and empirical results.

*Chapter 8*

This research was supported by grants from the National Science Foundation (NSF–SES–83–11428) and from the National Institute of Mental Health (NIMH MH 37188). Whilst accepting responsibility for errors, the author acknowledges useful discussions with Dan Heitjan and Mark Schluchter.

*Chapter 10*

It was on Jan Hoem's initiative that the authors undertook this study. They are grateful to him, and to Britta Hoem, for letting them use their data, and for their many helpful comments during the preparation of this chapter.

# Contents

# Editors and Contributors

| | |
|---|---|
| Elja Arjas | Department of Applied Mathematics and Statistics, University of Oulu |
| Daniel Courgeau | Institut National d'Études Démographiques, Paris |
| Ian D. Diamond | Department of Social Statistics, University of Southampton |
| James J. Heckman | Department of Economics, University of Chicago |
| Richard Hankinson | Office of Population Research, Princeton University |
| Britta Hoem | Statistics Sweden, Stockholm |
| Jan M. Hoem | Demography Unit, Stockholm University |
| Pekka Kangas | Department of Applied Mathematics and Statistics, University of Oulu |
| Éva Lelièvre | Institut National d'Études Démographiques, Paris |
| Roderick J. A. Little | Department of Biomathematics, School of Medicine, University of California at Los Angeles |
| John W. McDonald | Department of Social Statistics, University of Southampton |
| Kenneth G. Manton | Center for Demographic Studies, Duke University |
| Mark Montgomery | Department of Economics, State University of New York, Stony Brook |
| Michael Murphy | Department of Population Studies, London School of Economics and Political Science |
| Germán Rodríguez | Office of Population Research, Princeton University |
| Burton Singer | Department of Epidemiology and Public Health, Yale University |
| Judith Tilton | Office of Population Research, Princeton University |
| James Trussell | Office of Population Research, Princeton University |
| Barbara Vaughan | Office of Population Research, Princeton University |
| James R. Walker | Department of Economics, University of Wisconsin |
| Max A. Woodbury | Center for Demographic Studies, Duke University |

# Introduction

JAMES TRUSSELL

This book emanates from a seminar on Event History Analysis, which was sponsored jointly by the Institut National d'Études Démographiques (INED) and the International Union for the Scientific Study of Population (IUSSP), held in Paris from 14 to 17 March 1988. A selection of the papers presented at that seminar, some of which have been extensively revised to reflect the discussion there, forms this volume.

During the past few years, advances have been made in the study of individual life histories (e.g. family or occupational histories) for two reasons. First, the number of surveys undertaken throughout the world to collect detailed information on the timing of events in individual lives (including fertility surveys, surveys on the family, and occupation and migration histories) is increasing. Such detailed information cannot easily be analysed with conventional statistical methods such as ordinary linear regression, so that the increase in data has not necessarily led to commensurate advances in knowledge. Simultaneously, however, there has been great progress in developing methods to analyse such data. Hazard models (or multivariate life tables) permit the investigator to disentangle the effects of several explanatory variables on the risk that an event will occur; they also provide an attractive alternative to conventional simultaneous-equations techniques for analysing concurrent processes such as female labour force participation and fertility.

Although recent work has greatly advanced the analytical power of the tools available to demographers, two challenges remain. First, there are unresolved technical and practical issues apparent in the literature, particularly revolving around the problems of unmeasured heterogeneity and assessing goodness of fit. Second, most demographers and other social scientists have only limited experience with the new techniques and have not applied them in their own work. Therefore, the IUSSP working group on event history analysis thought that the time was ripe for the publication of a volume that illustrates the use of the new techniques, and that contains work on the current frontiers of methodological understanding. Nevertheless, this volume is *not* intended to be a textbook on the analysis of event history data; instead, those interested are referred to any of several excellent standard references (Kalbfleisch and Prentice 1980; Allison 1984; Cox and Oakes 1984; Tuma and Hannan 1984; Namboodiri and Suchindran 1987; Courgeau and Lelièvre 1989).

The volume, like the seminar, divides naturally into three distinct parts: a summary of the work on incorporating unmeasured heterogeneity into the analysis of event histories; a series of 'competitions' in which pairs of teams are assigned to analyse the same topic using the same data; and a discussion of other methodological issues such as the treatment of missing data, the analysis of current-status data, and the relation between discrete and continuous time models.

Chapter 1, by Kenneth Manton, Burton Singer, and Max Woodbury, contains a clear statement of the issues involved in identifying, controlling, and estimating the effects of unobserved variables in demographic modelling. The authors argue that model specification must involve considering the likelihood and testing for the presence of unobservable variables in order to be considered complete. They propose methods for explicitly incorporating such effects into the analysis, and they argue that there is no generic instability in the estimation of the parameters of such models. They conclude by examining the estimation of models in which the heterogeneity variables are changing. Another perspective on the identification issue and the necessity of explicitly incorporating unobservables in event history analysis was originally contained in an appendix to the paper on union dissolution in Sweden by Trussell, Rodríguez, and Vaughan presented at the seminar and included in this volume; their arguments, since published in detail elsewhere (Trussell and Rodríguez 1990), are summarized in Chapter 2 of this volume and discussed briefly at the end of this introduction. Yet other views— some stated quite strongly—are sprinkled throughout the other five papers in the paired competitions in the second part of this book. These conflicting views illustrate vividly that the issue of how to incorporate unobservables in a substantive analysis is still far from resolved.

The next section of the volume consists of three 'contests' in which pairs of teams were assigned to address the same topic using the same data. The purpose of these competitions, all conducted by careful and highly experienced investigators, was to see whether the analytical strategies chosen by the investigators would affect the results. The naïve expectations of all involved were that major differences in methodological approaches (such as the explicit inclusion of unobservables in a statistical model) could influence the results in a major way, but that the routine decisions that all investigators make during the course of any study (such as how to categorize variables and which variables to include) would have little effect. The lesson to be learned is that even such seemingly innocuous decisions can affect results.

This lesson is illustrated nicely by the pair of papers on union dissolution in Sweden. Both teams employed categorical covariates and neither modelled unobserved heterogeneity explicitly. Their conclusions were generally quite similar, except in two cases. Trussell, Rodríguez, and Vaughan (Chapter 2) concluded that the presence of children did not increase marital or union stability, but that higher education did decrease the rate of union dissolution. Hoem and Hoem (Chapter 3) reached the opposite conclusions. Further work by Vaughan and Britta Hoem resolved these differences. Vaughan (1988) found that different categorization of the civil-status variable and the exclusion of an occupational status variable in the Hoem and Hoem analysis accounted for the apparently opposite effects of children on union stability. Hoem (1988) found quite different models of union stability before and after entry into motherhood. In particular, she found a very low dissolution risk among highly educated childless women. Therefore, the primary reason for the opposite effects of education in the two analyses is that Hoem and Hoem considered only women with children. The more detailed classification of social background used by Trussell, Rodríguez, and Vaughan further increased the positive impact of increased education on union stability.

These sets of competitions are also very useful in illustrating different approaches to presentation: the extent to which authors describe and assess limitations of the data, the detail in which statistical models are explicated, the depth of substantive discussion of results. Some investigators provide measures of goodness of fit of their models to the data, while most do not. Some explicitly model unobserved heterogeneity, while others do not. These contrasts are interesting in themselves and, more importantly, should prove useful to any who wish to adopt the best elements of each when crafting papers summarizing their own research.

Montgomery (Chapter 4) and Courgeau and Lelièvre (Chapter 5) estimate quite different models of home-ownership in relation to family formation and evolution. Montgomery estimates models that explicitly seek to capture the effects of unmeasured heterogeneity. The two concurrent processes he models are home-ownership and first marriage among males. He concludes that men who, for unobserved reasons, tend to delay marriage acquire homes more quickly. Courgeau and Lelièvre model the birth of the last child and home-ownership among females as concurrent processes, and they do not explicitly model unmeasured heterogeneity. Instead, they split their sample into broad social classes in an attempt to reduce its impact. They show the different opportunities attached to specific professional groups for home-ownership, and conclude that birth of the last child does depend on home-ownership but that the acquisition of a home does not depend on the timing of the birth of the last child. Readers must decide for themselves how best to interpret the results of Courgeau and Lelièvre's hazard model with age at last birth as the event. While it is clear that age at last birth is a random variable and as such has a distribution characterized by a hazard, it is not prospectively defined, since one cannot (except under exceptional circumstances such as sterilization at that time) ever be sure that a particular birth will, in fact, prove to be the last one. Hence, theirs is a model in which the hazard— which in fact will depend on future variables—is instead assumed to depend on current covariates.

Murphy (Chapter 6) and Heckman and Walker (Chapter 7) study the progression to the third birth in Sweden. Heckman and Walker estimate models with explicit controls for unobserved heterogeneity. In all cases these models collapse to simple mover–stayer models, in which a fraction of the population is estimated to be at no risk of a birth for physiological or behavioural reasons. The fact that they do not find unmeasured heterogeneity that persists over time means that the third birth transition can be analysed in isolation, which is the approach assumed by Murphy. Nevertheless, the two teams reach different conclusions about the effect of wages on the transition to the third birth. Heckman and Walker find two alternative models that fit the data equally well. The first omits wages but includes the length of previous birth intervals as regressors. The second includes wages with no lagged birth intervals. Heckman and Walker prefer the model with wages for theoretical reasons, because it is more parsimonious, and because there is less serial dependence in time-series residuals. Murphy finds no effect of wages, although he does not include lagged birth-interval length as a covariate. The difference in results appears to stem from cohort drift. Heckman and Walker find that different cohorts behave differently and that, in particular, the fertility response to wages has become dampened over time (probably as a result of changes in pronatalist policies in Sweden). Murphy pooled all cohorts, thereby missing the changing effect of wages on fertility.

The book concludes with three methodological papers. In Chapter 8, Little reviews general tools for handling incomplete data, discusses methods for analysing event history data when data are complete, and then proposes modifications to these methods when incomplete information is available on the times of events or when covariates are missing. In Chapter 9 Diamond and McDonald consider methods for analysing event histories when these 'histories' are both left- and right-censored. Such 'histories' collapse to current-status data. Diamond and McDonald provide examples that show that event histories can involve severe misreporting of dates. They then review arguments that current-status data are likely to be more accurate than are retrospective event histories. Finally, they propose several methods for assessing the effects of covariates for current-status data and show how to estimate these models using readily available software. In Chapter 10, Arjas and Kangas propose an alternative to the treatment of event histories as continuous processes. Specifically, they show that virtually identical estimates can be obtained from logit regressions and hazard regressions, provided that each month in the history provides one observation in the logit framework.

What lessons does this volume provide to the demographer who wishes to estimate a behavioural model using event history data? Two seem particularly pertinent. First, there is still great disagreement about the necessity of explicitly modelling the effects of unobservables:

model specification evaluation must involve . . . testing for the presence of effects of unobservable variables in order to be considered complete.   (Manton, Singer, and Woodbury, Chapter 1)

moreover, the functions B(t) (for our purposes, the hazard function) and p(u) (for our purposes, the distribution of the unobservable) are clearly unidentifiable from data only on T (survival time).   (Oakes 1989: 487)

How can these two views possibly be consistent? The answer lies in how much external knowledge the investigator can assume. It can be shown that (for analyses of non-repeated events) there is one model without unobservables and infinitely many other models with different distributions of the unobservables (and hence different underlying hazard functions) that fit observed data *identically* (Trussell and Rodríguez 1990; illustrated in Chapter 2). Yet these models have very different behavioural implications. One can choose among them only on the basis of external knowledge either about the shape (functional form) of the hazard or about the distribution of the unobservable. Hence, one's degree of confidence in believing the behavioural implications of estimated parameters depends directly on one's confidence in these underlying assumptions. My own view is that existing theories provide little guidance in choosing among equally well-fitting alternative models. The implication of this reasoning is not that one can ignore unobservables. Rather, it is that one cannot simply explicitly model them and claim to have a better understanding of behaviour. Instead, a careful investigator must always be aware that different behavioural models could generate the same observed outcomes.

There are two compelling reasons why one may want to model unobservables explicitly. First, on no occasion could a social scientist be confident that all factors behaviourally related to an outcome of interest are in fact included in a statistical model. Hence, it is tempting to add an unobservable to capture the effects of these omitted factors. However, it is clear that this approach is not a solution to the problem of omitted variables because these models can capture only those sources of variation that are independent of the included covariates. One could, of course, go further, to build a model in which the unobservables and the observables were jointly dependent; but the form of this dependence would have to be assumed. Second, a model with unobservables might be more parsimonious than one without. If one has the modest goal of describing behaviours rather than establishing causal relationships, then a simpler model is compelling. If one's goal is the more ambitious attempt to establish 'truth', then the principle of parsimony may lead one astray.

Finally, the careful analyst must be concerned with the goodness of fit of a model to the data. One cannot simply compare the likelihood of a current model with the likelihood of the null model to conclude that the current model fits well. This lesson is nicely illustrated by the 'instability issue' discussed by Manton, Singer, and Woodbury in Chapter 1. Heckman and Singer (1982; 1984) observed that covariate effects estimates in a model of unemployment duration were sensitive to the distribution assumed for the unobservable. They proposed that the distribution of the unobservable be modelled as a discrete probability function with mass concentrated at relatively few points. Trussell and Richards (1985) and Montgomery and Trussell (1986) carried this analysis further. They reasoned that models estimated with the Heckman–Singer correction for heterogeneity could be sensitive to the choice of functional form for the shape of the hazard, just as Heckman and Singer had found that results can be sensitive to the choice of distribution for the unobservable. Those suspicions were confirmed in analyses of the determinants of birth-interval length and of child mortality in Korea.

The Heckman–Singer and Trussell–Richards–Montgomery instability findings illustrate the point that an analyst may achieve nothing but a false sense of security by examining a first model with only observed covariates and a second model with both observed covariates and an unobservable, and then concluding that the second model allows better inference because it has corrected for unobserved heterogeneity. The instability results do not generalize much further, because there was no test of goodness of fit of the models. Such tests might reveal that none of the models fits. Alternatively, the tests might reveal that several models fit the data well, although the estimated coefficients appear dissimilar. As discussed above, even if such tests did not reveal the latter outcome, it is always possible to find many models incorporating unobserved heterogeneity and one model not incorporating unobserved heterogeneity that fit equally well because they yield identical unconditional distributions of the outcome variables. Only external information (perhaps biological or genetic, as contrasted with social or cultural) seldom available to the analyst could be used to distinguish among these alternative models.

## References

Allison, P. (1984), *Event History Analysis: Regression for Longitudinal Event Data* (Beverly Hills, Calif.).

Courgeau, D., and Lelièvre, E. (1989), *Analyse Démographique des Biographies* (Paris).

Cox, D., and Oakes, D. (1984), *Analysis of Survival Data* (London).

Heckman, J., and Singer, B. (1982), 'Population Heterogeneity in Demographic Models', in K. Land and A. Rogers (eds.), *Multidimensional Mathematical Demography* (New York), 567–99.

———— (1984), 'Econometric Duration Analysis', *Journal of Econometrics*, 24: 63–132.

Hoem, B. (1988), 'The Effect of a Woman's Educational Level on Conjugal Union Dissolution in Sweden' (Section of Demography, Stockholm University).

Kalbfleisch, J., and Ross Prentice, R. (1980), *The Statistical Analysis of Failure Time Data* (New York).

Montgomery, M., and Trussell, J. (1986), 'Models of Marital Status and Childbearing', in O. Ashenfelter and R. Layard (eds.), *Handbook of Labor Economics*, i (New York), 205–70.

Namboodiri, K., and Suchindran, C. M. (1987), *Life Table Techniques and Their Applications* (New York).

Oakes, D. (1989), 'Bivariate Survival Models Induced by Frailties', *Journal of the American Statistical Association*, 84. 406: 487–93.

Trussell, J., and Richards, T. (1985), 'Correcting for Unmeasured Heterogeneity in Hazard Models Using the Heckman–Singer Procedure', in N. Tuma (ed.), *Sociological Methodology 1985* (San Francisco).

Trussell, J., and Rodríguez, G. (1990), 'Heterogeneity in Demographic Research', in J. Adams *et al.* (eds.), *Convergent Questions in Genetics and Demography* (New York), 111–32.

Tuma, N., and Hannan, M. (1984), *Social Dynamics: Models and Methods* (New York).

Vaughan, B. (1988), 'The Effect of Children on the Rate of Dissolution of First Unions in Sweden' (Office of Population Research, Princeton University).

# 1 Some Issues in the Quantitative Characterization of Heterogeneous Populations

KENNETH G. MANTON, BURTON SINGER, MAX A. WOODBURY

In this chapter we discuss the analytic issues that arise in identifying, controlling, and—under certain circumstances—estimating the effects of unobserved variables in demographic analyses of a wide variety of time-to-occurrence data. In this discussion, we will argue that the treatment of the effects of unobservable variables in demographic modelling is a direct and natural extension of the evaluation of model specification for analyses where all relevant variables are assumed to be observed. Indeed, it will be suggested that model specification evaluation must involve considering the likelihood and testing for the presence of effects of unobservable variables in order to be considered complete. We begin by identifying necessary steps in the general evaluation of demographic time-to-occurrence models based on observed variables alone. With this foundation at hand, we then introduce the additional subtleties associated with unobservable variables.

In very general terms, the fundamental issue in describing the relation of select variables to the time-to-occurrence of an event (whether it be death, birth, change in marital status, or any other socio-demographic change in status of substantive interest) is to determine the identity of variables from a substantively prescribed list, that influence, alter, or determine the time (age)-of-occurrence of the event. After identity of critical variables is determined, estimates of their quantitative impact can be made. The strategies presented in this paper are directed to the question of impact (or influence) of variables within specific demographic contexts. However, the basic principles are widely applicable in the social and health sciences.

The first principle to be addressed is that, to assess the influence that selected variables have on the time-to-occurrence of events, one can proceed by simultaneous stratification on multiple variables and examine the time-to-occurrence distribution for each stratum. Such stratification represents a wholly agnostic attitude towards the relationships of the variables with the time-to-occurrence of the event, in that no model, or even a class of models, is used to represent, smooth, or summarize relationships in a parsimonious and interpretable manner.

Stratification as a tool for understanding the influence of the variables is, however, severely limited in both substantive and operational terms. Operationally, stratification is severely limited by sample size. For example, even the very large samples of the US National Health Interview Survey (~100,000 cases), will not support, for low-prevalence health conditions or events, more than three- or four-way stratification in terms of producing rate estimates for the cross-classification cells with adequate precision. Indeed, though federal health surveys have classically been designed with sample sizes determined by the ability to resolve differences in means and/or rates in low-order stratifications with adequate power, the large samples are currently proving cost-ineffective because most of the interesting questions require stratification for much larger numbers of variables. Indeed, as the knowledge in specific substantive areas expands, the need for higher-order stratification is likely to increase, making such an approach, with any plausibly large sample size, infeasible. The second problem with such an approach is that description via stratification provides no model structure that can help us to generalize critical aspects of the situation to other times, places, and populations, i.e. the distribution described in this way is fully parameterized (saturated) and provides no direct test of an underlying stochastic process that might have generated the particular data configuration observed. Thus, to proceed beyond the descriptive phase we must construct some model, i.e. a mathematical structure describing the stochastic processes that generate both the observable data configuration and potentially other data configurations within appropriate stochastic limits.

An example of such a model for evaluating the influence of many variables on the time-to-occurrence of an event of interest is the class of additive models. In these models the outcome $Y$ or a function of it, $F(Y)$, is related to a $K$-vector of characteristics of individuals $\mathbf{X}$ via the representation $f(Y) = \mathbf{X}\beta$. A coefficient, $\beta_k$, in the vector $\beta$, which is 'significantly' different from '0' (i.e. having an effect or influence on the time-to-outcome) is identified with an influential variable, $X_k$, with the magnitude of $\beta_k$ interpreted as quantifying its influence holding the other $K - 1$ variables constant. The statistical control of holding the other $K - 1$ variables constant is logically equivalent to the process of stratification except that the exact nature of the control for the other variables is dependent on the assumed form of the model. The model assumptions, even in very simple cases such as linear models, necessarily imply a theoretical view of the processes generating the data in that the model imposes constraints on parameterizations of the data. If the model did not impose constraints it would be no more parsimonious than stratification; and the model assumptions would yield nothing in terms of the efficient use of the statistical information available.

One effect of the mathematical structure of the model is to allow for control of more variables acting alone or in combination than is possible in stratification. This involves an analytic judgement that the degree of statistical control achieved is greater when more variables are controlled for under model constraints than when stratification is employed, to the very limited degree (i.e. with far fewer variables) permitted by most sample sizes.

It is important to recognize that, while the use of a model requires interpretation of the coefficients within the selected class of models, there is no guarantee that the model corresponds in fact to the phenomena being assessed where one may have the $K$ observed variables, and one or' more other variables, acting together. The failure to recognize the model-imposed constraints in the interpretation of coefficients does not alter the fact of those constraints, i.e. the use of generic models to describe data implies a description that is necessarily an interpretation constrained by model assumptions. For example, principal-components analysis is often used to describe multivariate data. Tests of the eigenvalues and eigenvectors of a given solution usually involve assumptions that the data have the multivariate normal distribution, with the variables' covariance matrix having a corresponding Wishart distribution. Though one may eschew such statistical tests and argue that the necessary calculations for a principal-components analysis can be carried out on any data set, regardless of its distribution (which reflects assumptions about the stochastic processes generating the data), one cannot escape the fact that those calculations involve only the second-order moments of the data distribution (i.e. the eigenvalues and eigenvectors for the covariance or correlation matrix). Thus it is mathematically impossible for the principal-components model directly to represent third- or higher-order moments, since that information is not utilized in the calculations and represents a necessary constraint on interpretation of the coefficients of the principal-components model.

An important consideration in the use of any model is to examine the possibility of the existence of one (or more) variables that, a priori, influence the outcomes of interest and that are not measured in the data set at hand. Indeed, there may be conceptually meaningful variables that are unmeasurable with available measurement technology. Despite the non-measurement of such variables, it may be that they both exist and are potentially important as influences on the outcomes of interest. In this common condition one must be concerned as to whether conclusions obtained about the influences of $X_k$ (e.g. the $\beta_k$ in the additive model) on the outcome may be incorrect when the influence of the unobserved variable is ignored in the analysis. Such concerns necessarily arise whether one is viewing the model as interpretable within some theory or whether one is employing the model as a parsimonious description of the data. In the first case, one will derive incorrect inferences about the nature of the underlying processes generating the events. In the second case, one will derive an incorrect description of the relationships among the variables. This issue is a central question in analysing duration data in demography. It is also a central issue in the evaluation of the adequacy of model specifications in any analytic context.

In the following discussion we will perform three tasks. First, we shall consider the notion of 'influence', and the misleading inferences that can arise with (and without) the inclusion of the effects of unobserved variables within the general class of duration models often used in demography, referred to as proportional-hazards models. This discussion will clarify the structure of a wide range of misspecification errors, and potentially misleading inferences, that can arise from the failure to represent the effects of unobserved variables within this class of models. It will also highlight the necessary role of mechanistic theories in guiding model specification in order to maximize (given the data, current theory, and the analysts' judgement) confidence about claims that $X_k$ influences $Y$ in a certain way in the presence of unobservable variables.

The second part of the discussion involves the presentation of tools and procedures for evaluating the presence of the effects of unobservables in proportional-hazards models. This is done with the aid of several concrete illustrations from specific analyses.

The third part generalizes the argument by introducing multivariate diffusion process models with 'killing' terms, i.e. terms that selectively remove probability mass by jump processes such as mortality. This type of model is based on more refined mechanistic theories about the structure of processes generating the events (and their durations) and the influences of one or more temporally varying covariates. This represents one widely used—in the chronic-disease epidemiology and mortality literature—class of models with a stronger theoretical base than the proportional-hazards models. These models, if one accepts the broad, associated theory, can alleviate some of the misspecification difficulties that arise with the proportional-hazard models.

## Principles for Assessing the Effects of Unobserved Variables in Proportional-Hazards Models

In general terms, the introduction of unobserved variables in proportional-hazards models leads to the problem of estimating the effects of observed variables in the presence of incidental parameters. Such incidental parameters are omnipresent in any empirical situation, i.e., there will always be potentially influential variables that are not measured. At this level of generality, the boundary between the statistical methodology and substantive input is difficult to define.

An important instance of an incidental-parameters problem arises in the simultaneous-equations literature in economics (Malinvaud 1970), where one estimates the parameters in just one equation that is embedded in a large a priori defined system of equations. Economic theory—or simply economic plausibility—dictates the entire equation system. The more complex structure, which may contain multiple unmeasured variables, is taken into account when estimating parameters in the single equation of interest, in order to avoid possible incorrect inferences arising from the influence of the global interconnected system on the parameters in the single equation. The global interconnected system is based on the a priori beliefs of the analyst about the underlying reality.

From this perspective, we may view the proportional-hazards model as representing certain beliefs about the nature of the process described. The parsimony

offered by the model structure and its efficient use of data are not useful properties unless it is reasonable to assume that the hazards of different individuals
increase (decrease) with time in a proportional way. Given belief in the reason-
ableness of the proportional-hazards specification, a number of technical issues
in their formulation must be solved. To make the ideas precise, we introduce some
mathematical formalism.

Define $T$ to be a random variable representing the time-to-occurrence of an
event of interest. Let the survivor function conditional on observable time-invariant covariates, $\mathbf{X}$, and unobservable time-invariant covariates, $\theta$, be defined as

$$S(t \mid \mathbf{X}, \theta) = \mathrm{Prob}(T > t \mid \mathbf{X}, \theta) \tag{1}$$

The survivor function can be written in terms of a conditional cumulated-hazard
function, $W(t \mid \mathbf{X}, \theta)$, according to

$$S(t \mid \mathbf{X}, \theta) = \exp\{- W(t \mid \mathbf{X}, \theta)\} \tag{2}$$

The conditional hazard rate—interpreted as the expected number of occurrences
of the event of interest per unit time per individual at risk in a population with
covariate characteristics $(\mathbf{X}, \theta)$—is the right derivative.

$$\frac{\partial^+ W(t \mid \mathbf{X}, \theta)}{\partial t} = \lim_{h \downarrow 0} \frac{W(t + h \mid \mathbf{X}, \theta) - W(t \mid \mathbf{X}, \theta)}{h} \tag{3}$$

### Identifiability

From data one observes, in principle,

$$S(t \mid \mathbf{X}) = \mathrm{Prob}(T > t \mid \mathbf{X}) = \int_{\Theta} S(t \mid \mathbf{X}, \theta)\, d\mu(\theta \mid \mathbf{X}) \tag{4}$$

where $\mu(\theta \mid \mathbf{X})$ is the conditional distribution of $\theta$ given values of the observed
covariates, $\mathbf{X}$; and $\Theta$ is the set of possible values of $\theta$. In order to assess the
influence of $(\mathbf{X}, \theta)$ on the durations, $T$, we require knowledge of $S(t \mid \mathbf{X}, \theta)$ and
$\mu(\theta \mid \mathbf{X})$. This immediately leads to the basic identifiability question: under what
minimal restrictions on $S(t \mid \mathbf{X}, \theta)$ and on the conditional distributions $\mu(\theta \mid \mathbf{X})$
can one uniquely determine these quantities from a knowledge of $S(t \mid \mathbf{X})$? The
question is fundamental to model specification, since it delineates those classes
of models within which qualitatively different interpretations of the same data,
i.e. observational equivalence, cannot arise.

This particular identifiability question has only been addressed within two
forms of proportional-hazards models. They are defined by the factorizations

$$W(t \mid \mathbf{X}, \theta) = A(t, \mathbf{X})\theta \tag{5}$$

and

$$W(t \mid \mathbf{X}, \theta) = H(t)U(\mathbf{X})\theta \tag{6}$$

In (5) it is assumed that the time-dependent component of the hazard can vary
only with levels of the observed covariates, $\mathbf{X}$. However, the same shape curves,
$A(t, \mathbf{X})$, characterize event rates for all levels of the unobserved variable $\theta$. The

more widely utilized factorization (6) presumes that the same time-dependent shape of curve, $H(t)$, describes event rates for all levels of observed and unobserved covariates. Furthermore, $\theta$ and $\mathbf{X}$ are assumed to influence the event rate via the multiplicative scaling factor $U(\mathbf{X})\theta$. Identifiability analyses to date have also imposed the further strong restriction that $d\mu(\theta \mid \mathbf{X}) \equiv d\mu(\theta)$, i.e. $\theta$ and $\mathbf{X}$ are independent as random variables.

In the context of (5), Heckman and Singer (1984*b*) established that $A(t, \mathbf{X})$ and $\mu(\theta)$ can be uniquely determined from $S(t \mid \mathbf{X})$ where

$$A(t, \mathbf{X}) = \int_0^t \exp\left\{\gamma_{\mathbf{X}}\left(\frac{s^{\lambda_x - 1}}{\lambda_{\mathbf{X}}}\right)\right\} ds \tag{7}$$

with $0 < \lambda_{\mathbf{X}} < j$ for each stratum, $\mathbf{X}$ and

$$\mu \in \left[\mu : \int_0^\infty \theta^k d\mu(\theta) < +\infty \text{ for } 1 \leqslant k \leqslant j + 1), \int_0^\infty \theta d\mu(\theta) \text{ known a priori}\right]$$

The essential feature of the factorization (5) is that it allows for an agnostic position, i.e. stratification analysis, on the observed covariates, but at the price of strong parametric assumptions about the time-dependent form of the hazard within each stratum of $\mathbf{X}$ to secure identifiability. One might be able to trade strong within-stratum assumptions about $A(t, \mathbf{X})$ for strong parametric assumptions about $\mu$ while maintaining identifiability. However, escape from strong parametric assumptions in both expressions is impossible if one insists on an agnostic position about $\mathbf{X}$.

The factorization (6) is much more restrictive than (5); however, it leads to identifiability of $H(t)$, $U(\mathbf{X})$ and $\mu(\theta)$ without imposing strong parametric assumptions on any of these terms. In particular, Elbers and Ridder (1982) show that if

$$\mu \in \left[\mu : \int_0^\infty \theta d\mu(\theta) = 1\right]$$

$$H(t) = \int_0^t \Psi(s) ds \text{ for some non-negative integrable function, } \Psi(s)$$

and $U(\mathbf{X})$ is non-negative and non-constant on an open set in $K$-dimensional Euclidean space (where $\mathbf{X} = (x_1, \ldots, x_K)$), then $H(t)$, $U(\mathbf{X})$ and $\mu(\theta)$ are uniquely determined from $S(t \mid \mathbf{X})$. This implies that, within the class of proportional-hazard models (6), no strong parametric assumptions about $H$, $U$, or $\mu$ need to be imposed, in principle, in order to secure identification. From a practical point of view, however, the sample sizes necessary to secure reasonably precise estimates of all three components ($H$, $U$, and $\mu$) appear to be inordinately large ($> 20\ 000$ observations). Nevertheless, it would be useful to study the trade-offs between increasingly strong parametric assumptions on one or more of the three identifiable components and the sample sizes necessary to achieve a priori given levels of precision of estimation. Knowledge of these trade-offs lies in the future.

A final point concerning identifiability, even within the specifications (5) and (6), is the need to consider conditional distributions $\mu(\theta \mid \mathbf{X})$ where $\theta$ and $\mathbf{X}$ are not assumed to be independent random variables. The importance of the problem was pointed out by Montgomery, Richards, and Braun (1986), in the context of logistic models with unobserved covariates, but no rigorous identification analysis has been carried out for specific classes of conditional distributions, $\mu(\theta \mid X)$. In the context of the proportional-hazard assumption, model misspecification, where $\theta$ and $X$ are assumed to be independent when this is not the case, can have profound consequences in empirical analyses. Indeed, as discussed in the next section, parameter estimates within parametric proportional-hazards models can exhibit extreme sensitivity to minor perturbations in the model assumptions in the presence of this kind of misspecification.

## Misleading Inferences and Omitted Variables

A deeper understanding of the use of proportional-hazards models to assess the possible influence of one or more observed covariates on times-to-occurrence of events requires that we be precise about the word 'influence'. To this end we will say that $X_j$ influences $T$, in principle, if

$$\left.\frac{\partial S(t \mid \mathbf{x})}{\partial x_j}\right|_{x_j = x_j^*} \neq 0 \tag{8}$$

for some value $x_j^*$ and some values $x_i$, $i \neq j$. Within the class of proportional-hazards models without unobserved variables, this is equivalent to

$$\left.\frac{\partial U \bullet (\mathbf{x})}{\partial x_j}\right|_{x_j = x_j^*} \neq 0 \tag{9}$$

where the survivor function has the general specification $S(t \mid \mathbf{x}) = \exp\{-H \bullet (t) U \bullet (\mathbf{x})\}$ and $H \bullet (t)$ and $U \bullet (\mathbf{x})$ satisfy the assumption of the Elbers–Ridder identifiability theorem mentioned in the previous sub section. The stipulation influences 'in principle' is introduced to distinguish the conceptual idea of influence from the additional details of practical assessment, where the partial derivatives would be replaced by finite differences and where it is necessary to quantify the extent of deviation of such differences from zero before one has confidence that a signal is visible above the noise.

Now suppose that observations are generated by a proportional-hazards model with unobserved covariate $\theta$ which is statistically independent of the observed covariates. Thus, the correct survivor function has the specification

$$S(t \mid \mathbf{x}) = \int_{\Theta} \exp\{-H(t) U(\mathbf{x}) \theta\} \, d\mu(\theta) \tag{10}$$

for some non-degenerate mixing distribution $\mu$ where the triple $(H, U, \mu)$ satisfies the Elbers–Ridder identifiability conditions.[1] If an investigator fits

---

[1] It will be important to observe that $\mu$ must have a finite mean but the constant $\int_{\Theta} \theta d\mu(\theta)$ need not necessarily be equal to 1 to secure identification. Thus, $\mu \in \{\mu : \int_{\Theta} \theta d\mu(\theta) = c\}$ and all mixing distributions in contention have the same mean $c$.

$$S^\bullet(t\mid\mathbf{x}) = \exp\{-H^\bullet(t)U^\bullet(\mathbf{x})\} \tag{11}$$

to such data and assesses whether $\mathbf{x}$ influences $T$, we would like to understand the circumstances under which the resulting inference would be correct, in principle, despite the misspecification of ignoring the unobserved variable, $\theta$.

A minimal requirement for correct inferences would be

$$\text{sgn}\left|\frac{\partial U^\bullet(\mathbf{x})}{\partial x_j}\right| = \text{sgn}\left|\frac{\partial U(\mathbf{x})}{\partial x_j}\right| \tag{12}$$

where for any real number, $a$, we define

$$\text{sgn}[a] = \begin{cases} +1 & \text{if } a>0 \\ \phantom{+}0 & \text{if } a=0 \\ -1 & \text{if } a<0 \end{cases}$$

Condition (12) would clearly hold if every non-degenerate mixture (10) was observationally equivalent to some proportional-hazards specification (11). However, averaging over $\theta$ with $d\mu(\theta)$ does *not*, in general, yield a factorization such that

$$-ln\int_\Theta \exp\{-H(t)U(\mathbf{x})\theta\}\,d\mu(\theta) = H^\bullet(t)U^\bullet(\mathbf{x}) \tag{13}$$

where $0 < H^\bullet(t)\uparrow$ and $U^\bullet(\mathbf{x})$ is non-negative and non-constant. Nevertheless, to within a first-order Taylor series approximation we have

$$-ln\int_\Theta \exp\{-H(t)U(\mathbf{x})\theta\}\,d\mu(\theta) \approx H(t)U(\mathbf{x})\int_\Theta \theta d\mu(\theta). \tag{14}$$

Thus (12) holds to a first approximation.

Now suppose that the investigator's belief system suggests that

$$S(t\mid\mathbf{x}) = \int_\Theta \exp\{-H(t)U(\mathbf{x})\theta\}\,d\mu(\theta\mid\mathbf{x}) \tag{15}$$

where $\theta$ and $\mathbf{x}$ are correlated. Then, again, to within a first-order Taylor approximation we have

$$-ln\int_\Theta \exp\{-H(t)U(\mathbf{x})\theta\}\,d\mu(\theta\mid\mathbf{x}) \approx H(t)U(\mathbf{x})\int_\Theta \theta d\mu(\theta\mid\mathbf{x}) \equiv$$
$$H(t)U(\mathbf{x})E(\theta\mid\mathbf{x}) \tag{16}$$

However,

$$\frac{\partial\{-ln\,S(t\mid\mathbf{x})\}}{\partial x_j} = H(t)\left\{\frac{\partial U}{\partial x_j}E(\theta\mid\mathbf{x}) + U(\mathbf{x})\frac{\partial}{\partial x_j}E(\theta\mid\mathbf{x})\right\} \tag{17}$$

Thus, finding $\partial U^\bullet(\mathbf{x})/\partial x_j \neq 0$ from proportional hazards without unobservables does *not* necessarily imply that $\partial U/\partial x_j \neq 0$. Indeed the apparent (i.e. from a model ignoring unobservables) inference that $x_j$ influences the observed durations via the hazard

$$W(t\mid\mathbf{x},\theta) = H(t)U(\mathbf{x})\theta \tag{18}$$

could be an artefact resulting from the correlation of $\theta$ with $\mathbf{x}$.

Inference from $\partial U^\bullet(\mathbf{x})/\partial x_j \equiv 0$ that $x_j$ does not influence $S(t \mid \mathbf{x})$ could be false and be a consequence of correlated $\theta$ and $\mathbf{x}$ yielding

$$\frac{\partial U(\mathbf{x})}{\partial x_j} E(\theta \mid \mathbf{x}) + U(\mathbf{x}) \frac{\partial}{\partial x_j} E(\theta \mid \mathbf{x}) \equiv 0 \qquad (19)$$

Thus, ignoring unobservables when $\theta$ and $\mathbf{x}$ are correlated can give qualitatively incorrect inferences. The importance of the underlying belief system and its role in interpreting the analyses is made very manifest here, since

$$\int_\Theta \exp \{-H(t)U(\mathbf{x})\theta\} \, d\mu(\theta),$$

$$\int_\Theta \exp \{-H(t)U(\mathbf{x})\theta\} \, d\mu(\theta \mid \mathbf{x}),$$

and $\exp \{-H^\bullet(t)U^\bullet(\mathbf{x})\}$ could fit a given set of duration data almost equally well.

As a final point we observe that, under the weaker proportionality specification (5), i.e. $W(t \mid \mathbf{x}, \theta) = A(t, \mathbf{x})\theta$, there is no observational equivalence even to within first-order Taylor approximation between $\exp \{-H^\bullet(t)U^\bullet(\mathbf{x})\}$ and $\int_\Theta \exp \{-A(t, \mathbf{x})\theta\} d\mu(\theta \mid \mathbf{x})\}$. In particular,

$$- \ln \int_\Theta \exp \{-A(t, \mathbf{x})\theta\} \, d\mu(\theta \mid \mathbf{x}) \approx A(t, \mathbf{x})E(\theta \mid \mathbf{x}) \qquad (20)$$

using $\ln(z) = z - 1 + (z - 1)^2/2 + \ldots \approx z - 1$,

$$1 - e^{-z} = z - \frac{z^2}{2!} + \frac{z^3}{3!} + \ldots \approx z.$$

$A(t, \mathbf{x})$ does not, in general, factor into a form $H^\bullet(t)U^\bullet(\mathbf{x})$. Hence sgn $[\partial U^\bullet(\mathbf{x})/\partial x_j]$ and

$$\operatorname{sgn} \left[ \left( \frac{\partial}{\partial x_j} A(t, \mathbf{x}) \right) E(\theta \mid \mathbf{x}) + A(t, \mathbf{x}) \frac{\partial}{\partial x_j} E(\theta \mid \mathbf{x}) \right]$$

need have no clear relationship to each other.

## Mixtures of Proportional-Hazards Models: Types of Misspecification for Specific Models

A widely used strategy for assessing whether or not some combination of observed variables influences waiting times until occurrence of events is to fit a parametric version of (6)

$$\operatorname{Prob}(T > t \mid \mathbf{X} = \mathbf{x}) = \int_0^\infty \exp \{-\Lambda_\alpha(t)e^{\mathbf{X}\beta}\theta\} \, d\mu(\theta) \qquad (21)$$

to data on the time ($T$) to events and covariates ($X$) and interpret the coefficients of the regression vector, $\beta$, which are found to be significantly different from zero (or a theoretically appropriate null hypothesis). The variable $\theta$ is interpreted as an unobserved source of heterogeneity whose incorporation in (21) is motivated by a desire to reduce or eliminate misspecification bias in $\beta$ and $\alpha$ that could arise by ignoring unobservables. The analysis presumes, of course, that the proportional-hazards specification

$$\text{Prob}(T > t \mid X = x, \theta = \vartheta) = \exp\{-\Lambda_\alpha(t)e^{x\beta}\vartheta\} \tag{22}$$

is a reasonable representation of the investigator's beliefs about the underlying phenomena. Leaving aside, for the moment, the problem of the scientific basis for (22), modelling with (21) has led to difficulties that can arise from any one of several forms of misspecification, as will be explained below.

As part of an analysis of durations of spells of unemployment, Heckman and Singer (1984$a$) demonstrated that estimates of $\beta$ and $\alpha$ with $\Lambda_\alpha(t) = t^\alpha$ could be very sensitive to the family of mixing distribution selected to fit (21) to data on the timing of events ($T$) and covariates ($X$). In a subsequent analysis of infant mortality, Trussell and Richards (1985) demonstrated that, with $\mu$, the distribution of unobservables, only restricted to the family of distributions where $\mu(\theta)$ is a step function with at most four points of increase, $\beta$ and the sign of the first derivative of $\Lambda_\alpha'(t)$ could be very sensitive to the choice of the parametric family (i.e. Weibull v. Gompertz) for $\Lambda_\alpha(t)$ in (21). These particular examples have often been interpreted as evidence of a generic instability in estimates of $\beta$ and $\alpha$ in (21) resulting from selection of special parametric families of distributions, $\mu$, and integrated hazards, $\Lambda_\alpha(t)$.

The sensitivity exhibited in the analyses in Heckman and Singer (1984$a$) and Trussell and Richards (1985) is by no means generic, but can result from one or more forms of model misspecification. Clearly, more than one type of misspecification can be present in a given study. A thorough understanding of the interaction of multiple types of misspecification is a topic for future research. In the next two subsections we discuss two sources of misspecification, and indicate strategies for eliminating undue parameter sensitivity.

## Selection of the Incorrect Hazard Function

To focus on the basic idea, consider a hypothetical survivor function of the form shown in Fig. 1.1($a$). Associated with the survivor function is a cumulated hazard $\Lambda^*(t) = -\ln S(t)$ shown in Fig. 1.1($b$). Superimposed on the step function in Fig. 1.1($b$) are two Weibull cumulated hazards (i.e. $\Lambda_\alpha(t) = t^\alpha$, $\alpha > 0$), one with $\alpha < 1$ and the other with $\alpha > 1$. These correspond, respectively, to decreasing and increasing hazard rates. Despite the qualitative difference in mechanisms associated with $\alpha < 1$ v. $\alpha > 1$, the two curves represent equally good (or bad) fits to the data defined by $\Lambda^*(t)$.

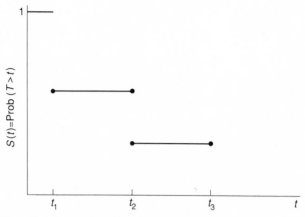

Fig. 1.1(*a*) Discontinuous survivor function.

The relevance of this example to our investigation of sensitivity of parameter estimates to modest changes in model specification can be seen if we consider the classes of mixture models

$$S(t) = \int_0^\infty \exp(-t^\alpha \theta) d\mu(\theta), \quad \alpha > 0 \tag{23}$$

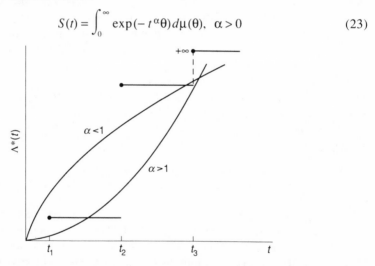

Fig. 1.1(*b*) Cumulated hazard for $S(t)$ in Fig. 1.1(*a*) and Weibull cumulated hazards.

where $\mu(\theta)$ is a member of either

$M_1 = (\mu : \mu$ has two points of support in the interval $0 < \theta < 1)$ or
$M_2 = (\mu : \mu$ has two points of support in the interval $1 < \theta < 10)$

If (23) is fitted to data where the empirical log survivor function is a discontinuous function $\Lambda^*(t)$, then the maximum likelihood estimate of $\alpha$ can satisfy $\alpha < 1$ when $\mu \in M_1$ and $\alpha > 1$ when $\mu \in M_2$. In particular, suppose that

$$\Lambda^*(t) = \left\{ \begin{array}{ll} 0 & \text{for } 0 \leq t < 1 \\ ln\,2 & \text{for } 1 \leq t < 3 \\ +\infty & \text{for } t \geq 3 \end{array} \right. \tag{24}$$

Thus, half of the population experiences the event of interest at $t = 1$ and the remainder experience it at $t = 3$.

Now if we fit the misspecified class of models

$$S(t \mid \theta) = \exp(-t^\alpha \theta) \tag{25}$$

to data generated by $\Lambda^*(t)$ for a priori fixed values of $\theta$, we find that the log-likelihood

$$ln\,L = N \left\{ ln\,\alpha + \left( \frac{\alpha - 1}{2} \right) ln\,3 + ln\,\theta - \frac{\theta}{2} (1 + 3^\alpha) \right\} \tag{26}$$

where $N$ = size of population, has a maximum with $\alpha < 1$ when $\theta < 1$ and a maximum with $\alpha > 1$ when $\theta > 1$. Thus, when mixture models (23) are fitted to (24), we can obtain $\hat{\alpha} < 1$ when $\mu \in M_1$ and $\hat{\alpha} > 1$ when $\mu \in M_2$.

In contrast to (24), suppose that the class of models (23) is fitted to data generated according to $S(t) = \exp(-t^2)$. Then for $\mu \in M_1 \cup M_2$ the maximum-likelihood estimate of $\alpha$ satisfies $\hat{\alpha} > 1$ (i.e. it is qualitatively correct). The essential point is that, by fitting smooth models (23), which qualitatively behave in the same manner as the mechanism generating the data, the phenomenon exhibited in Fig. 1.1(b) cannot occur.

Further theoretical insight into the sensitivity of parameter estimates to hazard misspecifications such as those exhibited above can be seen if we compare $\partial\,ln\,L^{(1)}/\partial\theta$ with $\partial\,ln\,L^{(2)}/\partial\theta$ where $L^{(1)}$ = likelihood for $\exp(-t^\alpha\theta)$ fitted to (24) and $L^{(2)}$ = likelihood for $\exp(-t^\alpha\theta)$ fitted to $\exp(-t^2)$. A straightforward calculation shows that the difference in their sensitivity to changes in $\theta$ is

$$\Delta = \frac{\partial\,ln\,L^{(1)}}{\partial\theta} - \frac{\partial\,ln\,L^{(2)}}{\partial\theta} = \sum_{j=1}^{N} t_j^\alpha - \frac{N}{2}(1 + 3^\alpha) \tag{27}$$

where $t_j$ are the event times for a process governed by $S(t) = \exp(-t^2)$. Indeed, if we define $t_j$ via $\exp(-t_j^2) = j/N$, we have $t_j = \{-ln(j/N)\}^{1/2}$ as one concrete realization of such event times. Then $\Delta > 0$ is a precise way of saying that the likelihood is more sensitive to perturbations in $\theta$ when a model with smooth cumulated hazard is fitted to a discontinuous function such as $\Delta^*(t)$ than when it is fitted to data generated by a qualitatively similar (i.e. smooth) mechanism. Large values of $\Sigma_{j=1}^{N} t_j^\alpha$ arise due to the fact that, under the model, $S(t) = \exp(-t^2)$, event-times are much more spread out than in the model associated with (24).

An obvious resolution of the sensitivity problem when data exhibit discontinuities in the survivor plot is to fit mixture models of the form

$$S(t) = \int_0^\infty \exp\{-\Lambda_0(t)\theta\}\, d\mu(\theta) \tag{28}$$

where $\Lambda_0(t)$ is a step-function. This would mean that the investigator takes the discontinuities to be associated with some specific mechanism. Examples of such naturally occurring discontinuities are:

  (i) dates following initiation of spells of unemployment when unemployment benefits expire;

 (ii) durations following live births when maternal antibodies are no longer protecting infants in developing countries and thus leaving them at much greater risk of death;

(iii) maximum length of reimbursable hospital stay under Medicare for specific diagnosis-related groups;

(iv) maximum length of Medicare reimbursable nursing-home stay for non-critically ill patients.

The issue of sensitivity in parameter estimates in the general class of models,

$$S(t \mid \mathbf{x}) = \int_0^\infty \exp\left\{-\Lambda(t)e^{\mathbf{x}'\beta}\theta\right\} d\mu(\theta) \tag{29}$$

or

$$S(t \mid \mathbf{x}) = \int_0^\infty \exp\left\{-\Lambda(t)e^{\mathbf{x}'\beta+\theta}\right\} d\mu(\theta) \tag{30}$$

to modest changes in $\Lambda(t)$ or $\mu(\theta)$ was demonstrated empirically in Heckman and Singer (1984a) and Trussell and Richards (1985). In Heckman and Singer's analysis of duration of spells of unemployment, a possible source of sensitivity in estimates of a Weibull parameter $\alpha$ in $\Lambda(t) = t^\alpha$ and in the regression coefficients, $\beta$ in (30) under changes in parametric families of mixing distributions—gamma v. log-normal v. normal—are the natural discontinuities associated with expiration of unemployment benefits at 13, 26, 39, and 52 weeks. In an analysis of infant and child mortality, Trussell and Richards (1985) used (29) with $\mu$ restricted to the class of discrete mixtures with at most four points of support and exhibited sensitivity in the sign of $\Lambda'(t)$ and in $\beta$ when $\Lambda(t)$ varied between the Weibull and Gompertz families. A possible source of this sensitivity could be the jump discontinuity in the survivor plot, which is not being modelled by either the Weibull or the Gompertz hazards. We use the word 'possible' when attempting to account for the parameter sensitivity in both of these analyses as arising from the special misspecification of fitting smooth hazards to data with discontinuities (analogous to Fig. 1.1). Our hesitancy arises from the fact that such sensitivity can arise from more than one source, a notable one being the assumption that $\theta$ and $\mathbf{x}$ are independent when this is, in fact, false. Such an independence assumption was made in both the Heckman and Singer and Trussell and Richards analyses.

It is important to understand that the sensitivity in parameter estimates exhibited in the above-mentioned empirical studies is not generic to modelling with (29) and (30). In this regard, Marini (1985) replicated Heckman and Singer's sensitivity analysis, but on duration-to-marital-disruption data in a cohort of

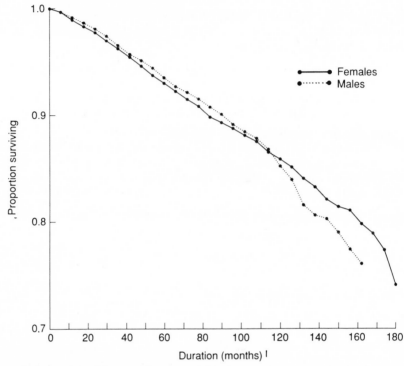

Fig. 1.2 Proportion of first marriages surviving, by sex.
*Source*: Marini (1985).

1950s high school graduates. The survivor plot (Fig. 1.2) indicates no apparent discontinuities; and the parameter estimates—β and Weibull parameter, α—are not sensitive to the choice of gamma v. log-normal mixing distributions. The same insensitivity was exhibited when the hazard specification was changed from Weibull to Gompertz curves.

Although it is tempting to follow up Marini's analysis with strong statements about the influence of covariates with significant coefficients on marital disruptions, this has—quite properly—not been done. The difficulty here is that (29) and (30) are not based on any cohesive theory of marital disruption. Furthermore, these models are not the basis of any theory of unemployment durations or of infant and child mortality. Thus, alleviating sensitivity of β parameters in Heckman and Singer's unemployment example by fitting cumulative hazards with jumps at the times when unemployment benefits terminate would not give confidence about the impact of observed covariates unless there is also an economic-theoretic basis for (29) and (30).

An analysis of mortality at older ages that is based on (29) with no observed covariates, where no parameter sensitivity of the kind exhibited by either Heckman and Singer (1984) or Trussell and Richards (1985) occurs, but where the

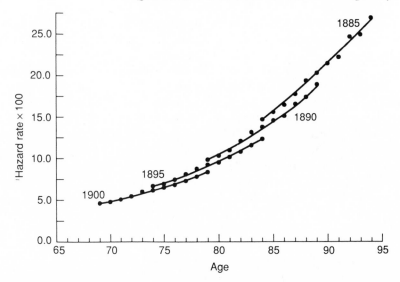

Fig. 1.3 Fit of the gamma/Weibull model to Medicare mortality data for four male cohorts born in 1885, 1890, 1895, and 1900. The four smooth lines show the age trajectory of the marginal-hazard rate function within the age range of observation for each of the four cohorts.
*Source*: Manton, Stallard, and Vaupel (1986).

models derive from theories of human mortality, is given in Manton, Stallard, and Vaupel (1986). They fitted the specification

$$\text{Prob}(T > t) = \int_{0}^{\infty} \exp\{-\Lambda_{\alpha}(t)\theta\} \, d\mu(\theta) \tag{31}$$

to mortality data for multiple cohorts of elderly people as recorded in the Medicare files. For $\Lambda_{\alpha}(t) = t^{\alpha}$, $\alpha > 0$ and $\mu$ being a member of the family of gamma or inverse Gaussian distributions, they demonstrate that the estimated value of $\alpha$ is not sensitive to the class of distributions to which $\mu$ is assumed to belong. For $\Lambda_{\alpha}(t) = (e^{\alpha t} - 1)/\alpha$, i.e. the Gompertz family of cumulated hazards (and $\mu$ again restricted to the gamma or inverse Gaussian families), estimates of $\alpha$ are again found to be insensitive to the class membership of $\mu$. An important feature of the Medicare mortality data is that the empirical survivor plots for all cohorts decay smoothly, i.e. there is no evidence of discontinuities such as those exhibited in Fig. 1.1. Thus, smooth families of monotone functions, $\Lambda_{\alpha}(t)$, are being fitted to smooth data. The smoothness of the data is illustrated in Fig. 1.3.

The models are based on theories of human mortality that lead either to the Gompertz (e.g. Strehler 1977: ch. 7) or to the Weibull (Rosenberg *et al.* 1973; Economos 1982) specification. Thus, testing between these two hazard functions represented a test of competing theories and not an exploratory search for a hazard model or the use of a flexible and convenient hazard form. Furthermore, the parameter estimates derived under the different specifications could be compared against other types of data. The Gompertz and Weibull parameters can be used to estimate rates of loss of physiological functions. These rates can then be compared to direct estimates of such loss rates obtained from specialized studies (e.g. Manton, Woodbury, and Stallard 1989).

In Table 1.1 we present the estimates of the male Gompertz hazards with different assumed mixing distributions. We see that, while the Gompertz hazards give similar estimates of the rate-of-ageing parameter, $\alpha$, for the selected mixing distributions, the homogeneous-population model yields estimates that, for individuals, are biologically infeasible (i.e., the confounding of heterogeneity in the population with the age dependence of the hazard for the individual gives values that are too low to be plausible and are inconsistent with estimates based on mortality from age 30 to 90, e.g. Wetterstrand 1981).

TABLE 1.1. *Alternative estimates of Gompertz rate parameter $\beta$ under three marginal distributions of frailty, for males.*

| Cohort/ age range | Gamma | $\beta \times 10^2$ Inverse Gaussian | Degenerate |
|---|---|---|---|
| 1902 | 7.34 | 7.96 | 6.26 |
| 65–76 | (0.10) | (0.24) | (0.06) |
| 1900 | 7.38 | 8.03 | 6.11 |
| 67–77 | (0.11) | (0.26) | (0.06) |
| 1898 | 7.73 | 8.40 | 6.26 |
| 69–79 | (0.12) | (0.28) | (0.06) |
| 1896 | 7.88 | 8.54 | 6.18 |
| 71–81 | (0.14) | (0.30) | (0.06) |
| 1894 | 8.20 | 8.84 | 6.22 |
| 73–83 | (0.15) | (0.31) | (0.06) |
| 1892 | 8.65 | 9.24 | 6.32 |
| 75–85 | (0.18) | (0.33) | (0.06) |
| 1890 | 9.14 | 9.67 | 6.44 |
| 77–87 | (0.21) | (0.35) | (0.07) |
| 1888 | 9.48 | 9.83 | 6.34 |
| 79–89 | (0.24) | (0.36) | (0.07) |
| 1886 | 9.81 | 9.90 | 6.17 |
| 81–91 | (0.28) | (0.35) | (0.08) |
| 1884 | 10.29 | 10.06 | 6.09 |
| 83–93 | (0.32) | (0.35) | (0.09) |

*Note*: Standard errors are given in parentheses.
*Source*: Manton, Stallard, and Vaupel (1986).

In Table 1.2 we consider consequences of the choice of different mixing distributions. In particular, we see that the inverse Gaussian model shows a sharp drop with age in $\gamma^2(x)$ (i.e. squared coefficient of variation) while the gamma has a constant $\gamma^2(x)$. Two types of evidence suggest that the gamma, with a constant $\gamma^2(x)$, is the better theoretical choice. One type of evidence is derived from studies of the health characteristics of elderly persons where significant heterogeneity is observed at even very advanced ages. Second, most theoretical models of human ageing and mortality suggest that heterogeneity, due to loss of homeostatic control, should increase except for the balancing force of selection. Thus, distinctions between the gamma and inverse Gaussian specifications could be made based upon qualitative theoretical statements about the moments of the mixing distribution. Empirically, the gamma mixing distributions, regardless of the hazard function employed, produced superior fits to the data.

TABLE 1.2. *Alternative estimates of $\gamma^2(x)$, squared coefficient of variation of conditional inverse Gaussian frailty distribution for persons born in 1900: lung cancer mortality 1950–1977, US white population.*

| Age | Males | | Females | |
|-----|-------|--|---------|--|
| | Gompertz | Weibull | Gompertz | Weibull |
| 0 | 37.8 | 39.2 | 146.8 | 31.0 |
| | (4.5) | (6.7) | (73.8) | (22.2) |
| 45 | 35.3 | 38.2 | 142.0 | 30.9 |
| 65 | 35.3 | 22.9 | 108.4 | 28.9 |
| 75 | 12.9 | 13.3 | 74.3 | 25.7 |
| 85 | 7.0 | 7.5 | 44.0 | 21.0 |
| 95 | 3.7 | 4.4 | 20.3 | 15.9 |
| | *Gamma model* | | | |
| | 27.6 | 16.7 | 86.7 | 28.7 |
| | (1.3) | (1.0) | (19.1) | (16.1) |
| | [58.6] | [70.9] | [71.5] | [65.9] |

*Note*: Standard errors are given in parentheses. Values in square brackets indicate ages at which $\gamma^2(x)$ for the inverse Gaussian model are the same values as for the gamma model.
*Source*: Manton, Stallard, and Vaupel (1986).

A more complex example of this type of modelling is summarized in Fig. 1.4, where we present the fit of a compound hazard function to US breast cancer data for 1969 (Manton and Stallard 1980). Two Weibull functions, representing two distinct types of disease, are required to fit this complex curve; and the 'premenopausal' disease has a high degree of heterogeneity associated with it. The gamma-shape parameter in this case (0.00386) is consistent with detailed genetic studies of the family pedigree of the disease which suggest that persons with specific pedigrees may have a 50 to 1 relative risk. The fact that breast cancer before age 55 is a mixture of the two disease types is consistent with the finding that about 35% of young women who get breast cancer and are diagnosed with small lesions and no positive lymph nodes will die of the disease within 10 years.

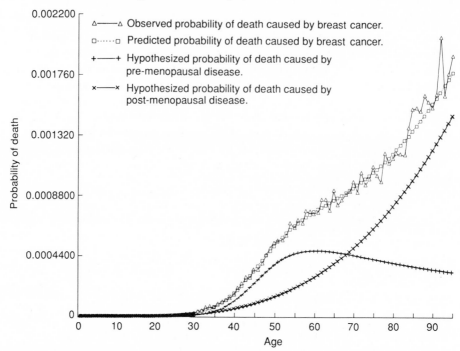

Fig. 1.4 Observed and predicted single year of age probabilities of death due to breast cancer for white females in the USA in 1969.
*Source*: Manton and Stallard (1980).

This is due to the extremely aggressive nature of the disease in such cases. Laboratory tests are now being developed to identify the characteristics of tumour cells with this aggressiveness. This also means that alternative models, where the 'hook' was modelled as the effect of menopausally related hormonal changes on a single disease process (e.g. Moolgavkar *et al.* 1979; De Lisi 1977) were probably incorrect.

### Misspecification Due to the Dependence Between Observed and Unobserved Variables

A potentially serious defect in the class of models (21) is that they are based on the frequently untested assumption that $\theta$ and $\mathbf{X}$ are independent random variables. Sensitivity in estimates of $\beta$ and/or $\alpha$ within the class of models (21) can arise simply due to a substantial mismatch between the marginal distribution $\mu(\theta)$ and the conditional distribution $\mu(\theta \mid \mathbf{X})$ that should be utilized in the specification,

$$\text{Prob}(T > t \mid \mathbf{X} = \mathbf{x}) = \int_0^\infty \exp\left\{- \Lambda_\alpha(t)e^{\mathbf{x}'\beta}\theta\right\} d\mu(\theta \mid \mathbf{x}). \tag{32}$$

Note that this model assumes that $\theta$ is determined by $X$ and thus the unobserved variables are endogenous to the observed variables. For the present discussion we will assume that the actual phenomena can be characterized by a formal theory whose mathematical image is the class of models where the conditional distribution, $\mu(\theta \mid X)$, is not equal to the unconditional distribution $\mu(\theta)$.

The potentially major consequences of ignoring dependence between $\theta$ and $X$ can be seen in the following example. Suppose data are generated from the specification

$$\text{Prob}(T > t \mid X = x) = \int_0^\infty \exp(-te^{x\beta}\theta)d\mu(\theta \mid x) \qquad (33)$$

where $X$ and $\theta$ are both dichotomous variables assuming the possible values 0 or 1. Then let

$$d\mu(\theta \mid X) = \begin{array}{ll} 1 & \text{if } X = \theta = 1 \text{ or } X = \theta = 0 \\ 0 & \text{otherwise.} \end{array} \qquad (34)$$

Thus, the true model will be

$$\text{Prob}(T > t \mid X = x) = \begin{array}{ll} \exp(-te^{\beta\,\text{true}}) & \text{for } x = 1 \\ 1 & \text{for } x = 0. \end{array} \qquad (35)$$

Ignoring the dependence between $\theta$ and $X$ is equivalent to setting $d\mu(1 \mid 1)$ equal to $d\mu(1 \mid 0)$ (and, by implication, $d\mu(0 \mid 1) = d\mu(0 \mid 0)$). The appropriate specialization of (21) to be fitted to data generated by (35) is

$$\text{Prob}(T > t \mid X = x) = \begin{array}{ll} \zeta e^{-te^\beta} + (1 - \zeta) & \text{for } x = 1 \\ \zeta e^{-t} + (1 - \zeta) & \text{for } x = 0 \end{array} \qquad (36)$$

$$\text{where } \zeta = d\mu(1).$$

If we now introduce two classes of mixing distributions:

$$M_1 = \left\{\zeta : \zeta > \frac{3}{4}\right\} \qquad (37)$$

and

$$M_2 = \left\{\zeta : \frac{1}{3} < \zeta < \frac{2}{3}\right\} \qquad (38)$$

then, as illustrated in Fig. 1.5, fitting (36) with $\zeta \in M_1$ yields an estimate of $\beta$ substantially larger than $\beta_{\text{true}}$. Constraining $\zeta$ to $M_2$ yields an estimate of $\beta$ less than $\beta_{\text{true}}$.

The sensitivity in estimates of $\beta$ to perturbations in the class of mixing distributions arises from the fact that no independence model of the form (36) could closely approximate the dependence specification (35). The substantial misspecification of using $\mu(\theta)$ instead of $d\mu(\theta \mid X)$ could be detected by simply examining plots of $\text{Prob}(T > t \mid X = x)$ over time for $x = 0$ and for $x = 1$. General diagnostic criteria are not currently available for determining when dependence

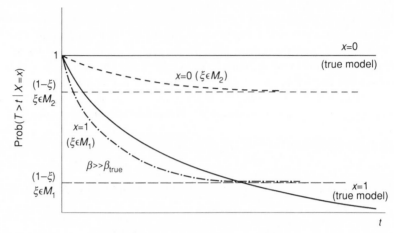

Fig. 1.5 Comparison of independence and dependence specifications.

mismatches are so severe that estimates of $\beta$ will be both biased relative to $\beta_{true}$ in the general class of models (32) and sensitive to perturbations in the class of distributions to which $\mu$ in (21) is assumed to belong. This is an important research problem, whose resolution would facilitate a deeper understanding of recent attempts (Montgomery, Richards, and Braun 1986; Foster 1985) to consider dependence between $\theta$ and $X$ in logistic models and in specifications of the form (32).

## Heterogeneity and Small-Area Estimates

Many spatial processes are only measured on a rather coarse scale relative to the level of detail required by scientific and/or policy analysis. Common examples of functionals of spatial processes where coarseness is problematic are site-specific cancer mortality rates, unemployment durations, and fertility rates. Country- or district-level rates, stratified by at least age and sex, are important economic and demographic indicators; however, their direct assessment, either by survey or even by a census of administrative records, frequently yields numerically unstable estimates as a result of both small numerators and small denominators.

Stabilization of rates associated with spatially heterogeneous processes involves the intuitive idea of borrowing information from neighbouring sites to adjust raw site-specific estimates and thereby produce more defensible values for each location. The word 'neighbouring' is not restricted to meaning simply geographical proximity. Any collection of variables for which neighbourhoods can be meaningfully defined, such as similar ages and disease histories, can be the information base for 'borrowing' to adjust initially unstable rates.

Borrowing, of course, requires a defensible model that constrains relationships among possible variables to be used for adjustment. Furthermore, judgements about the possible influence of unobserved variables on what are to be interpreted as meaningful rates dictate the structure of spatial models and can play a critical role in the interpretation of patterns and trends. We illustrate these ideas in the context of two problems that lie at the interface of demography and epidemiology: (i) whether and for which age/race/sex groups there is a west–east gradient of increasing lung cancer mortality rates across the 100 counties of the state of North Carolina; and (ii) whether and where there are changes over time in SIDS (sudden infant death syndrome) cases per live birth, also in the state of North Carolina.

For problem (i), Manton, Woodbury, and Stallard (1981) sought to determine which of 24 age × race × sex groups exhibit a west–east gradient in lung cancer mortality across North Carolina. The age categories utilized were 35–44, 45–54, 55–64, 65–74, 75–84, and 85+. Exploratory evidence suggests that age-standardized cancer rates seem to increase in the west–east direction. The word 'seem' is used because many of the 100 county rates were based on few deaths and, consequently, were unstable. Furthermore, available epidemiological evidence (Fraumeni 1985) also suggests that within age × race × sex × county populations there are further sources of heterogeneity. Here, possible unobserved heterogeneity represents an interpretation of assessed extra-Poisson variation (see e.g. Dean and Lawless 1989).

Detection and defence of possible west–east gradients and the production of adjusted county-specific lung cancer mortality rates were (Manton, Woodbury, and Stallard 1981) based on the following model.

Within each of 2400 age × race × sex × county (6 age classes × 2 races × 2 sexes × 100 counties) cells, we assume that $Z =$ (number of lung cancer deaths in the period 1970–5) is Poisson-distributed but with a gamma-distributed parameter to account for unobserved within-cell heterogeneity. Thus

$$\text{Prob}(Z = k) = \int_0^\infty e^{-n\lambda} \frac{(n\lambda)^k}{k!} \, d\mu(\lambda) \tag{39}$$

where

$$d\mu(\lambda) = \frac{(\lambda/s)^{c-1} e^{-\lambda/s}}{s\Gamma(c)} \, d\lambda, \tag{40}$$

$c$ and $s$ are positive constants, and $n =$ number of individuals in the cell.

The mixture-model defined by (39) and (40) is a negative-binomial model for $Z$. Indeed, we may rewrite (39) and (40) as

$$\text{Prob}(Z = k) = \left(\frac{1}{1+s}\right)^{kc} \frac{\Gamma(nc+k)}{\Gamma(nc)k!} \left(\frac{s}{1+s}\right)^k \tag{41}$$

Furthermore, if the gamma-distributed Poisson rate is denoted by $\Lambda$, then we have

$$E(\Lambda) = sc \quad \text{and} \quad \text{Var}(\Lambda) = s^2 c \tag{42}$$

Fitting (41) to a 2400-cell contingency table requires smoothing the 4800 $s$ and $c$ parameters—i.e. one $s$ and one $c$ per cell—across the variables age, race, sex, and county. To this end we identify the cell-specific parameters as $s_i$ and $c_i$, where $i = (i_1, i_2, i_3, i_4) \equiv$ (age, race, sex, county). Then we introduce the decomposition

$$ln\, E(\Lambda_i) = ln\, s_i c_i = ln\, s_{i_1} + b_{i_1, i_2, i_3} + b_{i_4} + B_{i_1, i_2, i_3}L \tag{43}$$

where $L$ = geographical longitude. This decomposition presumes that the scale parameter, $s_i$ only depends on age and that the gamma-shape parameter $c_i$ may be represented as

$$ln\, c_i = b_{i_1, i_2, i_3} + b_{i_4} + B_{i_1, i_2, i_3}L. \tag{44}$$

In (43), 'significantly' non-zero values of $B_{i_1, i_2, i_3}$ define the age/race/sex categories for which there is a west–east gradient. Manton, Woodbury, and Stallard (1981) found a 'significant' west–east spatial gradient for three white male age groups—55–64, 65–74, and 75–84—and one white female age group, 65–74.

The adjusted cell-specific lung cancer mortality rates are given by

$$\hat{\lambda}_i = \frac{\hat{s}_{i_1}}{1 + \hat{s}_{i_1}} \frac{y_i}{n_i} + \left(1 - \frac{\hat{s}_{i_1}}{1 + \hat{s}_{i_1}}\right)\widehat{E(\Lambda_i)} \tag{45}$$

where

$$ln\, \widehat{E(\Lambda_i)} = \widehat{ln\, s_{i_1}} + \hat{b}_{i_1, i_2, i_3} + \hat{b}_{i_4} + \hat{B}_{i_1, i_2, i_3}L \tag{46}$$

and $y_i$ = number of lung cancer deaths during 1970–5 in cell $i$. The term $s_i$ may be viewed as a measure of within-cell extra Poisson variation. The decomposition (46) represents the borrowed information used to adjust $y_i/n_i$. In particular, the averaging over levels of one or more variables that yield the estimates in (46) is the precise quantification of the word 'borrowing'. Equation (45) may also be viewed as an empirical Bayes estimate of $\lambda_i$ where the gamma distribution (40) is interpreted as a prior distribution.

An important comparison of conclusions between (39) and (40)—which incorporates unobserved within-cell heterogeneity—and a homogeneous Poisson contingency table model is that white females aged 75–84 exhibit a significant west–east gradient in the latter but not the former model. This qualitative difference in conclusions between a model that incorporates unobserved within-cell heterogeneity and one that does not is—given the unstable raw cell-specific rates—resolvable only by appeal to the a priori belief systems of the investigator. The within-cell-homogeneous Poisson model that was used in the comparison (Manton, Woodbury, and Stallard 1981) is

$$ln\, \lambda_i = \beta_{Age/Race/Sex} + \beta_{County} + \gamma_{Age/Race/Sex}L. \tag{47}$$

An alternative strategy for modelling spatial variation and borrowing information to adjust unstable rates can be based on a variety of random field specifications (Besag 1972; 1974). In this connection, Cressie and Chan (1989) study the spatial distribution of SIDS rates in two periods, 1974–8 and 1979–84, in the same 100 counties discussed above. Small numerators—including zero entries for some counties—suggest the desirability of transforming the raw rates to achieve, if possible, additivity over all scales of variation in a two-way decomposition for spatial trend. In this regard, the Freeman–Tukey deviates

$$Y_i = \sqrt{1000 \frac{s_i}{n_i}} + \sqrt{1000(s_i + 1)/n_i} \tag{48}$$

satisfy

$$\mathrm{Var}(Y_i) \approx \tau^2/n_i \tag{49}$$

where $n_i$ = (number of live births in county $i$ in a given period), $s_i$ = (number of SIDS cases in county $i$ in a given period), and $\tau^2$ is a constant invariant across counties. In terms of the transformed data, $Y_i$, it is useful to think of these values as decomposable into a component identified with large-scale spatial variation and a second component that captures local spatial dependencies. This rough idea is formalized in a Markov random-field model for $\mathbf{Y} = (Y_1, \ldots, Y_{100})$ defined by

$$\mathbf{Y} = m\mathbf{1} + b\mathbf{X} + \boldsymbol{\varepsilon} \tag{50}$$

where $\boldsymbol{\varepsilon}$ is Gaussian distributed with mean vector 0 and covariance matrix $(\mathbf{I} - \mathbf{C})^{-1}\mathbf{D}\tau^2$. The entries in $C = \| c_{ij} \|$ may be interpreted as conditional correlation coefficients between the SIDS-event counts in counties $i$ and $j$ given the counts in all other counties, $\mathbf{D} = \mathrm{diag}(n_i^{-1})$, $\mathbf{X}$ is an observed covariate (Freeman–Tukey transformed non-white live-birth rate), and $m$ is a grand mean of the transformed rates. $m\mathbf{1} + b\mathbf{X}$ models the largescale trends and $\mathbf{C}$ characterizes small-scale variation. (See Cressie and Chan 1989 for a detailed discussion of (50) as an instance of Besag's auto-Gaussian models.)

In terms of this specification the adjusted rates are estimated via

$$\hat{\mathbf{Y}}_{\mathrm{adj}} = \mathbf{X}\hat{b} + \hat{C}(\mathbf{Y} - \mathbf{X}\hat{b}) \tag{51}$$

where $\mathbf{Y}$ are the original transformed rates. The intuitive idea of borrowing information is formalized by the use of observed covariates, $\mathbf{X}$, from all counties and the near-neighbour conditional correlations, $\mathbf{C}$, to specify an adjusted rate for each county. Under the auto-Gaussian model (50), the estimator (51) generates minimum mean square error predictions of transformed rates for individual counties. In terms of these rates, the 1974–8 period involved significant influence of the non-white live-birth rate on the values of $\hat{Y}_i$ for $1 \leq i \leq 100$. The influence of race of the baby is no longer important in 1979–84.

The above analysis did not involve inclusion of within-county unobserved covariates. In the Cressie–Chan analysis, there was one county that exhibited SIDS rates that were inordinately deviant from the other counties and that substantially violated the auto-Gaussian model as a representation of spatial SIDS rates. Incorporation of an unobserved covariate, even in one county, could certainly influence estimates of adjusted rates; however, in analyses to date of SIDS rates, this strategy has not been pursued. A strong scientific basis for such specifications is currently lacking. Hence, the caution in pursuing this direction exhibited by Cressie and Chan is quite appropriate.

## Modelling the Evolution of Covariates

A common criticism of proportional-hazards specifications is that they are not derived from a formal theory that relates the structure of covariates to the time-to-occurrence of events. In many demographic contexts there is not currently a sufficiently developed theory or set of theories that could provide a deeper basis for model specification. However, chronic-disease mortality is a setting where a somewhat richer theoretical base and modelling literature allows us to examine the conclusions derived from a proportional-hazard specification when a qualitatively quite different process is viewed as correct. In addition, we illustrate the much more extensive understanding of demographic events that can be discerned where only a modestly tight, but substantively driven, theoretical framework dictates the class of allowed model specifications.

To fix these ideas we consider the evolution of a vector of physiological-status variables to be governed by a time-inhomogeneous stochastic differential equation

$$d\mathbf{x}(t) = \mathbf{u}\{t, \mathbf{x}(t)\}\,dt + \mathbf{D}\{t, \mathbf{x}(t)\}\,d\mathbf{W}(t) \tag{52}$$

for $0 \le t < T$, where $\mathbf{W}(t)$ is a multi-dimensional standard Brownian motion, $\mathbf{u}(t, \mathbf{x})$ governs local drift in the neighborhood of $\mathbf{x}$ at time $t$, $\mathbf{D}(t, \mathbf{x})$ is a bounded matrix of local variances and covariances in the neighborhood of $\mathbf{x}$ at time $t$, and $T$ is a positive random variable whose conditional survivor function is

$$P(T > t \mid \mathbf{x}(s), s < t) = \exp\left[-\int_0^t h\{s, \mathbf{x}(s)\}\,ds\right] \tag{53}$$

The function $h(t, \mathbf{x})$ is a hazard rate that, in the context of chronic disease mortality, will be assumed to have the functional form

$$h(t, \mathbf{x}) = h_0(t) + \mathbf{b}^T(t)\mathbf{x} + \frac{1}{2}\mathbf{x}^T\mathbf{B}(t)\mathbf{x} \tag{54}$$

The basic motivation for (54) is that large excursions by the physiological variables away from age-dependent homeostatic points are to be associated with a high risk of death. Thus, if we think of the quadratic form (54) describing a bowl, the bottom of which represents states of healthy physiological functioning, then large values of one or more coordinates in $\mathbf{x}$ will correspond to risky states represented by points on the quadratically increasing sides of the bowl. The restriction to quadratic forms, as opposed to cubic or higher-order non-linearities, is motivated by the necessity of modelling accelerating risk with increasing deviation from homeostatic points while at the same time recognizing that neither current theory or mortality data to date will allow for more refined distinctions among non-linearities.

The drift term, $\mathbf{u}(t, \mathbf{x})$, models age-dependent trends in physiological variables and, in the context of the evolution of risk factors for chronic diseases (Woodbury and Manton 1977; Manton, Stallard, and Woodbury 1986), has been restricted to the form

$$\mathbf{u}(t, \mathbf{x}) = \mathbf{u}_0(t) - \mathbf{A}(t)\mathbf{x}(t) \qquad (55)$$

Specification (55) represents the average rate of change of physiological status of those individuals at status-level $\mathbf{x}$. The diffusion term is usually assumed to satisfy $\mathbf{D}\{t, \mathbf{x}(t)\} \equiv \mathbf{D}(t)$. Thus it characterizes age-dependent changes in homeostatic stability of individuals.

A comparison of the relative influence of the drift and diffusion terms with each other and with specifications such as proportional hazards can be seen from a comparison of the columns in Table 1.3. Four different sets of restrictions are imposed within (52)–(55), and each specification is fitted to survival and covariate data (pulse pressure, diastolic blood pressure, Quetelet index, serum cholesterol, glucose tolerance, etc.) on a male population in Kaunas, Lithuania (Manton and Woodbury 1984). Then residual life expectancies in a cohort aged 30 years beyond the reference ages, $t$, were calculated under the four alternative sets of assumptions.

TABLE 1.3. *Residual life expectancies in a cohort aged 30 years under four alternative assumptions about the mixture of diffusion and regression contributing to the total variance of the survival with covariates; based on parameters derived from the survival experience of males in the Kaunas Study.*

| $t$ | Age | Assumption | | | |
|---|---|---|---|---|---|
|  |  | (1) | (2) | (3) | (4) |
| 0 | 30 | 44.84 | 51.83 | 52.14 | 55.32 |
| 5 | 35 | 40.05 | 47.08 | 47.60 | 50.39 |
| 10 | 40 | 35.47 | 42.42 | 42.94 | 45.52 |
| 15 | 45 | 31.13 | 37.87 | 38.39 | 40.74 |
| 20 | 50 | 27.10 | 33.46 | 33.99 | 36.08 |
| 25 | 55 | 23.40 | 29.24 | 29.77 | 31.57 |
| 30 | 60 | 20.09 | 25.24 | 25.77 | 27.28 |
| 35 | 65 | 17.18 | 21.50 | 22.03 | 23.23 |
| 40 | 70 | 14.66 | 18.06 | 18.59 | 19.49 |
| 45 | 75 | 12.52 | 14.96 | 15.49 | 16.09 |
| 50 | 80 | 10.70 | 12.21 | 12.73 | 13.06 |
| 55 | 85 | 9.16 | 9.82 | 10.31 | 10.42 |

Assumptions:
(1) $\mathbf{u}(t,\cdot) = 0$: Diffusion dominates over drift.
(2) Diffusion and regression in equilibrium.
(3) No diffusion, no regression, fixed covariate values.
(4) Homogeneous population.
*Source*: Manton, Stallard, and Woodbury (1986).

In case (1), the diffusion fluctuations are not counterbalanced by a force except mortality. These estimates are very close to those obtained in an unconstrained version of (52)–(55)—(not shown in Table 2). In case (2), the diffusion and regression components—$\mathbf{A}(t)\mathbf{X}(t)$—are in equilibrium and the age-dependent drift term $\mathbf{u}_0(t)$ is set equal to zero. Here, for example, the life expectancy at age 30 increases by 7 years (to 51.8 years), indicating that the combined action of diffusion and regression in equilibrium can have a major influence on mortality.

Case (3) corresponds to fixed covariates and differs very little from case (2). This means that, at least for the Kaunas male population, a mixture of proportional-hazard models of the kind discussed earlier in this paper can provide reasonable approximations at least for the mortality experience of a population governed by (52)–(55), subject to the restriction set of case (2).

Finally, case (4) corresponds to a homogeneous population model where, in most instances, the projected life expectancies are three years longer than in case (2), which corresponds to an a priori belief system supporting the diffusion specification (52)–(55). The principal lesson of these comparisons is that the richer chronic-disease-based specification (52)–(55) is much closer to the scientific subject-matter than the models presented earlier in the paper, and only leads to the same projections under very restrictive constraints. Furthermore, the uncertainty about the influence of covariates on survival that plagued the statistical models (proportional hazards and mixtures of them) is now changed to uncertainty about the defensibility of the biological rationale for (52)–(55). In our opinion, deeper understanding is obtained via empirical challenges to more biologically and/or social-theoretically driven models. Furthermore, Table 1.3 is only one of many possible examples indicating that the sensitivity of conclusions resulting from small changes in model assumptions, but in the presence of major model misspecification, does not manifest itself when the models and the science are much closer together—i.e. (52)–(55) and chronic-disease mortality.

## Conclusions

There has been considerable recent debate about the feasibility of estimating event history models in the presence of significant unobserved heterogeneity. Concerns were voiced that there was a generic instability in the estimation of the parameters of such models.

In this chapter we have shown that no such generic instability exists. In particular, we have shown that no instability results when there is adequate theory and ancillary data to get reasonable specifications of the deterministic and stochastic components of the model selected. This is illustrated with a number of examples in the analysis of chronic-disease morbidity and mortality. We furthermore described how, in a number of analyses that showed instability, that the instability resulted from model misspecification that could be easily diagnosed and repaired by an appropriate respecification. For example, in the case of unemployment data, instability could result from a smooth hazard being fitted to data with spikes at the times where unemployment benefits expired. Parameter-sensitivity problems could be eliminated if the spikes were included in an appropriate model respecification (Meyer 1986).

In addition to the problems produced by a given data structure, we also examined the issue of estimating models when the heterogeneity variables were changing. This was done by applying a multivariate diffusion process model of human mortality to longitudinal data on risk-factor change and mortality, and showing the magnitude of the bias introduced as the parameters describing risk-factor changes were constrained. This showed that, in certain types of multivariate process, the averaging of risks over the multivariate distribution function can be closely approximated by a hazard model with fixed frailty. This seemed to hold in the case of human mortality because the heterogeneity of the population was in necessary equilibrium with mortality selection. In other substantive areas where such equilibrium is likely to exist, the fixed-frailty model may be a reasonable approximation.

In addition to the hazard model with a fixed-frailty distribution, there are new analytic schemes that seem capable of dealing with unobserved heterogeneity. One such approach, due to Heckman and Singer (1984*a*), involves estimating non-parametric mixing functions. This removes bias in the structural coefficients by allowing for the effect of nuisance-mixing parameters. The advantage of the approach is that no assumption about the form of the mixing distribution is needed. Of course, it is still necessary to specify correctly the hazard function, and it is not possible to gain insights into the mixing distribution from the nuisance parameters.

A major issue raised by the paper is what the analyst should do if strong theory and ancillary data are not available to the analyst in the model construction and validation phase. It is often asked if generic, flexible model forms might not be employed. If the analyst's interest is to simply describe data, then use of such a generic model simply represents the calculation of statistics to summarize a complex distribution function. In this case, any model specification sensitive to the features of the data will suffice. In most cases, however, the analyst will want to go beyond description—to make generalizations beyond one's data set to other data sets, to develop theory or hypotheses, or to make predictions and forecasts. In this case a generic, 'flexible' model cannot be meaningfully employed, because any model embodies assumptions about the phenomena to be studied which, if wrong, will lead to seriously biased parameter estimates. In these cases, the analyst must use theory and ancillary data to motivate his model specification. If existing theory is weak this will be difficult, but it is necessary.

## References

Besag, J. (1972), 'Nearest-Neighbor Systems and the Auto-Logistic Model for Binary Data', *Journal of the Royal Statistical Society*, ser. B, 34. 1: 75–83.

Besag, J. (1974), 'Spatial Interaction and the Statistical Analysis of Lattice Systems', *Journal of the Royal Statistical Society*, ser. B, 36. 2: 192–236.

Cressie, N., and Chan, N. H. (1989), 'Spatial Modeling of Regional Variables', *Journal of the American Statistical Association*, 84. 406: 393–401.

Dean, C., and Lawless, J. (1989), 'Tests for Detecting Overdispersion in Poisson Regression Models', *Journal of the American Statistical Association*, 84. 406: 467–72.

De Lisi, C. (1977), 'The Age Incidence of Female Breast Cancer: Simple Models and Analysis of Epidemiological Patterns', *Mathematical Bioscience*, 37. 1–2: 245–66.

Economos, A. C. (1982), 'Rate of Aging, Rate of Dying and the Mechanisms of Mortality', *Archives of Gerontological Geriatrics*, 1: 13–27.

Elbers, C., and Ridder, G. (1982), 'True and Spurious Duration Dependence: The Identifiability of the Proportional Hazard Model', *Review of Economic Studies*, 49. 3: 403–10.

Foster, A. (1985), *Unobserved Heterogeneity and Dependent Covariates: A State–Space Model of Infant Growth*, Tech. Report WP-85–87, International Institute for Applied Systems Analysis (Laxenburg).

Fraumeni, J. F. (1985), *Persons at High Risk of Cancer: An Approach to Cancer Etiology and Control* (Academic Press, New York).

Heckman, J., and Singer, B. (1984*a*), 'A Method for Minimizing Distributional Assumptions in Econometric Models for Duration Data', *Econometrica*, 52. 2: 271–320.

—— and —— (1984*b*), 'The Identifiability of the Proportional Hazard Model', *Review of Economic Studies*, 51. 2: 231–41.

Malinvaud, E. (1970), *Statistical Methods of Econometrics* (Amsterdam).

Manton, K. G., and Stallard, E. (1980), 'A Two-Disease Model of Female Breast Cancer: Mortality in 1969 among White Females in the United States', *Journal of the National Cancer Institute*, 64. 1: 9–16.

—— —— and Vaupel, J. (1986), 'Alternative Models of the Heterogeneity of Mortality Risks Among the Aged', *Journal of the American Statistical Association*, 81. 395: 635–44.

—— —— and Woodbury, M. A. (1986), 'Chronic Disease Evolution and Human Aging: A General Model for Assessing the Impact of Chronic Disease in Human Populations', *Mathematical Modeling*, 7: 1155–71.

—— and Woodbury, M. A. (1984), *Models of the Process of Risk Factor Change and Risk Selection for Multiple Disease End-Points in the Kaunas Study Population*, WHO Report for Development of an Integrated Programme for Non-Communicable Disease Prevention and Control (Geneva).

—— —— and Stallard, E. (1981), 'A Variance Components Approach to Categorical Data Models with Heterogeneous Cell Populations: Analysis of Spatial Gradients in Lung Cancer Mortality Rates in North Carolina Counties', *Biometrics*, 37. 2: 259–69.

—— —— —— (1989), 'Forecasting the Limits to Life Expectancy: Modeling Mortality from Epidemiological and Medical Data', in S. R. Johansson (ed.), *Aging and Dying: The Biological Foundations of Human Longevity* (University of California Press, Berkeley, Calif.).

Marini, M. (1985), 'Determinants of Marital Disruption', paper presented at Population Association of America Annual Meeting, Mar. 1985, Boston.

Meyer, B. (1986), 'Semi-Parametric Estimation of Hazard Models', Ph.D. dissertation, Dep. of Economics, Massachusetts Institute of Technology.

Montgomery, M., Richards, T., and Braun, H. (1986), 'Child Health, Breast-Feeding, and Survival in Malaysia: A Random-Effects Logit Approach', *Journal of the American Statistical Society*, 81. 394: 297–309.

Moolgavkar, S. H. *et al.* (1979), 'Effect of Age on Incidence of Breast Cancer in Females', *Journal of the National Cancer Institute*, 62: 493–501.

Rosenberg, G., Kemeny, G., Smith, L. G., Skurnick, J. D., and Bandurski, M. J. (1973), 'The Kinetics and Thermodynamics of Death in Multicellular Organism', *Mechanisms of Aging and Development*, 2: 275–93.

Strehler, B. L. (1977), *Time, Cells, and Aging* (Academic Press, New York).

Trussell, T. J., and Richards, T. (1985), 'Correcting for Unobserved Heterogeneity in Hazard Models: An Application of the Heckman–Singer Procedure to Demographic Data', in N. Tuma (ed.), *Sociological Methodology, 1985* (Jossey-Bass, San Francisco).

Wetterstrand, W. H. (1981), 'Parametric Models for Life Insurance Mortality Data: Gompertz Law over Time', *Transactions of the Society of Actuaries*, 33: 159–75.

Woodbury, M. A., and Manton, K. G. (1977), 'A Random Walk Model of Human Mortality and Aging', *Theoretical Population Biology*, 11. 1: 37–48.

# 2 Union Dissolution in Sweden

JAMES TRUSSELL, GERMÁN RODRÍGUEZ, BARBARA VAUGHAN

In sharp contrast to marital dissolution, about which there are many articles and books, the study of non-marital union dissolution has received relatively little attention. The reason for such an omission in the literature is largely due to the absence of high-quality data. Whereas numerous fertility surveys have collected the dates of marriages and separations (or divorces), the collection of such dates for non-marital unions is uncommon, except in those developing countries (largely in the Caribbean) where such unions are prevalent and can be viewed as marriage equivalents.

As it does for many types of data, Sweden provides a refreshing exception. A 1981 fertility survey entitled *Women in Sweden* collected a union history, in addition to pregnancy and occupation histories and information on numerous other background variables. However, the rich variety of analyses of these data has included only one study of union dissolution, and it focused on the relatively narrow question of whether premarital cohabitation increased or decreased subsequent marital dissolution rates (Bennett, Blanc, and Bloom 1988). This focus is understandable, since a marked trend toward increased non-marital cohabitation has been evident in many countries, particularly those in Scandinavia. For example, in Sweden non-marital unions comprised 1% of all unions in 1960, 6–7% in 1969, and 15–16% in 1979 (Trost 1980).[1] As such unions become more prevalent, it becomes more important to study their role in the life cycle of families.

The goal of the present inquiry is to examine the covariates of union dissolution in Sweden, the only population with data suited for such an analysis. The remaining part of the chapter is divided into four sections. The first describes the data available for analysis and presents preliminary analyses of these data. The second discusses the hazard model, the statistical model (equivalent to a multivariate life table) that we use in the subsequent analyses, and the process of selecting variables for inclusion in this model. The third presents the final results and a discussion thereof. The chapter concludes with a summary.

---

[1] Actually, it is not possible to infer from the text the reference year for the 15–16% figure; it could be as early as 1975 or as late as 1979.

## The Data

The 1981 Swedish survey was conducted by the Central Bureau of Statistics (now Statistics Sweden). It was based on a sample of 4966 women aged 20–44 who were resident in the country in February 1981. Interviews were conducted with 4300 respondents, primarily in March, April, and May 1981 (Statistics Sweden

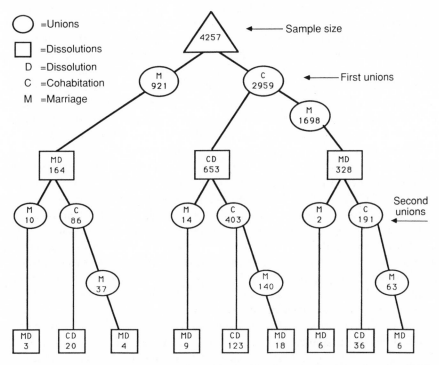

Fig. 2.1 Union histories in the 1981 Swedish Fertility Survey (Statistics Sweden 1981).

1981). The data obtained from 43 respondents were irreparably incomplete, and so only 4257 cases were available for further analysis. We must emphasize at this point that the respondents were women, and that, although there is a wealth of information in the survey, it is confined to respondents and excludes partners.[2] Our subsequent analyses of these covariates does not imply that the characteristics of men can be ignored when studying union stability, only that we have no data on the characteristics of men. While this omission is regrettable, it is by no means uncommon.

---

[2] There are 4 topics in the survey about the current partner (sharing household work, occupation, education, and sharing responsibilities for children). Information that is confined to the current partner is, however, useless for the analysis of union dissolution, because such information is available only for open intervals.

Women were asked to supply the dates (month and year) at which they 'moved in together', married, and 'split up' for all periods of time exceeding one month in which they 'lived together with a man, either as married or without being formally married'. From these data, we constructed Fig. 2.1, a tree diagram that shows the union histories of the 4257 women in the sample. A total of 3880 women had a first union; 921 of the 3880 entered directly into marriage and the remaining 2959 started a period of cohabitation, with 1698 of them proceeding to marry their partners at a later date. Note that, as a matter of definition, we consider first marriages following cohabitation as an integral part of the first union (not a second union). Of the 3880 first unions, 1145 ended in dissolution and the rest remained intact at the time of the survey in 1981. Among the 1145 women whose first unions were dissolved, 706 entered second unions. A large majority of these women came from (417 of 706) or entered into (680 of 706) cohabitation rather than marriage; 403 of 706 both came from and entered into cohabitation. Of the 706 second unions, 225 had dissolved by the time of the interview.

Scrutiny of this tree focuses attention on the life cycle of unions, and it forces one to think about the samples one should select for further analysis. For example, Bennett, Blanc, and Bloom (1988) analyse marriages. But, as can be seen from Fig. 2.1, such a sample must be plucked from many parts of the tree. Some marriages are first unions, while others are second or third unions. Even among first marriages, some occur after a period of cohabitation while others do not. For the former, duration may be counted from either the start of marriage or the start of cohabitation, and which choice is correct is not at all evident. Henceforth, we will analyse three primary samples: 3880 first unions, 706 second unions, and 2785 first marriages (of a total of 2913 marriages of all orders). We choose to analyse first marriages because marriage is still the primary reproductive unit, even in Sweden (Etzler 1987) and because the effect of premarital cohabitation on subsequent marriage stability is a topic of interest in itself. In addition, we will analyse first marriages in two ways. In the first, we measure duration from the start of marriage in the conventional way. In the second, women enter the marriage life table at their duration of cohabitation at the time of marriage. This multiple-increment approach allows one to test whether the finding by Bennett, Blanc, and Bloom (1988) (and also by Balakrishnan *et al.* (1987) among Canadian women) that cohabitation shortens the duration of marriage would hold if the entire duration of the union (including its premarital exposure) were examined.[3]

Under the assumption that the rate of union dissolution is constant across women and over duration, the monthly rate of first-marriage dissolution is 0.001497. The monthly rate of first-union dissolution is 0.002614, or 75% higher. The monthly dissolution rate for second unions is 0.005686, 3.8 times the rate for first marriages and 2.2 times the rate for first unions. Therefore, we see clearly

---

[3] Having not seen their paper until our analyses were completed, we were not aware that they had tested the same hypothesis; their results are reported in their n. 4.

from this preliminary analysis that first marriages are much less likely to fail than are first unions, which in turn are much less likely to fail than are second unions. Whether (and how much) this conclusion is altered by relaxing the assumption that the dissolution rate is constant will be explored in the next section.

Information on factors likely to influence dissolution is abundant in the Swedish survey, at least in comparison with other fertility surveys. Our preliminary analysis of such factors was guided by the literature on marital dissolution (Balakrishnan *et al.* 1987; Becker, Landes, and Michael 1977; Cherlin 1977; 1981; McCarthy 1978; McCarthy and Menken 1979; Menken *et al.* 1981; Morgan, Lye, and Condran 1988; Morgan and Rindfuss 1985; Murphy 1985; Teachman 1982; Thornton 1977; Waite, Haggstrom, and Kanouse 1985). There are three demographic variables that we hypothesize would affect dissolution rates: birth cohort, union cohort, and age at union. These three are perfectly collinear, with the date of birth plus the age at union being equal to the date of union; without special restrictive assumptions, age, period, and birth cohort effects cannot be identified. The question of identification will not be pursued further here; our goal is merely to decide which two best describe the data.

We expect that a young age at union signals relatively greater emotional or social immaturity and will be associated with higher rates of dissolution, but that this effect might be confined to those who form unions at the very youngest ages. In addition to mere immaturity, a young age at union is also an index of the life cycle changes that the union must undergo in order to survive (Morgan and Rindfuss 1985). We also expect that later birth or union cohorts will experience higher rates of dissolution, because of the generally observed tendency for dissolution rates to increase in the recent past. One might expect that birth cohort (with other factors held equal) would pick up the effects of norms and values transmitted through the family of orientation during childhood; as these norms (and behaviours as well) have changed over time, in part because the importance of family has weakened and economic prosperity has increased (period effects), then rates of dissolution should rise among later birth cohorts. Union cohort might be expected to reflect period effects more directly.

We would expect other variables as well to reflect norms and attitudes transmitted through the family. For example, we would be surprised not to find differences in union stability among various socioeconomic status (SES) categories of the family of orientation. Our expectation is that the higher the SES, the more likely one is to develop a 'modern' view about relationships, one that values commitment *per se* only so long as a relationship supplies satisfaction to both partners. Hence, we expect dissolution rates to rise with SES of the family of orientation. Preliminary life table analysis suggested that the two categories of blue-collar worker could be combined, and that two categories of white-collar worker could also be collapsed. Hence, we were left with five categories of SES: blue-collar, white-collar, professional, farmer, and small businessman.[4]

[4] Actually, there are 3 white-collar categories; we simply labelled the highest category 'professional' and found that the other 2 categories could be combined.

We would expect that, when the mother in the family of orientation worked outside the home, less traditional family values would be inculcated. Here the Swedish survey provided us with three options: information about the primary breadwinner during the respondent's childhood, about the mother's work before the respondent went to school, and about the mother's work after the respondent went to school. Preliminary life table analysis showed that the later variable was most discriminating, so it alone was retained for further analysis. One other set of factors partly transmitted through the family of orientation is attitudes toward children. At the time of the survey, respondents were asked to respond to six related assertions, only two of which ('having kids is one of the purposes of life' and 'something is missing in a relationship if there are no children') showed much power to discriminate. Clearly, attitudes about children expressed at the time of the interview could embody the accumulated experience in unions of the respondent, so cause and effect are not separable. Nevertheless, the former variable was the single most discriminating factor in our preliminary life tables, and it was retained for further analysis.

The variables discussed thus far are all time-fixed variables, whose values for a couple do not change during the union. In addition, the occupation/education and fertility histories allowed us to construct several other variables whose values could change over time. These time-changing variables were completed education, work/study status, and the age composition of children during the union. Of these, education poses by far the biggest challenge to the analyst. We are indebted for the help offered by Jan Hoem, both in his paper on this subject (Hoem 1986) and in subsequent conversations. The problem is that the answers to the question about the level and type of education completed at the time of the survey are not consistent with the histories of periods of study collected in the occupation history. The survey never asks the dates at which educational milestones (e.g. graduation from secondary school) were attained, so that these must be inferred by constructing completed years of education from the occupation history. To do so, Hoem tallied one month of schooling when the respondent reported that she was a full-time student, one-half a month of schooling when the respondent reported she was a part-time student, and one-quarter of a month of schooling when the respondent reported school as a sideline activity. Since the predicted milestones correlated so poorly with the reported milestones (in part because women with varied education histories (e.g. secondary school followed by typing school) had difficulty in deciding which education is the 'highest'), he employed only a trichotomous factor indicating low, middle, or high, based on his constructed years of schooling completed since age 16. The problem is further compounded because the Swedish education system underwent substantial change during the period in question; we refer the reader to Hoem's excellent discussion. Despite his bad experience with the education data, we bravely sought to reconstruct the milestones. We followed the same algorithm he used, except that we did not allocate any credit toward the next educational milestone when a study spell lasted less than five months; nor did we distinguish between part-time and sideline study, giving instead a half-month credit for both. Surprisingly, our results correlated more closely than Hoem's with the women's reports, though whether this outcome is a success is questionable, because these reports are themselves of dubious quality. Nevertheless, we retained our educational milestones for further analysis.

On the basis of previous research on marriage (e.g., Menken *et al.* 1981; Teachman 1982; Morgan and Rindfuss 1985), we would expect that union stability would be positively associated with educational attainment. Both Menken *et al.* and Teachman, in analyses of US data, found in their final models that having not graduated from high school raised dissolution rates significantly, but that education beyond high school did not increase marital stability further. Therefore, instability might be associated with only very low educational attainment. It is possible that very low educational attainment has little to do with education *per se*, and merely signals poor adaptation that could be due to personal, social, or economic factors; in the much more homogeneous society characteristic of Sweden, such an effect may be much weaker. Moreover, it is plausible that those with more education would develop more modern attitudes towards relationships so that the effect would be reversed.

Our children variable was constructed somewhat arbitrarily. We eventually decided on five categories: no children under 16, own children under 5 (whose father is the current-union partner), any children under 5, own children aged 5–15 (whose father is the current-union partner), and any children aged 5–15. We reasoned that children would affect union dissolution only if they were still at home, so we confined attention to children under age 16. We also wanted to test for different effects of young and older children, and we somewhat arbitrarily chose age 5 as the dividing age between toddler and child. Our expectation is that children will depress the rates of dissolution. However, it is certainly possible that couples have children to try to salvage their faltering relationship, in which case children might signal instability rather than the reverse. This signal of instability ought, however, to be confined primarily to the youngest age category of children. Our naïve expectation was that having children under age 5 would most strongly depress dissolution rates (despite the possibility of the reverse signal), that having no children under 16 would be associated with the greatest union instability, and that the partner's own children provide stronger glue than do children from a prior union (or liaison). Our expectations were only partly confirmed by Cherlin (1977) for US data; he found that having children under 5 did increase marital stability, but that having children of older ages made no difference whatsoever. Likewise, our expectations were partly confirmed by Murphy's (1985) discovery that having no children decreased marital stability among British couples; however, he also found that those with many children (a situation unlikely to be observed in Sweden) also experienced high rates of marriage dissolution.

TABLE 2.1. *Means of variables used in models of first marriage, first union, and second union dissolution, Sweden.*

| | First marriage | First union | Second union |
|---|---|---|---|
| *Fixed covariates* | | | |
| Birth cohort 1946–50 | 0.28 | 0.25 | 0.28 |
| Birth cohort 1951+ | 0.24 | 0.38 | 0.38 |
| Age at union < 20 | 0.17 | 0.36 | 0.06 |
| Age at union 20–4 | 0.58 | 0.52 | 0.39 |
| Age at union 25–9 | 0.20 | 0.10 | 0.30 |
| Union cohort 1966–70 | 0.28 | 0.26 | 0.08 |
| Union cohort 1971–5 | 0.22 | 0.28 | 0.28 |
| Union cohort 1976+ | 0.25 | 0.24 | 0.61 |
| Education at union: secondary 3–4 | 0.23 | 0.23 | 0.22 |
| Education at union: university | 0.06 | 0.04 | 0.07 |
| SES background: white-collar | 0.18 | 0.19 | 0.21 |
| SES background: professional | 0.06 | 0.07 | 0.09 |
| SES background: small businessman | 0.14 | 0.14 | 0.14 |
| SES background: farmer | 0.14 | 0.13 | 0.09 |
| Attitude toward kids: immaterial | 0.24 | 0.29 | 0.33 |
| Attitude toward kids: a drag | 0.03 | 0.05 | 0.06 |
| Mom worked a lot while woman in school | 0.31 | 0.34 | 0.42 |
| Cohabit with husband < 2 years before marriage | 0.42 | — | — |
| Cohabit with husband ⩾ 2 years before marriage | 0.25 | — | — |
| Previously married | — | — | 0.41 |
| First union lasted < 24 months | — | — | 0.32 |
| First union lasted 60+ months | — | — | 0.34 |
| No. of cases[a] | 2 720 | 3 788 | 687 |
| *Changing covariates* | | | |
| Study only | 0.07 | 0.10 | 0.10 |
| Any work | 0.54 | 0.55 | 0.60 |
| Full-time work/study | 0.38 | 0.47 | 0.52 |
| Part-time work/study | 0.23 | 0.19 | 0.19 |
| Education: secondary 3–4 | 0.23 | 0.23 | 0.22 |
| Education: university | 0.09 | 0.08 | 0.07 |
| No kids ⩽ 16 | 0.25 | 0.39 | 0.32 |
| Own kid < 5 | 0.50 | 0.42 | 0.30 |
| Any kid < 5 | 0.52 | 0.44 | 0.41 |
| Own kid 5–16 | 0.21 | 0.16 | 0.06 |
| Married | — | 0.67 | 0.36 |
| No. of spells[a, b] | 14363 | 20648 | 2366 |

[a] *After* cases with missing covariate information have been discarded.
[b] No. of spells: a spell is created whenever a time-varying covariate changes.

The occupation variable has six categories: none, full-time study, part-time study, full-time work, part-time work, and full-time combination of study and work. Not all categories can be considered simultaneously, because cell sizes for some categories are too small. We reason that working would increase the rate of dissolution, since one would be more likely to have the resources to live alone. But both working and studying ensure that one is more likely to encounter other men who might prove irresistibly attractive. Hence the trichotomy no/part-time/full-time work or study might be more discriminating than the trichotomy no work or study/study only/work. For the moment, we retain all six categories for further analysis.

Four other variables round out our set of candidates for multivariate analysis. The first, premarital cohabitation, applies only to the marriage samples. We employ a trichotomous categorization (none, less than two years, and two years or more) to test the effect of prenuptial cohabitation on first-marriage dissolution. We expect that longer cohabitation would increase rates of dissolution when duration is measured since the start of marriage. But we are agnostic about the effect on marriage stability when those who have cohabited enter the marriage life table at the duration of the union at the time of marriage. The second variable, married (which is a changing variable that takes the value 0 until marriage occurs, when it takes the value 1), applies to the samples of first and second unions. We expect that being married substantially lowers rates of dissolution, since marriage signals a greater commitment than merely living together. Another dummy variable, previously married, applies only to the sample of second unions. We expect that it signals a more traditional attitude toward relationships, so that we expect it to enhance second-union stability. The final covariate, the duration of the first union (with three categories: short (< 24 months), medium (24–59 months), and long (≥ 60 months)) likewise applies only to second unions. We expect that the lengths of first and second unions would be positively related, perhaps because we will have omitted important explanatory factors that have similar effects on dissolution rates in both unions and that also persist over time.

Means of all these fixed and changing variables are displayed in Table 2.1. Note that the sample sizes are always somewhat smaller than the numbers in Fig. 2.1 would imply, because cases with missing covariate values were excluded before the means were calculated.

## The Statistical Model and Variable Selection

The model we employ is the now familiar piece-wise exponential-hazards model in which the hazard is represented as a step function. More precisely, we model the natural logarithm of the hazard or risk of union dissolution ($\lambda_{ik}$) for individual $i$ with vector of covariates $\mathbf{Z}_{ik}$ in duration category $k$ (where $d_k \leq d < d_{k+1}$) as

$$ln(\lambda_{ik}) = \alpha_k + \gamma_k' \mathbf{Z}_{ik} \tag{1}$$

TABLE 2.2. *Summary of model selection.* $\chi^2$ *and df pertain to the comparison of the given model with a null model (no covariates and constant hazard).*

| Model | First marriage | | First union | | Second union | | Multiple increment first marriage[a] | |
|---|---|---|---|---|---|---|---|---|
| | $\chi^2$ | df | $\chi^2$ | df | $\chi^2$ | df | $\chi^2$ | df |
| *Final proportional hazards* | 215.4 | 26 | 905.8 | 26 | 116.3 | 27 | 209.5 | 26 |
| Drop duration | 198.8 | 19 | 889.4 | 19 | 112.5 | 21 | 198.8 | 19 |
| Drop covariates | 14.6 | 7 | 134.4 | 7 | 27.2 | 6 | 15.3 | 7 |
| Add 3 more duration categories | 215.5 | 29 | 908.0 | 29 | — | — | 212.3 | 29 |
| Drop covariates | 14.9 | 10 | 144.6 | 10 | — | — | 18.3 | 10 |
| Add own kid > 5 | — | — | — | — | 116.7 | 28 | — | — |
| *Final proportional hazards* | 215.4 | 26 | 905.8 | 26 | 116.3 | 27 | 209.5 | 26 |
| With union cohort instead of birth cohort[b], or vice versa[c] | 209.2 | 27 | 898.9 | 25 | 111.7 | 27 | 203.5 | 27 |
| With work/study instead of part-time/full-time | 192.2 | 26 | 878.9 | 26 | 108.7 | 27 | 186.0 | 26 |
| With any kid < 5 instead of own kid < 5 | 215.0 | 26 | 904.8 | 26 | 115.8 | 27 | 208.9 | 26 |
| With own kid > 5 instead of own kid < 5 | 214.4 | 26 | 904.2 | 26 | 116.4 | 27 | 208.3 | 26 |
| With time-varying education instead of education at start | 214.0 | 26 | 901.5 | 26 | 115.3 | 27 | 208.0 | 26 |

[a] Exposure status at duration of union, instead of at duration 0.
[b] First marriage.
[c] First and second unions.

Note that the covariates have a subscript $k$ to allow for the fact that some or all of them may change with duration. Likewise, the parameter vector of effects estimates has a subscript $k$ to allow for the possibility that the effect of a particular value of a variable might change with duration. If the subscript on the parameter vector is dropped, then we have a proportional-hazards model, in which the effect of a covariate is to raise or lower the baseline hazard (traced out by $\exp(\alpha_k)$) by a constant proportion at all durations. We estimate such models by maximizing the likelihood function (based on equation (1)) using the software package RATE (Tuma 1979). For a further discussion of this model in terms familiar to demographers, see Menken *et al.* (1981) or Trussell and Hammerslough (1983).

Among other choices not addressed or left unresolved in the previous section are: (i) how many duration intervals are needed, and where the steps should be located; (ii) which two of the three variables, birth cohort, union cohort, and age at union, perform best; (iii) whether the time-varying education variables perform better than their counterparts that are fixed at the beginning of the union; (iv) whether the work/study dichotomy outperforms the full/part-time dichotomy; and

(v) which categories of the children variable work best. To address these questions we estimated proportional-hazards models on the three samples (first marriage, first union, second union) described earlier. The results are summarized in Table 2.2.

We first estimated proportional-hazards models with eight duration categories for the first marriage and first union samples: 0, 1, 2, 3, 4, 5–9, 10–14, and 15+ years. For the sample of second unions the categories were 0, 1, 2, 3, 4, 5–6, and 7+ years. These were chosen after examining the preliminary life tables, which did not show much variation of the hazard with duration (or any heaping at specific durations). This preliminary observation was supported by the results from the proportional-hazards models. First, dropping duration categories altogether had only a small effect on the likelihood, when compared with the much larger reduction caused by dropping the covariates. For first marriages and first unions, the assumption of a constant hazard is rejected by a likelihood ratio test, but then only barely ($x^2 = 16.6$ and $X^2 = 16.4$, respectively, with 7 $df$). In no sample did the assumption of a constant hazard alter the estimated covariate effects. This finding of a constant hazard in itself was unexpected, because our previous work on marital dissolution in the United States showed a definite decline in the hazard (Menken *et al.* 1981). Second, adding three more intervals (at the longer durations after 5 years) did not improve the likelihood for the marriage or first-union samples.[5] As a result of these comparisons, we decided to retain eight intervals for these two samples.

Similar experiments showed that birth cohort was a better discriminator in the marriage models than was marriage cohort, but that the reverse was true for the union models. As expected, union and birth cohort together always performed more poorly than did either variable when combined with age at union (results not shown). The trichotomy no children/own children under five/other proved to be best for all samples. Likewise, the trichotomy no/part-time/full-time work or study outperformed the trichotomy no work or study/work/study only in all samples. Finally, the time-varying education variables did not discriminate as well as the education variables fixed at the start of the union in any of the samples. We suspect that this finding is not real, but in fact is caused by our inability to construct education milestones with any precision from the available data. With these choices made, we proceeded to search for final models, those that in our estimation best capture the data.

## Final Models and Results

Variables selected according to the discussion in the previous section were included in our final proportional-hazards models. The effect estimates and selected

---

[5] More intervals could not be added to second unions, because the sample is too small.

$\chi^2$ statistics are presented in Tables 2.3–2.6. We discuss briefly the goodness of fit of the final models and then turn to examine the effects estimates for each in turn.

## Goodness of Fit

The $\chi^2$ statistics (shown at the bottom of Tables 2.3–2.6) comparing the final models with the null (where all durations and combinations of values of the covariates are assumed to have the same risk) are all highly significant, indicating that our models have captured important sources of variation in the data. On the other hand all models pass the usual goodness of fit test based on the $\chi^2$ (or deviance) statistic, comparing the final with the saturated models (where each combination of values of the covariates at each duration has its own hazard rate).

These statistics must be interpreted with considerable caution, however, for two reasons. First, tests of significance are not strictly applicable when the model has been selected after looking at the data, and therefore provide more an informal orientation than a rigorous test. Second, our data tables have a large number of relatively sparse cells, which inflate the number of degrees of freedom and shed doubt on the validity of asymptotic $\chi^2$ approximations to the sampling distribution of the goodness of fit or deviance statistic. In the final analysis we are reasonably confident that the models selected provide a reasonable description of the data, but our conclusion rests more on the lack of improvement noted after the addition of further effects than on the fact that the models pass the goodness of fit tests.

## First Marriage

Table 2.3 shows the estimated final proportional-hazards model of first-marriage dissolution, in which all women enter the life table at duration 0. As expected, the longer one cohabits before marriage, the greater is the instability of the subsequent marriage. Compared with no prenuptial cohabitation, cohabiting for less than two years raises the hazard by 57%, while cohabiting for two years or longer doubles it, with the estimated 97% increase being significantly greater than the estimated 57% increase. Marriages to women born after 1950 exhibit rates of dissolution 69% higher than those to women born earlier. Rates of dissolution among those who marry before age 20 are 93% greater than those among women who marry at later ages.

Those with university education and those with three to four years of secondary education experienced rates of dissolution only 58% and 77% as high, respectively, as those with two or fewer years of secondary education, although the rate for the best educated is not significantly lower than the rate for those with intermediate education. As expected, those who strongly agree that having children is important have the greatest marital stability; those who merely agree or do not know (whose attitude we label 'kids immaterial') have risks of dissolution

TABLE 2.3. *Final proportional-hazards model of first-marriage dissolution.*

|  | Exp (Coeff) | Z–Stat (Coeff/se) |
|---|---|---|
| *Fixed covariates* | | |
| Didn't cohabit with husband before marriage | 1.00 | — |
| Cohabit with husband < 2 years before marriage | 1.57 | 4.33 |
| Cohabit with husband ⩾ 2 years before marriage | 1.97 | 4.63 |
| Birth cohort < 1946 | 1.00 | — |
| Birth cohort 1946–50 | 1.06 | 0.54 |
| Birth cohort 1951+ | 1.69 | 3.58 |
| Age at marriage: < 20 | 1.93 | 3.96 |
| Age at marriage 20–4 | 0.99 | − 0.05 |
| Age at marriage 25+ | 1.00 | — |
| Education at marriage: < secondary 3 | 1.00 | — |
| Education at marriage: secondary 3–4 | 0.77 | − 1.98 |
| Education at marriage: university | 0.58 | − 2.01 |
| Attitude toward kids: light of life | 1.00 | — |
| Attitude toward kids: immaterial | 1.40 | 3.32 |
| Attitude toward kids: a drag | 2.01 | 3.30 |
| Mom worked a lot while woman in school | 1.36 | 3.19 |
| Mom hardly ever, never worked while woman in school | 1.00 | — |
| SES background: white-collar | 1.47 | 3.05 |
| SES background: blue-collar | 1.00 | — |
| SES background: professional | 2.02 | 3.60 |
| SES background: small businessman | 1.27 | 1.81 |
| SES background: farmer | 0.95 | − 0.32 |
| *Changing covariates* | | |
| Not working/studying | 1.00 | — |
| Part-time work/study | 1.07 | 0.53 |
| Full-time work/study | 1.90 | 5.51 |
| No kids < 16 | 0.74 | − 1.82 |
| Own kid < 5 | 0.88 | − 1.01 |
| Any kid 5–16, other kid < 5 | 1.00 | — |
| *Duration of marriage* | | |
| 0–11 months | 0.00032 | − 28.94 |
| 12–23 months | 0.00050 | − 29.27 |
| 24–35 months | 0.00064 | − 28.91 |
| 36–47 months | 0.00063 | − 28.44 |
| 48–59 months | 0.00058 | − 27.48 |
| 60–119 months | 0.00053 | − 34.18 |
| 120–79 months | 0.00067 | − 34.30 |
| 180+ months | 0.00063 | − 30.33 |

*Notes*:
− *In* likelihood = 3659.6.
$\chi^2$ against null model = 215.4 with 26 df.
$\chi^2$ against saturated model = 2632.2 with 9142 df.

40% higher; and those who disagree (labelled 'kids a drag') have rates twice as high. Having a mother who worked always or most of the time (labelled 'mom worked a lot') while the respondent was in school during childhood raises the risk of subsequent marital dissolution by 36%, when compared with those whose mother worked sometimes or never. Finally, the SES background variables perform as expected. Those from white-collar backgrounds split up at a 47% greater rate than those with blue-collar backgrounds, while those with professional backgrounds split up twice as fast. The rates for those with a small-business background are intermediate, and the rates for those with a farm background do not differ from the rates for those with a blue-collar background.

Women who study or work full-time experience marital breakups at nearly twice the rate of those who either do not work or study or do so only part-time. While we expected that full-time work or study would raise the hazard most, we would have expected a more intermediate effect for a part-time occupation. This conflict with our expectation is, however, not nearly as severe as the unexpected results for children. Those with husband's own (or any) children aged 5–15 did not experience lower rates of marriage dissolution than did those with no kids (who actually experienced a statistically lower rate). Nor are both our expectation and Cherlin's (1977) finding that having children under age 5 increases marital stability supported; in the Swedish data, having no children increases marital stability most, while having children under 5 decreases the hazard only half as much as having no children, when compared with having children aged 5–15 (and the contrast between children under 5 and children aged 5–15 is not statistically significant). The clear implication here is that having children is stressful to a marriage.

It is worth examining the estimated hazard with some care, as will become evident later (when we discuss the implications in greater detail). We see that it rises, falls, rises, and falls again. The pattern is the same if eleven duration categories are employed (results not shown). Many of the pair-wise contrasts are not significantly different from each other, but a few are. As stated earlier, the imposition of a constant hazard is not a significant constraint. Evidently, the hazard does not decline with duration, as it does in US data (Menken *et al.* 1981).[6] A similar pattern is displayed by the hazard when there are no covariates in the model (data not shown); in particular, the addition of covariates does not cause a very marked flattening of the hazard.

Let us return to the effect of cohabitation by examining the results in Table 2.4, in which marital exposure starts not at 0 but instead at the duration of prenuptial cohabitation achieved at the start of marriage. We need not examine

[6] After controlling for the effects of covariates, Balakrishnan *et al.* (1987) found that the hazard rose as duration increased among Canadian women. Aaberge, Kravdal, and Wennemo (1989) did not find much evidence of a declining hazard among Norwegian couples married from 1968 to 1970. Their analysis is confined to first marriages and ignores the first 2 years of marriage; when parameterized as a step-function, the hazard rose during years 2–6 and essentially levelled off afterwards. After controlling for the effects of unobserved heterogeneity, they found that the hazard rose monotonically.

TABLE 2.4. *Final proportional-hazards model of first-marriage dissolution. Exposure starts at the duration of first union instead of at duration 0.*

|  | Exp (Coeff) | Z–Stat (Coeff/se) |
| --- | --- | --- |
| *Fixed covariates* | | |
| Didn't cohabit with husband before marriage | 1.00 | — |
| Cohabit with husband < 2 years before marriage | 1.52 | 4.02 |
| Cohabit with husband ⩾ 2 years before marriage | 1.73 | 3.66 |
| Birth cohort < 1946 | 1.00 | — |
| Birth cohort 1946–50 | 1.05 | 0.41 |
| Birth cohort 1951+ | 1.64 | 3.40 |
| Age at marriage: < 20 | 1.98 | 4.14 |
| Age at marriage 20–4 | 1.01 | 0.08 |
| Age at marriage 25 + | 1.00 | — |
| Education at marriage: < secondary 3 | 1.00 | — |
| Education at marriage: secondary 3–4 | 0.77 | − 1.95 |
| Education at marriage: university | 0.58 | − 2.00 |
| Attitude toward kids: light of life | 1.00 | — |
| Attitude toward kids: immaterial | 1.40 | 3.31 |
| Attitude toward kids: a drag | 1.99 | 3.27 |
| Mom hardly ever, never worked while woman in school | 1.00 | — |
| Mom worked a lot while woman in school | 1.36 | 3.19 |
| SES background: white-collar | 1.47 | 3.05 |
| SES background: blue-collar | 1.00 | — |
| SES background: professional | 2.01 | 3.59 |
| SES background: small businessman | 1.27 | 1.81 |
| SES background: farmer | 0.95 | − 0.31 |
| *Changing covariates* | | |
| Not working/studying | 1.00 | — |
| Part-time work/study | 1.07 | 0.52 |
| Full-time work/study | 1.90 | 5.54 |
| No kids < 16 | 0.74 | − 1.84 |
| Own kid < 5 | 0.87 | − 1.09 |
| Any kid 5–16, other kid < 5 | 1.00 | — |
| *Duration of marriage* | | |
| 0–11 months | 0.00030 | − 22.05 |
| 12–23 months | 0.00041 | − 26.52 |
| 24–35 months | 0.00045 | − 27.65 |
| 36–47 months | 0.00056 | − 28.11 |
| 48–59 months | 0.00064 | − 28.05 |
| 60–119 months | 0.00057 | − 33.96 |
| 120–79 months | 0.00066 | − 34.91 |
| 180 + months | 0.00062 | − 31.13 |

*Notes*:
− *ln* likelihood = 3662.6.
$\chi^2$ against null model = 209.5 with 26 df.
$\chi^2$ against saturated model = 2487.3 with 8642 df.

this table in great detail, because the covariate effects, except for the two cohabitation categories, are virtually identical to those already discussed (from Table 2.3). The effect of cohabiting two years or more prior to marriage is diminished, and the effect of short cohabitation is no longer significantly lower than the effect of long cohabitation. The results of both ways of defining exposure do lead us to conclude unambiguously that cohabitation raises the risk of marital disruption, probably because those who cohabit are selected for less traditional values (Carlson 1986). It may nevertheless be true that only the most stable cohabiting couples marry (Cherlin 1981), a hypothesis considered further below.

## First Unions

The estimated parameters of our final proportional-hazards model of first-union dissolution are shown in Table 2.5. As expected, union stability decreases with advancing union cohorts. Those whose unions were formed in 1971–5 and in 1976 or after experience rates of dissolution 36% and 72% higher, respectively, than those whose unions were formed earlier. Those who formed unions when they were less than 20 years old split up at a rate 86% higher than those who formed unions at later ages. Those with a university education at the start of the union experience rates of dissolution 41% lower than those with less education. Attitudes toward children have less of an impact on first-union dissolution than on first-marriage dissolution, but their impact is still in the expected direction. Compared with those who agree strongly that having children is one of the purposes of life, those who merely agree or do not care (labelled 'kids immaterial') split up at rates 27% higher, and those who do not agree (labelled 'kids a drag') split up at rates 76% higher. Those whose mother worked experience rates of dissolution 16% higher.

The effects of background SES on first-union stability are quite similar to their effects on stability of first marriage. As with first marriage, those whose families of orientation were farmers have the most stable unions (this time significantly more so than blue-collar workers), followed in order by blue-collar workers, small businessmen, white-collar workers, and professionals. As with first marriages, full-time work or study doubles the risk of dissolution. Furthermore, as with first marriages, having partner's own (or any) children aged 5–15 is not associated with lower rates of dissolution; with unions, however, having children does not seem to increase instability.

Being married has a profound impact on first-union dissolution; those married experience rates of dissolution 67% lower than those not married. This estimate is altered only slightly to 64% under the assumption of a constant hazard. If all other covariates are dropped as well, then the estimate falls to only 44% lower; thus, controlling for the effects of other covariates substantially raises the difference in dissolution rates between the married and the unmarried.

TABLE 2.5. *Final proportional-hazards model of first-union dissolution.*

|  | Exp (Coeff) | Z–Stat (Coeff/se) |
|---|---|---|
| *Fixed covariates* | | |
| Union cohort < 1966 | 1.00 | — |
| Union cohort 1966–70 | 1.09 | 0.89 |
| Union cohort 1971–5 | 1.36 | 3.03 |
| Union cohort 1976+ | 1.72 | 4.66 |
| Age at first union < 20 | 1.86 | 4.93 |
| Age at first union 20–4 | 1.07 | 0.54 |
| Age at first union 25+ | 1.00 | — |
| Education at start of union: < secondary 3 | 1.00 | — |
| Education at start of union: secondary 3–4 | 0.94 | – 0.78 |
| Education at start of union: university | 0.59 | – 2.27 |
| Attitude toward kids: light of life | 1.00 | — |
| Attitude toward kids: immaterial | 1.27 | 3.61 |
| Attitude toward kids: a drag | 1.76 | 4.61 |
| Mom hardly ever, never worked while woman in school | 1.00 | — |
| Mom worked a lot while woman in school | 1.16 | 2.28 |
| SES background: white-collar | 1.28 | 2.97 |
| SES background: blue-collar | 1.00 | — |
| SES background: professional | 1.93 | 5.65 |
| SES background: small businessman | 1.26 | 2.56 |
| SES background: farmer | 0.82 | – 1.78 |
| *Changing covariates* | | |
| Cohabiting | 1.00 | — |
| Married | 0.33 | – 13.13 |
| Not working/studying | 1.00 | — |
| Part-time work/study | 1.18 | 1.54 |
| Full-time work/study | 1.99 | 7.34 |
| No kids < 16 | 0.87 | – 1.26 |
| Own kid < 5 | 0.87 | – 1.34 |
| Any kid 5–16, other kid < 5 | 1.00 | — |
| *Duration of union* | | |
| 0–11 months | 0.00145 | – 32.83 |
| 12–23 months | 0.00171 | – 31.56 |
| 24–35 months | 0.00184 | – 30.45 |
| 36–47 months | 0.00204 | – 29.32 |
| 48–59 months | 0.00209 | – 28.27 |
| 60–119 months | 0.00200 | – 31.45 |
| 120–79 months | 0.00243 | – 30.65 |
| 180+ months | 0.00217 | – 27.90 |

*Notes*:
– *ln* likelihood = 7251.1.
$\chi^2$ against null model = 905.8 with 26 df.
$\chi^2$ against saturated model = 3894.8 with 10099 df.

A moment's thought makes one realize that it is difficult to test Cherlin's simple hypothesis that the most stable cohabiting couples marry. Clearly, those cohabiters who marry cannot have had a dissolution while cohabiting, so as a matter of logic their (zero) rates of dissolution while cohabiting are lower than the rates of those who do not subsequently marry. While we observe that the rates of dissolution are subsequently lower for those who marry than for those who continue to cohabit, this finding does not necessarily validate the hypothesis. It is possible, for example, that the mere act of marrying would cause one to struggle harder to avoid dissolution, either because one has just made a new commitment or because dissolution of marriages is still socially less acceptable than dissolution of nonmarital unions. Despite this possibility, we would regard the estimated effect of marriage as lending support for the Cherlin hypothesis.

Examination of the estimated hazard reveals that (like the hazard for first marriage) it rises, falls, rises, and falls again. A model with eleven duration intervals (not shown) shows this pattern even more clearly. As before, many of the estimated hazards for separate duration intervals do not differ significantly. The imposition of a constant hazard proves to be a significant restriction, though barely so, in contrast to the results for the first-marriage sample. In contrast to marriages, the hazard in a model with no covariates monotonically declines when there are eight duration categories (although when there are eleven categories it rises at the higher durations and then falls again). The addition of covariates, therefore, does flatten the hazard, as expected.

## Second Unions

Because of the small sample size, virtually none of the effects estimates for second unions is significantly different from 1.0, as can be seen from Table 2.6. Unions formed in 1976 or later break up at a faster rate than those formed before 1976. As was true of both first marriages and first unions, those who were raised in a farming family exhibit the lowest rates of dissolution (in this case, at less than half the rates experienced by women raised in blue-collar families). In contrast to the two earlier analyses, those whose SES background was small-business exhibit significantly lower rates of dissolution than those with blue-collar backgrounds. As expected, being previously married lowers the hazard (by 40%), and being married lowers it still further (by 62%, compared with 67% for first unions). Curiously, part-time work or study lowers the hazard significantly, whereas full-time work or study has no effect, when compared with no work or study. As with first unions, the presence and age composition of children has no significant impact on second-union stability. The estimated hazard falls and then rises; it might subsequently fall again, but we lack sufficient observations to estimate rates at the higher durations. All of these findings hold regardless of whether the length of the first union is included as a covariate; in fact, the parameter estimates are nearly identical in the two models.

TABLE 2.6. *Final proportional-hazards model of second-union dissolution.*

|  | Exp (Coeff) | Z–Stat (Coeff/se) |
|---|---|---|
| *Fixed covariates* | | |
| Union cohort < 1971 | 1.00 | — |
| Union cohort 1971–5 | 1.12 | 0.49 |
| Union cohort 1976+ | 1.76 | 2.31 |
| Age at second union < 25 | 1.05 | 0.17 |
| Age at second union 25–9 | 1.35 | 1.28 |
| Age at second union 30+ | 1.00 | — |
| Education at start of union: < secondary 3 | 1.00 | — |
| Education at start of union: secondary 3–4 | 0.75 | − 1.47 |
| Education at start of union: university | 1.24 | 0.66 |
| Attitude toward kids: light of life | 1.00 | — |
| Attitude toward kids: immaterial | 1.27 | 1.56 |
| Attitude toward kids: a drag | 1.17 | 0.56 |
| Mom hardly ever, never worked while woman in school | 1.00 | — |
| Mom worked a lot while woman in school | 1.16 | 1.04 |
| SES background: white-collar | 1.05 | 0.27 |
| SES background: blue-collar | 1.00 | — |
| SES background: professional | 1.08 | 0.28 |
| SES background: small businessman | 0.62 | − 1.94 |
| SES background: farmer | 0.46 | − 2.29 |
| Never married before | 1.00 | — |
| Previously married | 0.60 | − 2.61 |
| First union lasted < 24 months | 1.51 | 2.31 |
| First union lasted 24–59 months | 1.00 | — |
| First union lasted 60+ months | 1.45 | 1.73 |
| *Changing covariates* | | |
| Cohabiting | 1.00 | — |
| Married | 0.38 | − 4.76 |
| Not working/studying | 1.00 | — |
| Part-time work/study | 0.64 | − 1.72 |
| Full-time work/study | 1.20 | 0.86 |
| No kids < 16 | 1.00 | 0.00 |
| Own kid < 5 | 1.17 | 0.72 |
| Any kid 5–16, other kid < 5 | 1.00 | — |
| *Duration of union* | | |
| 0–11 months | 0.00447 | − 12.67 |
| 12–23 months | 0.00443 | − 12.48 |
| 24–35 months | 0.00401 | − 12.18 |
| 36–47 months | 0.00315 | − 11.96 |
| 48–59 months | 0.00326 | − 11.46 |
| 60–83 months | 0.00468 | − 11.61 |
| 84+ months | 0.00537 | − 11.77 |

*Notes:*
− *ln* likelihood = 1249.8.
$\chi^2$ against null model = 116.3 with 27 df.
$\chi^2$ against saturated model = 1191.8 with 3112 df.

We had expected that second-union length would be positively correlated with the length of the first union, a circumstance that might be caused by unmeasured factors that persist over time and that have the same (or similar) effects on dissolution rates in both unions. We were very surprised, therefore, to discover that, although having had a short first union was associated with higher second-union dissolution rates, having had a long first union was definitely not associated with lower rates of dissolution in the subsequent union. In fact, those with long first unions dissolved their second unions more quickly than those with first unions of intermediate length, and the second-union dissolution rates did not differ significantly among those with short and long first unions. Such a U-shaped pattern could not be caused by persistent unmeasured heterogeneity. A plausible explanation frankly eludes us.

### Next Steps

When we embarked on this project, we assumed that we would find declining rates of dissolution as duration increased (as economic theory suggests), variables whose effect changed with duration, and, among second unions, effects that could be interpreted as evidence of unobserved heterogeneity. As we have earlier discussed, we do not find any evidence of a declining hazard. Given that duration as a main effect is insignificant, we would ordinarily not search for interactions. Nevertheless, we did estimate several models with duration-varying effects to test particular hypotheses.

For example, Bennett, Blanc, and Bloom (1988) found that the effect of the cohabitation variable diminished as the duration of marriage increased. We found (weak) evidence of a similar pattern, but a $\chi^2$ test revealed that the imposition of constant effects was not a significant constraint. We ran separate models of first marriage for those who married before and after 1976, but the parameter estimates for the two models did not differ significantly (except for a higher baseline hazard for those who married later). We thought that the effect of children might vary with duration, particularly since Murphy (1985) concluded that early childbearing was particularly disruptive to marriages, but allowing for duration-dependent effects did not significantly improve the fit in any of the three samples. This conclusion holds regardless of whether either the effect of no children, or the effect of own children under 5, or the effects of both are allowed to vary with duration. These models do, nevertheless, powerfully suggest that early childbearing is not disruptive; effects estimates in the first two or three years are not significant, and the effect of own children under 5 is to increase stability thereafter.

We tested whether the effect of being married varied with duration in the samples of first and second unions. We reasoned that the marriage effect might become more pronounced with increased duration; however, there was no significant improvement in the fit for either union sample. Among first unions the estimated effects did rise gently during the first five years, but they displayed no regular pattern thereafter. Among second unions, the estimates showed no marriage effect in the first year (but only 26 women started a second union by marrying without first cohabiting) and no regular pattern thereafter. We also tested whether the effect of having been previously married varied by duration in the sample of second unions; it did not. These findings about second unions hold regardless of whether the length of the first union is included as a covariate. Finally we tested whether the (puzzling) effects of the length of the first union on the length of the second union varied with duration. Neither the effect of a short first union nor the effect of a long first union (nor both together) displayed significant variation across duration categories. Given all these findings, we decided that it would be largely fruitless to keep searching for effects that varied by duration of union.

We likewise concluded that the further search for unmeasured heterogeneity would be unlikely to bear fruit. We initially added to the final proportional-hazards models an unobserved variable $\theta_i$,

$$\ln(\lambda_{ik}) = \alpha_k + \gamma_k' \mathbf{Z}_{ik} + \theta_i \qquad (2)$$

where $\exp(\theta_i)$ was assumed to have a gamma distribution with mean 1. Countless hours spent trying to get the model to converge finally led us to conclude that there is a programming error in RATE that prohibits convergence when there is a constraint imposed on the estimates.[7] However, we were able to achieve convergence under the assumption of a constant hazard. We suspected that, because the hazards in the final proportional-hazards models did not decline, it would not be possible to find any unmeasured heterogeneity unless the estimated hazard actually rose, a condition that is ruled out by the imposition of a constant hazard. Our suspicion proved to be correct; the estimated variance of the gamma was very small (of the order of 0.02) in all four models, and the covariate effects were virtually identical to those reported in Tables 2.3–2.6. It is possible that there is unobserved heterogeneity so that the underlying hazard really rises, but such a model would fit no better than the best model we could find without explicit incorporation of unobserved heterogeneity. Therefore, there would be no empirical reason to prefer one model to the other. Our reasons for this conclusion are described extensively elsewhere (Trussell and Rodríguez 1990), but we summarize the argument briefly here.

For simplicity, suppose we accept the proportional-hazards model with a constant hazard as our final model. This model could also be represented as an accelerated failure-time model with Gompertz baseline risk and gamma-distributed unobserved heterogeneity[8] or as a model with linear hazards and inverse

---

[7] In RATE there is a constant in the equation of proportional effects and in the equations for each duration category. Hence, to obtain estimates, one must constrain one of these constants to be zero.

[8] The hazard in this model is $\lambda(d) = \gamma_i \exp(\mathbf{Z}_i' \beta) \exp\{d\sigma^2 + \exp(\mathbf{Z}_i' \beta)\}$, where the unobservable $\gamma$ is gamma-distributed with mean 1 and variance $\sigma^2$. Note that we place a distribution on $\gamma_i = \exp(\theta_i)$ rather than $\theta_i$ as in equation (2).

Gaussian-distributed unobserved heterogeneity.[9] Our final model has constant risks of dissolution for groups with identical observed covariates. In the first and second alternative models with unobserved heterogeneity, groups with identical observed covariates have exponentially increasing and linearly increasing risks of dissolution, respectively. These three models have very different behavioural implications. In order to estimate the models with unobserved heterogeneity or assess their goodness of fit, however, the analyst must first obtain the unconditional distribution of failure-times by integrating over the unobservable. The two models with unobserved heterogeneity have the same unconditional distribution of failure-times as does our simple final model with no unobserved heterogeneity. This fundamental identification problem cannot be resolved without external non-statistical information that is simply unavailable. We conclude that, in the present case, the proportional-hazards models presented in Tables 2.3–2.6 adequately describe the data.

Before concluding, we tarry to discuss the hazard itself. We initially postulated two theories regarding the risk of union dissolution over time. The first, which we label the theory of accumulated irritations, postulates that the hazard will rise as the duration of union increases because the partners become increasingly frustrated with each other's shortcomings and behaviours (until the straw finally breaks the camel's back). A variant of this theory is that the partners simply drift apart as their lives take different paths and as the initial glue loses its sticking ability. The fact that the observed hazard does not rise with duration casts doubts on this notion but is not sufficient to disprove it, because, as we noted earlier, such a pattern could result from a rising hazard combined with substantial unmeasured heterogeneity.

The other hypothesis, which we label the theory of growing acceptance, postulates that persons come to accept their partner's faults, realizing that everyone is human and that there is no Mr Right or Ms Right, and come to value the promise of an old age with a partner who will have shared their past. A slight variant of this theory is that the longer a union lasts, the greater is the investment of the partners in its success (Becker, Landes, and Michael 1977); this investment is union-specific and not transferable to a new partner. The implication of this theory is that the hazard should fall, and unmeasured heterogeneity would only make it fall more steeply. Because we do not find evidence of a declining hazard, the theory of growing acceptance finds little support in the Swedish data. There is some hint that there may be a decline after many years (more than seventeen), so perhaps the theory does not hold until the unions are quite mature; there are insufficient observations at the longest durations to settle this matter. Or perhaps what would have been a decline had conditions not changed has simply been obscured by a secular rise in dissolution rates at all durations.

---

[9] The hazard in this model is $\lambda(d) = \gamma_i \exp(\mathbf{Z}_i'\beta)\{1 + d\sigma^2 \exp(\mathbf{Z}_i'\beta)\}$, where the unobservable $\gamma$ is inverse Gaussian-distributed with mean 1 and variance $\sigma^2$. Note that we place a distribution on $\gamma_i = \exp(\theta_i)$ rather than $\theta_i$ as in equation (2).

## Conclusion

In this chapter, we estimated hazard models of first-marriage dissolution, of first-union dissolution, and of second-union dissolution. In all cases, we concluded that a proportional-hazards assumption adequately described the data. Furthermore, the estimated hazard was virtually flat. This finding leads us to conclude that there is little evidence to support the hypothesis that dissolution rates fall as the duration of the union increases (the theory of growing acceptance). On the other hand, unless there is substantial unmeasured heterogeneity, there is little support for the opposite hypothesis that rates of dissolution rise with duration (the theory of accumulated irritations).

The effects of covariates were largely as expected. Dissolution rates increased with decreased age at union formation, with increased date of birth or date of union formation, with increased socio-economic status, and with decreased perceptions of the importance of children. Union stability increased with educational attainment, and it was higher when the respondent's mother did not usually work when the respondent was in school. Working or studying full-time substantially increased rates of dissolution. These effects were much weaker (and much less consistent) in second unions.

In addition, prenuptial cohabitation decreased the stability of the subsequent marriage, regardless of whether women entered the marriage life table at duration 0 or at the duration of their prenuptial cohabitation. Being married substantially increased the stability of first and second unions, and having been previously married increased the stability of second unions still further. Having children did not affect the stability of either first or second unions and lowered the stability of first marriages. The length of the first union, to our surprise, was not positively associated with the length of the second union; instead, the pattern was U-shaped, with both long and short first unions associated with short second unions.

## References

Aaberge, R., Kravdal, O., and Wennemo, T. (1989), *Unobserved Heterogeneity in Models of Marriage Dissolution*, Discussion Paper No. 42, Central Bureau of Statistics (Oslo).

Balakrishnan, T. R., Rao, K. V., Krotki, K. J., and Lapierre-Adamcyk, E. (1987), 'A Hazards Model Analysis of the Covariates of Marriage Dissolution in Canada', *Demography*, 24. 3: 395–406.

Becker, G. S., Landes, E. M., and Michael, R. T. (1977), 'An Econometric Analysis of Marital Instability', *Journal of Political Economy*, 85. 6: 1141–87.

Bennett, N., Blanc, A. K., and Bloom, D. E. (1988), 'Commitment and the Modern Union: Assessing the Link between Premarital Cohabitation and Subsequent Marital Stability', *American Sociological Review*, 53. 1: 127–38.

Carlson, E. (1986), 'Couples Without Children: Premarital Cohabitation in France', in K. Davis (ed.), *Contemporary Marriage: Comparative Perspectives of a Changing Institution* (Russell Sage Foundation, New York).

Cherlin, A. (1977), 'The Effect of Children on Marital Dissolution', *Demography*, 14. 3: 265–72.

—— (1981), *Marriage, Divorce, Remarriage* (Harvard University Press, Cambridge, Mass.).

Etzler, C. (1987), *Education, Cohabitation, and the First Child: Some Empirical Findings from Sweden*, Stockholm Research Reports in Demography No. 34, University of Stockholm, Section of Demography.

Hoem, J. M. (1986), 'The Impact of Education on Modern Family-Union Initiation', *European Journal of Population*, 2. 2: 113–33.

McCarthy, J. (1978), 'A Comparison of the Probability of the Dissolution of First and Second Marriages', *Demography*, 15. 3: 345–59.

—— and Menken, J. (1979), 'Marriage, Remarriage, Marital Disruption, and Age at First Birth', *Family Planning Perspectives*, 11. 1: 21–30.

Menken, J., Trussell, J. T., Stempel, D., and Babakol, O. (1981), 'Proportional Hazards Life Table Models: An Illustrative Analysis of Socio-Demographic Influences on Marriage Dissolution in the United States', *Demography*, 18. 2: 181–200.

Morgan, P., Lye, D., and Condran, G. (1988), 'Sons, Daughters and the Risk of Marital Disruption?', *American Journal of Sociology*, 94. 1: 110–29.

—— and Rindfuss, R. R. (1985), 'Marital Disruption: Structural and Temporal Dimensions', *American Journal of Sociology*, 90. 5: 1055–77.

Murphy, M. (1985), 'Demographic and Socio-Economic Influences on Recent British Marital Breakdown Patterns', *Population Studies*, 39. 3: 441–60.

Statistics Sweden (1981), *Women in Sweden* (Stockholm).

Teachman, J. D. (1982), 'Methodological Issues in the Analysis of Family Formation and Dissolution', *Journal of Marriage and the Family*, 44. 4: 1037–53.

Thornton, A. (1977), 'Children and Marital Stability', *Journal of Marriage and the Family*, 39. 3: 531–40.

Trost, J. (1980), 'Cohabitation Without Marriage in Sweden', in J. Eekelaar and S. Katz (eds.), *Marriage and Cohabitation in Contemporary Societies* (Butterwash, Toronto).

Trussell, J., and Hammerslough, C. (1983), 'A Hazards Model Analysis of the Covariates of Infant and Child Mortality in Sri Lanka', *Demography*, 20. 3: 391–406.

—— and Rodríguez, G. (1990), 'Heterogeneity in Demographic Research', in J. Adams, A. Hermalin, D. Lam, and P. Smouse (eds.), *Convergent Questions in Genetics and Demography* (OUP, New York).

Tuma, N. (1979), *Invoking RATE* (SRI International, Menlo Park, Calif.).

Waite, L. S., Haggstrom, G. W., and Kanouse, D. (1985), 'The Consequences of Parenthood for the Marital Stability of Young Adults', *American Sociological Review*, 50. 6: 850–7.

# 3 The Disruption of Marital and Non-Marital Unions in Contemporary Sweden

BRITTA HOEM, JAN M. HOEM

In this chapter, we study the extent and structure of the general decline in the stability of marital and non-marital unions in Sweden over the quarter-century between the 1950s and the late 1970s, a period marked by much change in many respects of demographic behaviour. We focus on the event that a conjugal union breaks up and the partners stop living together[1] and use hazard regression techniques to analyse dissolutions among a reasonably large number of Swedish women from all walks of life, taken from the 1981 Swedish Fertility Survey.[2]

Our analysis takes into account the fact that a breakup is a terminal event in an observed sequence that starts with union formation and that may also include marriage and child-bearing as well as transitions in other arenas, mainly in the job market and in the educational system. When the majority mode of union formation changes, this is bound to alter the incidence of dissolution. For instance, while Swedes certainly lived in non-marital cohabitation in the late 1950s and early 1960s,[3] the phenomenon did not have much public visibility at that time. This changed quickly in the late 1960s and early 1970s. By the mid-1970s, the usual way to start a union was to move in together without marriage, and very few married without previously cohabiting. Simultaneously, the consensual union developed into a prevalent institution in its own right, largely replacing the phase when young people used to go steady or were engaged, as well as the early stages of a marriage. It lost some of its function as a preamble to a lifelong relationship,

[1] Our concern is with the occurrence and timing of any dissolution (as reported by the respondents) even for marriages, and not with separations and divorces in the legal sense. In fact, we do not even know when the latter kinds of event occurred in the individual life histories.

[2] The survey, which was conducted by Statistics Sweden, contains usable records for 4223 women, distributed with 490, 990, 1014, 1030, and 699 respondents from the 5 quinquennial cohorts born between 1936–40 and 1956–60. The target sample was selected by simple random sampling from each of these 5 cohorts, among women born in Sweden and of Swedish nationality as of Feb. 1981. The uneven size of the 5 groups of respondents is due mainly to differential sampling fractions in the strata. After some quite extensive cleaning operations (J. Hoem 1985), we have information about each respondent's family of origin, some of her educational history, her complete cohabitation and marriage history, employment and educational activity (largely month by month from Sept. of the year in which she reached the age of 16), and much else. For more information, see Lyberg (1984) and World Fertility Survey (1984). Popenoe (1987: 1988) has also been concerned with family stability in Sweden and has provided many accurate observations.

[3] In fact, this living arrangement has traditions documented more than a century back in time and probably extending much further. See Wikman (1937) and references in J. Hoem (1985: n. 1).

and moved towards becoming a practical arrangement for enjoying many of the trappings of a marriage with many fewer of its bonds. Finally, some kind of bandwagon effect may have developed towards the end of the 1970s, as entering a consensual union became the normal way to start a new relationship.

Evidently, the nature of a consensual union is different from that of a marriage.[4] A marriage entails greater legal (and, for many, also moral) obligations, and is a public expression of stronger commitments than those signalled by a consensual union. Everyone would expect the dissolution risk to be higher in a non-marital than in a marital union when there are no children, and of course this turns out to be the case, as we have shown elsewhere (J. Hoem 1990). It may not be so equally generally realized, even in Sweden, that consensual unions have higher dissolution risks than marriages also when children have arrived. Marriage formation acts as a process that selects those less prone to dissolution. It also serves as a signal that the partners soon plan to have children. Even though child-bearing has increasingly occurred in consensual unions, at low parities fertility is much lower among cohabitants than among the married in our study population (Etzler 1988; Hoem and Hoem 1989).

The dramatic restructuring of the mode of union formation has had important consequences for dissolutions. As consensual unions without children became ever more prevalent, their symbolic and practical commitment value fell, and we have shown (J. Hoem 1989) that their dissolution risks rose, even when we control for the fact that the unions were started at ever younger ages. But what happened to the cohesion structure of marriages? Has premarital cohabitation served as a sorting ground where the more durable unions have been converted into marriages, or have other forces been more strongly at work? And how strongly has the arrival of children affected the cohesion of a union, for marital and for non-marital unions? This chapter sketches our main results concerning such issues. We concentrate on first unions after entry into motherhood, for it turns out that the impacts of some of the factors involved have a different structure in unions before this stage. We also include some material on second unions.

## Theory and Main Findings

The predictions that social theory would suggest for periods after the advent of children in a union should be simple in principle, so let us address them first. In the terminology of economic theory, children are investments common to the partners in a union; they are union-specific capital (Becker 1981) that may get lost, possibly in whole and certainly in part, by at least one of the partners in a union breakup. People would not want to make such an investment unless they perceive rewards for themselves and for their offspring (and perhaps for other

---

[4] For discussions, see Trost (1978) and particularly Macklin (1978).

family members as well), so the arrival of children should be a signal of a well-functioning relationship with a low dissolution risk, at least if the children were planned.[5] Similarly, the presence of common children should work in the same direction,[6] and if there were no other effects, each additional child should reduce the risk even further, at least so long as we are talking about the families with up to two or three children that dominate the Swedish scene.[7] Our empirical results (given in J. Hoem 1990) give empirical support to this argument. They show that entry into motherhood reduces dissolution risks considerably in our data, as they have done when this feature has been investigated by others (e.g. Murphy 1985; Morgan and Rindfuss 1985; Ermisch 1986).[8] The reduction is not monotonic, however, for three-child families have higher dissolution risks than unions with two children, *ceteris paribus*. We speculate that going beyond the two-child norm may put unforeseen extra strains on family life, or that perhaps having the additional child did not save a halting family relationship after all in some cases. Together, such features outweighed any 'investment effects' of the third child.

Turning now to other aspects of behaviour, we first note that one of the most consistently documented findings in the literature is that those who start family-building much earlier than is normally expected have increased risks of family breakdown.[9] Our analysis replicates this result. A respondent who started her first union as a teenager has a higher dissolution risk than others, *ceteris paribus*. Economic theory would explain this as a result of an insufficient mate search by the individuals involved (Becker, Landes, and Michael 1977; Becker 1981; Ermisch 1986). They will not have made themselves sufficiently acquainted with the market of available partners before jumping into a conjugal union. Since the differences by starting age persist throughout the duration of the union, this can hardly be the whole story, however. As has been pointed out to us by Mike Murphy (personal communication), some persistent personality factor may be involved. Other elements of an explanation include insufficient maturity, differences in the continued individual development of the two partners, and retained attraction on the partner market (Booth and Edwards 1985; Morgan and Rindfuss 1985; Thornton and Rodgers 1987).

---

[5] We are grateful to Mike Murphy for the following information: the first reference in the literature to the idea that childlessness is associated with increased risks of marital breakdown is probably Wilcox (1891). Over the years, a number of other analysts rejected this conclusion (e.g. Monahan 1955; Chester 1972; Gibson 1980). This is one area where intensity regression has cleared up the issues.

[6] Carlson and Stinson (1982) seem to hold a different view.

[7] Four-child families are so few in our data set that we do not go beyond the arrival of the 4th child in our analysis.

[8] Thornton (1977) and Koo and Janowitz (1983) get mixed results.

[9] Here is a sample of contributions: Schoen (1975); Bumpass and Sweet (1972); Menken *et al.* (1981); Moore and Waite (1981); Teachman (1983); Booth and Edwards (1985); Morgan and Rindfuss (1985); Murphy (1985); Kiernan (1986); South and Spitze (1986); Balakrishnan *et al.* (1987); Kravdal (1988); Lehrer (1988); Martin and Bumpass (1989).

The same type of reasoning could be applied to the mode of entry into marriage. One could argue that women who marry after having lived with a partner in a non-marital union for a while ought to have a lower dissolution risk than comparable women who enter marriage directly (without preceding cohabitation) because the latter have taken less time to get to know their partner and his behaviour in situations important for daily family life. The information level and specific investment in the union of those who have cohabitational experience is simply greater. The less durable unions would be weeded out before marriage when the couple invests in a premarital trial period, while otherwise this weeding process is delayed into the early stages of the marriage. Let us call this *the weeding hypothesis*.

So long as one believes that individual human experience is cumulative, there will always be room for reasoning of this nature. In our data set, however, women who have married a cohabitational partner have much higher dissolution risks than comparable women who have married directly, i.e. the reverse of what the weeding hypothesis predicts. This points up a *ceteris paribus* clause implicit in the above argument, a clause that is problematic for an empirical investigation; even when all factors that one can control for have been taken into consideration, there will remain some element of unobserved heterogeneity, and its effects can dominate those of the weeding theory completely. When this is the case, the structure of the heterogeneity distribution and what happens to it as time goes by will be more interesting than the predictions of the weeding hypothesis. This is the basis of the following notions concerning the features we observe.

As part of the change in the mode of union formation, direct marriage must progressively have become a manifestation of particular religious or other convictions (or of particular regional or other cultural influences). As a consequence, we observe lower *and decreasing* dissolution risks for this group. Conversely, the growing acceptance of consensual unions as a possibly long-lasting predecessor of marriage, or in some cases even a replacement for it, is a reflection of what Lesthaeghe and Meekers (1986) have called ideational developments, namely changes in attitudes and norms (or in tastes and preferences) and possibly even in deeper life values in the general population.[10] In Sweden they have run the gamut from increasing tolerance of nonconformist modes of family formation to a complete changeover into a situation where to conform implies to behave in a manner that used to be rather deviant. As if by contagion, such ideational changes have extended to family cohesion, and have produced a higher and increasing incidence of dissolution even after entry into motherhood for those who marry only after they have started their initial union. This trend has been the vehicle of the deteriorating family stability that has been observed in Sweden as in most of the Western world.[11] All in all, our explanation is one of a progressive self-

---

[10] Preston (1986) has emphasized the role of changing values in recent population developments.

[11] This development started well before the 1st cohort in our data. The roots of current patterns of marital instability are much deeper than just recent changes in other domains, as has been emphasized by Sweet and Bumpass (1988: ch. 11).

selection in the choice of mode of union formation, and of consequential changes in norms concerning union dissolution. Let us call this *the (mode-of-entry) self-selection hypothesis.*[12]

If this hypothesis is correct, then the analysis of union dissolution must contend with a heterogeneity distribution that (i) depends on the form of initial union formation and (ii) changes over time or from cohort to cohort. A user of existing methodology, developed from ideas introduced by Heckman and Singer (1982; 1984), would perhaps try to disentangle the effects of the differential and changing heterogeneity distribution from other effects by a separate analysis for each cohort and each mode of family formation. We are not sure that such a procedure is feasible (cf. J. Hoem 1990), except possibly by introducing extra assumptions not warranted by current knowledge, or at the risk of leaving out important regressors; for even without the additional burden of a heterogeneity model, our investigation seems to be working close to the limit beyond which random noise drowns the information contained in the data. In any case, we have not struck out in this direction, but have tried to catch heterogeneity effects by other means.

To apply the life-course perspective (Elder 1985; Morgan and Rindfuss 1985), the following presentation starts with a brief account of the changing scene of family formation in Sweden. In our hazard regressions, which constitute the bulk of this paper, most of our investigation is concerned with the dissolution of the respondents' first unions,[13] for they are the most numerous and, in some respects, perhaps the most important in a consideration of union cohesion (at least in cohorts before our youngest). This analysis gives ample evidence of individual life-strategy selection, in that early behaviour is an important apparent determinant of later behaviour. This theme is picked up again in a brief presentation of similar hazard regressions of dissolution behaviour in second unions. Dissolution behaviour in a first union before entry into motherhood is sufficiently different from the behaviour after this watershed to merit separate consideration (Hoem and Hoem 1988*b*; J. Hoem 1990).

Our contribution concerns the insight that demographic reasoning and methodology can provide into conjugal-union dissolutions. Union stability has many other relevant aspects that we address at best indirectly in this paper, such as the psychological satisfaction of the partners, conflicts between them, everyday chore distribution, power relationships in the union, and property and child settlements on breakup. Such issues must be tackled by other approaches.

---

[12] Various versions of this contrasting hypothesis occur in the literature, at least as tentative propositions. See e.g. Cherlin (1981: 17) and Bennett, Blanc, and Bloom (1988).

[13] We know nothing about the number of unions experienced by their male partners. In fact, we know nothing about the characteristics of those men except for some information relating solely to the time of interview.

## The Changing Scene of Family Formation in Sweden

### Divorce Trends

Before we turn to the investigation of our own data, it will be sensible to take a brief look at what official statistics can tell us about trends in legal divorces. Sweden is commonly known to be among the countries most strongly affected by the rise in divorce over the last couple of decades (Sardon 1986; Festy 1985; Popenoe 1987; 1988). A change in the divorce law in 1974 speeded up the divorce procedure.[14] The new law reflected and abetted profound attitudinal changes in the population, changes that work towards easier acceptance of marriage dissolution. It also reflected a consensus concerning the role of public policies relevant to union dissolution that placed divorce firmly in the private domain, outside the area where public authority should guide individual behaviour.[15] This consensus generally extends to all aspects of family life, including the more ready acceptance of previously unconventional forms of union formation.[16]

By the same token, however, the dramatic growth in consensual unions means that a study of formal divorces alone can give only a progressively more incomplete picture of union cohesion in Sweden, as it would in other populations that follow the Swedish lead on this front. Unfortunately, official population statistics contain little information concerning disruption among those who live in consensual unions, even in Sweden. In fact, the population statistics that we do have give only a meagre picture of the essential features of real divorce trends during the last twenty years since the composition of the group that gets married has changed so much. For instance, teenage marriages have almost disappeared and the median age at first marriage has increased by almost five years for both men and women. It is now almost 30 years for men and 27 years for women. Correspondingly, it has become progressively more common for those who marry to

---

[14] Under the regulations introduced in 1974 (Agell 1989a; 1989b), a divorce is granted immediately when requested by both partners, unless they have children together. In the latter case, or when one partner refuses to accept the divorce request of the other, there is a waiting period of six months. There is no mandatory mediation or other mandatory involvement by public authorities in the divorce request *per se* beyond the registration of the change in civil status. Because previous legislation required a waiting period of at least 12 months before a divorce could take effect, the introduction of the new law led to an upsurge in divorces in 1974 as those who had previously been waiting were granted the change in marital status that they requested.

[15] Consideration of the interests of the weaker party in any conflict is very much regarded as being in the public domain. This is reflected in current regulations concerning children's rights in divorce settlements, for instance, and also in their rights and even the rights of the adult parties involved in the breakup of a non-marital union.

[16] This reflects a particular set of standpoints concerning the division between areas that are of public concern and areas that belong in the private sphere. We claim elsewhere (Hoem and Hoem 1988a) that, in many respects, this division has been different in Sweden from what it has been in many other countries, or that its manifestations in public policies have appeared earlier or more noticeably.

have lived together for a long time[17] and perhaps to have children together before marriage.

This could be the vehicle of a countervailing trend as regards divorce. The transition into formal marriage must have become more and more selective, in a way that could work toward making more recent marriages more cohesive. In fact, Swedish divorce rates have been levelling off since the late 1970s, and official statistics contain signs that may suggest a small decline during the last few years. Given the strength of the self-selection element in recent developments, it is actually rather remarkable that the trend did not go into reverse and divorce rates start to decline earlier and more strongly. What follows helps us to understand why.

## Modes of Union Formation

The complexity of the stage on which union breakups take place is apparent from Fig. 3.1. It displays some of the different life paths that can lead up to the dissolution of the first union for a woman who was childless when she entered that union. The boxes depict the various life statuses involved, and the lines between them represent possible direct transitions (or their corresponding events). Dissolutions are represented by lines leading into boxes marked Dis. As we see, there are three different lines that correspond to dissolutions for women with no children, four different lines for women with one child, and further lines for women with two or more children. Hazard regression can capture this complexity of behaviour as well as the patterns of influence of the covariates we observe.

The women in our data set have moved through this state space in streams that have reallocated themselves in reflection of recent behavioural developments. Table 3.1 presents some counts and Table 3.2 a few basic facts about marriage, preceding cohabitation, and subsequent child-bearing among respondents who reported that they entered motherhood while in their first union.[18] In our oldest cohort (born in 1936–40), most women started their family life by marrying directly, i.e. without living in a consensual union first. This changed in the next cohort (born in 1941–5), and the most common behaviour became to enter cohabitation and then to marry before any first birth arrived. This remained the mainstream pattern in the subsequent cohort (born in 1946–50), but people spent a longer time in a consensual union before they married, more women entered motherhood while the union was still consensual, and the proportion that married directly decreased even further. By our fourth cohort (born in 1951–5), it had become somewhat more common to have a child in the consensual union than to

---

[17] According to our survey data, as many as 45% of the women who married for the 1st time in 1980 had lived in a consensual union with the same man for at least 3 years before marriage, while only 4% had done so among those who married for the 1st time in 1965.

[18] For more information on the emergence of the new style of union continuation and of Swedish family stability, and for references to the existing literature, see Hoem and Hoem (1988*a*). The following description uses some general information not directly contained in Tables 3.1 and 3.2.

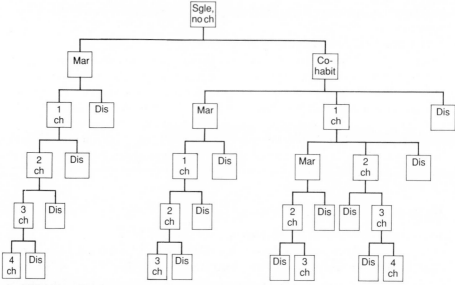

ch=child/children; Dis=first union dissolved; Mar=married; Sgle=single

Fig. 3.1 Statuses and transitions leading up to first-union dissolution for women who have not entered motherhood before first-union formation. (Read figure from top down in terms of sequential life transitions (events), and think of figure as continuing beyond its lower row of states.)

convert the union into a marriage before any entry into motherhood. After the arrival of the first child, the next step usually was to marry, though in the fourth cohort almost as many had a second birth in their consensual union.[19]

TABLE 3.1. *Some basic counts concerning first conjugal unions.*

| Cohort born in | Nos. of individuals | | | | | |
|---|---|---|---|---|---|---|
| | Useable recorded life histories | Married without preceding cohabitation | Cohabitation[a] as first event | Next event after entry into cohabitation[b] | | |
| | | | | Marriage | First birth | Dissolution |
| | (1) | (2) | (3) | (4) | (5) | (6) |
| 1936–40 | 490 | 234 | 187 | 143 | 33 | 9 |
| 1941–5 | 990 | 360 | 505 | 334 | 116 | 45 |
| 1946–50 | 1014 | 155 | 698 | 358 | 210 | 112 |
| 1951–5 | 1030 | 66 | 832 | 269 | 280 | 179 |
| 1956–60 | 699 | 16 | 493 | 67 | 124 | 136 |

[a] Entry into cohabitation.
[b] Out of the no. in col. 3. Next event not known for censored observations.

[19] The women in this cohort were only 25–9 years old at interview, and we do not know whether this pattern continued at higher ages.

TABLE 3.2. *First marriage, preceding cohabitation, and subsequent child-bearing: differential behaviour according to cohort and level of religious activity among women who have reported a first birth in their first conjugal union (%).*

| Cohort born in | Marriages not preceded by cohabitation[a] | | | Married by the time of first child-bearing[b] | | | Married by second birth[c] | Religiously active |
|---|---|---|---|---|---|---|---|---|
| | All[d] women | Religiously active? | | All[d] women | Religiously active? | | All[d] women | |
| | | No | Yes | | No | Yes | | |
| | (1) | (2) | (3) | (4) | (5) | (6) | (7) | (8) |
| 1936–40 | 59 | 57 | 85 | 91 | 91 | 97 | 86 | 9 |
| 1941–5 | 45 | 42 | 78 | 85 | 84 | 100 | 76 | 7 |
| 1946–50 | 22 | 18 | 69 | 69 | 67 | 94 | 59 | 8 |
| 1951–5 | 10 | 6 | 69 | 49 | 45 | 94 | 45 | 6 |

[a] % of respondents with a 1st birth in their 1st union who did not report that they had cohabited with their husband before the marriage. We know nothing about any previous cohabitational experience of her husband.

[b] % who were in their 1st marriage on entry into motherhood among respondents who reported a 1st birth in their 1st union.

[c] Note that this is the % of our respondents who had married by the time of their 2nd birth among those who reported that they had their 1st birth in a consensual union and a 2nd birth in the same union. Concerns 1st unions only.

[d] Counting only respondents who reported a 1st birth in their 1st union.

Our youngest cohort was born in 1956–60 and was only 20–4 years of age at interview, so one would think that they had not had much time for union formation and family-building. Nevertheless, seven out of ten of them had already started a consensual union, and among those who experienced a further demographic event, it was more common to return to the single status again than to have a child or to marry. The latter fact is one item out of several that reflect the increasing incidence and changing form of union dissolution.

The strong attraction that marriage used to have as a framework for family-building weakened over our cohorts as a consensual union became an acceptable alternative even when children started to arrive.[20] This has been a massive change, extending over most of our study population. The only exception we have noticed is the group who have reported themselves as religiously active.[21] We have incorporated this variable as an indicator of religiosity to capture the different marital behaviour in a small (though not negligible) minority (Table 3.2, column 8). In this group, almost everyone was married at entry into motherhood (column 6). Relatively few of them reported that they lived together with their husband before marriage (column 3), though to non-Scandinavians it may be

[20] Very few of our respondents had children outside any conjugal union. See the subsection below on the basic time variable, and B. Hoem (1987*b*).

[21] A subsection below contains a discussion of the information on religious activity in our data.

more interesting to note that some 30% actually reported that they had lived in a consensual union in our third and fourth cohorts.[22]

## Definitions of Basic Factors

Here is an account of the factors used in most of our dissolution hazard regressions. We describe additional factors used in particular analyses as we go along.

### Birth Cohort of the Respondent

We have used the five conventional quinquennial birth cohorts conveniently provided by the sampling plan to capture the progression of cohorts as well as secular trends. We have not included calendar period as an additional factor. This is not because we fail to recognize the possibility of period effects, underlined so strongly by Thornton and Rodgers (1987), or because we have a theory that the observed behavioural changes are brought about with the birth cohort as its main vehicle, in the manner that Ingelhart (1985) considers cohort progression as the vehicle of the development of values in a population.[23] However, the small size of our data set and the priority given to other factors whose effects we want to assess leave no room for an additional period factor in most of our investigation. We also want to avoid any identification problems that may arise if we include it. Unfortunately, this procedure precludes addressing questions about period effects such as the impact of legislative reforms or changes in public benefits.

As an alternative to the respondent's birth cohort, we could have used union formation cohorts instead, the way others have done before for marriage cohorts (e.g. Teachman 1983; Morgan and Rindfuss 1985; Thornton and Rodgers 1987; Balakrishnan *et al.* 1987; Martin and Bumpass 1989). We tried this out in a model where we included a factor to indicate the calendar year in which a respondent started her first union, in addition to her birth cohort and other factors (not displayed here). We could not discern that the union-starting year had any separate influence worth mentioning, and left it out in our subsequent work.

### Number of Births Experienced (Parity)

According to their own reports, 326 of our 4223 respondents entered motherhood before they started any conjugal union (B. Hoem 1987*b*). Even though some 30% of them lived together with a man six months after the arrival of their first child (B. Hoem, 1987*c*: 6), we suspect that their behaviour may have been different

---

[22] The Swedish State Church does not unequivocally condemn non-marital cohabitation.

[23] Lesthaeghe and Surkyn (1988) similarly consider cohort progression as the vehicle of fertility change.

from that of other respondents later in life as well, and we have excluded their recorded life histories from our analysis of first unions.[24]

In some of our regressions, nulliparae and mothers have been kept together; in others we have analysed them separately. Whenever respondents with different parities have been included in the same regression, we have also used the parity variable as a time-varying regressor.[25] In line with our treatment of all other regressors, it has appeared as a categorical variable measured on a nominal scale. When a factor actually is ordinal, the way parity is, we look for gradients in the effects estimates for its various levels.

Our analysis is mostly confined to parities one to three, though parity zero is included in a preliminary analysis in the next section as well as in our analysis for second unions in this chapter's penultimate section. This covers most months of observation. It means that a respondent history is censored on the arrival of the fourth child.

## Civil Status

To capture impacts of current civil status as well as some of the personal history leading up to it, we have used a time-varying regressor with the following levels.

(1) Currently cohabiting.
(2) Currently married with no report of a previous period of cohabitation.
(3) Currently married after premarital cohabitation, with marriage starting before entry into motherhood.
(4) Currently married after premarital cohabitation, with marriage starting between first and second birth.

The very few cohabiting women who married after the second birth have been censored in the wedding month if they subsequently married.

## The Basic Time Variable

The next section reports on an introductory analysis where periods of parity zero have been kept together with periods of parities one and above. In that situation, our spontaneous choice of the basic time variable of the hazard regression has been the number of months since the start of the union. When the investigation moves to parities one and above, there is more of a choice to be made. We have settled for time since first birth, which, of course, is also the age of the first child. Since the most profound role changes at this stage of a woman's life are connected to her entry into motherhood, we believe that this time variable is more

[24] Some of them were included in the analysis of 2nd unions, by which stage after-effects of the early births should have disappeared. See our concluding remarks.

[25] For each month of observation, a time-varying regressor is entered with the value that is current in that month. We have been surprised to discover that many previous authors have omitted the parity factor from their analyses of divorce or marriage dissolution.

pertinent than options like duration of current union or marriage duration.[26]
Union duration appears among the regressors indirectly as a combination of our
time variable and a factor representing the number of months between the entry
into the union and the arrival of the first birth.

## An Introductory Regression

For a general overview of the levels of relative dissolution risks in the data, we
first present a very simple, completely multiplicative model with factors that arise
directly from Fig. 3.1. They and their levels appear in Table 3.3. We see that there
has been a strong overall increase in dissolution risks over the cohorts, with a
particularly pronounced jump from the fourth to the fifth cohort, where risks
increased by 64%.

TABLE 3.3. *Relative risks of dissolution of a first conjugal
union in an introductory model.*

| Factor | Level | Relative risk |
|---|---|---|
| Cohort | 1936–40 | 0.78 |
| | 1941–5 | 0.84 |
| | 1946–50 | 1.00 |
| | 1951–5 | 1.24 |
| | 1956–60 | 2.03 |
| Civil status | Married, no previous cohabitation | 0.68 |
| | Married after previous cohabitation: | |
| | before first birth | 1.00 |
| | between 1st and 2nd birth | 1.61 |
| | Currently cohabiting | 3.05 |
| No. of children | 0 | 1.52 |
| | 1 | 1.00 |
| | 2 | 0.72 |
| | 3 | 0.96 |

*Time variables*: months since entry into 1st union (grouped).
*Overall level of baseline risk*: 18 dissolutions per 10 000 women per
month.

In this model, those who live in a consensual union have a dissolution risk
estimated to be about four-and-a-half times that of those who report that they
have married directly. The coefficients of the various categories of married

---

[26] The respondent's own current duration has been strongly recommended by Thornton and Rodgers
(1987).

[27] Blanc (1985: 75–9) and Bennett, Blanc, and Bloom (1988) first published on the increased marital
dissolution risk for women with premarital cohabitation in the same data set. Balakrishnan *et al.* (1987)
have a similar result for Canadian data.

women support the mode-of-entry self-selection hypothesis.[27] Preceding cohabitation seems to be more of a signal of liberal individual values than a sorting ground for successful marriages.[28]

As expected, having children reduces the dissolution risk, either because children serve as a focus of communality between the partners[29] or because children are produced more often in unions of some expected permanence. As noted above, however, more children do not necessarily reduce the dissolution risk monotonically. Our finding that unions with three children are less cohesive than those with two children turns out to be a consistent feature of all the models we have fitted that include these parities. It is not an artefact produced by the unrealistic simplicity of the current introductory model.

When one starts from this model and adds other factors and relevant interactions, it quickly becomes apparent that women of parity zero have dissolution patterns quite different from those of women who have entered motherhood. This shows up in the form of many meaningful and statistically significant interactions between parity and other factors in the intensity model. Due to space limitations, our analyses of dissolutions of childless first unions will not be reported here.[30] The following section focuses on first unions with children.

## Disruptions after Entry into Motherhood

### Model Selection

For a consideration of the development of family cohesion in Sweden, the most interesting part of our investigation is the analysis of disruption risks for women who have entered motherhood. Table 3.4 contains a sequence of ten models fitted to the available life histories on the basis of the reasoning of the section on the definitions of basic factors. Starting with Model 1, which includes only the cohort factor and the basic time variable (age of the first-born), we have added one more factor at a time, stopping with the ten factors of Model 10. With one exception, we have introduced the factors in a sequence that is meant largely to reflect their temporal appearance in the respondent's life, and to capture gradual causal proximity to the current situation in any month of observation. This allows us to see how the inclusion of a later factor modifies the estimated effects of earlier factors. It reveals the direct effects of the earlier factors by removing from the estimates indirect influences that work via the later factor.

---

[28] We do not want to read too much into the fact that the dissolution risk was actually larger when the marriage was started only after rather than before the advent of the 1st child (but still before the 2nd birth) according to Table 3.3. We believe this to be an overestimate mostly produced by random deviations in some life histories in the 5th cohort. We return to this topic in the subsection on trends over birth cohorts and effects of civil status.

[29] Cf. such an interpretation of a similar finding by Morgan and Rindfuss (1985: 1070).

[30] See J. Hoem (1990) instead.

TABLE 3.4. Relative risks of dissolution of a first union in a sequence of nested multiplicative-intensity models.

| Factor | Levels | Model 1 | Model 2 | Model 3 | Model 4 | Model 5 | Model 6 | Model 7 | Model 8 | Model 9 | Model 10 |
|---|---|---|---|---|---|---|---|---|---|---|---|
| Cohort | 1936–45 | 0.68 | 0.68 | 0.69 | 0.76 | 0.75 | 0.73 | 0.71 | 0.72 | 0.73 | 0.90 |
| | 1946–50 | 1.00 | 1.00 | 1.00 | 1.00 | 1.00 | 1.00 | 1.00 | 1.00 | 1.00 | 1.00 |
| | 1951–5 | 1.64 | 1.64 | 1.62 | 1.44 | 1.43 | 1.43 | 1.39 | 1.40 | 1.41 | 1.05 |
| Social origin | Up + middle[a] | | 1.15 | 1.19 | 1.32 | 1.32 | 1.28 | 1.32 | 1.24 | 1.22 | 1.33 |
| | Other | | 1.00 | 1.00 | 1.00 | 1.00 | 1.00 | 1.00 | 1.00 | 1.00 | 1.00 |
| Religiously active? | Yes | | | 0.40 | 0.44 | 0.45 | 0.44 | 0.45 | 0.44 | 0.46 | 0.57 |
| | No | | | 1.00 | 1.00 | 1.00 | 1.00 | 1.00 | 1.00 | 1.00 | 1.00 |
| Age at start of union | 16–19 yrs. | | | | 1.80 | 1.72 | 1.53 | 1.53 | 1.59 | 1.56 | 1.51 |
| | 20–5 | | | | 1.00 | 1.00 | 1.00 | 1.00 | 1.00 | 1.00 | 1.00 |
| | 26–35 | | | | 1.03 | 1.03 | 1.11 | 1.09 | 1.04 | 1.07 | 1.96 |
| Months between start of union and first birth | ≤ 7 mths. | | | | | 1.21 | 1.04 | 0.94 | 0.96 | 0.97 | 1.05 |
| | 8–35 mths. | | | | | 1.00 | 1.00 | 1.00 | 1.00 | 1.00 | 1.00 |
| | ≥ 36 mths. | | | | | 0.82 | 0.92 | 0.86 | 0.84 | 0.85 | 0.88 |
| First birth planned? | Yes | | | | | | 1.00 | 1.00 | 1.00 | 1.00 | 1.00 |
| | No | | | | | | 1.93 | 1.86 | 1.83 | 1.76 | 1.66 |
| No. of children born | 1 | | | | | | | 1.00 | 1.00 | 1.00 | 1.00 |
| | 2 | | | | | | | 0.51 | 0.51 | 0.58 | 0.64 |
| | 3 | | | | | | | 0.65 | 0.64 | 0.80 | 0.87 |
| University-level education | None | | | | | | | | 1.00 | 1.00 | 1.00 |
| | Some | | | | | | | | 1.28 | 1.10 | 1.12 |
| Current work-force status | Full-time job | | | | | | | | | 1.83 | 1.81 |
| | Part-time job | | | | | | | | | 1.00 | 1.00 |
| | Housewife | | | | | | | | | 1.12 | 1.13 |
| | Other | | | | | | | | | 2.72 | 2.51 |
| | Pregnant | | | | | | | | | 0.33 | 0.35 |
| | In maternity period | | | | | | | | | 0.65 | 0.62 |
| Civil status and history | Married, no preceding cohabitation | | | | | | | | | | 0.65 |
| | With preceding cohabitation, married since before first birth | | | | | | | | | | 1.00 |
| | With preceding cohabitation, married since between first and second birth | | | | | | | | | | 1.02 |
| | Currently cohabiting | | | | | | | | | | 2.62 |
| − 2 ln likelihood: | | 5179.7 | 5178.7 | 5165.4 | 5134.6 | 5127.6 | 5099.0 | 5072.7 | 5070.3 | 4996.9 | 4930.3 |

Time variable: Mths. since 1st birth (grouped).

[a] Upper- and middle-level white-collar employees.

The one exception is the factor 'civil status and history', which should logically appear at least one step before it actually does in this sequence. The civil-status factor is involved in an interaction with the birth cohort in the model we like best (Model 11), and we have preferred to include the interaction (and therefore also the corresponding factor) last. The interaction does not change the estimated effects of the other factors in Model 10 in any essential manner, so we only report the estimated interaction effects in the form of the relative risks in Table 3.5. Except for a minor overall increase in risks, dissolution behaviour turned out to be very similar in our two oldest cohorts, so we have combined them.[31] We have eliminated our youngest cohort, born in 1956–60, because it contributed very little information about this stage in life.

TABLE 3.5. *Relative risks of first-union dissolution with the cohort and civil-status factors in interaction (Model 11).*

| Civil status and history | Cohort born in years | | |
|---|---|---|---|
| | 1936–45 | 1946–50 | 1951–5 |
| Married, no preceding cohabitation | 0.58 | 0.54 | 0.34 |
| Married, with preceding cohabitation: | | | |
|     starting before first birth | 0.75 | 1.00 | 1.47 |
|     start between first and second birth | 0.94 | 0.82 | 1.00 |
| Currently cohabiting | 2.53 | 2.70 | 2.32 |
| − 2 *ln* likelihood: 4922.6 | | | |

*Overall level of baseline risk*: 15 dissolution per 10 000 women per month.
*Note*: Model 11 contains the same factors as Model 10 but also has the interaction terms of this table. The estimated effects of other factors are much the same as those of Model 10.

We have also experimented with extending the regressor space and with including a number of other interaction terms, such as those between civil status and parity, between parity and work-force status, and between age at the start of the union and the time factor (months since first birth). We will mention a couple of the extra regressors below, but none of them significantly improved the fit of the model, nor have we found any estimated patterns that have caught our interest. The outcome was very similar when interactions were fitted. None of them significantly improved the model, and only two of them had interesting estimated patterns, namely the interaction in Model 11 and the one between starting age and time since entry into motherhood (see the subsection on union starting age that appears later in this chapter). Any further patterns in our data may have been drowned by random variation due to small group sizes. We appear to be close to a complete exploitation of the information contained in our data.

[31] With this many regressors there is a point in reducing the number of levels of each factor whenever possible. Combining the 2 cohorts also helps us avoid problems that could arise from the fact that we only have half as many respondents in our oldest cohort as in the 2nd, 3rd, and 4th cohorts, and from the fact that their distribution over the levels of the civil-status factor is much more concentrated among the directly married and among those who marry after a brief period of preceding cohabitation than in later cohorts.

Perhaps only strong effects can be detected when we use so many regressors. It is also costly to go any further, since computer runs become very long even with an efficient program like LOGLIN, which we have used in this study (Olivier and Neff 1976; Laird and Olivier 1981).

## Trends over Birth Cohorts and Effects of Civil Status

There is a strong overall increase in dissolution risks over our cohorts when we take the other factors into account, just as there was in the simple model described in the previous section. This shows up in all models up to Model 9, inclusive. The increase almost disappears when civil status is added in Model 10, but that is because the differing trends in the various civil statuses interfere with each other. As we can see from Model 11 (Table 3.5), those who have married without a preceding period of cohabitation actually have a decreasing dissolution risk, well in line with our notion that, in our population, direct entry into marriage has become progressively selective in favour of those with high marriage cohesion. Cohabiting mothers have much higher dissolution risks, as expected, and according to Table 3.5 their risks have essentially been stable across our cohorts. In the group that represented the mainstream during our study period, namely, those who were married after a preceding cohabitation but before entry into motherhood, dissolution risks increased over our cohorts, and by as much as almost 100%. As we noted already in the previous section, they have higher dissolution hazards than the directly married, *ceteris paribus*. In the fourth cohort their risk ratio is as much as 4.

The dissolution risks of those who have married only after the advent of the first child (but before the second birth) have been quite stable over our cohorts. Note how their risk level is about the same as for the mainstream group that married before entry into motherhood. When a consensual union is converted into a marriage, the existence of a premarital first-born in the union is no indicator of an increased marital dissolution risk, as the introductory analysis in the previous section makes it appear. The result in that previous model was affected by features that have now been brought under better control.[32]

Together with the difference between the messages of our Models 10 and 11, this demonstrates the importance of including all influential factors and interactions in the analysis. In particular, developments over time are exposed and secular trends are unravelled when the respondent's birth cohort or some other suitable factor (and appropriate interactions) are included as hazard regressors. Otherwise, effects of other factors may be confounded with cohort developments.[33]

## Social Origin

To capture any direct influence of the respondent's family of orientation, we have included a factor based on the occupation of the main breadwinner in the family

---

[32]   We have not been able to uncover similar misrepresentations of other effects in the section in which we presented an introductory regression.

[33]   For a case in point, see Hoem and Hoem (1988*b*: s. 6.2).

in which the respondent grew up. This characterization of social status originally had seven levels, comprising unskilled and skilled workers, lower-, middle- , and higher-level white-collar employees (including independent academics and members of the educated liberal professions), farmers, and the self-employed with small business enterprises (Lyberg 1984; J. Hoem 1985). We used a several-level factor based on this grouping in some of our preliminary analyses. Because of small group sizes, it became necessary to combine the respondents into just two groups for this variable in most of our investigation, however. On the basis of preliminary analyses of differentials in dissolution behaviour, we have chosen a grouping into (i) daughters of middle- and higher-level employees, and (ii) other respondents.

The former group turned out to have dissolution risks that are higher than the latter.[34] Presumably, there is something in the bourgeois culture that more easily makes dissolution an acceptable alternative when a union does not function as desired.

## Religious Activity

The religiously active have much lower dissolution risks than others after entry into motherhood, though the risks are not negligible even for this group. It is interesting to note the somewhat reduced importance of religious activity after the inclusion of the civil-status factor in Model 10. Apparent dissolution risks of those who are not religiously active drop from over twice the level of the active to about one-and-three-quarters of their level, due, of course, to the much greater concentration of the religiously active in the group of the directly married. As expected, manifest religiosity influences dissolution risks directly as well as indirectly, such as via its influence on the mode of marriage formation.

At this stage, it may be informative to note how religious activity was measured in our data set and what we take it to represent. In the interview, a respondent was asked the following question:

Are you religiously active? ([Do you] go to religious services or other meetings, [do you] work for a religious society, take Holy Communion, or [participate in similar activities]?)[35]

It appeared in a sequence of questions concerning leisure activities along with sports, political work, course-work, etc., towards the very end of the questionnaire, well after the sequences on demographic and other behaviour. A follow-up question elicited the extent of religious activity, but we have only used the yes/no response here. It should be understood that nominally, the target population overwhelmingly belongs to the (liberal Protestant) Swedish State Church, and

---

[34] This was the case at parity zero as well. See J. Hoem (1990).

[35] Our translation with our elucidations in square brackets.

that singling out Catholics or non-Christians, for instance, would be impossible in our data and virtually meaningless for our analysis.

The purpose of including this factor is to assess the influence of religious values on union dissolution behaviour. The manifestation of such values in professed religious activity should be a measure of some merit[36] beyond essentially being the only indicator available to us. There is a potential problem in the fact that the question refers to activities at the time of the interview, not at the time when the behaviour occurred.[37] What we seek is a causal relation running from religious values to family behaviour, and we cannot rule out the possibility that family and other adult life experiences may influence subsequent religious observance. If the experience of a painful divorce makes individuals turn to religion for consolation, support, and perhaps atonement, then the inclusion of our religious-activity indicator in the regression analysis of a dissolution intensity will tend to underestimate the impact of religious values on family cohesion because some of those recorded as religiously active were not so when the divorce decision was made. Conversely, a divorce could alienate some previously religious individuals if there is some residual disapproval of divorce in the religious population, which would work towards biasing the effect of a religious commitment in the opposite direction. However, since our respondents live in a society where the religiosity profile is very low, we believe, perhaps heroically, that religious values are ingrained before adulthood in most cases, and that later conversions to or from manifest religious behaviour play a minor role. The fact that our respondents were all at most 44 years old at the time of the interview may be an argument in our favour, for presumably repentant conversions mostly occur later in life.

Other parts of the questionnaire could tap a dimension that we might call 'family orientation'. For instance, the respondent was asked to take a stand on several statements like 'To have children is part of the meaning of life' and 'The joy of having many children compensates for economic and other sacrifices'. Presumably, women who strongly endorse statements of this nature and live up to them throughout their adult life might be less prone than others to accept family dissolution. We suspect, however, that, unlike assessments of religious activity, interview responses to such statements may be more strongly influenced by temporary sentiments and changeable norms than by deeply ingrained values. We also believe that posterior rationalization built on the outcome of the life course may play a more important role in the response to such items. This makes the direction of influence between dissolution behaviour and such statements of attitudes much more problematic. In the competition for space in our regressions, therefore, a representation of these responses has lost out.

---

[36] Lesthaeghe and Surkyn (1988: 14) have pointed out the increasing adequacy of this indicator in a modern society.

[37] A similar concern has been voiced by Balakrishnan et al. (1987: 400).

## Union Starting Age

Since starting age is a well-known determinant of subsequent child-bearing and divorce behaviour,[38] we have included age at the start of the first union as a factor in our regressions, grouped into ages 16–19, 20–5, and 26–35 years. The partition was mainly chosen for practical reasons, such as group sizes and expected age gradients of behaviour. We have deleted the respondents who have reported that they started their first union before age 16 or after age 35 because there are very few of them, and because we suspect a different dissolution behaviour from such outliers.

As expected, starting the first conjugal union as a teenager gave our Swedish female respondents a dissolution risk that was considerably higher than for those who started later, even after entry into motherhood and even when the rest of our factors are taken into account. (We made the same finding at parity zero; see J. Hoem 1990.) Age at marriage is often regarded as an indicator of preparation for marriage. A few previous authors have found that at least some of the factors that reflect the degree of such preparation have effects that taper off at higher marital durations in their data. Morgan and Rindfuss (1985) and South and Spitze (1986) found diminishing effects of initial educational level, and Morgan and Rindfuss (1985) as well as Kravdal (1988) found declining effects of the timing of the first birth relative to entry into marriage. While South and Spitze (1986) also found some reduction in the effect of age at marriage as marital duration increases, Morgan and Rindfuss (1985) interpreted the corresponding starting-age effects in their data as essentially persistent over all marital durations and all ages attained, and so apparently did Kravdal (1988). Given the size limitations of our data, we have not pursued this topic systematically, but we can at least report one item of this nature, namely that the effect of teenage union formation weakens over the fifteen years after entry into motherhood that we follow the respondents in our current analysis (Hoem and Hoem 1988*b*: table 10).

## Circumstances Surrounding Entry into Motherhood

It is a common finding that the marital dissolution risk is increased if the woman had a child before marriage or if she was pregnant at marriage.[39] This is commonly attributed to an insufficient partner search before a forced marriage, and to a lower attractiveness of unmarried mothers as marriage partners, both of which can lead more easily to mismatches and to marital strain. (See Furstenberg 1976 for a review of explanations.) The second paragraph of the subsection on trends over birth cohorts and effects of civil status shows that there is no such effect in our data if the first birth occurred in the same conjugal union. It is

---

[38] See references in the subsection above on theory and main findings.

[39] Bumpass and Sweet (1972); Menken *et al.* (1981); Teachman (1983); Morgan and Rindfuss (1985); Murphy (1985); Ermisch (1986); Balakrishnan *et al.* (1987); Bennett, Blanc, and Bloom (1988); Kravdal (1988); Lehrer (1988); Martin and Bumpass (1989); and others.

essentially immaterial, then, for the marital-dissolution risk whether the first birth occurred before or after the union was converted into a marriage.

This is different if the woman's first child was born before she entered the union in question. In that case, the dissolution risk is appreciably higher in our data. We have no information on who the biological father of such a child is. The child's presence in a union may indicate either that the woman's current partner is not the child's father or that, if he is, the couple has had problems that lead them not to start living together before the child was born. In either case, increased dissolution risks are expected.

In the analysis reported here, we concentrate on respondents who were nulliparous when they entered into their first union, and we do not give the details of how we arrived at the above empirical observation. However, one supporting indication can be found in Bennett, Blanc, and Bloom (1988: table 7). They show that a premarital first birth gives an estimated increase of 58% in the risk of dissolution for those who married without preceding cohabitation in our data set.

Some respondents who married directly without any recorded preceding cohabitation were pregnant at marriage, but most non-marital births and premarital conceptions in Sweden will have taken place in consensual unions. Pregnancy at marriage is unlikely to be very important for subsequent dissolution risks if the child was conceived in the same union.[40] To concentrate on the most interesting features of our data set in this analysis of union dissolution after entry into motherhood, we have included as a regressor the number of months spent in the union up to the first birth, grouped as indicated in the fifth panel of Table 3.4. This should allow us to capture any effect of pregnancy at entry as well as any effect of an unusually long delay of the arrival of the first birth.

The considerable effect of the timing of the first birth in the union in Model 5 largely disappears when its planning status[41] is brought into consideration (Model 6). Evidently, an unplanned first birth carries a high dissolution potential with it (Model 10), but beyond that effect, it is not very important whether the woman was pregnant at entry into the union. Again, this is the kind of effect that search theory would predict, for an admission that the first birth was unplanned would suggest that the respondent had not completed assessing potential partners before pregnancy interfered.

---

[40] Billy, Landale, and McLaughlin (1986), Kiernan (1986), and McLaughlin *et al.* (1986) have found no significant difference in marital breakup between those who were pregnant at marriage and those who were not. In a much more extensive data set for Norway, Kravdal (1988) did get noticeable effects of premarital pregnancy.

[41] The planning status of a birth was determined from the response to the following question: 'Pregnancies do not always occur at the time one has planned. When you discovered that you were pregnant with your [1st, 2nd, 3rd . . .] child, did you then feel that you wanted it but that it had appeared too early, that you wanted it and that the time was suitable, or would you say that in reality you did not want the pregnancy?' The births were coded as unplanned if the pregnancy was reported as unwanted or mistimed. Our faith in the responses is modified by the usual caveats about subsequent rationalization, etc. See Ryder (1979).

**Parity and Children's Ages**

The parity effects for families with children in Table 3.4 have the same pattern as in Table 3.3, which we discussed in the previous section. In fact, all our models (including some not reported here) suggest that being a family with two children vouches for family stability more than having only one child. As a family goes beyond the two-child norm, the dissolution risk increases again.[42]

In most intensity regression analyses, we would include a plot of the baseline hazard to give an impression of the direct effect of the time variable, in this case the age of the first child in the family. It is noteworthy, however, that in our data the risk of union dissolution after entry into motherhood has no interesting time pattern. In fact, deleting this factor would not significantly reduce the fit of the model or appreciably change other effect estimates. We conclude that the age of the oldest child does not have an important direct effect on dissolution behaviour over the segments of the life span during which we follow our respondents. We cannot find any clear direction in the relation between duration and union break-down. It looks as if explanations that include duration effects in dissolution behaviour at this stage can concentrate on the development of our time-varying covariates. An understanding of the time-pattern of union dissolutions must then build on an explanation of birth timing, of labour force participation, of how and when respondents seek to improve their education, and so on.

In this connection, one should note that we should expect little impact of the empty nest in our data set. In fact, most women will have their oldest child living in their household throughout the life segments when they contribute to our observations, for we censor all life histories fifteen years after entry into motherhood.

The employment-status factor (see later in this chapter) gives a clue to the age of the youngest child, for it indicates whether the family has a baby under one year old. In preliminary work, we have experimented with various more complete representations of the age of the youngest child, but to our disappointment we have not found any sensible patterns in the outcome.[43]

**Educational Level**

Theoretical considerations and previous investigations suggest that the risk of union dissolution may depend on the individual's educational level. More highly educated individuals can perhaps better afford the expense of establishing separate homes. Better educated women (as well as their men) may also generally be more confident that they are able to cope with the other difficulties involved, as

---

[42] A similar U-shape has been noted before by Thornton (1977), Becker, Landes, and Michael (1977), and Murphy (1984; 1985), while Kravdal (1988) finds a monotonic decrease in divorce risks as parity increases.

[43] Again, this outcome may reflect our small group sizes. Becker, Landes, and Michael (1977) and Cherlin (1977) found that only preschool children deter marital separation or divorce. Kravdal (1988) similarly found clear gradients in divorce risks by age group of youngest child. Morgan and Rindfuss (1985) and Waite, Haggstrom, and Kanouse (1985) made similar findings.

well as to cash in on the potentials of a new start. These items would make us expect that dissolution risks should increase with educational level, and we observe a mild effect in this direction.[44] This is rather unusual, for the most common empirical pattern for *divorce* risks is that they are highest for the least well-educated.[45]

To capture any effects of educational level, we have included a time-varying regressor that measures a woman's current educational level in any month of observation. This factor appears in many contexts in the larger project from which this chapter reports on one part. As described elsewhere (J. Hoem 1985), we have developed a trichotomous characterization based on a grouping of the number of months that a respondent has reported she has been in school since September of the calendar year in which she reached age 16.[46] When this characterization was used in a study of second and third births in the same data set (Hoem and Hoem 1989), it turned out that the crucial distinction was between women who had received some education at university level and those who had not. Preliminary analyses have suggested that this may be the case for dissolution behaviour as well, so our present report uses this dichotomous representation.

### Effects of Employment, of Pregnancy, and of Having a New-Born Family Member

When everything else is equal, a woman's labour force situation is likely to affect her dissolution risk in much the same way as does her educational level. We would expect a woman with a secure foothold in the labour force to have a higher dissolution risk than others, both because of her better economic position and her higher general ability to cope with family breakup and to utilize its potential, and also because of her more extensive opportunities to meet and get to know men other than her husband or partner through a partly independent social life.[47]

---

[44] The influences just mentioned may have been partly counterbalanced in our data if the more highly educated make a better choice of living partner (Becker 1981). It would also work in the opposite direction after entry into motherhood if the more highly educated are more hesitant to have children in an unsatisfactory relationship. As indicated by Ermisch (1986), current theory cannot predict the direction of the impact of education on dissolution risks, for it depends on the balance between countervailing effects.

[45] Menken *et al.* (1981); Moore and Waite (1981); Teachman (1982); Morgan and Rindfuss (1985); Ermisch (1986); Martin and Bumpass (1989). South and Spitze (1986) found that divorce risks had a falling gradient over educational levels at short marital durations, but that this changed into an increasing gradient at long durations. We trust that their educational variable essentially refers to level at entry into marriage.

[46] Records of employment and educational activities before that age are less reliable, and a suitable grouping of months recorded since that age will help guard against an unwarranted impression of the accuracy of reports at later ages. The grouping was chosen to fit with the Swedish educational system.

[47] In a population less overwhelmingly dominated by general female labour force participation than in Sweden, it is also possible that a woman in a faltering union may seek a job to establish a better financial basis for a breakup and for her life afterwards.

Women in part-time jobs may have all of these elements in a reduced dose, and the fact that they have chosen to work part-time may be a manifestation of a stronger family orientation. To assess arguments such as these, we have included a time-varying covariate that in any month of observation after entry into mother-hood indicates whether the respondent was in a full-time job, was in a part-time job, was a housewife, or had some other main activity, all according to her own report.

In a study of marital and consensual union dissolution, such a classification is not so relevant for the months just before and after a birth. First of all, the reliability of reports concerning such a period are manifestly less accurate than otherwise.[48] Secondly, the fact that a couple knows that the woman is pregnant is surely going to influence the dissolution risk much more profoundly than any labour force connection of hers at the time. Thirdly, dissolution risks should be low when the family has a new-born child. For reasons of this nature, we have extended the four-level work-force characterization to a factor with two more levels: 'pregnant' and 'in maternity period'. The factor takes the first of these additional levels during the seven months preceding a birth and the second level during the first year after the birth.[49]

Our expectation concerning the effects of a pregnancy turns out to be war-ranted: the risk level during the pregnancy period is only about one-third that of a non-pregnant housewife or woman in part-time work and only a fifth that of a non-pregnant woman in full-time work. Similarly, we observe a reduced dissol-ution risk when the family has a baby that is under a year old.[50]

The increased dissolution risks of the full-time job-holders is what we pre-dicted, though we would have expected a gradient such that the risks of part-time job-holders would be somewhere between those in full-time work and house-wives, as was found by South and Spitze (1986). A woman who holds a part-time job is likely to have the duties of a full-time housewife as well. We would have thought that this kind of work-load could be conducive to conflicts between the partners. We find no such gradient, however. Housewives and those with a part-time job have much the same dissolution risks. Perhaps we should be more open to the effects of job satisfaction and to partner equality, as well as to discontent with 'merely' being a housewife and with presumably having the correspondingly less satisfactory economic situation in a population where the overwhelming majority of women hold a job and full-time housewives are a small minority.

---

[48] For instance, the questionnaire invites the respondent to report periods during which she was on paid maternity leave separately from months in which she was a housewife, but reporting accuracy was so low that we have never ventured to utilize this distinction. Some women even reported that they continued working in their jobs with no interruption caused by their births.

[49] For the purposes of our analysis, the detailed treatment of the month of the birth is unimportant, but we may mention that, for reasons mainly of programming convenience, it was split in 2 equal parts, which makes the pregnancy period last for 7.5 months and the maternity period for 11.5 months.

[50] This contrasts with previous findings by Koo and Janowitz (1983).

It is no surprise that women in the employment status 'other' have elevated dissolution risks. Women in this group are non-pregnant, have not had a child during the preceding year, and are mostly students, whose attention may be directed elsewhere than to their living partner and whose personal development may lead to other male contacts. Other (smaller) contributions in this category are from the unemployed, the institutionalized, and so on. These groups could easily be prone to high dissolution risks as well, and are so on average.

A woman's employment status in any month must be an incomplete characterization of work-force influences in her dissolution behaviour. One would suspect that her labour force history would have an impact as well. Ermisch (1986) found that British women with a longer work experience generally tend to face a greater risk of subsequent marital breakdown, and that work experience after entry into motherhood is more important at the longer marriage durations. South and Spitze (1986) found that a recent entry into the labour force was associated with an elevated divorce risk for a married woman. Since most Swedish women spend most of their time as students or in jobs before first birth in any case, one of us (B. Hoem 1986; see also Hoem and Hoem 1989) has developed a representation of the job history since first birth that seeks to capture both the woman's labour force attachment and any signals of recent changes in personal plans. This representation turned out to provide much additional insight into the advent of the third birth, and unpublished work concerning the fourth birth demonstrates corresponding effects for that birth order also. We have included this feature in preliminary analyses of union dissolution as well, but have failed to achieve similar results, and have not pursued the issue.[51]

## Dissolution of the Second Union

There were 626 second unions among the respondents in our first four cohorts. We have deleted from our analysis of second unions the 64 life histories whose first unions lasted for nine months or under to avoid respondents whose first-union history seems to signal unusually high dissolution proneness. Because we censor all life histories at the advent of any fourth birth, we have also excluded nine respondents who entered their second union at parity four or more. On the other hand, we have included respondents who entered a first union after the advent of their first child, unless they were excluded under any of the two criteria just mentioned. For simplicity, and to avoid reducing a small data set even further, we have also included any periods in second unions before entry into motherhood.

Most second unions start out as consensual unions in our data, but many are converted into marriages later.[52] The cohesion of second unions depends on

---

[51] Cf. again our remarks concerning small group sizes at the end of the section on the dissolution of the 2nd union.

[52] For accounts of the formation of 2nd unions in our data set, see Blanc (1985) and Larsson (1986).

whether dissolution behaviour is dominated by transference or by learning. In other words, are people who leave a first union and start a second one more dissolution-prone than others in general,[53] or has the experience of the first union and its breakup largely made them more careful in the selection of the second

TABLE 3.6. *Relative risks of dissolution of second unions*

| Factor | Level | Relative risk |
|---|---|---|
| Cohort born in | 1936–40 | 0.51 |
| | 1941–5 | 0.58 |
| | 1946–50 | 1.00 |
| | 1951–5 | 1.04 |
| Family of origin | Up + middle | 1.33 |
| | Others | 1.00 |
| No. of children in the first union | 0 | 1.20 |
| | 1 | 1.00 |
| | 2 or 3 | 1.16 |
| Duration of first union | 10–29 mths. | 1.31 |
| | 30 mths. or more | 1.00 |
| Civil status at the conclusion of first union | Married | 1.00 |
| | Cohabiting | 1.56 |
| Age at start of second union | 24 or under | 0.63 |
| | 25–30 | 1.00 |
| | 31 or over | 1.28 |
| Any children so far in the second union? | No | 1.00 |
| | Yes | 0.81 |
| University-level education | None | 1.00 |
| | Some | 0.66 |
| Current civil status (second union) | Married | 1.00 |
| | Cohabiting | 2.99 |

*Time variable*: months since start of 2nd union.
*Overall level of baseline risk*: 24 dissolution per 10 000 women per month.
*Notes*: Life histories whose 1st unions lasted for 9 mths. or less have been excluded from this analysis. All records have been censored at any 4th birth. Periods of pregnancy have not been removed.

partner and in their behaviour in the second union, and perhaps more appreciative of the benefits of living in a union? After all, they have taken the step of starting anew. What is the effect if the decision to start a new partnership takes place

---

[53] Cf. arguments in this direction by Halliday (1980) and by Furstenberg and Spanier (1984).

while the first one still exists?[54] It is a common observation that second marriages have higher divorce risks than first marriages.[55] In line with this, net of the compositional effects controlled by our many hazard regressors, our respondents turn out to have an overall baseline dissolution risk that is considerably higher in second than in first unions.

As Table 3.6 shows, many factors influence dissolution risks in second unions in much the same way as in first unions. The dissolution risk has increased over the cohorts. Daughters of middle- and upper-level white-collar employees have a somewhat elevated risk when everything else is equal. The arrival of a child in the union is associated with a reduced dissolution risk,[56] and consensual second unions have much higher dissolution risks than marital second unions.

For second unions, some factors work in the opposite direction to what they did for first unions. Women with some university-level education now have somewhat reduced dissolution risks,[57] as if their ability to make a suitable second choice of mate or to learn to cope with the problems of union stability is a bit better than that of others, *ceteris paribus*. It is even more striking that the general age effect has now been reversed: the dissolution hazard for second unions increases as the age at the start of the second union goes up. As we see from panels A and B in Table 3.7, this effect is produced by those who have no child in the second union, or by those who live in a consensual second union. When the second union is converted into a marriage (or in the rare case that it is a marriage from the outset), then age is an advantage for union cohesion.[58] It looks as if the durable unions with the more experienced partners are generally successfully converted into marriages, while other unions remain consensual.

The dissolution risk of the second union is adversely affected if the first union remained consensual until it broke up. The effect on the second union is the same, irrespective of its character: marital second unions are affected as badly as consensual second unions by the final civil status of the first union. We see this as another manifestation of mode-of-entry self-selection. The character of the first union gives a signal about the character of the individuals involved in it.

Panel C of Table 3.7 suggests that having a child in the second union is particularly advantageous for union cohesion if one has some university education. Perhaps the more highly educated are more cautious about having children in second unions unless they see the union as quite durable.

Cherlin (1978) identified stepchildren as the principal destabilizing element in remarriage, and Becker, Landes, and Michael (1977) and White and Booth (1985)

---

[54] Beside common everyday observation, see Monahan (1952) for an early reference.

[55] Bumpass and Sweet (1972); Becker, Landes, and Michael (1977); Cherlin (1977); McCarthy (1978); Lehrer, (1988); Kravdal and Noack (1988).

[56] Cf. a similar finding by Becker, Landes, and Michael (1977).

[57] Martin and Bumpass (1989) similarly show a falling gradient for second US marriages.

[58] The panels in Table 3.7 have been produced by fitting separate models to the data set. As indicated in a note to the table, the 3 models there have included the same factors but have different interaction terms. Small group sizes have not supported the simultaneous estimation of 2 or more interaction tables in 1 model.

have supported his finding. Like Furstenberg and Spanier (1984) and Martin and Bumpass (1989), we find otherwise, In our data, how many children the woman had before her second union has little impact on its cohesion so long as we stick to the small family sizes represented here. How many children she has had altogether is not important either.[59] What counts is the arrival of any children in the current union. A longer duration of the first union gives a somewhat improved prognosis for the cohesion of the second.

TABLE 3.7. *Relative risks in three separate models, each with an interaction between a single pair of factors.*

A. *Interaction between age at start of second union and current number of children in that union*

| Age at start of second union | Current no. of children in second union | |
|---|---|---|
| | *None* | *1 or more* |
| 24 or under | 1.00 | 1.16 |
| 25–30 | 1.73 | 1.04 |
| 31 or over | 2.24 | — |

B. *Interaction between age at start of second union and that union's current civil status*

| Age at start of second union | Current civil status of second union | |
|---|---|---|
| | *Marital* | *Consensual* |
| 24 or less | 1.00 | 1.69 |
| 25–30 | 0.61 | 2.92 |
| 31 or more | 0.45 | 3.66 |

C. *Interaction between educational level and current number of children in second union*

| University-level education | Current no. of children in second union | |
|---|---|---|
| | *None* | *1 or more* |
| None | 1.00 | 1.89 |
| Some | 0.89 | 0.14 |

*Notes*: Each model has the factors and levels of Table 3.6 (except family of origin, duration of 1st union, and the time variable, which gave no significant contributions) and the single interaction indicated in one of the panels of this table. Estimated effects of factors not included in interactions were hardly changed by the interactions. No interactions other than those of this table were significant. A dash indicates no occurrences.

[59] If it were, an interaction between the 2 factors involving children would have appeared in the model, which it does not.

Preliminary analyses suggested that the interval between the two unions has very little impact on the survival chances of the second union, and that it also does not matter whether the woman was pregnant when she started her second union. In the interest of restricting the number of regressors, we have not even included these two factors in the analyses reported in our tables.

## Concluding Remarks

The monthly risk that a conjugal union will dissolve depends on the character of the union and on the characteristics of the partners. Consensual unions have much higher dissolution risks than marriages, unions with children have lower dissolution risks than comparable unions without children, and so on. Risks vary by social origin and by educational level; respondents with bourgeois origins, or with some education on the university level, or who are currently receiving education, have higher risks than others in first unions, *ceteris paribus*.[60] Many of these effects can be interpreted in terms of rational expectations. The less committed do not marry and have higher dissolution risks; the more favourably situated can better handle a dissolution and can profit more from it. Children represent an investment and a bond, so their presence reduces the dissolution risk. Some differentials can be ascribed to manifest differences in values. The religiously active have lower risks of union dissolution than others, both in marital unions and when they cohabit, which they do less frequently than others.

All of these features contribute to differentials in dissolution risks, but mode-of-entry selection effects are stronger. Individuals differ in ways that are not caught by the factors included in our hazard regressions, and these differences manifest themselves as the individual life courses progress. This helps explain why we find that premarital cohabitation gives higher marital-dissolution risks, that starting a first union at a very young age makes it particularly dissolution-prone even later in life, that second unions have higher dissolution risks than first unions, and that a second union following after a first consensual union that was not converted into a marriage has a higher dissolution risk than other second unions.

There are similar elements in our explanation of the general increase in dissolution intensities over our cohorts. Improved living standards, and in particular the increasing availability of housing, surely have contributed to it. When one can better afford a dissolution and can regard its financial aftermath and one's subsequent housing situation with greater equanimity, one is less prone to remain in an unsatisfactory union. Many features suggest that the stronger driving forces behind these developments have deeper roots and are of an ideational nature, however, as has been contended by Lesthaeghe and Meekers (1986) for the populations of the European Community and by Sweet and Bumpass (1988: ch.

---

[60] The effect of educational level was not significant.

11) for the United States. It is hard to explain the massive growth in consensual unions purely in terms of items like improving wealth and more available housing. Instead, it is natural to see it more as reflecting the rapidly increasing acceptability of a living arrangement that was rather unconventional before. In its wake follow similar attitudes to problems encountered in conjugal life. More than before, it becomes mainstream behaviour to assert one's independence and break up a relationship when its future seems too bleak, even if it has been converted into a marriage since it started. When marrying directly becomes rather unusual, those who do so progressively come from a select group whose ideational position differs from the crowd's. Surely, the change in general norms will have affected members of this group as well, but its composition has shifted sufficiently toward classical family values to make its group-level risk decrease over our cohorts.

Union formation behaviour has shifted from modes of entry connected with a relatively good prognosis for union cohesion to modes with a less favourable outlook. For the latter, increasingly the mainstream group, developments have additionally been linked to deteriorating cohesion. To summarize, therefore, it is our assessment that both structural changes and economic trends have contributed to the rapidly increasing general dissolution risks of Swedish conjugal unions over our study period, but that developments have primarily been dominated by ideational changes.

## References

Agell, A. (1989*a*), *Äktenskaps-och samboenderätt enligt 1987 års lagstiftning* (Justus förlag, Uppsala).

—— (1989*b*), 'On Divorce: Background Notes on Swedish Law to a Colloquium in Bellagio, Italy, 3–7 April, 1989', Faculty of Law, Uppsala University.

Balakrishnan, T. R., Rao, K. V., Lapierre-Adamcyk, E., and Krotki, K. J. (1987), 'A Hazards Model Analysis of the Covariates of Marriage Dissolution in Canada', *Demography*, 24. 3: 395–406.

Becker, G. S. (1981), *A Treatise on the Family* (Harvard University Press, Cambridge, Mass.).

—— Landes, E. M., and Michael, R. T. (1977), 'An Economic Analysis of Marital Instability', *Journal of Political Economy*, 85. 6: 1141–87.

Bennett, N., Blanc, A. K., and Bloom, D. E. (1988), 'Commitment and the Modern Union: Assessing the Link between Premarital Cohabitation and Subsequent Marital Stability', *American Sociological Review*, 53. 1: 127–38.

Billy, J. O. G., Landale, N. S., and McLaughlin, S. D. (1986), 'The Effect of Marital Status at First Birth on Marital Dissolution among Adolescent Mothers', *Demography*, 23. 3: 329–49.

Blanc, A. K. (1985), *The Effect of Nonmarital Cohabitation on Family Formation and Dissolution: A Comparative Analysis of Sweden and Norway* (Ann Arbor, Mich.).

Booth, A., and Edwards, J. N. (1985), 'Age at Marriage and Marital Instability', *Journal of Marriage and the Family*, 47. 1: 67–76.

Bumpass, L. L., and Sweet, J. A. (1972), 'Differentials in Marital Instability: 1970', *American Sociological Review*, 37. 6: 754–66.

Carlson, E., and Stinson, K. (1982), 'Motherhood, Marriage Timing and Marital Stability: A Research Note', *Social Forces*, 61. 60: 258–67.

Cherlin, A. (1977), 'The Effect of Children on Marital Dissolution', *Demography*, 14. 3: 265–84.

—— (1978), 'Remarriage as an Incomplete Institution', *American Journal of Sociology*, 84. 3: 636–50.

—— (1981), *Marriage, Divorce, Remarriage* (Harvard University Press, Cambridge, Mass.).

Chester, R. (1972), 'Is There a Relationship between Childlessness and Marriage Breakdown?', *Journal for Biosocial Science*, 4. 4: 443–54.

Elder, G. H. (1985) (ed.), *Life Course Dynamics* (Cornell, Ithaca, NY).

Ermisch, J. (1986), *The Economics of the Family: Applications to Divorce and Remarriage*, Discussion Paper No. 140, Centre for Economic Policy Research (London).

Etzler, C. (1988), 'Första barnet. En demografisk studie av barnafödandet bland svenska kvinnor födda 1936–60', in H. Moors and J. Schoorl (eds.), *Lifestyles, Contraception and Parenthood* (NIDI & GBDS, The Hague), 351–71.

Festy, P. (1985), *Divorce, Judicial Separation and Remarriage: Recent Trends in the Member States of the Council of Europe*, Population Studies No. 17, Council of Europe (Strasbourg).

Furstenberg, F. F. (1976), 'Premarital Pregnancy and Marital Instability', *Journal of Social Issues*, 32. 1: 67–86.

—— and Spanier, G. B. (1984), 'The Risk of Dissolution in Remarriage: An Examination of Cherlin's Hypothesis of Incomplete Institutionalization', *Family Relations*, 33. 3: 433–41.

Gibson, C. (1980), 'Childlessness and Marital Instability: A Re-examination of the Evidence', *Journal of Biosocial Science*, 12. 2: 121–32.

Granath, F. (1986), *Analys av separationsbenägenheten hos barnlösa svenska kvinnor*, Section of Demography, Stockholm University.

Halliday, T. C. (1980), 'Remarriage: The More Complete Institution?', *American Journal of Sociology*, 86. 3: 630–5.

Heckman, J. J., and Singer, B. (1982), 'Population Heterogeneity in Demographic Models', in K. Land and A. Rogers (eds.), *Multidimensional Mathematical Demography* (Academic Press, New York), 567–604.

—— —— (1984), 'A Method for Minimizing the Impact of Distributional Assumptions in Economic Models for Duration Data', *Econometrica*, 52. 2: 271–320.

Hoem, B. (1986), *Tredjebarnsfödslar bland svenska kvinnor födda 1936–50*, Stockholm Research Reports in Demography No. 30, Stockholm University.

—— (1987a), *Sysselsättningshistoriens betydelse för tvåbarnsmödrars fortsatta barnafödande bland svenska kvinnor födda 1936–50*, Stockholm Research Reports in Demography No. 32, Stockholm University.

—— (1987b), *Streams of Demographic Events to Respondents in the Swedish Fertility Survey of 1981*, Internal Memorandum 870521, Section of Demography, Stockholm University.

—— (1987*c*), *Graviditetens betydelse för barnlösa svenska kvinnors civilståndsändringar*, Stockholm Research Reports in Demography No. 38, Stockholm University.

—— and Hoem, J. M. (1988*a*), 'The Swedish Family: Aspects of Contemporary Developments', *Journal of Family Issues*, 9. 3: 397–424.

—— —— (1988*b*), *Dissolution in Sweden: The Break-up of Conjugal Unions to Swedish Women Born in 1936–60*, Stockholm Research Reports in Demography No. 45, Stockholm University.

—— —— (1989), 'The Impact of Women's Employment on Second and Third Births in Modern Sweden', *Population Studies*, 43. 1: 47–67.

Hoem, J. M. (1985), *The Impact of Education on Modern Family-Union Initiation*, Stockholm Research Reports in Demography No. 27, Stockholm University. For a briefer version, see *European Journal of Population*, 2. 2: 113–33 (1986).

—— (1990), 'Limitations of a Heterogeneity Technique: Selectivity Issues in Conjugal Union Disruption at Parity Zero in Contemporary Sweden', in J. Adams, D. A. Lam, A. I. Hermalin, and P. Smouse (eds.), *Convergent Issues in Genetics and Demography* (OUP, Oxford), 133–53.

Ingelhart, R. (1985), 'Aggregate Stability and Individual-Level-Flux in Mass Belief Systems: The Level of Analysis Paradox', *American Political Science Review*, 79. 1: 97–116.

Kiernan, K. (1986), 'Teenage Marriage and Marital Breakdown: A Longitudinal Study', *Population Studies*, 40. 1: 35–54.

Koo, H. P., and Janowitz, B. K. (1983), 'Inter-Relationships between Fertility and Marital Dissolution: Results of a Simultaneous Logit Model', *Demography*, 20. 2: 129–45.

Kravdal, Ø. (1988), 'The Impact of First Birth Timing on Divorce: New Evidence from a Longitudinal Analysis Based on the Central Population Register of Norway', *European Journal of Population*, 4. 3: 247–69.

—— and Noack, T. (1988), *Skilsmisser i Norge 1964–1984. En demografisk analyse*, Report 88(6), Central Bureau of Statistics of Norway (Oslo).

Laird, N., and Olivier, D. (1981), 'Covariance Analysis of Censored Survival Data Using Log-Linear Analysis Techniques', *Journal of the American Statistical Association*, 76. 374: 231–40.

Larsson, R. (1986), *Analys av svenska kvinnors benägenhet att ingå nytt samboende efter det första parförhållandets upplösning*, Section of Demography, Stockholm University.

Lehrer, E. L. (1988), 'Determinants of Marital Instability: A Cox-Regression Model', *Applied Economics*, 20. 2: 195–210.

Lesthaeghe, R., and Surkyn, J. (1988), 'Cultural Dynamics and Economic Theories of Fertility Change', *Population and Development Review*, 14. 1: 1–45.

—— and Meekers, D. (1986), 'Value Changes and the Dimensions of Familism in the European Community', *European Journal of Population*, 2. 2: 255–68.

Lyberg, I. (1984), 'Att fråga om barn. Teknisk beskrivning av undersökningen Kvinnor i Sverige', *Bakgrundsmaterial från Prognosinstitutet*, 1984(4), Statistics Sweden (Stockholm).

McCarthy, J. (1978), 'A Comparison of the Probability of the Dissolution of First and Second Marriages', *Demography*, 15. 3: 345–59.

Macklin, E. D. (1978), 'Nonmarital Heterosexual Cohabitation', *Marriage and Family Review*, 1. 2: 1–12.

McLaughlin, S. D., Grady, W. R., Billy, J. O., Landale, N. S., and Winges, L. D. (1986), 'The Effect of the Sequencing of Marriage and the First Birth during Adolescence', *Family Planning Perspectives*, 18. 1: 12–18.

Martin, T. C., and Bumpass, L. (1989), 'Recent Trends and Differentials in Marital Disruption', *Demography*, 26. 1: 37–51.

Menken, J., Trussell, T. J., Stempel, D., and Babakol, O. (1981), 'Proportional Hazards Life Table Models: An Illustrative Analysis of Socio-Demographic Influences on Marriage Dissolution in the United States', *Demography*, 18. 2: 181–200.

Monahan, T. P. (1952), 'How Stable are Remarriages?', *American Journal of Sociology*, 58. 3: 280–8.

—— (1955), 'Is Childlessness Related to Family Stability?' *American Sociological Review*, 20. 4: 446–56.

Moore, K. A., and Waite, L. J. (1981), 'Marital Dissolution, Early Motherhood and Early Marriage', *Social Forces*, 60. 1: 20–40.

Morgan, S. P., and Rindfuss, R. R. (1985), 'Marital Disruption: Structural and Temporal Dimensions', *American Journal of Sociology*, 90. 5: 1055–77.

Murphy, M. (1984), 'Fertility, Birth Timing and Marital Breakdown: A Reinterpretation of the Evidence', *Journal of Biosocial Science*, 16. 4: 7–500.

—— (1985), 'Demographic and Socio-Economic Influences on Recent British Marital Breakdown Patterns', *Population Studies*, 39. 3: 441–60.

Olivier, D. C., and Neff, R. K. (1976), *LOGLIN 1.0 User's Guide*, with later updates, Harvard University Public Health Science Computing Facility (Cambridge, Mass.).

Popenoe, D. (1987), 'Beyond the Nuclear Family: A Statistical Portrait of the Changing Family in Sweden', *Journal of Marriage and the Family*, 49. 1: 173–83.

—— (1988), *Disturbing the Nest: Family Change and Decline in Modern Societies* (Aldine de Gruyter, New York).

Preston, S. H. (1986), 'Changing Values and Falling Birth Rates', in K. Davis, M. S. Bernstam, and R. Ricardo-Campbell (eds.), *Below-Replacement Fertility in Industrial Societies; Causes, Consequences, Policies*, 176–95. Supplement to *Population and Development Review*, 12.

Ryder, N. B. (1979), 'Consistency of Reporting Fertility Planning Status', *Studies in Family Planning*, 10. 4: 115–28.

Sardon, J. P. (1986), 'Évolution de la nuptialité et de la divortialité en Europe depuis la fin des années 1960', *Population*, 41. 3: 463–82.

Schoen, R. (1975), 'California Divorce Rates by Age at First Marriage and Duration of First Marriage', *Journal of Marriage and the Family*, 37. 3: 548–55.

South, S. J., and Spitze, G. (1986), 'Determinants of Divorce over the Marital Life Course', *American Sociological Review*, 51. 4: 583–90.

Sweet, J., and Bumpass, L. (1988), *American Families and Households* (Russell Sage, New York).

Teachman, J. D. (1982), 'Methodological Issues in the Analysis of Family Formation and Dissolution', *Journal of Marriage and the Family*, 44. 4: 1037–53.

—— (1983), 'Early Marriage, Premarital Fertility and Marital Dissolution: Results for Blacks and Whites', *Journal of Family Issues*, 4. 1: 105–26.

Thornton, A. (1977), 'Children and Marital Stability', *Journal of Marriage and the Family*, 39. 3: 531–40.

—— and Rodgers, W. L. (1987), 'The Influence of Individual and Historical Time on Marital Dissolution', *Demography*, 24. 1: 1–22.

Trost, J. (1978), 'A Renewed Social Institution: Non-Marital Cohabitation', *Acta Sociologica*, 21. 4: 303–15.

Waite, L. J., Haggstrom, G. W., and Kanouse, D. E. (1985), 'The Consequences of Parenthood for the Marital Stability of Young Adults', *American Sociological Review*, 50. 6: 850–7.

White, L., and Booth, A. (1985), 'The Quality and Stability of Remarriages: The Role of Stepchildren', *American Sociological Review*, 50. 5: 689–98.

Wikman, R. (1937), *Die Einleitung der Ehe. Eine vergleichend ethnosoziologische Untersuchung über die Vorstufe der Ehe in der Sitten des schwedischen Volkstums*, Åbo Akademi, Acta Academia Aboensis (Turku), Humaniora xi.1, 1–395.

Wilcox, W. (1891), 'The Divorce Problem', *Economics and Public Law*, 1. 1, Columbia University Studies in History (New York).

World Fertility Survey (1984), *Fertility Survey in Sweden, 1981: A Summary of Findings*, No. 43 (International Statistical Institute, Voorburg).

# 4 Household Formation and Home-Ownership in France

MARK MONTGOMERY

Demographic variables are unquestionably important to the economic behaviour of households. Marital status and parity are among the most important predictors of female labour supply. Migration and employment decisions are inextricably linked. This chapter will consider a third type of linkage: the connection between household formation through marriage and the demand for housing. Separate models of age at marriage and age at first home-ownership are estimated. I shall also specify a joint model of marriage and ownership and will discuss the conceptual and statistical differences that are implied by the joint approach. The data for the study are drawn from a retrospective survey of the French population conducted by the Institut National d'Études Démographiques (INED) in 1981, and concern first home-ownership for cohorts of men born between 1911 and 1935.

This chapter is mainly concerned with methodological issues, although it also has a substantive focus. The substantive question to be considered is a simple one: does higher socioeconomic status promote earlier home-ownership? As will be seen, the answer to this simple question is surprisingly complex. Background factors that encourage earlier marriage appear to discourage or delay home-ownership. As regards methodology, the issues that arise are inherent in any joint consideration of household formation and economic behaviour. A change in demographic status—say, a transition from being never-married to married—is properly viewed as endogenous in nature. The demand for a particular type of housing is also endogenous. Decisions in each sphere depend on the characteristics of the economic environment and on a set of individual traits and attitudes, some of which inevitably go unmeasured. There is the possibility that persistent unobserved traits may influence both the timing of demographic events (e.g. a marriage) and the nature of housing demand. In consequence, it may be quite difficult to disentangle the empirical associations between demographic and economic behaviour. A strong correlation between marriage and the rate of accession to home-ownership may reflect a causal linkage, or a dependence of each decision on common but unmeasured background factors.

In short, models that attempt to assess the impact of demographic decisions on economic decisions must come to grips with the problem of heterogeneity. This is an area of current controversy. Even in the simplest, single-spell duration models, the techniques required to control for heterogeneity present computational difficulties. There is much disagreement, and as yet not much accumulated experience, concerning the fragility of these techniques. Still less is known about the empirical importance of heterogeneity in multiple-state or multiple-spell models. One of the goals of this chapter is to add to the body of results concerning the substantive importance of controls for heterogeneity in demographic work.

How does one know whether controlling for heterogeneity does or does not make a substantive difference? I shall argue that the simple controls for heterogeneity developed by Heckman and Singer (1984*a*) are valuable, because they provide a check on results from models that assume homogeneity. It is important to understand that the types of heterogeneity that can be controlled for are, at present, highly restricted. One can allow the population of interest to be divided into unobserved groups or classes, but only in a manner that is independent of the observed explanatory covariates. Further, membership in a group is held fixed through the period of observation; in a sense, individuals are 'tagged' and retain their (unobserved) labels over time. If the estimated effect of a covariate alters sign or undergoes a large change in magnitude when the population is permitted to be heterogeneous in this seemingly innocuous fashion, then something of substance has been learned from the effort to accommodate heterogeneity. Covariate effects that resist change are more robust and therefore of greater substantive interest ex post.

Are there choices made by the analyst that affect the sensitivity of results? Trussell and Richards (1985) and Montgomery and Trussell (1986) have argued that in some circumstances the estimated effects of covariates can be disturbingly sensitive to the specification of the structural hazard. Alternate structural models which make use of the flexible heterogeneity correction of Heckman and Singer, and which produce roughly equivalent fits to the data, may display strikingly different effects estimates. Although duration models with heterogeneity are not necessarily so vulnerable to specification, there are clear advantages in comparing results using different functional forms for the underlying hazard. At each step in the analyses to follow, two functional forms will be considered, the log-logistic and the gamma. The intent is to determine whether the effects estimates are robust to changes in specification.

The chapter is in four parts. The data are discussed in the first part, and methods in the second. The third part gives the results of the analysis, and conclusions follow in the fourth.

## Data

The data are drawn from a large retrospective survey conducted in early 1981 by Daniel Courgeau at INED. The sample is representative of the French population born between 1911 and 1935 and surviving to the date of the survey. The INED survey is unusually rich in demographic detail. In addition to marriage and fertility histories, it contains comparable information on the housing, employment, and migration histories of some 4602 individuals. Most events are dated to the month. Although information is available for both men and women, in what follows I shall consider only the histories for men.

An extract from the full sample has been made available for this analysis by Daniel Courgeau and Éva Lelièvre. There are certain limitations on the research that follow from the absence of complete event histories in the data extract. But the subsample is representative of a 'typical' demographic data set in the sense that it contains a mix of full- and partial-event histories. Thus the restrictions imposed on the analysis are familiar restrictions likely to be encountered in one form or another in much applied demographic work.

## Housing

There is information available on the month and year of first home-ownership, for cases in which the respondent owned the home at the time he first moved into it. In a number of instances, however, a home was not owned upon initial habitation, and the transition to ownership was made at some later date. For such cases the precise date of first ownership is not known; an approximate date is provided in the survey extract.[1]

The full housing history, encompassing dates, locations, and types of tenure, is not included in the extract. Hence one cannot draw from these data a complete picture of the demand for housing over the life cycle. Neither are the characteristics of the home first owned (e.g. number of rooms) known. Therefore, of the numerous factors that together describe the demand for housing, only the aspect of ownership can be considered here.

## Employment and Education

The respondent's first professional occupation is coded in broad categories, as is his occupation at the time of first home-ownership. However, age at entry into first professional employment is not included. The type of education completed by the respondent is available, but not the date at which it was completed.

## Marriage

Year and month of first marriage and characteristics of the spouse are provided in the survey extract. If a divorce occurred its date is also provided, but dates of remarriage are not supplied.

[1] The full survey includes, for each lodging, the date of first habitation by the respondent $t_f$; the date at which it was last inhabited $t_e$, which may be the date of survey; and the respondent's tenure status at these two endpoints. If tenure status changed (to ownership) in the interim, the midpoint year was entered as an approximate date on the data extract prepared at INED. Cases with such a change in tenure status are treated separately in estimation, as discussed in n. 4 below.

## Family Background

The professions of the respondent's father and mother are known, as is the date of the father's death.

In short, these data can provide useful detailed information on the link between marriage and first home-ownership. Some limitations are implied by the absence of complete marriage histories for those individuals whose first marriage dissolved, but these limitations do not appear to be serious.[2]

TABLE 4.1(*a*). *Descriptive statistics: dependent variables.*

| Dependent variable | 25th percentile | Median | 75th percentile |
|---|---|---|---|
| Age at first home-ownership[a] | 34.8 | 44.5 | 64.3 |
| Age at first marriage[a] | 23.3 | 25.4 | 29.9 |
| Duration between first marriage and first home-ownership[a] (yrs.) | 10.5 | 19.8 | 39.0 |

[a] Derived from life-table estimates.

TABLE 4.1(*b*). *Descriptive statistics: covariates.*

| Covariate | Means |
|---|---|
| Birth year | 24.3 |
| Father's occupation | |
|   Unskilled | 15.0 |
|   Qualified | 15.3 |
|   Tradesman | 17.8 |
|   White-collar | 11.7 |
|   Agriculture | 40.2 |
| Schooling | |
|   No schooling | 34.0 |
|   Primary | 46.9 |
|   First general | 7.8 |
|   Baccalaureate | 11.3 |
| First occupation | |
|   Unskilled | 38.4 |
|   Qualified | 4.6 |
|   Tradesman | 6.4 |
|   White-collar | 15.5 |

Table 4.1 presents descriptive statistics on the variables to be considered. The sample contains information on 2049 men. A case is omitted from the analysis if any of the variables listed in Table 4.1 is missing.

[2] Only 10% of this sample ever experienced a divorce.

As can be seen, acquisition of a home occurs rather late in this sample. The median age at first ownership is 44.5, and even by age 64 some 25% of men have not owned a home. Life-table estimates suggest that 24% of men never become owners; that is, the distribution of age at ownership is a defective distribution.

By contrast, first marriage occurs considerably earlier in the life cycle (the median age is 25.4) and the transitions are concentrated in a relatively brief age span. By age 30 less than 25% of men remain unmarried; life-table estimates put the proportion never marrying at just over 9%, and the hazard is essentially 0 after age 50.

First marriage precedes home-ownership in the vast majority (95%) of cases. The median duration from marriage to ownership (leaving aside the individuals whose ownership came before marriage) is nearly 20 years.

The remaining variables in Table 4.1 comprise a set of fixed covariates to be considered in the analysis. Among these are the respondent's birth year (ranging from 11 to 35), his schooling, and first professional occupation. Also included is the profession of the respondent's father, with agriculture being the excluded category.

## Methods

I will first consider single-spell models of age at home-ownership $T_h$ and age at marriage $T_m$. In such models there is a single type of transition: for $T_h$ it is the transition between never-owning and ever-owning a home, while for $T_m$ the change in status is from single to married. I shall also specify a joint model of marriage and ownership in which marital status acts as an endogenous influence on the propensity to acquire a home. The joint model is set out in a multiple-state or 'competing-risk' framework.

### Single-Spell Models

Estimation is restricted to the class of duration models known as proportional-hazards models. In such models the hazard function $r(t \mid X)$ for duration $t$, given covariates $X$, may be written

$$r(t \mid X) = r_0(t)\, \Delta(X) \tag{1}$$

where $r_0$ is a baseline hazard function and $\Delta(X) = \exp(X'\delta)$. The implied relationship between the hazard and survivor function is

$$S(t \mid X) = \exp\left\{ -\int_0^t r(s \mid X)\,ds \right\} = S_0(t)^{\Delta(X)} \tag{2}$$

where $S_0(t) = \exp\{-\int_0^t r_0(s)\,ds\}$ is the baseline survivor function.

There is a two-part justification for restricting attention to proportional models. First, it simplifies the task of comparing covariate effects estimates when the estimates are derived from different baseline hazards. Furthermore, it is not yet clear whether non-proportional models that incorporate a correction for hetero-geneity are identified (Heckman and Singer 1984*b*). The proof that establishes identification, that of Elbers and Ridder (1982), applies to proportional-hazards models in which an unobserved variable $U$ enters the shift factor $\Delta(X, U)$ as $\Delta_1(X)\Delta_2(U)$. The proportionality assumption plays a key role in the Elbers–Ridder proof.

As mentioned above, the analysis will rely on two parametric models of dura-tion, the log-logistic and the gamma. The properties of each distribution are briefly summarized here.

## The Log-Logistic

The baseline log-logistic model is characterized by the survivor function given in (3):

$$S_0(t) = 1/\{1 + (\beta t)^p\}. \tag{3}$$

Its density is given in (4) and hazard function in (5):

$$f_0(t) = p\,\beta^p\,t^{p-1}/\{1 + (\beta t)^p\}^2 \tag{4}$$

$$r_0(t) = p\,\beta^p\,t^{p-1}/\{1 + (\beta t)^p\} \tag{5}$$

Note from (3) that the median of the baseline distribution is $\beta^{-1}$. The parameter $p$ functions as a measure of dispersion about the median. It can be shown that, as $p$ increases, holding $\beta$ constant, the distribution becomes more concentrated about its median. Finally, with $p > 1$ the hazard of the log-logistic rises from zero to a maximum at $t = (p - 1)^{1/p}\beta^{-1}$ and declines thereafter.

## The Gamma

The baseline gamma is also determined by two parameters. Its survivor function, density, and hazard are respectively

$$S_0(t) = 1 - \Gamma(p)^{-1}\int_0^{\beta t} u^{p-1}e^{-u}du \tag{6}$$

$$f_0(t) = \beta^p t^{p-1}e^{-\beta t}\Gamma(p)^{-1} \tag{7}$$

and

$$r_0(t) = f_0(t)/S_0(t) \tag{8}$$

where $\Gamma$ is the gamma function. The mean and standard deviation of the gamma are given as $\mu = p/\beta$ and $\sigma = p^{1/2}/\beta$. With $p > 1$ the hazard function for the gamma rises monotonically to an upper asymptote equal to $\beta$ (Cox 1962: 20). With $p = 1$ the gamma distribution collapses to an exponential.

Thus the distributions to be considered share certain properties: the parameters of each have a location-and-scale interpretation, and with $p > 1$ both hazard functions have a upward-sloping portion beginning at duration zero. However, these are not nested models and one cannot rely on conventional likelihood-ratio tests to discriminate between them. Furthermore, the two models may be expected to yield different results at long durations, since the hazard for the log-logistic eventually declines while that of the gamma does not. As will be seen, these features of the hazards have implications for the estimation of unobserved heterogeneity.

## Unobserved Heterogeneity

The treatment of unobservables will follow the approach of Heckman and Singer (1984a). It is assumed that all persistent unobserved influences on spell durations can be summarized in a single unobserved variable $U$, which takes on the discrete values $(u_1, u_2, \ldots, u_k)$ with associated probabilities $(\pi_1, \pi_2, \ldots, \pi_k)$. The elements of $u$ and $\pi$ are viewed as additional model parameters. By assumption $\pi$ is not a function of covariates $X$; that is, $U$ and $X$ are assumed to be independent. The unobservable $U$ exerts a proportional influence on the hazard, so that

$$r(t \mid X = x, U = u) = r(t \mid x) \exp(u) \tag{9}$$

and the survivor function $S(t \mid X, U) = \exp\{-\int_0^t r(s \mid X, U)ds\}$. To calculate the probability contribution made by an observation to the sample likelihood, one 'integrates out' the unobservable; for instance,

$$S(t \mid X) = \sum_{i=1}^{k} S(t \mid X, u_i)\pi_i \tag{10}$$

is the contribution made by an observation with covariates $X$ that is right-censored at duration $t$. As (10) shows, the probabilities attached to each observation are mixtures of the underlying or 'structural' probabilities specific to each category of $U$.

The simplest discrete mixture in the Heckman–Singer class is the two-point mixture. Individuals fall into one of two 'latent' classes, indexed by values $u_1 = 0$ and $u_2 = \theta$, with probabilities $\pi$ and $1 - \pi$ respectively. In this case the survivor function at duration $t$ is the mixture of the survivor functions for $U = 0$ and $U = \theta$, or

$$S(t \mid X) = \pi S(t \mid X, 0) + (1 - \pi) S(t \mid X, \theta). \tag{11}$$

A special case of the two-point mixture is the 'mover–stayer' model, in which one group is assumed never to be at risk of transition. This case may be represented as $\theta = -\infty$, yielding the survivor function

$$S(t \mid X) = \pi S(t \mid X, 0) + 1 - \pi \tag{12}$$

and hazard function

$$r(t \mid X) = \pi f(t \mid X, 0)/[\pi S(t \mid X, 0) + 1 - \pi]. \tag{13}$$

The mover–stayer model is a limiting case of the more general two-point mixture.

The mover–stayer mixture has had numerous applications in demography in connection with the Coale–McNeil (1972) model of first marriage. In the Coale–McNeil approach, the parameter $\pi$ measures the proportion of the population ever at risk of marriage, and the survivor function $S(t \mid X, 0)$ for the group of eligibles is derived from the convolution of a normal distribution with exponential delays. The Coale–McNeil survivor function $S(t \mid X, 0)$ is in fact closely related to the survivor function of the gamma distribution (Rodríguez and Trussell 1980). Indeed, the hazard functions for the gamma and Coale–McNeil models exhibit similar behaviour, in that both hazards rise monotonically toward an upper asymptote. The gamma model of first marriage with mover–stayer heterogeneity can therefore be interpreted as an approximation to the more familiar Coale–McNeil model.

Note that an application of the gamma mover–stayer model to marriage data will tend to show a greater fraction of the population to be ineligible than would its log-logistic counterpart. The reason is that the gamma hazard is monotonic. It rises with age (given $p > 1$) and remains high. Hence, in order to explain a given proportion unmarried at survey, the gamma tends to assign most such individuals to the group of ineligibles. The log-logistic hazard declines after $t = (p - 1)^{1/p}\beta^{-1}$, an age typically not too far from the median age at marriage, and therefore permits a greater proportion of those unmarried at survey to reside in the 'still eligible but at low risk' category. Log-logistic estimates of $\pi$ will tend to be higher. There is a general lesson here, that the shape of the structural hazard will influence the estimation of heterogeneity parameters. This point does not seem to have been fully appreciated by users of the Coale–McNeil model (e.g. Bloom 1982).

## Joint Models of Marriage and Home-Ownership

For a number of reasons marriage may increase the risk of home-ownership. Marriage may increase household income, alter the taxation rules facing the husband and wife, strengthen the commitment of the partners to a particular location, and encourage greater attention to activities that occur within the home as opposed to outside it. These and other factors produce what one could call a 'structural' relationship between marital status and ownership. However, un-measured factors affecting decisions to marry, on the one hand, and to acquire a home, on the other, may also induce a correlation between marital status and ownership. A separation of marital and ownership decisions in time is not enough, by itself, to reveal their structural relationship. If there is concern about un-measured background factors a more elaborate detection strategy is required.

The relationship between marriage and ownership may be described in a multiple-state framework. Consider a stochastic process in which individuals reside in one of three states at a point in time: (1) never-owned, never-married (NO, NM); (2) never-owned, ever-married (NO, EM); and (3) ever-owned (EO). A sample transition path is depicted in Fig. 4.1. The sample history shows a first

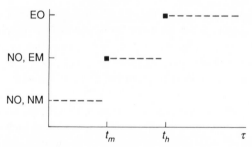

Fig. 4.1   Sample marriage–ownership history.

marriage at age $t_m$, and accession to home-ownership at $t_h$. The state EO is defined as an absorbing state, and so the portion of the history from $t_h$ to age at survey $\tau$ contributes no information on the stochastic process.

Let $r_h\{t \mid m(t)\}$ represent the transition intensity for ownership conditional on marital status at $t$, $m(t)$, and let $r_m(t)$ be the transition intensity for first marriage.[3] The indicator $m(t) = 1$ if the man has ever married as of $t$, and $m(t) = 0$ otherwise. We might also include age at marriage in the model for $r_h$ when $m(t) = 1$. (Dependence of the intensities on exogenous covariates is left implicit here.) We expect married individuals to have a greater propensity to acquire a home; that is, $r_h(t \mid m(t) = 1) > r_h(t \mid m(t) = 0)$. The difference between the transition intensity levels is one of the 'structural' effects of marriage.

In the absence of unobserved heterogeneity, the probability contribution of the sample path depicted above is the product $\rho_1 \rho_2$, where

$$\rho_1 = r_m(t_m) \exp\left[-\int_0^{t_m} \{r_m(s) + r_h(s \mid m(s) = 0)\} ds\right] \tag{14}$$

and

$$\rho_2 = r_h(t_h \mid m(t_h) = 1) \exp\left[-\int_{t_m}^{t_h} r_h(s \mid m(s) = 1) ds\right] \tag{15}$$

Similar expressions can be derived for other sample paths. As is well known, the likelihood function for the model is separable in the parameters entering $r_m$ and $r_h$. Hence these transition intensities can either be estimated separately, making proper allowance for exposure times, or estimated jointly. The point is that, in the absence of unobservables, it makes little difference whether one views a change in marital status as being endogenous or not.

Of course, the worry about endogenous variables is that they are likely to depend on the unobserved determinants of choice as well as on the observed determinants. In linear models, a problem arises when one fears that an explanatory variable is correlated with the regression disturbance. The issue is precisely

---

[3] As the figure shows, there are 3 possible transitions to consider. I use $r_h(t \mid m(t) = 0)$ to represent the transition intensity for moves from (NO, NM) to EO, and $r_h(t \mid m(t) = 1)$ for transitions from (NO, EM) to EO.

the same here, but the techniques required to address the problem are considerably more complicated in hazard models than in the linear context. For consistent estimation one must model the dependence of the endogenous variables (that is, the time path of $m(t)$) on the unobservables.

To continue the approach outlined above, suppose that the transition intensities $r_m$ and $r_h$ are influenced by a common unobserved variable $U$. In the one-factor correlation scheme proposed by Heckman and Singer (1984a), $U$ would enter the transition intensity for marriage as $r_m(t \mid U)$ and enters the transition intensity for ownership multiplied by a constant, or as $r_h(t \mid m(t), \lambda U)$. (Suppose there are two latent classes, i.e., $U$ takes on two values. Then $U$ enters $r_m$ and $r_h$ as $(0, 0)$ for individuals in one class and as $(u, \lambda u)$ for the individuals in the other.) As is the case with single-spell models, $U$ must be integrated out to derive the sample likelihood. The contribution of the sample path above becomes

$$\sum_U \left( r_m(t_m, u_i) \exp\left[ \int_0^{t_m} \{ r_m(s \mid u_i) + r_h(s \mid m(s) = 0, \lambda u_i) \} \, ds \right] \right.$$

$$\left. r_h(t_h \mid m(t_h) = 1, \lambda u_i) \exp\left[ -\int_{t_m}^{t_h} r_h(s \mid m(s) = 1, \lambda u_i) ds \right] \right) \pi_i \qquad (16)$$

The likelihood function is the product of such expressions across all observed sample paths. The likelihood function is not separable in the parameters entering $r_m$ and $r_h$; all parameters must therefore be estimated jointly.

## Results

We begin with the simplest models of age at first home-ownership, and proceed to consider transitions in marital status and joint models of marriage and first

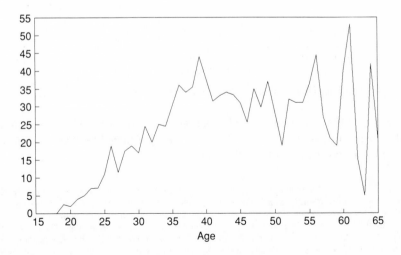

Fig. 4.2 Empirical hazard function for first home-ownership.

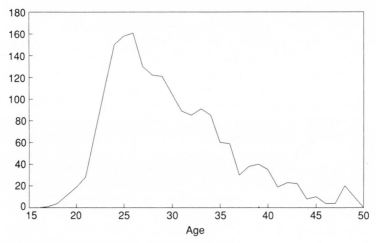

Fig. 4.3 Empirical hazard function for first marriage.

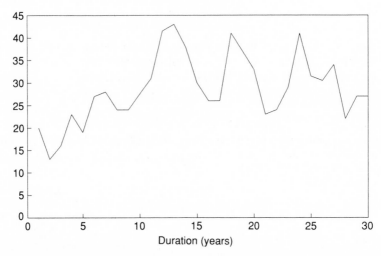

Fig. 4.4 Empirical hazard function for marriage duration at home-ownership.

ownership.[4] The empirical hazard functions for first ownership, first marriage, and duration from marriage to ownership, each estimated by ordinary life-table methods, are presented in Figs. 4.2–4.4.

---

[4] The models were estimated by maximum-likelihood methods using the optimization algorithms available in GQOPT (Goldfeld and Quandt 1972). The starting-point for exposure is assumed to be exact age 17 (the assumption eliminates 1 case). Age is measured in terms of months in the estimation. Cases in which tenure status changed during habitation (see n. 1) are treated as follows. All that is actually known about such cases is that by the end of the period in question the respondent had made his transition to ownership. Strictly speaking, the probability to assign to such an event is $F(t_e) - F(t_f)$, where $t_e$ is the respondent's age at the end of the period, $t_f$ is his age at the beginning of

## First Ownership

The hazard function for first ownership is somewhat irregular with respect to age, but certain broad features are apparent. The hazard is zero until age 17, rises, and then appears to flatten or slightly decline. How well do the baseline log-logistic and gamma models, without covariates, approximate this hazard?

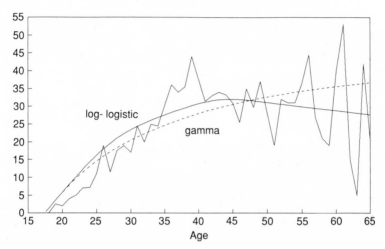

Fig. 4.5 Log-logistic and gamma models for first home-ownership.

The dotted lines in Fig. 4.5 show the results. The estimated median age at ownership is 43.7 for the log-logistic and 44.8 for the gamma model. These figures bracket the life-table estimate of 44.5 years.[5] Fig. 4.5 reveals the characteristic shapes of the log-logistic and gamma hazard functions. The log-logistic hazard reaches its peak at age 45 while, of course, the gamma hazard rises throughout.

In Table 4.2, a set of fixed covariates is introduced in the log-logistic model. The model in the first column includes the respondent's year of birth and completed schooling. The profession of the respondent's father is added next, and the third model includes the respondent's first professional occupation.

The results in column 1 show a clear positive effect associated with birth cohort: a decade's worth of difference in birth year increases the risk function for first ownership by 19% (exp(.172)). The effects of schooling are somewhat less clear. Primary schooling increases the hazard by some 15% relative to no

the period, and $F$ is the cumulative distribution function. Unfortunately neither the end-of-period of age $t_e$ nor the start point $t_f$ is included on the data extract. As a compromise, I have taken $F(t_{e'})$ as the probability contribution, where $t_{e'}$ is the respondent's age at the end of the midpoint year. Roughly 12% of the 2049 cases in the sample are supplied with a midpoint date.

[5] The hazard functions graphed in Figs. 4.2–4.4 are calculated as if midpoint dates (see n. 4 above) were the actual dates of transition. It would be straightforward, although tedious, to apply the midpoint correction. The consequence of not doing so is that the ordinary life-table estimates presented for descriptive purposes in Table 4.1 and Figs. 4.2–4.4 are somewhat inaccurate.

schooling, and attainment of the baccalaureate by 22%; yet men with an inter-mediate level of schooling show no difference in behaviour from those without schooling. As will be seen, this pattern of schooling effects persists in several of the analyses below.

TABLE 4.2. *Log-logistic estimates of age at first home-ownership. Asymptotic t-statistics in parentheses.*

|  | (1) | (2) | (3) |
|---|---|---|---|
| *Baseline* | | | |
| Log $p$ | 0.653 | 0.677 | 0.693 |
| | (23.04) | (31.19) | (23.92) |
| Log $\beta$ | − 6.159 | − 6.075 | − 6.023 |
| | (76.90) | (109.50) | (84.27) |
| *Covariates* | | | |
| Father's occupation | | | |
| Unskilled | | − 0.315 | − 0.124 |
| | | (3.77) | (1.30) |
| Qualified | | − 0.357 | − 0.171 |
| | | (4.24) | (1.77) |
| Tradesman | | − 0.064 | 0.091 |
| | | (0.62) | (0.97) |
| White-collar | | − 0.210 | − 0.028 |
| | | (2.28) | (0.27) |
| Birth year[a] | 0.172 | 0.170 | 0.170 |
| | (4.06) | (4.96) | (4.56) |
| Schooling | | | |
| Primary | 0.140 | 0.181 | 0.217 |
| | (2.33) | (2.95) | (3.42) |
| First general | 0.039 | 0.104 | 0.155 |
| | (0.36) | (0.93) | (1.37) |
| Baccalaureate | 0.202 | 0.215 | 0.227 |
| | (2.27) | (2.01) | (2.13) |
| First occupation | | | |
| Unskilled | | | − 0.356 |
| | | | (4.52) |
| Qualified | | | − 0.276 |
| | | | (1.90) |
| Tradesman | | | − 0.167 |
| | | | (1.21) |
| White-collar | | | − 0.254 |
| | | | (2.44) |
| Log-likelihood | − 8285 | − 8271 | − 8261 |

[a] Divided by 10.

TABLE 4.3. *Gamma estimates of age at first home-ownership. Asymptotic* t-*statistics in parentheses.*

|  | (1) | (2) | (3) |
|---|---|---|---|
| *Baseline* | | | |
| Log $p$ | 0.696 | 0.712 | 0.724 |
|  | (18.79) | (17.50) | (19.32) |
| Log $\beta$ | $-5.766$ | $-5.683$ | $-5.627$ |
|  | (65.27) | (62.37) | (61.56) |
| *Covariates* | | | |
| Father's occupation | | | |
| Unskilled | | $-0.297$ | $-0.111$ |
|  | | (3.55) | (1.17) |
| Qualified | | $-0.342$ | $-0.162$ |
|  | | (4.12) | (1.68) |
| Tradesman | | $-0.046$ | 0.103 |
|  | | (0.61) | (1.09) |
| White-collar | | $-0.190$ | $-0.015$ |
|  | | (2.10) | (0.15) |
| Birth year[a] | 0.244 | 0.247 | 0.250 |
|  | (6.22) | (6.35) | (6.26) |
| Schooling | | | |
| Primary | 0.171 | 0.210 | 0.244 |
|  | (2.76) | (3.30) | (3.81) |
| First general | 0.064 | 0.127 | 0.176 |
|  | (0.61) | (1.15) | (1.55) |
| Baccalaureate | 0.238 | 0.245 | 0.252 |
|  | (2.65) | (2.56) | (2.35) |
| First occupation | | | |
| Unskilled | | | $-0.347$ |
|  | | | (4.41) |
| Qualified | | | $-0.281$ |
|  | | | (1.93) |
| Tradesman | | | $-0.158$ |
|  | | | (1.14) |
| White-collar | | | $-0.236$ |
|  | | | (2.26) |
| Log-likelihood | $-8293$ | $-8281$ | $-8270$ |

[a] Divided by 10.

The addition of father's profession to the model, in column 2, produces some interesting and unanticipated results. The omitted category of profession is agricultural. Relative to men whose fathers were in agriculture, those with unskilled or 'qualified' fathers show considerably lower propensities to own a home: the hazards are reduced by 27% and 30% respectively. Men with fathers in white-collar professions are also less likely to acquire a home, with the risk being diminished by 19%. From column 3 it is evident that the respondent's first profession functions much like the profession of the father in its effect on the hazard.[6]

These findings hint at a complex relationship between initial socioeconomic position, as measured by schooling and father's profession, and age at first ownership. One feature of the results is clear: ownership occurs earlier for men with fathers in agriculture rather than in the urban-based occupations. Why this should be so is less clear. There may be fewer alternatives to owner-occupied housing in rural areas. It should certainly be the case that the relative price of housing is lower outside urban areas, and perhaps these price effects counterbalance what are, in general, lower rural incomes. Cityward migration during the period may have contributed to a tightening of urban housing markets and opened vacancies in rural markets. (According to Blanchet and Bonvalet (1985), there were few net additions to the stock of housing in France in 1919–40, and a rather slow expansion of the housing stock until the 1960s.) These issues merit further exploration.

The gamma estimates of first ownership are presented for comparison in Table 4.3. The results are qualitatively similar: no covariate effect changes its sign or statistical significance when the underlying hazard is specified to be gamma rather than log-logistic, and the changes in the magnitude of the effects are not large.

In Table 4.4, two forms of heterogeneity are considered for the log-logistic and gamma models. In the columns labelled 'Model I' are the estimates from two-point mover–stayer models. Columns labelled 'Model II' are the less restrictive two-point mixtures. Two questions arise in considering the results. First, are the covariate effects sensitive to the inclusion of heterogeneity? Second, with heterogeneity included, do the results of the gamma and log-logistic models diverge?

The answer to both questions is, on the whole, no. The qualitative pattern of effects estimates for father's occupation, birth year, and schooling remains similar to that shown in Tables 4.2 and 4.3. The positive influence of birth year on the hazard is evident across models, as is the non-monotonic effect of schooling. An agricultural family background remains conducive to earlier home-ownership, just as shown in the models without heterogeneity controls. Thus the covariate effects do not exhibit the extreme sensitivity to changes in functional form that has been found in other applications (Trussell and Richards 1985).

Why are these results relatively robust? One factor that must be considered is the form of the empirical hazard function for first ownership. The empirical hazard has an initial positive slope. That upward slope could not be produced by any mixture of flat or negatively sloped structural hazards.[7] Therefore, we need

---

[6] On balance, the addition of respondent's first occupation adds little in the way of substantive insights. There is a further difficulty in terms of the potential endogeneity of first occupation in models of first marriage. Therefore, the models that follow do not include first occupation.

[7] Recall that the unobservables are restricted to be time-invariant.

consider in estimation only those structural hazards that exhibit (initial) positive duration dependence. By contrast, in the most extreme case of parameter sensitivity reported by Trussell and Richards having to do with analyses of mortality,

TABLE 4.4. *Log-logistic and gamma estimates of age at first home-ownership, with correction for heterogeneity. Asymptotic* t-*statistics in parentheses.*

|  | Log-logistic | | Gamma | |
|---|---|---|---|---|
|  | Model I | Model II | Model I | Model II |
| *Baseline* | | | | |
| Log $p$ | 0.855 | 0.945 | 1.037 | 1.201 |
|  | (22.59) | (15.24) | (19.95) | (18.35) |
| Log $\beta$ | − 5.937 | − 5.654 | − 5.007 | − 4.583 |
|  | (77.08) | (37.19) | (43.38) | (37.43) |
| *Covariates* | | | | |
| Father's occupation | | | | |
| Unskilled | − 0.429 | − 0.356 | − 0.452 | − 0.440 |
|  | (3.96) | (3.52) | (3.98) | (3.95) |
| Qualified | − 0.512 | − 0.417 | − 0.552 | − 0.522 |
|  | (4.81) | (3.79) | (5.06) | (4.60) |
| Tradesman | − 0.192 | − 0.061 | − 0.233 | − 0.117 |
|  | (1.93) | (0.69) | (2.36) | (1.14) |
| White-collar | − 0.325 | − 0.253 | − 0.347 | − 0.369 |
|  | (2.80) | (2.24) | (2.94) | (2.99) |
| Birth year[a] | 0.299 | 0.246 | 0.337 | 0.316 |
|  | (4.85) | (4.47) | (6.14) | (6.57) |
| Schooling | | | | |
| Primary | 0.212 | 0.236 | 0.183 | 0.265 |
|  | (2.56) | (3.26) | (2.11) | (3.11) |
| First general | 0.039 | 0.102 | − 0.004 | 0.064 |
|  | (0.29) | (0.81) | (0.03) | (0.44) |
| Baccalaureate | 0.158 | 0.242 | 0.105 | 0.248 |
|  | (1.33) | (2.19) | (0.86) | (1.95) |
| Unobserved factor | | | | |
| $\theta$ | | − 1.286 | | − 1.797 |
|  | | (6.49) | | (14.71) |
| $\pi$ | 0.802 | 0.344 | 0.772 | 0.440 |
|  | (32.63) | (1.94) | (42.32) | (10.72) |
| Log-likelihood | − 8255 | − 8254 | − 8254 | − 8252 |

[a] Divided by 10.

the empirical hazard displayed negative duration dependence throughout. It is inherently more difficult to discriminate among the various mixture models that can yield negative duration dependence. Indeed, it is theoretically possible for a mixture of positively sloped structural hazards to exhibit negative duration dependence; this is one of the extreme and implausible cases encountered by Trussell and Richards in their mortality analyses.

What can be gleaned from these results about the distribution of heterogeneity? One expects the two-point mixture with $\theta$ freely estimated to dominate the mover–stayer model with $\theta$ set equal to $-\infty$. A first point to notice, then, is that likelihood values are very little improved by the more flexible model. For all practical purposes the two approaches describe the data equally well. Yet the implications of these models for the distribution of unobservables in the population are quite different. The mover–stayer findings suggest that 80% of the population is at risk of owning a home, while the remaining 20% are effectively out of the market, with a hazard rate of zero. The more general model finds 34% of the population to be characterized by the baseline hazard and 66% by a hazard that is positive but only 28% of the baseline. The data do not permit these rather different possibilities to be distinguished. Heckman and Singer (1984a) have cautioned that discrete mixture models do not capture the underlying heterogeneity distribution with any reliability. The results presented here help to illustrate their point.

Note that the mover–stayer estimate of $\pi$ for the log-logistic exceeds the estimate under the gamma specification. The difference, while not large in this instance, reflects the behaviour of the underlying structural hazards.

Appendix A includes a brief discussion of exogenous time-varying covariates. Results are presented for models that include two such variables—an indicator for whether the respondent's father is alive, and a dummy variable for the period 1939–50. One might expect home-ownership to be passed to sons via inheritance, but no such tendency appears in these data: the indicator for father's death is insignificant. In contrast, the time period dummy is significant, taking the negative sign one would expect. It is worth mentioning here that the inclusion of a variable for the war years renders the coefficient on respondent's year of birth insignificant. The result suggests that the older men in the sample (born near 1911) were affected by the dislocations of the war during ages which would otherwise have been their prime ages for first home-ownership. A detailed exploration of these time period effects is left to future research.

### First Marriage

The hazard function for first marriage shown in Fig. 4.3 is decidedly non-monotonic. Thus, if it is to be fitted at all by a model based on the gamma distribution, that model must include a correction for heterogeneity. It is less clear whether a log-logistic model might agree with the data, but Fig. 4.6 shows that, without allowance for heterogeneity, the fit is rather poor. In contrast, a log-logistic model with mover–stayer heterogeneity reproduces the empirical hazard reasonably well.

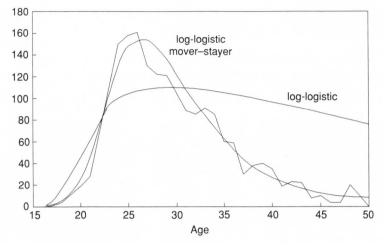

Fig. 4.6 Log-logistic models for first marriage.

Table 4.5 gives the estimates of log-logistic and gamma models for first marriage with covariates. Three models of each type are shown: a bench-mark model without correction for heterogeneity, a model with mover–stayer heterogeneity, and the two-point mixture.

Note that the influences of father's occupation and schooling on marriage are just the reverse of their effects on home-ownership. This is most clearly seen in the two-point mixture models. When father's occupation is unskilled, the risk function for first marriage is increased by 53% (exp(.422)) relative to the baseline. The effect is somewhat larger if the father is qualified and somewhat smaller (49%) when the father's occupation is white-collar. In short, while men whose fathers were in agriculture tend to acquire a home earlier than others, Table 4.5 shows that their ages at first marriage are apt to be older.

Respondents who attained a baccalaureate tend to marry later, with the level of the hazard being reduced by about 24% in the models with a control for heterogeneity. Lower levels of education do not appear to influence the hazard. Recall that schooling to baccalaureate level is associated with earlier home-ownership; here again, the effects of a covariate on marriage and ownership differ in direction.

The estimates of the heterogeneity parameters $\theta$ and $\pi$ are highly significant in these models. The mover–stayer models place 10% of the population in the stayer category, a figure that is close to the life-table estimate of the proportion never-married at age 50. The results from the gamma and log-logistic mover–stayer models are quite similar. Consideration of general two-point mixtures improves the likelihood values to a much greater extent than in the models of first home-ownership. However, the qualitative result is similar: whereas the mover–stayer models assign 10% of the population to the zero-hazard category, the two-point models suggest that 14%–16% of the population has a positive hazard that is .02–.06 of the baseline hazard.[8]

TABLE 4.5. *Log-logistic and gamma estimates of age at first marriage, with and without correction for heterogeneity. Asymptotic* t-*statistics in parentheses.*

| | Log-logistic models | | | Gamma models | | |
|---|---|---|---|---|---|---|
| | I | II | III | I | II | III |
| *Baseline* | | | | | | |
| Log $p$ | 1.323 | 1.291 | 1.323 | 0.746 | 1.465 | 1.638 |
| | (40.54) | (42.67) | (41.66) | (21.03) | (41.38) | (40.43) |
| Log $\beta$ | −4.525 | −4.806 | −4.876 | −4.500 | −3.571 | −3.404 |
| | (20.44) | (14.81) | (12.50) | (52.72) | (53.15) | (45.47) |
| *Covariates* | | | | | | |
| Father's occupation | | | | | | |
| Unskilled | 0.103 | 0.201 | 0.422 | 0.210 | 0.198 | 0.422 |
| | (1.53) | (2.88) | (4.38) | (2.97) | (2.87) | (4.80) |
| Qualified | 0.258 | 0.226 | 0.464 | 0.384 | 0.234 | 0.453 |
| | (3.81) | (3.25) | (4.69) | (5.46) | (3.43) | (5.06) |
| Tradesman | 0.039 | 0.088 | 0.201 | 0.159 | 0.100 | 0.203 |
| | (0.60) | (1.26) | (2.19) | (2.34) | (1.51) | (2.41) |
| White-collar | 0.183 | 0.216 | 0.399 | 0.303 | 0.239 | 0.403 |
| | (2.35) | (2.73) | (3.83) | (3.83) | (3.11) | (4.12) |
| Birth year[a] | −0.317 | 0.083 | 0.152 | −0.046 | 0.178 | 0.225 |
| | (13.92) | (2.65) | (3.89) | (1.38) | (5.67) | (6.12) |
| Schooling | | | | | | |
| Primary | 0.121 | 0.046 | 0.118 | 0.310 | 0.080 | 0.113 |
| | (2.45) | (0.86) | (1.68) | (5.86) | (1.54) | (1.75) |
| First general | 0.076 | −0.023 | −0.017 | 0.245 | 0.008 | −0.027 |
| | (0.83) | (0.25) | (0.14) | (2.63) | (0.086) | (0.24) |
| Baccalaureate | −0.041 | −0.251 | −0.280 | 0.168 | −0.245 | −0.278 |
| | (0.51) | (2.89) | (2.60) | (2.02) | (3.09) | (2.67) |
| Unobserved factor | | | | | | |
| $\theta$ | | | −2.884 | | | −3.850 |
| | | | (15.01) | | | (28.47) |
| $\pi$ | | 0.903 | 0.840 | | 0.901 | 0.862 |
| | | (14.82) | (52.95) | | (28.22) | (95.75) |
| Log-likelihood | −10648 | −10435 | −10417 | −11071 | −10494 | −10433 |

[a] Divided by 10.

The introduction of heterogeneity in these marriage models appears to make a substantive difference: the effects of schooling change in sign and significance,

[8] The mover–stayer estimates of $\pi$ produced by the log-logistic and gamma models are essentially equal, although in general the shape of the hazards should produce a higher $\pi$ in the log-logistic case.

as do the effects of year of birth. This is in some contrast to the models of home-ownership discussed above, in which the covariate effects estimates were relatively insensitive to the inclusion or exclusion of a heterogeneity control. By the criterion set out in the introduction, such a reversal in effects estimates should demonstrate the value of controlling for heterogeneity. But I would argue that there is in fact less here than meets the eye. The change in coefficient sign and significance in the first-marriage models has less to do with heterogeneity *per se* than with an inadequate initial specification of the structural hazard. The results differ because, without heterogeneity, these two parametric models simply do not possess the flexibility required to reproduce the empirical risk function. No one would suppose that an unadorned gamma model could possibly fit the hazard function of Fig. 4.3. That kind of model is not a sensible starting-point; it should be no surprise that the coefficient estimates it produces are badly distorted.

### Joint Models of Marriage and Home-Ownership

In this section, I consider two transition intensities, $r_m(t)$ for marriage and $r_h\{t \mid m(t)\}$ for ownership. Marriage is viewed as an endogenous influence on the transition to home-ownership. The key comparison is therefore between a separable model, in which persistent heterogeneity plays no role, and a joint model, in which the transition intensities are linked by a dependence on a common unobservable.

Table 4.6 presents estimates of the conventional model in which marital status enters as a time-varying variable in the transition intensity $r_h\{t \mid m(t)\}$. Two covariates summarize the marital history: a dummy variable taking the value '1' upon marriage, and an interaction between this variable and age at marriage. Both covariates are set equal to zero until marriage occurs.

The results show that marriage sharply increases the likelihood of home-ownership. The risk is elevated by 80% (exp(.59)) in the log-logistic model and 95% in the gamma. We expect this effect to be large, as only 5% of the men in the sample acquired a home before marriage. Age at marriage has a positive influence on the risk as well: men who marry at older ages tend to acquire a home sooner after marriage. The result can be compared to Murphy (1984), who found a nonlinear association between age at marriage and home-ownership in a sample of British data.

Are these findings concerning the influence of an endogenous variable contaminated by heterogeneity? If transitions to marriage depend on unmeasured background factors, and such factors also affect the propensities to own a home, then the estimated effects of marriage presented in Table 4.6 confound the effects of unmeasured variables with the direct influence of marriage. The bias is like that encountered in regression models in which an explanatory variable is correlated with the regression disturbance. The aim of a joint model is to purge the estimates of such spurious correlation.

TABLE 4.6. *Log-logistic and gamma estimates of age at home-ownership, with marital status entered as time-varying. Asymptotic t-statistics in parentheses.*

|  | Log-logistic | Gamma |
|---|---|---|
| *Baseline* | | |
| Log $p$ | 0.201 | 0.101 |
|  | (2.88) | (1.21) |
| Log $\beta$ | $-7.031$ | $-7.275$ |
|  | (42.43) | (30.97) |
| *Covariates* | | |
| Father's occupation | | |
| Unskilled | $-0.347$ | $-0.344$ |
|  | (4.08) | (4.15) |
| Qualified | $-0.414$ | $-0.414$ |
|  | (4.90) | (5.00) |
| Tradesman | $-0.072$ | $-0.068$ |
|  | (0.93) | (0.89) |
| White-collar | $-0.253$ | $-0.249$ |
|  | (2.76) | (2.73) |
| Birth year[a] | 0.210 | 0.230 |
|  | (5.19) | (6.72) |
| Schooling | | |
| Primary | 0.162 | 0.170 |
|  | (2.59) | (2.73) |
| First general | 0.083 | 0.094 |
|  | (0.77) | (0.87) |
| Baccalaureate | 0.215 | 0.221 |
|  | (2.26) | (2.33) |
| Married | 0.590 | 0.667 |
|  | (3.03) | (3.52) |
| Age at marriage[b] | 0.021 | 0.021 |
|  | (2.74) | (2.84) |
| Log-likelihood[c] | $-8209$ | $-8211$ |

[a] Divided by 10.
[b] In years.
[c] Strictly speaking, that portion of the log-likelihood in which the parameters of $r_h$ appear.

Estimates from the joint model are given in Table 4.7. The findings suggest that the direct influence of marital status on ownership is much stronger than is shown by the conventional estimates of Table 4.6. The influence of marital status is understated by the conventional techniques. Furthermore, the effect of age at marriage on the propensity to acquire a home, positive in the conventional model, now vanishes. Note that the estimates of $\theta_m$ and $\theta_h$ suggest that men who for unobserved reasons tend to delay marriage ($\theta_m < 0$), are quicker to acquire a home

TABLE 4.7. *Log-logistic estimates of joint model for marriage and home-ownership. Asymptotic t-statistics in parentheses.*

|  | Marriage | Home-ownership |
|---|---|---|
| *Baseline* | | |
| Log $p$ | 1.330 | 0.416 |
|  | (40.23) | (2.01) |
| Log $\beta$ | − 4.824 | − 7.129 |
|  | (11.72) | (37.88) |
| *Covariates* | | |
| Father's occupation | | |
| Unskilled | 0.404 | − 0.386 |
|  | (4.47) | (3.78) |
| Qualified | 0.417 | − 0.447 |
|  | (4.54) | (4.32) |
| Tradesman | 0.230 | − 0.078 |
|  | (2.02) | (0.74) |
| White-collar | 0.447 | − 0.269 |
|  | (3.87) | (2.67) |
| Birth year[a] | 0.113 | 0.244 |
|  | (2.69) | (4.89) |
| Schooling | | |
| Primary | 0.069 | 0.197 |
|  | (1.32) | (2.03) |
| First general | − 0.045 | 0.137 |
|  | (0.87) | (0.58) |
| Baccalaureate | − 0.276 | 0.284 |
|  | (2.23) | (2.05) |
| Married | | 1.777 |
|  | | (5.32) |
| Age at marriage[b] | | − 0.019 |
|  | | (0.37) |
| *Unobservable* | | |
| $\theta_m$ | − 2.795 | |
|  | (13.35) | |
| $\theta_h$ | | 1.122 |
|  | | (3.32) |
| $\pi$ | 0.806 | |
|  | (43.32) | |
| Log-likelihood | − 17899 | |

[a] Divided by 10.
[b] In years.

($\theta_h > 0$). What has happened here? In essence, the effect that had been located in the age-at-marriage coefficient of the conventional model has been shifted to $\theta_m$ and $\theta_h$. The estimate of $\pi$ puts 20% of the population into the delayed marriage/earlier ownership category.

Perhaps too much should not be read into this result. Certainly the one-factor characterization of heterogeneity employed here is highly restrictive. But the finding about unobservables is nevertheless interesting because it mimics the findings about the observed covariates: later-marrying men (such as those with fathers in agriculture) tend to acquire homes at younger ages.

## Conclusions

While this chapter has been narrowly focused on the relation between marriage and home-ownership, the larger point being made concerns estimation strategies in models with time-varying endogenous variables. A number of endogenous influences on ownership might be considered. Propensities to migrate and to own a home appear related (see Appendix B). There is a positive relationship (evident in models not reported here) between parity levels and transitions to ownership. Each of these relationships merits investigation; neither is difficult to investigate, given the event history data, if persistent unobservables are assumed away. But if the researcher intends to deal head-on with such unobservables, the estimation task is formidable indeed.

In considering the results of the joint modelling exercise, I find it difficult to conclude that the pay-off has been high. A cautious interpreter of the conventional model presented in Table 4.6 would have stressed the possibility that a positive association between age at marriage and home-ownership could be ascribed to heterogeneity. There is some merit in confirming this suspicion through a joint modelling exercise. The pay-off to the joint strategy is, of course, much enhanced if there is a serious theoretical proposition at stake. I suspect that, as the empirical relations between demographic and economic variables become better documented—and the task of documentation is one for which conventional event history models are perfectly well suited—these relationships will also attract closer theoretical scrutiny. The popularity of the joint modelling strategies will increase in proportion to the number of testable theoretical propositions.

## Appendix A

This appendix briefly describes models of first ownership that include exogenous time-varying covariates. Few computational difficulties are presented by such variables unless they change continuously with time. The covariates considered here change, if at all, at discrete points. As in the text, let the survivor function be $S(t \mid X)$, suppressing dependence on parameters. Suppose that at the beginning of a spell the covariate vector is $X_0$ and then changes at age $t_1$ to $X_1$. The probability of surviving to age $t > t_1$, given the time-path of the covariates $\{X(s)\}$, is

$$S[t \mid \{X(s)\}] = \exp\left\{ -\int_0^{t_1} r(s \mid X_0)ds \right\} \exp\left\{ -\int_{t_1}^{t} r(s \mid X_1)ds \right\} \tag{A1}$$

TABLE 4.8. *Log-logistic and gamma estimates of age at home-ownership, with time-varying variables. Asymptotic* t-*statistics in parentheses.*

|  | Log-logistic | Gamma |
|---|---|---|
| *Baseline* | | |
| Log $p$ | 0.664 | 0.554 |
| | (14.30) | (10.34) |
| Log $\beta$ | − 5.601 | − 5.626 |
| | (58.21) | (49.73) |
| *Covariates* | | |
| Father's occupation | | |
| Unskilled | − 0.349 | − 0.319 |
| | (4.07) | (3.72) |
| Qualified | − 0.393 | − 0.370 |
| | (4.59) | (4.30) |
| Tradesman | − 0.102 | − 0.073 |
| | (1.29) | (0.91) |
| White-collar | − 0.235 | − 0.199 |
| | (2.52) | (2.19) |
| Birth year[a] | − 0.036 | 0.122 |
| | (0.82) | (2.86) |
| Schooling | | |
| Primary | 0.173 | 0.216 |
| | (2.75) | (3.31) |
| First general | 0.106 | 0.144 |
| | (0.95) | (1.29) |
| Baccalaureate | 0.208 | 0.253 |
| | (2.14) | (2.56) |
| Father dead | 0.085 | 0.066 |
| | (1.46) | (1.07) |
| Year 1939–50 | − 0.974 | − 0.793 |
| | (8.73) | (6.92) |
| Log-likelihood[b] | − 8004 | − 8026 |

[a] Divided by 10.
[b] Not strictly comparable to levels in Tables 4.2–4.4, as sample size is smaller, due to missing data on year of father's death.

or

$$S[t \mid \{X(s)\}] = S(t_1 \mid X_0) \, S(t_1 \mid X_1)^{-1} \, S(t \mid X_1). \tag{A2}$$

A transition to ownership at age t occurs with density

$$f[t \mid \{X(s)\}] = S(t_1 \mid X_0) \, S(t_1 \mid X_1)^{-1} \, r(t \mid X_1) \, S(t \mid X_1). \tag{A3}$$

The gamma or log-logistic survivor and hazard functions are inserted in (A2) and (A3) in estimation.

In Table 4.8, results are given for a model with two time-varying covariates: a dummy variable which takes the value '1' if the respondent's father has died, and another dummy indicator that is '1' during 1939–50. The latter variable is highly significant. Note, as discussed in the text, that respondent's year of birth loses statistical significance upon inclusion of the 1939–50 dummy.

## Appendix B

A descriptive regression suggests that there is a positive relation between the propensity to move and the likelihood of home-ownership. The evidence comes from a model in which the dependent variable $Y$ is the cumulative number of moves made as of the time of the survey or first ownership (whichever is the earlier) and the explanatory variables include the respondent's age (at survey or at the time of first ownership), age squared, and a dummy variable 'Own' taking the value '1' if the respondent owned his home at the age in question. Regression results, with $t$-statistics in parentheses, are:

$$Y = \begin{array}{ccccc} 0.436 & + & 0.162\,\text{Age} & - 0.0007\,\text{Age Squared} & + & 1.377\,\text{Own} \\ (0.63) & & (5.10) & (2.05) & & (8.31) \end{array}$$

with age being measured in years. The model has an $R^2$ of 0.11.

To understand the model, imagine that the propensity to migrate and to own a home are entirely independent. Under this assumption, age at first home-ownership (or at survey) merely indexes length of exposure to the risk of migration. One therefore expects the age variable to be positively related to the cumulative number of moves. (For instance, if the risk of migrating were constant with respect to age, the number of moves could be described by the Poisson distribution.) The fact that the migration histories for some men are sampled up to the point of home-ownership, while for others the histories are sampled up to the date of survey, is irrelevant if, indeed, the propensities to move and to own a home are independent. Under an assumption of independence, the variable 'Own' should not exert a significant influence on the number of moves, holding length of exposure constant. Clearly, however, the ownership variable is statistically significant: with length of exposure held constant, men who had owned a home moved more often (by 1.4 moves on average) than men who never owned a home. This is the case despite the fact that men who are censored without ever owning a home (Own = 0) tend to be censored at older ages than the typical ages of first ownership. In other words, censored cases tend to have a longer exposure to the risk of migrating, and, if all else were equal, would therefore have more moves in total rather than fewer moves.

The positive relationship between the 'Own' variable and the total number of moves is quite robust. Adding higher-order polynomial terms in age did not alter the association; neither did the introduction of background covariates for the respondent's birth year, schooling, and father's occupation much reduce the coefficient. With the other covariates included, the coefficient on 'Own' equals 1.134 with a $t$-statistic of 5.68. In short, although an investigation into the relationship cannot be pursued further with the data in hand, a link clearly exists between the propensities to move and to own a home.

## References

Blanchet, D., and Bonvalet, C. (1985), 'Croissance démographique et marché du logement en France depuis 1954', *Population*, 40. 6: 911–36.

Bloom, D. (1982), 'What's Happening to the Age at First Birth in the United States? A Study of Recent Cohorts', *Demography*, 19. 3: 351–70.

Coale, A., and McNeil, D. (1972), 'The Distribution by Age of the Frequency of First Marriage in a Female Cohort, *Journal of the American Statistical Association*, 67. 340: 743–9.

Cox, D. R. (1962), *Renewal Theory* (Methuen, London).

Elbers, C., and Ridder, G. (1982), 'True and Spurious Duration Dependence: The Identifiability of the Proportional Hazards Model', *Review of Economic Studies*, 49. 3: 403–9.

Goldfeld, S., and Quandt, R. (1972), *Nonlinear Methods in Econometrics* (North-Holland, Amsterdam).

Heckman, J., and Singer, B. (1984a), 'Econometric Duration Analysis', *Journal of Econometrics*, 24. 1, 2: 63–132.

—— —— (1984b), 'The Identifiability of the Proportional Hazard Model', *Review of Economic Studies*, 51. 2: 231–41.

Montgomery, M., and Trussell, J. (1986), 'Models of Marital Status and Childbearing', in O. Ashenfelter and R. Layard (eds.), *Handbook of Labor Economics* (Elsevier Science Publishers, Amsterdam).

Murphy, M. (1984), 'The Influence of Fertility, Early Housing-Career, and Socioeconomic Factors on Tenure Determination in Contemporary Britain', *Environment and Planning A*, 16. 10: 1303–18.

Rodríguez, G., and Trussell, J. (1980), 'Maximum Likelihood Estimation of the Parameters of Coale's Model Nuptiality Schedule from Survey Data', World Fertility Survey Technical Bulletin No. 7 (London).

Trussell, J., and Richards, T. (1985), 'Correcting for Unobserved Heterogeneity in Hazard Models: Using the Heckman–Singer Procedure', in N. Tuma (ed.), *Sociological Methodology 1985* (Jossey-Bass, San Francisco).

# 5 Interrelations between First Home-Ownership, Constitution of the Family, and Professional Occupation in France

DANIEL COURGEAU, ÉVA LELIÈVRE

An important aim in the life of a Frenchman or Frenchwoman is to become the owner of his or her own home. Nevertheless, in 1982, only 50.6% of French households were home-owners, and among households whose head was between 55 and 64 years old, this proportion rose to 63.5%. These results, which reflect a behaviour pattern toward home-ownership distinct from other European countries, are well known from census data. Nevertheless, the processes that lead to the fulfilment of this ambition to own a home are more difficult to study. To analyse this process of first home-ownership, longitudinal data are necessary. In order to obtain such data, we conducted a survey that collected retrospective information on the entire family, professional career, and migration histories of the interviewees. The sample consists of the life histories of 4602 individuals, and is representative of the population living in France in 1981 and born between 1911 and 1935. These data will enable us to explore in more detail the process of home-ownership.

The first step consists of the identification of ways in which the building of a family interacts with the fact of becoming a home-owner. Qualitative as well as economic studies have stressed the problems of costs involved. The cost of rearing children competes with the cost of purchasing a home, and thus plays an important role in the timing of the purchase. Previous sociological studies (Culturello and Godard 1982), using the last birth as a time-reference, have identified the timing differentials of buying a home for different social groups. These results concerned earlier generations of individuals between the ages of 24 and 44. For our study of the factors affecting the process of first home-ownership, we also chose the last birth in the family as the event of interest (other choices being marriage, births of successive children, and final departure of children from the parental home).

The validity of the choice of the last birth has provoked some controversy (Hoem 1985). In our case, the women surveyed were at least 45 years old at interview and therefore most of them are past reproductive age.[1] Consideration

---

[1] Only for women born between 1931 and 1936. Some late births may introduce a slight bias. However, as we are working on a retrospective survey, the selection by virtue of survival introduces an equivalent bias.

of the last birth in this study does not, therefore, constitute a bias due to incomplete birth histories. It should be emphasized here that the use of such information to define family completion is unlike using the last previous birth, which is obviously subject to length bias. Such a bias could also occur with our data if we use information concerning men, since there is no such age limitation on men's ability to father children. For that reason, the results that we obtained for men are given here only as indicative trials, and we will concentrate on the results for women. We consider women without children as censored at the date of the survey. Another possible choice could have been to consider their family constituted at the date of marriage. However, this option seemed less realistic.

We will also take into account job characteristics that determine the ownership propensity of individuals. From census data we know that 77.5% of the households whose head is a farmer are home-owners, whereas the proportion of home-owners drops to 41.3% if the head of the household is a manual worker. But these cross-sectional data give no information about the timing of home-ownership. Our concern here is not focused on the study of how a professional change may induce a change in the probability of becoming a home-owner,[2] and so we consider the professional occupation of the husband at marriage when studying the subsample of women. This allows us to distinguish five different professional groups (farmers, unskilled manual workers and domestic staff, qualified manual workers, white-collar and management, and craftsmen and small tradesmen), all of which are studied separately. The different timing observed for the purchase of a home by each of these groups justifies the disaggregation of the population according to the professional occupation of the householder. It is important not to consider occupation merely as a categorical variable in the framework of a proportional-hazards model. Such a model could lead to inconsistent results as the timing effect of occupation may not act proportionally on the rates. Only the first professional occupation of men is available in the data set (in addition to their occupation at marriage). As many changes in occupation may occur before marriage (Courgeau and Lelièvre 1986), this first occupation is a more unreliable indicator than occupation at marriage for the husbands of the married women in the sample. This constitutes another justification for the choice of the subsample of married women.

We have adopted both non-parametric and semiparametric methodologies in this analysis. These approaches are complementary. The non-parametric methods represent a generalization of demographic longitudinal analysis. They are used to study complex interactions among events, including those that do not generate or impede the phenomenon under observation. We will use a bivariate model here that allows the study of interactions between the end of the formation of the family and the first purchase of a home. Using the semiparametric method, we introduce into the previous bivariate model a study of the relationship between the rates of home-ownership or the rates of last child birth, and a variety of

---

[2] The data used here did not give the whole professional life of the individuals.

observable variables (e.g. education, birth order, number of siblings, place of birth, and mobility during childhood).

The following questions are explored in this chapter. First, is there a strong dependence whereby the end of the constitution of the family precedes becoming a home-owner, so that the following sequence would mainly be observed?

family formation → last birth → becoming home-owner

Or is the dependence between the two events even more complex? Or is there a total independence between the two processes? Second, does social class differentiation allow us to find different behaviours toward home-ownership that permits the use of proportional-hazard models? Given that each social class corresponds roughly to a different mean family size, how does this influence the likelihood of becoming a home-owner? Third, France was for a long time a mainly rural country, populated primarily by small-farm owners. Does the preference for home-ownership still prevail when the urbanization process has become more important? The methods and variables that we intend to use in the study of these questions will next be presented in more detail.

## Non-Parametric Analysis

Non-parametric bivariate models are particularly appropriate in the study of the interactions between life course events, here the birth of the last child and the first purchase of a home. These models formalize two stochastic processes developing with time. Each of these processes may influence the local development of the other, leading to different concepts of dependence or independence. Stochastic independence between the two processes is observed when the occurrence of one type of event is wholly unrelated to the occurrence of the other and vice

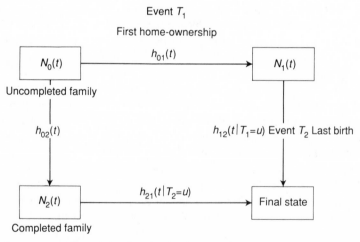

Fig. 5.1 State–space diagram for the bivariate case.

versa. When a stochastic process influences the local development of another process while the converse is not true, we say that there is local dependence (Schweder 1970). If this ever occurs, then we are able to say that there is a one-sided influence of the first process on the second one. In contrast, we have stochastic dependence if the two processes are mutually dependent. We are working here in terms of the state–space diagram presented in Fig. 5.1, which considers the relationship between the birth of the last child and the first purchase of a home. In this case, we have two failure times represented by the random variables $T_1$ and $T_2$, and four possible states (not owner before the end of the family completion; owner before the end of the family completion; not owner after the end of the family completion; and owner after the end of the family completion).

The hazard function, defined in the univariate case as the instantaneous rate of failure conditional upon survival to time $t$, can be generalized into four hazard functions:

$$h_{01}(t) = \lim_{\Delta t \to 0} \frac{\Pr(T_1 < t + \Delta t \mid T_1 \geq t, T_2 \geq t)}{\Delta t} \tag{1}$$

with a similar one for $h_{02}(t)$ and

$$h_{12}(t \mid u) = \lim_{\Delta t \to 0} \frac{\Pr(T_2 < t + \Delta t \mid T_1 = u, T_2 \geq t)}{\Delta t} \quad \text{with } t \geq u \tag{2}$$

with a similar one for $h_{12}(t \mid u)$, where $u$ stands for the time of the previous event. If we do not take into account the time $u$ of the previous event, then these two series of hazard functions become $h_{12}(t)$ and $h_{21}(t)$. In a later phase, it would be interesting to study the hazards indexed by the duration since the previous event. Unfortunately, doing so leads to small-sample problems that render the estimates unstable.

Let us now consider the ways of estimating these hazard functions from our yearly data.[3] Let $N_i(t)$ $i = 0, 1, 2, \ldots$, be the population in state $i$ at the beginning of year $t$, and let $n_{ij}(t)$ $j = 1, 2, \ldots$, be the number of events of type $j$ occurring in the population of state $i$ during the year $t$. To simplify the presentation, we assume here that the behaviour of the observed individuals will depend only on their age and not on the time at which the previous event occurred. The approximate estimates of the continuous distribution with piecewise-constant hazard rates at time $t$ are given as follows:[4]

$$h_{0j}(t) = n_{0j}(t) / \left| N_0(t) - 1/2 \sum_i n_{0i}(t) \right| \tag{3}$$

$$h_{ij}(t) = n_{ij}(t) / \{ N_i(t) - 1/2 \, (n_{ij}(t) - n_{0i}(t)) \} \tag{4}$$

---

[3] In the questionnaire, every date is recorded on a monthly and yearly basis. However, the use of monthly data does not appear to improve the estimation.

[4] See Courgeau and Lelièvre (1988) for the assumptions leading to such an estimation, and Cox and Oakes (1984: 53–6) for the estimation of such rates.

We can also include censored individuals that are then assumed to be exposed to risk for approximately 0.4 years, because the survey took place during the spring of 1981. We can cumulate these rates from the beginning of the observation. These cumulative rates will give smoother curves than the annual ones. We can then test the equalities $h_{01}(t) = h_{21}(t)$ and $h_{02}(t) = h_{12}(t)$. If both equalities hold true, we can conclude that there is stochastic independence between the two processes. If only one holds true, we can conclude that there is local dependence. If neither holds true, we have a stochastic dependence between the two processes. The following test statistic, for example, can be used for the first hypothesis:

$$U(t) = (h_{01}(t) - h_{21}(t)/\left[ \frac{h_{01}(t)}{N_0(t) - 1/2 \sum_i n_{0i}(t)} \right.$$

$$\left. + \frac{h_{21}(t)}{N_2(t) - 1/2 \{n_{21}(t) - n_{02}(t)\}} \right]^{1/2} \tag{5}$$

and the cumulative:

$$U = \frac{1}{\sqrt{n}} \sum_{t = t_0}^{t = t_0 + n} U(t) \tag{6}$$

which is asymptotically normal $N(0,1)$ when the equality holds (Hoem and Funck Jensen 1982). The multivariate case may be formalized in a similar way (Courgeau and Lelièvre 1988; 1989). The tables given in the text will present the hazards and both the annual and the cumulated test statistics. The hypothesis of equality between the hazards is rejected when $|U| > 1.96$ (when $\alpha = 5\%$).

## Non-Parametric Analysis Results

A preliminary investigation of the data gives some insights on the relevance of occupational categories. Of the married couples observed, 30.8% were not home-owners at interview, but the proportion is far from being evenly distributed among the professional groups. Less than a quarter of the farmers or craftsmen at marriage had not yet purchased a dwelling of their own at the time of the interview, but nearly half of the unskilled workers remained tenants; 30% of the skilled workers as well as the white-collar workers are not yet home-owners.

For the married couples in our sample, the acquisition of a house normally either preceded the birth of the first child or followed the birth of the last child. The financial expense involved in the upbringing of the children clearly makes the purchase of a property difficult for all professional subgroups. And, conversely, one might expect that once the financial means are invested in a home, they are no longer available for eventual children. What we observe is here, again, the less favourable position of the white-collar and unskilled workers. Only women married to farmers or craftsmen are likely (30% of them) to own their home before the first birth. A bivariate non-parametric model is applied to the last birth and first home-ownership. In the first application, we compare the instantaneous rates of ownership before or after the birth of the last child and, reciprocally, the last birth rates before and after the change of status to ownership. We will, as explained in the introduction, concentrate mainly on the results for women. The reciprocal approach is conducted in order to disaggregate the correlation observed between the two events. In fact, its purpose is to confirm the assumption of proportionality made in the next step of the analysis, and to detect local dependencies between the two events. Is the last birth a compulsory step before becoming a home-owner? Does this new state favour a last birth? Both questions must be answered prior to the use of proportional-hazard models and the introduction of explanatory variables. The second application derives from the timing of the purchase of a home. As described above, for a large majority of the married couples, acquisition of a home occurs once the family is completed. In that context, it seems appropriate to conduct a univariate analysis of first home-ownership after the birth of the last child in different professional groups.

## First Home-Ownership

For only two professional groups does first home-ownership clearly appear to depend on the last birth. For couples where the husband is a craftsman or farmer at marriage, chances of becoming a home-owner are significantly greater before or during family constitution. Paradoxically, for these couples the process of becoming a home-owner seems to be independent of the financial capital invested in the children's upbringing. This corresponds in fact to the inheritance not only of a home but also of the family 'enterprise', either agricultural or artisanal, or at least to a share of this inheritance. This happens when the couple's parents let them take over certain responsibilities, and this change is relatively independent of the stage they have reached in their family life cycle. For farmers an additional phenomenon is observed. The national mean age at independence, defined as having their first independent dwelling, is 29 years, and they are more likely than others to be a home-owner at this age (Lelièvre 1987). They also constitute the professional group with the largest families. Consequently, the change to home-owner happens before the birth of the last child for those below the age of 33; at later ages the tendency reverses. This can be detected in Table 5.1 by the clear reversal of the test statistic sign. This confirms the relative independence of the two processes, which develop at their own pace. For farmers and craftsmen, becoming a home-owner is influenced by other factors and does not depend on the completion of the family.

For other couples, becoming a home-owner does not depend upon the birth of the last child. Fig. 5.2 shows the cumulated rates when the husband is a skilled worker as an example. It is clear that the two curves cannot be considered as different, and the test statistic allows the verification of this.

TABLE 5.1. *First home-ownership for wives—husband farmer : non-parametric rates before and after the last birth.*

| Age | Before last birth | After last birth | Test statistic : annual | Test statistic : cumulated $U$ | Test statistic : cumulated $U$ |
|---|---|---|---|---|---|
| $t$ | $h_{01}(t)$ | $h_{21}(t \mid u)$ | $U(t)$ | From age 15 | From age 33 |
| 28 | 0.0214 | 0.0181 | −0.2147 | 0.3772 | |
| 29 | 0.0363 | 0.0076 | −2.0076 | −0.6771 | |
| 30 | 0.0227 | 0.0066 | −1.3223 | −1.1970 | |
| 31 | 0.0407 | 0.0306 | −0.5103 | −1.3010 | |
| 32 | 0.0645 | 0.0172 | −2.1670 | −2.0236 | |
| 33 | 0.0270 | 0.0379 | 0.5539 | −1.6970 | 0.5539 |
| 34 | 0.0311 | 0.0417 | 0.4917 | −1.4361 | 0.7394 |
| 35 | 0.0563 | 0.0657 | 0.3176 | −1.2619 | 0.7870 |
| 36 | 0.0225 | 0.0347 | 0.5951 | −1.0238 | 1.9792 |
| 37 | 0.0130 | 0.0593 | 2.1544 | −0.3583 | 1.8393 |
| 38 | 0.0469 | 0.0596 | 0.3954 | −0.2345 | 1.8404 |
| 39 | 0.0189 | 0.0350 | 0.7001 | −0.0389 | 1.9685 |
| 40 | 0.0440 | 0.0457 | 0.0500 | −0.0247 | 1.8591 |

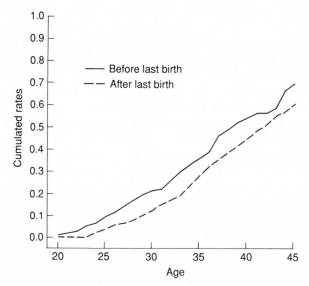

Fig. 5.2 First home-ownership for wives: husband skilled worker.

It has been suggested by qualitative research that home purchases might occur 10–20 years following, rather than soon after, the last birth. In fact, in our sample, among those who become owners after the end of family completion, 23% become home-owners within 10 years and 43% within 20 years after the birth of the last child. The results for the subsample of married men give an interesting indication of a selection effect among the men who started their professional career as unskilled workers. Table 5.2 shows a significant propensity to become a home-owner after the birth of the last child from age 35 onwards. In fact, couples from this professional background are less likely to become home-owners if they are still unskilled workers at marriage. Hence the influence detected at later ages for those who started in this disadvantaged subgroup may be due to those who ascended professionally and thus adopted the behaviour patterns of higher professional subgroups toward home-ownership.

TABLE 5.2. *First home-ownership for husbands—unskilled worker : non-parametric rates before and after the last birth.*

| Age | Before last birth | After last birth | Test statistic : annual | Test statistic : cumulated $U$ |
|-----|-----|-----|-----|-----|
| $t$ | $h_{01}(t)$ | $h_{21}(t \mid u)$ | $U(t)$ | From age 15 |
| 34 | 0.0287 | 0.0308 | 0.1416 | 1.1836 |
| 35 | 0.0168 | 0.0476 | 2.0652 | 1.7294 |
| 36 | 0.0098 | 0.0301 | 1.7189 | 2.1383 |
| 37 | 0.0281 | 0.0440 | 0.9388 | 2.3114 |
| 38 | 0.0324 | 0.0496 | 0.9142 | 2.4691 |
| 39 | 0.0224 | 0.0648 | 2.2418 | 2.9511 |
| 40 | 0.0084 | 0.0541 | 2.9849 | 3.5869 |
| 41 | 0.0094 | 0.0120 | 0.2353 | 3.5413 |
| 42 | 0.0435 | 0.0296 | − 0.5850 | 3.3127 |
| 43 | 0.0377 | 0.0419 | 0.1706 | 3.2670 |
| 44 | 0.0000 | 0.0306 | — | 3.2670 |
| 45 | 0.0150 | 0.0341 | 1.0468 | 3.4167 |

## Last Birth

While becoming a home-owner appears to happen independently of the last birth, the coming of the last child is for all groups (except unskilled workers, few of whom became home-owners) associated with a change in home-owner status. This influence becomes statistically significant at older ages, which suggests that becoming a home-owner may have a positive influence on building a larger family. Illustrative results are displayed in Table 5.3 for couples in which the husband was a craftsman or tradesman at marriage.

## Univariate Analysis

For couples who become home-owners after the birth of their last child, a univariate analysis for the five professional groups was performed. The results are shown in Fig. 5.3. The two extreme behaviour patterns occur among women

TABLE 5.3. *Last birth of wives—husband craftsman, tradesman :*
*non-parametric rates before and after the acquisition of a home.*

| Age | Before last birth | After last birth | Test statistic: annual | Test statistic: cumulated U |
|-----|-----|-----|-----|-----|
| $t$ | $h_{02}(t)$ | $h_{12}(t \mid u)$ | $U(t)$ | From age 15 |
| 27 | 0.0724 | 0.1013 | 0.5335 | 1.6350 |
| 28 | 0.0395 | 0.2308 | 2.4402 | 2.4887 |
| 29 | 0.0545 | 0.0263 | − 0.8826 | 1.9705 |
| 30 | 0.0658 | 0.1892 | 1.6570 | 2.4291 |
| 31 | 0.0879 | 0.1127 | 0.4008 | 2.4238 |
| 32 | 0.0992 | 0.1176 | 0.2824 | 2.3887 |
| 33 | 0.0837 | 0.0923 | 0.1427 | 2.3206 |
| 34 | 0.1099 | 0.1408 | 0.4303 | 2.3460 |
| 35 | 0.1781 | 0.1370 | − 0.5222 | 2.1091 |
| 36 | 0.1345 | 0.1818 | 0.5374 | 2.1760 |
| 37 | 0.0800 | 0.2759 | 1.8580 | 2.5820 |
| 38 | 0.0706 | 0.0357 | − 0.6436 | 2.3391 |
| 39 | 0.1714 | 0.1053 | − 0.7138 | 2.0961 |
| 40 | 0.1053 | 0.0351 | − 1.0000 | 1.8013 |
| 41 | 0.0400 | 0.1071 | 0.9115 | 1.9624 |
| 42 | 0.0435 | 0.0755 | 0.4648 | 2.0166 |

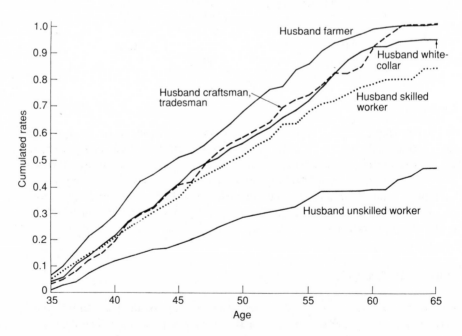

Fig. 5.3 First home-ownership for wives after birth of last child.

married to farmers and among women married to unskilled workers, whose chances of becoming a home-owner are half those of farmers. The rates for the intermediate groups tend to be closer to those of the farmers, and their behaviour patterns cannot be differentiated from one another.

## Semiparametric Analysis

To introduce some explanatory variables we use a semiparametric model. In the bivariate case, we can introduce a model using proportional hazards for the two rates we want to compare, $h_{01}$ and $h_{21}$ (or $h_{02}$ and $h_{12}$). Let $\mathbf{Z}$ be a row vector of explanatory variables $\mathbf{Z} = (\mathbf{Z}_1, \ldots, \mathbf{Z}_r, \ldots, \mathbf{Z}_s)$ with $r$ basic time-independent variables and $(s - r)$ variables depending on the second state reached at time $u$. These last variables are thus time-dependent. Under the hypothesis that individual behaviour will depend only on the age and not on the time the previous event occurred, we can write the following rates:

$$h_{01}(t \mid \mathbf{Z}, \beta_1) = h_0(t) \exp(\mathbf{Z}\beta_1) \tag{7}$$

$$h_{21}(t \mid u, \mathbf{Z}, \beta_2) = h_2(t) \exp(\mathbf{Z}\beta_2) \tag{8}$$

where $\beta_1$ and $\beta_2$ are two column vectors of estimated regression parameters, and $h_0(t)$ and $h_2(t)$ are two unspecified baseline hazard functions.

Some constraints on the parameter values may be desirable or necessary. A first constraint can be used to force the $(s - r)$ last parameters in the vector $\beta_1$ to be zero. As the variables corresponding to these parameters depend on the state reached at time $u$, they do not need to operate before this time. For example, when studying the risk of becoming a home-owner, the characteristic 'final family size' should not be introduced before the last birth. Such a variable will play a role only when family formation is finished.

It is interesting to consider the hazard function $h_{21}(t \mid u; \mathbf{Z}, \beta_2)$ separately from $h_{01}(t; \mathbf{Z}, \beta_1)$ for women older than 50 years as at these ages the second hazard function will be identically null. At younger ages it may also be interesting to compare the two hazard functions. If we verify that during the ages at child-bearing the two hazard functions are proportional, we can rewrite the two previous rates under a more concise formulation (Crowley and Hu 1977) thus:

$$h(t \mid u, \mathbf{Z}, \beta_1, \beta_2) = h_0(t) \exp\{\mathbf{Z}\beta_1 + H(t - u)(\beta_0 + \mathbf{Z}\beta_2)\} \tag{9}$$

where $H(t - u)$ is the Heaviside function that takes the value 0 when $t < u$ and 1 when $t \geqslant u$. For example, if the covariate is a dummy one, the rate (for those who have the characteristics) of becoming a home-owner before the last birth will be equal to $h_0(t) \exp(\beta_1)$; after the last birth the rate will be then equal to $h_0(t) \exp(\beta_1 + \beta_0 + \beta_2)$. The parameters $\beta_0, \beta_1, \beta_2$ as well as their covariance matrix can be estimated by partial likelihood methods (Cox 1972; Kalbfleisch and Prentice 1980). Some of the first $r$ parameters in vector $\beta_2$ may also be constrained to zero. In this case, the corresponding variables are considered as acting independently of the state of the individual. For example, some variables related to home-ownership may be assumed to operate independently of family formation. Thus, the model is flexible enough to cover different kinds of interactions among demographic phenomena. The variables used are displayed in Table 5.4. This table contains the measures of the different variables used in the semiparametric analysis.

TABLE 5.4. *Measures of variables for wives.*

| Variable | | Indicator for the study of | |
|---|---|---|---|
| | | Ownership | Birth of last child |
| Education | No grade of any kind | 0 | 0 |
| (continuous) | Primary school certificate | 1 | 1 |
| | Professional aptitude or first general educational level | 2 | 3 |
| | Baccalaureate or higher degrees | 3 | 2 |
| Elder | If not elder | 0 | 0 |
| | If elder | 1 | 1 |
| *No. of sibs (continuous)* | | | |
| Type of place | High fertility areas | 0 | 0 |
| | Low fertility areas | 1 | 1 |
| *No. of residences during childhood (continuous)* | | | |
| Father farmer | If not farmer | 0 | 0 |
| | If farmer | 1 | 1 |
| *No. of children (continuous)* | | | |
| Owner at the end of the period | If at the beginning | | 0 |
| | If not at the beginning | | 1 |
| Previously tenant | If not tenant | | 0 |
| | If tenant | | 1 |
| *No. of previous migrations (continuous)* | | | |
| Occupation when becoming owner (continuous) | Farmer and farmworker | | 0 |
| | Unskilled manual worker | | 1 |
| | Qualified manual worker | | 4 |
| | Craftsmen and small tradesmen | | 5 |
| | White-collar and management | | 3 |
| | Not working | | 2 |

## Effects of the Different Characteristics

The use of a proportional-hazards model allows us to pinpoint the main effects of the different characteristics of the individual and her family on both events, becoming a home-owner and the birth of the last child. We have here again disaggregated the population according to the husband's profession at marriage, as the non-parametric analysis showed us that this variable introduces non-proportional timing in the different rates of first home-ownership. First, we distinguish the child-bearing period during which women are subject to both risks, and second, we consider only the women who have completed their family before becoming a home-owner.

### Women of Reproductive Age

Table 5.5 gives the semiparametric results for the risks of becoming a home-owner before or after the child's birth. It presents 14 models, each including only one variable at a time. We will not discuss these results in detail here but try to pinpoint some of the more interesting ones.

Notice first that, when introducing only the change in family status variable (Model 1), we find results similar to those given by the non-parametric approach, namely, a very significant decrease in the probability of becoming a home-owner once family completion is achieved for women married to craftsmen or tradesmen, a less significant decrease for those married to farmers, and no significant decrease for other women.

The number of siblings (Model 4) has a very similar effect for every professional category. We observe a significant reduction in the probability of becoming a home-owner when the number of siblings increases. This reduction is maintained after the last child's birth for women married to farmers or unskilled workers, while it disappears for those married to craftsmen or tradesmen. A similar negative influence exists for all the indicators of large families. The probability of becoming a home-owner decreases when the number of the husband's siblings increases (Model 12), or when the number of children of the married couple increases (Model 11), but this is significant only for some professional groups. The first influence (Model 12) is observed when the husband is a skilled or unskilled worker, craftsman, or tradesman, and the second relation (Model 11) exists when the husband is a farmer or unskilled worker. Both are, however, always negative. We can relate these results to different motives. First, as the individual portion of inheritance decreases because the number of siblings increases, it is more difficult for those raised in large families to find enough money to become a home-owner. Second, it is more difficult for those who have a large family to put aside money when they have numerous dependent children. We will see later that, once the children are independent, this variable no longer deters acquisition of a home.

Birth order (Model 3) of the individual also affects the probability of becoming a home-owner. Before the birth of the last child, being the eldest child in a family generally increases the probability of becoming a home-owner, while after the last birth this effect disappears. Again, this is not true for every profession; there is no effect for the woman whose husband is a craftsman or tradesman. However,

TABLE 5.5. *First home-ownership for wives, before or after child's birth: semiparametric analysis values of the* $\beta_1$, $\beta_0$, *and* $\beta_2$ *parameters (single-variable analysis).*

| Variable | Model No. | Husband farmer | | | Husband unskilled | | | Husband skilled | | | Husband white-collar | | | Husband crafts–tradesman | | |
|---|---|---|---|---|---|---|---|---|---|---|---|---|---|---|---|---|
| | | $\beta_1$ | $\beta_0$ | $\beta_2$ | $\beta_1$ | $\beta_0$ | $\beta_2$ | $\beta_1$ | $\beta_0$ | $\beta_2$ | $\beta_1$ | $\beta_0$ | $\beta_2$ | $\beta_1$ | $\beta_0$ | $\beta_2$ |
| Last birth | (1) | | -0.221[a] | | | -0.159 | | | -0.090 | | | -0.023 | | | -0.368[b] | |
| Education | (2) | 0.219[b] | -0.124 | -0.187 | -0.022 | -0.347[b] | 0.273[a] | 0.029 | -0.119 | 0.040 | 0.057 | -0.177 | 0.115 | -0.058 | -0.752[b] | 0.287[a] |
| Elder | (3) | 0.217[a] | -0.172 | -0.145 | 0.178 | -0.083 | -0.209 | 0.272[a] | 0.052 | -0.331[a] | 0.299[a] | 0.082 | -0.210 | 0.049 | -0.302[a] | -0.145 |
| No. of sibs | (4) | -0.033[a] | -0.197 | -0.010 | -0.057[b] | -0.164 | -0.003 | -0.062[b] | -0.214 | 0.045 | -0.076[b] | -0.086 | 0.029 | -0.058[a] | -0.542[b] | 0.064 |
| Born in low-fertility area | (5) | -0.009 | -0.190[a] | -0.398 | -0.368[a] | -0.243[a] | 0.528[a] | -0.490[b] | -0.131 | 0.310 | 0.088 | 0.023 | -0.228 | -0.249 | -0.371[a] | -0.011 |
| No. of residences during childhood | (6) | -0.040 | -0.387[a] | 0.113 | 0.029 | -0.047 | -0.072 | -0.044 | -0.067 | -0.011 | 0.025 | -0.012 | -0.007 | 0.166[b] | -0.053 | -0.193[a] |
| Father born in low-fertility area | (7) | -0.419 | -0.239[b] | 0.328 | -0.598[a] | -0.271[a] | 1.069[b] | 0.009 | -0.113 | -0.177[b] | -0.570 | 0.107[b] | -0.688[b] | -0.249 | -0.399[b] | 0.083 |
| Mother born in low-fertility area | (8) | -0.426[a] | -0.251[a] | 0.403 | -0.392 | -0.258[b] | 0.945[b] | -0.382 | -0.111 | 0.288 | -0.633[b] | -0.084 | 0.529 | -0.095 | -0.296[a] | -0.594[a] |
| Father farmer | (9) | 0.203 | -0.272 | 0.064 | 0.262[a] | -0.145 | -0.010 | 0.250[a] | -0.008 | -0.324 | 0.144 | -0.022 | 0.002 | 0.203 | -0.348[b] | -0.070 |
| Husband's education | (10) | | -0.295[a] | 0.143 | | -0.375[b] | 0.316[b] | | -0.134 | 0.051 | | -0.149 | 0.078 | | -0.735[a] | 0.193[a] |
| Final no. of sibs | (11) | | -0.044 | -0.069[a] | | 0.304[a] | -0.206[b] | | 0.038 | -0.059 | | 0.050 | -0.034 | | -0.265 | -0.048 |
| Husband's no. of sibs | (12) | | -0.127 | -0.025 | | 0.095 | -0.076[b] | | 0.031 | -0.040[a] | | -0.088 | 0.025 | | -0.249[a] | -0.039 |
| Husband lives in low-fertility area | (13) | | -0.199[a] | -0.286 | | -0.144 | -0.060 | | -0.013 | -0.301[a] | | 0.010 | -0.109 | | -0.398[b] | 0.103 |
| Husband born in low-fertility area | (14) | | -0.191[a] | -0.515[a] | | -0.148 | -0.069 | | -0.041 | -0.243 | | -0.047 | 0.128 | | -0.431[a] | 0.281 |

[a] Significantly less than or greater than 0: 1-tailed test with size 5%.
[b] Significantly less than or greater than 0: 1-tailed test with size 1%.

TABLE 5.6. First home-ownership for wives, before or after last child's birth: semiparametric analysis values of the $\beta_1$, $\beta_0$, and $\beta_2$ parameters (optimal models).

| Optimal models | Husband farmer | | | Husband unskilled | | | Husband skilled | | | Husband white-collar | | | Husband crafts–tradesman | | |
|---|---|---|---|---|---|---|---|---|---|---|---|---|---|---|---|
| | $\beta_1$ | $\beta_0$ | $\beta_2$ | $\beta_1$ | $\beta_0$ | $\beta_2$ | $\beta_1$ | $\beta_0$ | $\beta_2$ | $\beta_1$ | $\beta_0$ | $\beta_2$ | $\beta_1$ | $\beta_0$ | $\beta_2$ |
| Education | -0.259[b] | | -0.290[a] | | | | | | | | | | -0.128[a] | | 0.317[a] |
| Elder | | | | | | | | | | | | | | | |
| No. of sibs | | | | -0.062[b] | | 0.010 | -0.075[b] | | 0.059[a] | -0.069[a] | | 0.014 | -0.070[a] | | 0.079[a] |
| Born in a low-fertility area | 0.573[b] | | -1.218[b] | | | | -0.720[b] | | 0.419 | 0.407[a] | | -0.743[b] | | | -0.266[b] |
| No. of residences during childhood | | | | | | | | | | | | | 0.187[b] | | |
| Father born in low-fertility area | | | | | | | 0.433[a] | | 0.156 | | | 0.916[b] | | | |
| Mother born in low-fertility area | | | 1.263[b] | | | | | | | -0.458 | | | -0.164 | | -0.662 |
| Father farmer | -0.760[b] | | -0.062 | 0.302[a] | | 0.079 | 0.284[a] | | -0.364[a] | -0.668[a] | | 0.460 | | | |
| Last birth | 0.273[a] | -0.121 | | | 0.212 | | | -0.175 | | | -0.065 | | | -0.824[b] | 0.176[a] |
| Husband's education | | | 0.153 | | | 0.239[b] | | | | | | | | | |
| Final no. of children | | | | | | -0.173[b] | | | | | | | | | |
| Husband's no. of sibs | | | | | | -0.060[b] | | | | | | | | | |
| Husband lives in low-fertility area | | | | | | | | | -0.342[a] | | | | | | |

[a] Significantly less than or greater than 0: 1-tailed test with size 5%..
[b] Significantly less than or greater than 0: 1-tailed test with size 1%.

TABLE 5.7. *Last child for wives, before or after becoming home-owner: semiparametric analysis values of the $\beta_1$, $\beta_0$, and $\beta_2$ parameters (single-variable analysis).*

| Variable | Model | Husband farmer | | | Husband unskilled | | | Husband skilled | | | Husband white-collar | | | Husband crafts–tradesman | | |
|---|---|---|---|---|---|---|---|---|---|---|---|---|---|---|---|---|
| | No. | $\beta_1$ | $\beta_0$ | $\beta_2$ | $\beta_1$ | $\beta_0$ | $\beta_2$ | $\beta_1$ | $\beta_0$ | $\beta_2$ | $\beta_1$ | $\beta_0$ | $\beta_2$ | $\beta_1$ | $\beta_0$ | $\beta_2$ |
| Home-owner | (1) | | 0.384[b] | | | 0.187[a] | | | 0.275[b] | | | 0.289[b] | | | 0.416[b] | |
| Education | (2) | -0.008 | 0.407[b] | 0.039 | 0.144[b] | 0.221[b] | -0.052 | 0.065 | 0.185 | 0.134 | -0.048 | 0.275 | 0.008 | -0.032 | 0.376[b] | 0.033 |
| No. of sibs | (3) | -0.019 | 0.296[b] | 0.023 | -0.008 | 0.079 | 0.033 | 0.017 | 0.492[b] | -0.076[b] | 0.003 | 0.283[b] | 0.004 | -0.052[b] | 0.289[a] | 0.047 |
| Father farmer | (4) | 0.067 | 0.338[b] | 0.055 | -0.102 | 0.086 | 0.290 | -0.044 | 0.249[b] | 0.097 | -0.024 | 0.313[b] | -0.111 | -0.110 | 0.308[b] | 0.562[b] |
| Occupation at becoming owner | (5) | | 0.494[b] | -0.149[b] | | -0.057 | 0.164[b] | | 0.273[a] | 0.001 | | 0.336[b] | -0.020 | | 0.459[b] | -0.018 |

[a] Significantly less than or greater than 0: 1-tailed test with size 5%.
[b] Significantly less than or greater than 0: 1-tailed test with size 1%.

this effect, when observed, may be a spurious one. To see if such is the case, we will have to consider the simultaneous effects of the number of siblings and the fact of being the eldest child. When this is done, we can verify that the only significant effect is the effect of sibship size. We can thus see in the optimum model (Table 5.6), which contains only the variables that have a simultaneous significant effect, that being the eldest does not in fact have an effect on the probability of becoming a home-owner.

It is also interesting to see that to have a father who is a farmer increases the probability of becoming a home-owner before the last child's birth particularly for the woman whose husband is a skilled or unskilled worker. Again this phenomenon may be due to the fact that those workers whose fathers are farmers get their portion of the inheritance before completing their family, thereby permitting them to become home-owners earlier than others.

Finally, we observe in Table 5.5 that the educational level affects home-ownership for farmers only before their last child's birth. Those who have achieved a better education become owners of their farm earlier than the others. We will see later the significant part that education plays in becoming an owner when individuals grow older.

Let us now consider the reciprocal interaction: the effect of becoming a home-owner on the birth of the last child, according to different characteristics. Table 5.7 gives the results of this analysis. First let us note that, when only the interaction of becoming a home-owner (Model 1) is introduced, we get results similar to those given by the non-parametric approach, namely, a significant increase in the probability of the last child's birth occurring after the parents have become home-owners. This is true to different degrees for every professional group. When we observe the effects of the other characteristics, we are surprised to see that each professional group is affected by a different cluster of variables. What we generally observe here is the lack of influence of the variables chosen, which are educational status, number of siblings, farmer father—the very characteristics that played an important role in the purchase of a home. The only significant interaction is the influence observed for the variable 'occupation when becoming a home-owner' for farmers and unskilled workers (Model 5). A woman married to a farmer who has left the agricultural sector has a decreasing probability of having the last child; in fact, the favourable effect of becoming a home-owner on the last birth is slightly but significantly decreased if they left their original environment. On the other hand, home-owners of the unskilled-workers group have greater chances of having a last birth if the husband has been promoted to a higher professional category. We also know that very few of them turn to the agricultural sector for advancement.

## Women after Last Child's Birth

We now introduce a semiparametric analysis of women who did not become a home-owner before completing their family. Table 5.8 gives the results for the

TABLE 5.8. *First home-ownership for wives, after last child's birth: semiparametric analysis values of the* $\beta_1$ *parameter (single-variable analysis).*

| Variable | Model No. | Husband farmer $\beta_1$ | Husband unskilled $\beta_1$ | Husband skilled $\beta_1$ | Husband white-collar $\beta_1$ | Husband crafts–tradesman $\beta_1$ |
|---|---|---|---|---|---|---|
| Education | (1) | 0.314[b] | 0.538[b] | 0.222[b] | 0.326[b] | 0.332[b] |
| Elder | (2) | 0.337[b] | 0.207 | 0.174 | 0.217[a] | 0.092 |
| No. of sibs | (3) | 0.000 | 0.005 | 0.029[a] | 0.030 | 0.047 |
| Born in low-fertility area | (4) | −0.052 | 0.360[a] | −0.045 | −0.042 | −0.123 |
| No. of residences during childhood | (5) | 0.282[b] | 0.220[b] | 0.130[b] | 0.135[b] | 0.143[b] |
| Father born in low-fertility area | (6) | 0.232 | 0.762[b] | 0.395[b] | 0.063 | 0.047 |
| Mother born in low-fertility area | (7) | 0.298 | 0.715[b] | 0.113 | −0.100 | −0.554[b] |
| Father farmer | (8) | 0.684[b] | 0.524[b] | 0.149 | 0.310[b] | 0.506[b] |
| Husband's education | (9) | 0.293[b] | 0.594[b] | 0.296[b] | 0.236[b] | 0.318[b] |
| Final no. of children | (10) | 0.021 | −0.002 | 0.007 | 0.053 | 0.069 |
| Husband's no. of sibs | (11) | 0.025 | 0.013 | 0.016 | 0.059[b] | 0.001 |
| Husband lives in low-fertility area | (12) | −0.118 | 0.206 | 0.037 | 0.040 | 0.144 |
| Husband born in low-fertility area | (13) | −0.236 | 0.002 | −0.116 | 0.154 | 0.323[a] |

[a] Significantly less than or greater than 0: 1-tailed test with size 5%.
[b] Significantly less than or greater than 0: 1-tailed test with size 1%.

various professional groups. The data mainly concern the behaviour of couples for whom the main expenses involved in building a family have begun to decrease, offering new possibilities of becoming a home-owner. For these couples, we observe an increasing similarity of behaviour patterns regardless of their professional occupation.

First, education (Model 1), whose effect was obvious only for farmers before the last child's birth, now has a very similar effect on all professional groups. The likelihood of becoming a home-owner increases with the educational level of individuals, whatever their professional group may be. The same is true for the husband's educational status (Model 9). In fact, educational status, as sociological studies show, is a good indicator of the future professional career.

TABLE 5.9. *First home-ownership for wives, after last child's birth: semiparametric analysis values (optimal models).*

| Optimal models | Husband farmer | Husband unskilled | Husband skilled | Husband white-collar | Husband crafts–tradesman |
|---|---|---|---|---|---|
| | $\beta_1$ | $\beta_1$ | $\beta_1$ | $\beta_1$ | $\beta_1$ |
| Education | $0.197^a$ | $0.442^b$ | 0.105 | $0.355^b$ | $0.246^b$ |
| Elder | $0.300^b$ | | | $0.209^a$ | |
| No. of sibs | | | | $0.048^a$ | |
| Born in low-fertility area | | | $-0.516^b$ | | |
| No. of residences during childhood | $0.255^b$ | $0.135^a$ | | | |
| Father born in low-fertility area | | | | $0.098^a$ | |
| Mother born in low-fertility area | | $0.750^b$ | $0.738^b$ | | $-0.747^b$ |
| Father farmer | $0.591^b$ | $0.579^b$ | | $0.313^b$ | $0.649^b$ |
| Husband's education | $0.227^b$ | $0.481^b$ | $0.203^b$ | | $0.280^b$ |
| Final no. of children | | | | | |
| Husband's no. of sibs | | | | $0.056^b$ | |
| Husband lives in low-fertility area | | | | | |
| Husband born in low-fertility area | | | | | |
| Log likelihood | $-956.41$ | $-739.20$ | $-1\,032.61$ | $-1\,054.43$ | $-541.17$ |

[a] Significantly less than or greater than 0: 1-tailed test with size 5%.
[b] Significantly less than or greater than 0: 1-tailed test with size 1%.

Second, to have a farmer father (Model 8) increases the probability of becoming a home-owner for all professional groups, even if it is not statistically significant for those whose husband is a skilled worker. This influence identified previously extends to most of the professional groups after the last child's birth.

Third, a new characteristic introduced into the analysis appears to have a similar effect on all professional groups. To have had a large number of different residences during childhood (Model 5) increases the probability of becoming a home-owner after the last child's birth. This characteristic appears also to be very significant for different migration behaviours (Courgeau 1985*a*; Courgeau 1985*b*). We observe that those individuals who have moved a lot are more inclined to become a home-owner in the latter phase of their life.

Fourth, the number of siblings (Models 3 and 11) no longer plays a significant role in the propensity for becoming a home-owner after the last child's birth. This is again very different from what we observed for women of reproductive age. However, for women whose husbands are in the white-collar or management category, we observe an interesting phenomenon. To have many siblings and to be the eldest are no longer inhibiting factors; instead, both characteristics increase the probability of becoming a home-owner when they are acting simultaneously (Table 5.9). For those social categories, having many siblings may be helpful in raising the money to buy a house.

## Conclusion

The approach used here to study a sample of married women allowed us to identify different behaviour patterns according to the professional occupation of the husband. If we had used a single model for the whole population, postulating a proportional effect of the profession on the hazard, we would have missed these differences and observed only the common features, such as the effect of the number of siblings on home-ownership. Some other characteristics might also have disappeared in an analysis of the entire population because they only affect some professional subgroups. Conversely, some factors could still appear to be important when in fact they characterize only a subgroup. It is only unfortunate that the size of the sample, as well as the characteristics available, did not allow us to go into further detail.

By splitting the sample into different professional groups we were able to reduce the problems of residual heterogeneity. The unobserved factors are not explicitly modelled here. Other qualitative disciplines, such as anthropology or psychology, would be more likely to identify the factors unobserved by quantitative approaches. They could provide insights into the problems of heterogeneity that modelling has not succeeded in solving satisfactorily. Nevertheless, the use of a reciprocal analysis has again proved its value here in clarifying a complex interrelation. Our search for local dependence led us to perform a reciprocal analysis of interactions among various events. In the present example we actually observe a local dependence of birth of the last child on home-ownership, whereas a relative independence exists between the purchase of a home and the completion of the family.

Analysis of the professional occupation of the husband at marriage shows that different opportunities attach to specific professional groups. Traditional patterns of home-ownership and inheritance in the agricultural sector not only enable young farmers to become home-owners more easily but also facilitate the buying of a home for those who have left this sector. Even for unskilled workers, coming from the agricultural sector constitutes one of their few advantages in trying to become a home-owner during the building of the family. The attachment to home-ownership and the strong link to rural antecedents is here confirmed.

Another important result of our analysis is the support for the controversial finding that confirms the favourable effect of home-ownership on the birth of the last child. It has been argued that couples without children constitute a large proportion of home-owners. This argument remains true, but couples with one or two children constitute an even higher proportion of home-owners.

Finally, one of the main advantages of our approach is its demonstration of the clear need for multidisciplinary analysis. The complex results we obtain demand collaboration with other researchers, especially those who work more qualitatively. For example, we observed previously that individuals who have moved frequently are more inclined than others to become home-owners in the latter phase of their lives. This finding cannot be interpreted with the information collected in this survey, and so a more anthropological approach might be helpful. On the other hand, an important benefit of our approach is its ability to confirm or deny through empirical analysis the behavioural hypotheses proposed by those working in other disciplines.

## References

Courgeau, D. (1985*a*), 'Interaction Between Spatial Mobility, Family and Career Life-Cycle: A French Survey', *European Sociological Review*, 1. 2: 139–62.

—— (1985*b*), 'Changements de logement, changements de département et cycle de vie', *L'Espace Géographique*, 4: 289–306.

—— and Lelièvre, E. (1989), *Manuel d'analyse démographique des biographies* (INED, Paris).

—— and —— (1986), 'Nuptialité et agriculture', *Population*, 41. 2: 303–26.

—— and —— (1988), 'Estimation of Transition Rates in Dynamic Household Models', in N. Keilman, A. Kuijsten, and A. Vossen (eds.), *Modelling Household Formation and Dissolution* (OUP, Oxford).

Cox, D. R. (1972), 'Regression Models and Life Tables' (with discussion), *Journal of the Royal Statistical Society*, B34. 2: 187–220.

—— and Oakes, D. (1984), *Analysis of Survival Data* (Chapman & Hall, London).

Crowley, J., and Hu, M. (1977), 'Covariance Analysis of Heart Transplant Data', *Journal of the American Statistical Association*, 72. 357: 27–36.

Culturello, P., and Godard, F. (1982), *Familles mobilisées, accession à la propriété du logement et notions de l'effort des ménages* (Ministère de l'Urbanisme et du logement, Paris).

Hoem, J. (1985), 'Weighting, Misclassification and Other Issues in the Analysis of Survey Samples of Life Histories', in J. Heckman and B. Singer (eds.), *Longitudinal Analysis of Labour Market Data* (CUP, New York).

Hoem, J., and Funck Jensen, U. (1982), 'Multistate Life Table Methodology: A Probabilist Critique', in K. Land and A. Rogers (eds.), *Multidimensional Mathematical Demography* (Academic Press, New York).

Kalbfleisch, J., and Prentice, R. (1980), *The Statistical Analysis of Failure Time Data* (John Wiley & Sons, New York).

Lelièvre, É. (1987), 'Bilan des connaissances sur la mobilité individuelle au cours du cycle de vie', in C. Bonvalet and A. M. Fribourg (eds.), *Stratégies Résidentielles* (Colloques et Congrès) (Paris).

Schweder, T. (1970), 'Composable Markov Processes', *Journal of Applied Probability*, 7. 2: 400–10.

# 6 The Progression to the Third Birth in Sweden

MICHAEL MURPHY

---

This chapter is concerned with the patterns of progression from second to third birth in Sweden during the period 1960 to 1980 from analysis of data from the 1981 Statistics Sweden (formerly Central Bureau of Statistics) survey *Women in Sweden* (Statistics Sweden 1981; WFS 1984), which is also described as the Swedish Fertility Survey. The approach adopted is the widely used one of hazard regression, which attempts to explain (at least in a statistical sense) patterns of differential progression to the third birth. Within this framework, a number of social, demographic, and economic factors that obtained prior to the third conception are included in a formal regression-type model that quantifies their relative and joint importance. Such techniques are both powerful and appropriate for fitting models to survival processes such as this one. However, they are not without their problems, and some of these will be brought out and illustrated in areas relating to the form of data source employed, the variables used in the analysis, and the transformation and interpretation of results.

A chapter like this can cover only a fraction of possible topics, and it can present only a selected group of results rather than a full set of alternative models. Its main purpose is to exemplify and assess the use of hazard models as an aid to further discussion. In particular, several more detailed and complicated models are not discussed, although they may be useful for substantive interpretation. For example, the woman's union status has substantial and clearly defined effects on the probability of conception, and even factors such as the sex distribution of the previous children also affects this progression (women with two children of opposite sexes being less likely to have a third child than women with children of the same sex); a number of models using such factors have been discussed by Hoem and Hoem (1987). However, such variables were found to have relatively little effect on the parameters in the models presented here.

## Specification of the Process

In recent years, two aspects of fertility have appeared to be particularly important in determining overall fertility trends in developed countries. The first is the increase in the age of mother at birth, especially for the first birth, and the second is the proportion of women going on from a second to a third birth (Festy 1979).

Thus there is considerable interest in the latter topic, which forms the focus of this chapter.

Of course, a necessary—but not necessarily sufficient—reason for a birth to take place was that the woman should have conceived around nine months before the birth, and prior to that she should have been in a susceptible state and sexually active; this observation follows from the Davis and Blake intermediate-variables framework (Davis and Blake 1956). Any variable that influences fertility must act through one or more of these intermediate variables. Some of the problems involved in specifying the process may be illustrated by considering separately factors that might affect fertility before and after a conception has taken place. The types of event that an analyst would want to include between conception and a subsequent birth are of a very different nature from those relevant to the pre-conception period. A fuller analysis of the set of potentially important covariates that affect the probability of a conception leading to a full-term pregnancy would include micro-level factors such as the woman's age at pregnancy, her physical condition at various stages of the pregnancy, and socioeconomic factors such as her union status. Macro-level factors are also likely to be relevant; environmental pollution and improved medical intervention may affect the outcome, and legislative, technical, and administrative changes may, for example, alter the likelihood of having an induced abortion. Over the period 1960–80 there was a substantial rise in induced abortion in Sweden, from a ratio per 100 live births of 2.7 in 1960 to 35.9 in 1980, and this trend was very similar to that of economic variables such as real wages, which are frequently used by economic demographers (see Fig. 6.1).

Those factors that are assumed to have an inhibiting effect on conception should also be expected to increase the probability of induced abortion if a

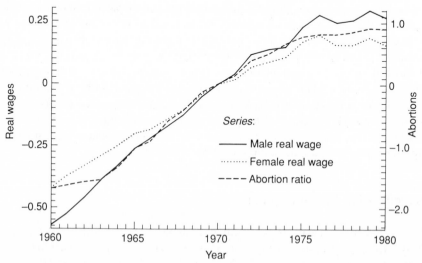

Fig. 6.1 Real male and female wages, and abortion ratio: Sweden (log values 1970 = 0).

conception has taken place. Attitudes to abortion clearly changed over this period, and this factor must have had some effect on birth rates, although the magnitude of this effect cannot be unambiguously determined. For example, the availability of abortion may change sexual behaviour and hence alter the probability of conception. Indeed, very efficient methods of preventing births could even increase some low-order birth rates by making it possible for women to have births early and then be confident of being able to avoid further unwanted births (Ní Bhrolcháin (1988) discusses this idea of 'contraceptive confidence' originated by Nathan Keyfitz). A number of potentially partially conflicting hypotheses about the role of induced abortion could be made. They include the hypothesis that abortion has risen because of changes in attitudes that are essentially independent of other socioeconomic changes, so that increased abortion has directly reduced fertility, and the hypothesis that abortion has risen because of altered views about the desired number of children, perhaps determined by labour market factors, and therefore that it has had little independent influence. It appears to be impossible to obtain useful data to elucidate such topics from large-scale fertility surveys, since such surveys cannot collect the sorts of information required (indeed, it is doubtful if such information could be collected at all). In spite of strongly held views on the importance of macro-economic influences on conception, the existence of effects of a similar magnitude acting on the decision whether or not to terminate a pregnancy remains unaddressed, even though some of the time trends such as those shown in Fig. 6.1 indicate a very high correlation between abortion and real wages over this period. On the other hand, if abortion is essentially independent of real wages, then incorporating only real wages as an explanatory variable for births would lead to the usual error in the interpretation of regression coefficients that arises owing to omitted variables.

Although induced abortions initially accounted for only a relatively small proportion of notified conceptions, they have increased substantially over the period covered here. Data constraints mean that such factors will have to be ignored in this exercise, but (as noted above), depending on the model assumed, it is likely to lead to biases, and possibly to large ones. Attempts to include abortion lead to major problems, in that surveys such as the 1981 Swedish Fertility Survey have not been able to obtain accurate data on induced abortions, and to use such deficient data could lead to various biases in the results. From a formal estimation point of view, therefore, it will be assumed that only events that occur and are measured nine or more months before the third birth are assumed to influence that birth. From a computational point of view, the simplest procedure is to lag the reported birth month by nine and define this new variable as the dependent one, which formally is the approximate live-birth conception date. Purists will rightly object that this procedure is conditioning on the future; but, for reasons set out above, these effects will be assumed to be relatively unimportant.

Other analysts have adopted different solutions to the specification of the time-dependency among the variables in the hazard process. Hoem and Hoem

(1987), for example, retained the date of birth, but 'froze' the woman's employment at six months before the birth, so the independent variable was close to the employment status at time of conception. Heckman, Hotz, and Walker (1985), on the other hand, appear to have made no adjustment of this sort and, not surprisingly, found that a woman who was recorded as working in a particular month was very unlikely to give birth in that particular month (it turned out that this variable was by far the most statistically significant in their analysis). Unfortunately, such procedures cannot easily be used if the covariates under study are essentially continuous functions of time rather than categorical covariates, because it is assumed that variables that change over the period of pregnancy should have no effects in that period.[1] The discussion of the importance of events occurring during the gestation period, particularly induced abortion, is illustrative: similar points could be made about other aspects of the determinants of the birth interval (although it would not be expected that the likely magnitude of change in factors such as possible male subfecundity due to environmental pollution or of female infecundity following pill discontinuation are of such a magnitude as to affect the form of the birth-interval distributions).

A final point regarding the definition of the dependent variable is that the timing of a major event of interest such as entry into risk, either by entering a non-contracepting union or by ceasing contraception (or one of the even more difficult-to-specify processes such as changing method of contraception and/or coital frequency), is not available.

## Inclusion of Multi-Level Factors

Almost any socioeconomic factor may be expected to have a (statistical) influence on fertility, however slight (Murphy 1987). Few of these factors are collected in a suitable form in retrospective cross-sectional surveys. Among these are income prior to the conception and gestation period (and also the perceptions of the individual about likely future income) and various attitudinal and cultural factors of the sort emphasized by scholars such as Lesthaeghe and Meekers (1986). For these sorts of variable, there are essentially no relevant data available

---

[1] It should be noted that the macro-level data for real male and female wages that are used in this exercise are annual data. A decision is required as to whether the data should be included as a series of annual step functions or whether some method of interpolating the data is to be used. Since it seems more plausible that real wages are not subject to step changes, these annual data were interpolated to monthly ones using a cubic spline. There may be objections to this procedure, since interpolation of a value at month $t$ uses information from periods both before and after time $t$ in general. It would be possible to interpolate data up to month $t$ using only information prior to time $t$, essentially expressing the values at time $t$ as a linear filter of earlier values of the series in question. However, the benefits of undertaking this procedure did not appear to be worthwhile; moreover, it could lead to possible discontinuities in the series as each new observation became available. The differences in the estimates produced by 1-sided compared to 2-sided filters was, in any case, small compared with the precision with which the effects of these series could be measured.

from such surveys (although in the case of the Swedish Fertility Survey some of these data, such as past income, could theoretically be made available by linkage to other register data). If it is argued that macro-level cultural and attitudinal data are useful for explaining behaviour at the individual level—presupposing, for example, that such factors are homogeneous among the population under study and that relevant data exist—then they could be included in the estimation process. Unfortunately, this does not appear to be the case. Although Sweden has a good set of cultural indicators relating in particular to the mass media (Rosengren 1984), no suitable long-running, consistent, and annually precise measures were found. For this reason, among others, the models estimated tend to utilize variables from areas where collection is easier and data are more readily available, namely for micro-level and macro-level economic data, especially those concerned with the labour force. There is the clear danger of attributing too much importance to such variables, simply because other relevant variables are omitted; hazard regression, as with regression models in general, will attempt to explain as much as possible in terms of those variables that happen to be included in the model. For example, Lesthaeghe and Surkyn (1988: 36) pointed out that an indicator of religious involvement used by John Simons in an analysis of English fertility (Easter communicants) was a better predictor for post-war fertility trends than conventional Easterlin-type measures.

The relative paucity of data available for inclusion in such models if a strict logical temporal ordering is imposed may be illustrated by listing the only ones available in the Swedish Fertility Survey (which is typical of such fertility surveys). These are community type at birth, number of siblings, mother's activity during childhood, father's socioeconomic status, birth history, union history, and activity history (including education). The number of topics collected on status at the time of the survey is, of course, much greater, but it is difficult to justify the inclusion of such variables as independent covariates in a hazard model since there is the problem of conditioning the process on the future. (However, Murphy (1987) does provide some evidence that current-status information from such surveys could often provide a useful proxy for the same variables at an earlier period in the life course.) Even with this restricted set of potential explanatory variables, a large amount of exploratory work could be undertaken on the sorts of factor that might be included, and on the various ways in which they might be specified (one of the particular difficulties of event history data is simply that they are capable of being transformed in many different ways). With data in categorical form, the fitting procedures appear to be simplified, since there is a paradigm of fitting main effects and then interactions until a satisfactory model is obtained. With this approach, however, the choice of categories can affect both the interpretation of results and the final form of the model fitted; there is possible loss of information due to the effect of categorizing continuous covariates; and since the response to a continuous covariate is usually assumed to be continuous, useful coefficients such as marginal responses cannot be directly estimated. This analysis includes what are essentially continuous covariates (such as the number of months worked) as continuous variables rather than categorizing them, particularly since previous work (Hoem and Hoem 1987) has treated these as categorical.

In an ideal world, a sufficiently well-specified model could be written down, fitted, and interpreted. However, most demographers would probably agree with Preston (1987: 177) that consideration of economic factors, contraceptive technology, and values 'is necessary for a complete understanding of recent fertility changes in these [developed] countries—and in most times and places'. Moreover, the various factors will also tend to act at different levels: individual, family, community, national, and supranational. In addition, the form of the relationship between variables at different levels is open to a number of possible interpretations. For example, it may be hypothesized that the primary way in which economic factors act is by promoting fertility when a large change occurs that leads to improved perceptions of prosperity, or that an improved standard of living needs to be experienced for a number of years before any major impact on fertility can be seen, or that it is relative rather than absolute standard of living that is important. Although such questions could, in theory, be settled by the incorporation of various lags in a hazard model, in practice this proved to be impossible in this case because of numerical instability.[2] This point is related to the problem of high correlations typically found in macro-level time-series, which can lead to major errors in both the estimated statistical significance of results and the interpretation of model parameters if unsuitable techniques are used.

In this chapter, a number of variables concerned only with the individual woman's activity history and macro-level wage series will be used, representing only two levels of variables, individual and national. In a relatively homogeneous society such as Sweden, subnational factors are likely to be less important than in more internally differentiated societies; for example, the existence of centralized wage-negotiating machinery means that macro-level series are a better indicator of individual-level wages than might be the case in other countries. The central point, however, remains that data appear to be largely unavailable for two out of the three main areas identified by Preston, namely contraception and values; this is a major problem to which I will return later after a brief discussion of the methods used.

## Method of Model-Fitting

There are a number of approaches to the fitting of hazard models. For example, the hazard function may be specified in parametric or non-parametric form, or as a class that is in some senses intermediate (piece-wise constant exponential).

---

[2] This problem was exacerbated by the fact that most theories that incorporate real wages as explanatory factors stress that both male and female wages should be entered into the model.

For the specification of covariates, a somewhat semantic distinction may be drawn between parametrically specified covariates (such as mathematical transformations of continuous ones) and less parametrically specified ones (such as categorizing continuous ones). In the case of the specification of covariates, in particular, an important consideration may simply be the operational one that some widely used programs (e.g. LOGLIN) can only handle categorical covariates, and users of these programs are therefore constrained to formulate their data in categorical form. Although it would usually be assumed that the relationship between the hazard rate and a continuous covariate process is continuous, the rigidity of widely used mathematical transformations (especially in regard to their behaviour at small and large values) and the lack of a clearly specified model means that the greater flexibility and ease of fitting of categorically specified covariates may outweigh the disadvantages.

For the hazard process of going from second to third birth, no parametric form is clearly suggested on either theoretical or empirical grounds, since a wide variety of forms have been used without any particular one being clearly superior. This, perhaps, is to be expected since, even for non-contracepting populations, the birth process has been specified as a complex set of convolutions of stochastic processes involving distributions for return to susceptibility, probability of conception, and probability of the outcome being a full-term birth, often incorporating individual variability in the probability distributions (or 'unobserved heterogeneity'). For contracepting populations, the process is yet more complex. Indeed, changes in contraceptive use and attitudes would seem to make the concept of a fixed 'true' distribution for birth intervals a meaningless one. Given that the true underlying distribution is unknown—and probably unknowable—at least for the foreseeable future, there is a need to establish the sensitivity of the interpretation of covariates to alternative specifications of the hazard process. The results of an experiment with a number of alternative hazard models are shown in the Appendix. In these cases, the parameter estimates for the variables shown here are essentially the same, and clearly their interpretation would be unaltered regardless of the form of model fitted. Within this class of models, the results would appear to be relatively robust to alternative hazard specifications. (I am grateful to Jan Hoem for suggesting the phrase 'harmless misspecification' for such cases.)

However, consideration of a wider set of models leads to different interpretations: Heckman, Hotz, and Walker (1985) found that the effect of the covariate of duration of previous birth interval, the sort of variable that is included in the Appendix, changed from being highly statistically significant to insignificant when a heterogeneity parameter was added to a model with a quadratic-hazard function. Heterogeneity models were not considered here for a number of theoretical, substantive, and practical reasons. The non-robustness of these models and the highly implausible interpretation of their parameters in some cases has been clearly demonstrated (Trussell and Richards 1985). As argued above, there are no good grounds for specifying the form of either the heterogeneity or the underlying parametric distributions, and therefore the technique was not used. On substantive grounds, the main effect of including a heterogeneity term is to extend the tail of the birth-interval distribution compared to a homogeneous population. Since individuals with longer previous intervals tend to have longer later intervals, it would be expected that the inclusion (1) of previous birth interval as a covariate in a hazard model, and (2) of a heterogeneity term together with a less skewed distribution than the overall observed might provide alternative explanations for observed birth-interval patterns, but in fact both approaches are deficient for interpretative purposes. The use of heterogeneity is a counsel of despair in that it interprets observed patterns in terms of unobserved variables. However, it may be useful to emphasize that the model fitted does not include all the relevant variables and may act as a stimulus to improve the information set used, although the model does require that the form of the hazard function is known.

Unfortunately, the use of portmanteau variables such as length of the previous birth intervals is not much more illuminating: the previous birth interval subsumes a wide class of other variables, including physiological difficulties in conceiving, continuity in terms of contraceptive usage, possible episodes of spousal separation, low coital frequency, stable attitudes to appropriate birth-interval length, and constraining and socialization factors due to differing educational and employment histories. Most, but not all, of these will tend to lead to a positive correlation between closed birth intervals: in this sense, the length of the previous birth interval is acting as a composite indicator for a range of different and perhaps more illuminating economic, technological, and attitudinal variables. As noted earlier, many of these are unavailable, but even if these variables are included separately in the analysis, the greater coherence of the previous interval variable will often tend to dominate the fitting process and lead to other variables being judged as not statistically improving the fit of the models with the sorts of sample size found here.

When the relationship of the first birth interval to later ones, or of the open interval to prior closed ones, is considered, the situation may be more complex, in that the observed patterns may reflect decisions about overall strategies for child-bearing. For example, it may be efficient for some women to delay the onset of child-bearing and then to have a small number of children quickly (Ní Bhrolcháin 1986), a pattern that would lead to a very different relationship between various birth intervals from the positive one usually found in developing countries and for most analyses of developed countries as well (which has been described as the engine of fertility by Rodríguez *et al.* (1984)). With the particular Swedish social and economic system, preferences about whether child-bearing should be concentrated or spread out might be expected to differ from those in other developed countries. If one believes that such strategies exist, even if they are not necessarily constant, then, in a homogeneous and efficiently contracepting population, these factors are the main determinants of child-bearing patterns, but they are ones that are not available from retrospective cross-sectional surveys. In these circumstances, it is argued that previous interval information is at least a partial indicator about some of these aspects (which, since they involve variability among women, would also be subsumed in an unobserved-heterogeneity model). Turning to the form of model fitted, the points above, plus the fact that continuous macro-level covariates were being used, suggest that the baseline hazard function used should be (*a*) flexible, and (*b*) non-parametric at each duration. For this reason, a Cox proportional-hazards model, which includes time-varying covariates, was chosen.

## The Population Analysed

Retrospective cross-sectional surveys produce a partial information set of fertility data, not only because certain variables are not included, but also because the information collected refers to the particular cohorts included in the sample. In this case, the survey comprises women born 1936–61 who were interviewed in 1981, so it covers all fertility in 1981 and stretches back to (for example) the fertility of women aged under 30 in 1956. Ignoring migration and selective mortality as well as non-response biases, the sample is therefore representative of the fertility of different age groups at different periods (see Fig. 6.2). Since younger women tend to have higher fertility, and since women who enter the risk of having a third birth at early ages are selected as 'fast movers', the use of simple

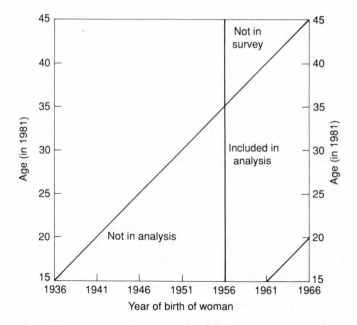

Fig. 6.2 Exposure analysed in 1981 Swedish Fertility Survey.

comparisons between different periods could be highly misleading. There are various ways of attempting to overcome this problem of selectivity. For example, confining the information set to that of the experience of women, say, aged under 30 would mean not only that a substantial amount of information would be ignored for later cohorts, but also that the characteristics of the groups of women who are at risk at the same age at different periods may be very different.

An alternative procedure that may also be intrinsically informative is to control the use of variables such as age at entry to various states. This will be correct only if the model that is fitted actually holds for that portion of exposure that is not available to the survey (the triangle labelled 'Not in Survey' in Fig. 6.2). This assumption cannot, of course, be established with a single data set such as this one; if there really are birth cohort effects, then those relating to the 1920s cohorts, for example, would affect fertility in the 1950s and 1960s, but their magnitude could not be assessed with the data available here. Once again the problem of fitting a correct model has to be ignored or assumed away. In certain cases, it can be argued that the biases that arise are likely to be relatively small, and that no corrections need to be made. Unfortunately, when looking at the effects of period factors, the need for as extensive a period for analysis as possible is important. In this case, therefore, a compromise was made by rejecting all those cases where the second birth took place before 1960 (the models were rerun with a cut-off date of 1965 but the effect of the additional five years' data did not seem to make much difference to the results obtained).

## Controls at the Micro-Level

It has been stated earlier that the main micro-level data included in the model were duration variables in various states. It is argued that these subsume a variety of diverse influences and therefore tend to be the most powerful variables without necessarily providing clear theoretical insights, in part because of their portmanteau nature. However, much attention has been given to the key role of female employment in certain theories of fertility. In this analysis, therefore, the time spent in employment by women was divided into three categories: employed (full- and part-time), student (including joint studying and working), and other (mainly homemaker but also including maternity leave, which had been found in practice frequently to be confused with homemaking by respondents, plus minor residual categories such as unemployment). Women with defective work histories were not included in the analysis because missing information could not be incorporated into the model used. Preliminary analysis showed that the amount of time spent as a homemaker was small before the first birth, and that time spent as a student was trivial between the first and second births. Since these two categories were relatively unimportant, they were combined with the non-student time in the pre-first-birth interval so that the two duration variables included were (1) months spent as a student between the September after which age 16 was reached and the date of the first birth, and (2) time spent doing something else in this period (see Table 6.1). On the other hand, time between the first and second births was dichotomized into months spent as a homemaker and other. A time-varying covariate for the number of months spent working after the second birth up to and including the third conception was also constructed and fitted: this variable turned out to be rather weak, as was one based on the current status at time of conception. These findings will be reported elsewhere.

TABLE 6.1. *Average number of months spent in various states: 1941–1945 birth cohort women with at least two births* (n = 632).

|  | Before first birth | Between first and second births |
|---|---|---|
| Studying | 64.1 | 1.4 |
| Working | 24.8 | 17.7 |
| Homemaker | 3.9 | 24.6 |

*Source*: Swedish Fertility Survey, 1981.

Results of fitting these simple variables are shown in Table 6.2. The main conclusion is that on average all delays lead to reduced third-birth intensities, but that the effects per month are less in the pre-first-birth period. Prior to the first birth, the inhibitory effect of studying per month is about half of that associated with working. Of course, because of the way in which the variables have been defined, there is linear dependency between the length of the pre-first-birth interval and its two components. If an alternative model had been used, for example, using total number of months and number of months spent studying, then the coefficient on the student variable would have turned out to be positive. While the relationship between the coefficients of these three variables is a simple arithmetic one, the most useful model for interpretation depends on an assumption about behaviour. If a woman decides that she does not wish to have her first birth before, say, age 25 and can choose to spend this time working or studying, then the second model formulation above would be more appropriate, since it shows that there is a positive effect of studying before the first birth on third-birth intensity (subject to the overall length being fixed). However, if on the other hand a woman waits to have her first birth until she has completed a particular length of time in the educational sector in order to obtain a particular qualification, and then she works for a period of time, a negative influence of studying on the third-birth intensity would be a more satisfactory, if superficial, explanation. In practice, different women are likely to have different motivations for delaying the first birth, an obvious one being the unavailability of a suitable partner, but even this is unlikely to be independent of the woman's activity status. Thus the interpretation and specification of such models is likely to be determined by a pre-existing view of the way in which socioeconomic factors influence fertility.

TABLE 6.2. *Parameter estimates for a fixed covariates proportional-hazard model for third-birth conceptions: Sweden, 1960–1980.*

| Variable | Coefficient (*t*-statistic) |
|---|---|
| Months studying prior to first birth | − 0.0066 (− 3.93) |
| Months not studying prior to first birth | − 0.0105 (− 7.86) |
| Months homemaker between first and second births | − 0.0314 (− 8.61) |
| Months not homemaking between first and second births | − 0.0242 (− 8.38) |
| Two girls born at first and second births | − 0.23 (2.41) |

*Notes*:
(1) Based on 1825 women whose 2nd birth occurred from 1960 onwards.
(2) The estimated maximum likelihood was − 3889.3.
(3) The 'two girls' variable is a dummy variable.
*Source*: Swedish Fertility Survey, 1981.

Turning to the second-birth-interval variables, we see that their influence per month spent is clearly much greater, with each additional month leading to a decrease in the third-birth hazard of about 2%–3% (time spent working having an effect closer to the lower figure and time spent as a homemaker having an effect closer to the higher one). By the same argument as before, if the interval is fixed for other reasons, such as medical advice about the minimum or preferred birth interval, then the effect of working is positive; if not, then it is best considered as negative on average.

When using continuous variables, the obvious way to extend the model is to fit more general variables, such as a sum of power-series transformations of the duration variables. While such transformed variables were found to lead to statistically significant non-linear effects, they did not affect the conclusion that each additional month was associated with a lower probability of progressing to the third birth. However, inclusion of additional factors such as a dummy variable for high-level education did not produce any substantial effects, presumably because such an effect was subsumed in the length-of-time-spent-studying variable.

The final set of models reported here include both micro- and macro-level factors. The basis for this formulation is the theory that higher male real wages should tend to increase fertility since the parents can afford more children, while higher female real wages tend to reduce fertility because of the increased opportunity costs of child-bearing and child-rearing (Becker 1960; Butz and Ward 1977). The results of including real male and real female wages are shown in Table 6.3. The high correlation between the two series makes separation of effects impossible: however, the main conclusion is that the male wage effect is relatively larger, and negative; increased male real wages tend to be associated with reduced fertility. The effect of female real wages is small. Once more, these two coefficients can be reformulated since the log of the ratio of female to male wages

TABLE 6.3. *Parameter estimates for a fixed and time-varying covariates proportional-hazard model for third-birth conceptions: Sweden, 1960–1980.*

| Variable | Coefficient (*t*-statistics) |
|---|---|
| Months studying prior to first birth | − 0.0041 (− 2.32) |
| Months not studying prior to first birth | − 0.0094 (− 6.82) |
| Months homemaker between first and second births | − 0.0297 (− 8.11) |
| Months not homemaking between first and second births | − 0.0216 (− 7.39) |
| Two girls born at first and second births | − 0.24 (2.55) |
| Log male real wages | − 2.30 (− 1.77) |
| Log ratio female to male wages | 1.81 (0.58) |

*Notes:*
(1) Based on 1825 women whose 2nd birth occurred from 1960 onwards.
(2) The estimated likelihood was − 3878.3.
(3) The 'two girls' variable is a dummy variable.
*Source:* Swedish Fertility Survey, 1981.

is simply given by the difference in the log of female and male wages. In this case also, the ratio of wage levels does not appear to be particularly useful. The sort of precision with which these effects can be measured is shown in Fig. 6.3, which gives a one-standard-error band around the fitted values of the wage series. This level of uncertainty is consistent with a number of possible alternative models and precludes fine distinctions between models. It could be argued that combining employment outside the home and child-rearing is easier in Sweden than almost anywhere in the world because of the high level of State support for child care, maternity (and paternity) leave arrangements, etc. Indeed, the need for two incomes to support a family may be the dominant factor in the decision by many Swedish couples whether to have an additional child (Hoem and Hoem 1987). Therefore, the lack of a clear effect of women's wages on fertility is perhaps not surprising. The sign of the male coefficient is inconsistent with the simple theory outlined above. However, it would not be sensible to reject the

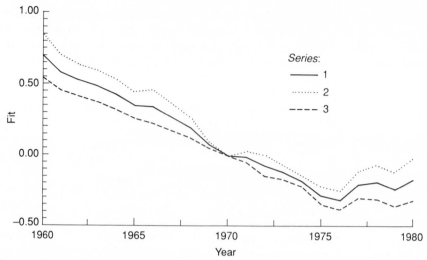

Fig. 6.3 Fitted effect for real male and female wages: Sweden. (Plus and minus one standard error estimate are also given.)

theory because of this finding (and, conversely, the opposite finding would not have confirmed it either), since a number of relevant and potentially important variables have been omitted from the model and the theory is based on the usual *ceteris paribus* assumptions.

Some scholars reject the primacy of these sorts of economic influence, emphasizing the role of cultural factors on fertility (Lesthaeghe and Surkyn 1988; Preston 1987). From such a viewpoint, observed phenomena such as the proportion of women in the labour force and the ratio of female to male wages may themselves be seen as consequences of cultural changes rather than determinants of fertility change—in other words, correlation does not imply causation. For example, materialism may tend to depress fertility and more than offset the hypothesized economic effects. Thus, theoretical models suggest that the impact of increased men's and women's wages may tend to be associated with increased and decreased fertility, and they might act to reinforce or to cancel each other. The precise effect would be expected to be specific to a particular time and place, and it would be inadvisable to try to generalise any empirical results.

## Conclusions

A primary focus of this chapter has been to discuss the level of precision with which factors affecting the differential progression to the third birth may be measured using data from surveys such as the 1981 Swedish Fertility Survey. Of the factors examined, it was concluded that the most powerful were the straightforward ones associated with the length of time spent before the first birth and between the first and second birth. Compared to these variables, the other ones considered were relatively unimportant when using conventional statistical criteria. This finding does not mean that other variables are substantively unimportant, or that variables not collectible in surveys like this one are also unimportant. The other main focus of this chapter concerns whether hazard models applied to standard-size, retrospective, cross-sectional fertility surveys can in fact be used to test that class of theories that assume (often implicitly) that the determinants of fertility change are identifiable from the information set that such surveys collect, perhaps augmented by certain macro-level data either as society-level data or as proxies for individual-level data not collectible in such surveys.[3] Although such effects may be estimated and interpreted, the conclusion would tend to be that the power of such models for discriminating between such theories is rather limited.

## Appendix: Comparison of Estimates Obtained Using Alternative Hazard Rate Specification

The coefficients obtained by fitting the following variables for the number of months in various states before the first birth and between the first and second births to data for the 1941–5 cohort for progression to the third conception were as follows:

TABLE 6.4

| Model | Before first birth | | Between first and second | |
|---|---|---|---|---|
| | Working | Studying | Homemaking | Working |
| Piece-wise constant | − 0.0125 | − 0.0063 | − 0.0357 | − 0.0256 |
| Exponential | − 0.0104 | − 0.0030 | − 0.0356 | − 0.0254 |
| Proportional hazards | − 0.0126 | − 0.0053 | − 0.0362 | − 0.0264 |
| Weibull | − 0.0121 | − 0.0040 | − 0.0398 | − 0.0286 |
| Log-normal | − 0.0137 | − 0.0040 | − 0.0363 | − 0.0226 |
| Log-logistic | − 0.0139 | − 0.0041 | − 0.0401 | − 0.0268 |

## References

Becker, G. (1960), 'An Economic Analysis of Fertility' in National Bureau for Economic Research, *Demographic and Economic Change in Developed Countries* (Princeton University Press, Princeton, NJ), 209–37.

[3] An example of the first type of variable might be the unemployment rate, which may affect directly only a trivial proportion of the sample in a country like Sweden, but may be assumed to have its primary effect by influencing the attitudes of the rest of the population. An example of the second type might be real wages in a society where wages of the whole labour force tend to move in very similar ways.

Butz, W. P., and Ward, M. P. (1977), *The Emergence of Counter-Cyclical US Fertility*, Rand Monograph, R–1605 (Rand Corporation, Santa Monica, Calif.).

Davis, K., and Blake, J. (1956), 'Social Structure and Fertility: An Analytic Framework', *Economic Development and Cultural Change*, 4. 3: 211–35.

Festy, P. (1979), *La fécondité des pays occidentaux de 1870 à 1970*, Cahier de l'INED No. 85 (Presses Universitaires de France, Paris).

Heckman, J. J., Hotz, V., and Walker, J. R. (1985), 'New Evidence on the Timing and Spacing of Births', *American Economic Review*, 75. 2: 179–84.

Hoem, B. and Hoem, J. M. (1987), *The Impact of Female Employment on Second and Third Births in Modern Sweden*, SRRD36, Section of Demography, University of Stockholm.

Lesthaeghe, R., and Meekers, D. (1986), 'Value Change and the Dimensions of Familism in the European Community', *European Journal of Population*, 2. 3–4: 225–68.

—— and Surkyn, J. (1988), 'Cultural Dynamics and Economic Theories of Fertility Change', *Population and Development Review*, 14. 1: 1–45, 220–1.

Murphy, M. J. (1987), 'Differential Family Formation in Great Britain', *Journal of Biosocial Science*, 19. 4: 463–85.

Ní Bhrolcháin, M. (1986), 'The Interpretation and Role of Work-Associated Accelerated Childbearing in Post-War Britain', *European Journal of Population*, 2. 2: 135–54.

—— (1988), 'The Contraceptive Confidence Idea: An Empirical Investigation', *Population Studies*, 42. 2: 205–25.

Preston, S. H. (1987), 'Changing Values and Falling Birth Rates', in K. Davis, M. S. Bernstam, and R. Ricardo-Campbell (eds.), *Below-Replacement Fertility in Industrial Societies: Causes, Consequences, Policies*, supplement to *Population and Development Review*, 12 (The Population Council, New York), 176–95.

Rodríguez, G., Hobcraft, J. N., McDonald, J. W., Menken, J., and Trussell, J. (1984), *Comparative Analysis of Determinants of Birth Intervals*, World Fertility Survey Comparative Studies No. 30 (International Statistical Institute, Voorburg).

Rosengren, K. E. (1984), 'Cultural Indicators for the Comparative Study of Culture', in G. Melischek, K. E. Rosengren, and J. G. Stappers (eds.), *Cultural Indicators: An International Symposium* (Verlag der Osterreichischen Akademie des Wissenschaften, Vienna).

Statistics Sweden (1981), *Women in Sweden* (Stockholm).

Trussell, J., and Richards, T. (1985), 'Correcting for Unmeasured Heterogeneity in Hazard Models Using the Heckman–Singer Procedure', in N. B. Tuma (ed.), *Sociological Methodology 1985* (Jossey-Bass, San Francisco), 242–76.

*World Fertility Survey* (1984), *Fertility Survey in Sweden, 1981: A Summary of Findings*, WFS Report No. 43 (International Statistical Institute, Voorburg).

# 7 Understanding Third Births in Sweden

JAMES J. HECKMAN, JAMES R. WALKER

This chapter estimates the determinants of third births in Sweden. Walker (1986) documents stability in the transition rates to the first and second births for the three most recent cohorts of Swedish women for which comprehensive fertility histories are available (women born in 1936–40, 1941–5, and 1946–50). There has been a secular decline in the transition rate to the third birth, accounting for a substantial portion of the recent decline in Swedish fertility.

A woman is at risk for a third birth only if she has already had two births. Several important demographic consequences follow from this truism. First, in order to estimate age-specific third-birth rates and their determinants, it is necessary to account for the effect of the first two births on placing women at risk for a third birth. The effects of socioeconomic variables on age-specific third-birth rates includes the effects of such variables on the timing and spacing of the first two births.

Second, even if attention focuses on the estimation of transition rates from the second birth to the third birth, it may be necessary to account for the history of a birth process up to the time a woman becomes at risk for the third birth. Parameters of transition rates may vary by parity. The age of a woman at the time she becomes at risk may affect third-birth fertility. So may the length of time spent waiting for the first two births, independently of any age effect.

Third, much demographic evidence has accumulated that person-specific unobservables ('heterogeneity') correlated across parities are important in accounting for life cycle fertility. Failure to account for these variables leads to biased estimates of parameters of socioeconomic variables determining third births. Heterogeneity has important implications for how to account for the history of a process in estimating transitions to the third birth. We can be much more casual about the history of a process if there is no heterogeneity.

We estimate the determinants of third births in Sweden using longitudinal data from the 1981 Swedish Fertility Survey (SFS). In work reported elsewhere (Heckman and Walker 1990a; 1990b), we fit a variety of multi-state duration models with time-varying covariates, general forms of duration dependence, and unobservables that are temporally dependent across birth intervals. The variety of models estimated in our work forces us to confront the largely unexplored problem of model selection in multi-state duration analysis. The most commonly used model selection criterion—comparing likelihoods—is inappropriate because many of our models are non-nested (i.e., often one model cannot be produced from a bigger model by constraining certain coefficients to be zero). We judge the fit of alternative models (*a*) by using the classical chi-square goodness-of-fit test applied to parity attainment distributions, (*b*) by considering the ability of models to produce parameter estimates that are stable across cohorts, (*c*) by considering their ability to forecast the aggregate time-series of birth rates, and (*d*) by using a model selection criterion that penalizes models with many parameters.

We find two strikingly different models that predict parity attainment distributions equally well in terms of the classical $\chi^2$ measure of fit often used in demographic studies. One model is consistent with neoclassical economic theory. It assigns a central role to the wages of men and women in explaining the timing and spacing of births. The other model is a purely demographic model that excludes wages and uses lagged birth durations as explanatory variables. This specification is consistent with models proposed by Rodríguez *et al.* (1984). The $\chi^2$ testing procedure cannot distinguish between them, and a model combining the regressors included in the two models fails to pass the goodness-of-fit tests. Using additional model selection criteria, we reject the demographic model in favour of a neoclassical model.

Because both models exhibit cohort drift, neither is an adequate framework for forecasting the fertility of future cohorts. The neoclassical economic model, augmented to allow for the impacts of pronatalist Swedish policies, offers a more promising vehicle for developing a framework that has the potential to account for future fertility. The estimated cohort drift found in our analysis is consistent with neoclassical explanations of the impact of recent Swedish policies on fertility.

The structure of this chapter is as follows. In the first section, we briefly discuss the formulation, estimation, and evaluation of multi-state duration models with time-varying regressors and unobservables that are correlated across spells. Our companion papers (Heckman and Walker 1990*a*; 1990*b*) develop the methodology in greater detail. We note the importance of accounting for the sampling frame used to collect the data, and of accounting for unobservables in deriving the correct likelihood function for analysing transition times to the third birth. We note the potential danger in adopting the widely used, low-cost, 'piecemeal' approach of analysing birth spells in isolation from each other. We exposit a $\chi^2$ goodness-of-fit test for a general multi-state duration model developed in our other work, and we consider alternative model selection criteria to pick the 'best' among a collection of non-nested models.

In the second section, we discuss the SFS data analysed in this paper. We present relevant institutional information on the Swedish economy and on Swedish fertility policy. The third section reports summary results from an extensive empirical analysis of the SFS data. The fourth section synthesizes our findings.

## The Formulation, Estimation, and Evaluation of Multi-State Duration Models for the Third Birth

The third birth is the outcome of a multi-state life cycle stochastic process. In making forecasts of age-specific third-birth rates, it is necessary to take account of the occurrence of the preceding births. Age-dependent fecundity, and the hypothesis of Rodríguez *et al.* (1984) that outcome times of previous births affect current birth-transition probabilities, suggest that it may be necessary to condition on the history of a process in order to produce empirically concordant models of fertility. The more interrelated the life cycle processes, and the greater the importance of age and previous durations in explaining transitions to the third birth, the more important it is to account for the occurrence and timing of prior events in predicting the occurrence and timing of third births.

The conventional demographic approach to the estimation of life cycle models is to estimate the components of life cycle processes in isolation from each other—the 'piecemeal' approach. This approach is often computationally cheaper than full estimation of interrelated life cycle processes. It also enables the analyst to focus on the transitions of interest to his or her study without having to worry about other transitions of secondary concern.

If there are variables that affect outcomes that are not observed by the demographer, and if they are temporally dependent across spells, the piecemeal approach is fraught with danger. Unobserved 'heterogeneity' is one name given to such variables in the recent literature. Gini (1924), Sheps (1965), and Sheps and Menken (1973) develop models of fertility in which persistent differences among women in unobserved fecundity give rise to unobserved heterogeneity. Heckman and Walker (1987) demonstrate that it is necessary to account for such variables to produce empirically concordant models of Hutterite fertility. This section briefly considers the dangers of the piecemeal approach when unobserved variables are part of the model specification.

We conduct our discussion within the context of estimating a life cycle birth process. We first present the basic statistical model that underlies our empirical analysis. Some of our estimated models have time-varying covariates. We state conditions for such models under which it is possible to integrate up hazards to form the survivor function in the 'usual' way—i.e., as is done in models without time-varying covariates. We then discuss the specification of multi-state models of fertility, and demonstrate how unobservables naturally arise in such models. In the context of the specification of unobservables that has been universally adopted in the empirical literature, we discuss the danger of the piecemeal approach in estimating component transitions of a model. We present our strategy for estimating multi-state duration models with time-varying variables, unobservables, censoring, and lagged durations. We conclude this section with a discussion of methods for evaluating alternative models.

## A Birth Process

We assume that a woman's conception history evolves in the following way. The woman becomes at risk for the first conception at calendar time $\tau = 0$. This is the age of menarche. For simplicity, we ignore the distinction between birth times and conception times in developing the model, although we distinguish between the two in our empirical work.

The basic building-block for multi-state duration models is the conditional hazard. Define $H(\tau)$ as the relevant conditioning set of explanatory variables at time $\tau$. The choice of the variables to include in the relevant conditioning set involves matters of judgement and context. For the moment, we assume that these are known. $H(\tau)$ may include variables that influence the woman's transition to the next birth. Anticipations about the future formed at time $\tau$ that affect transitions may be part of the $H(\tau)$. So may be the relevant past, including the history of the process up to time $\tau$ (previous birth intervals, etc.).

Denote the potential durations by $T_1, \ldots, T_C$. If a woman becomes at risk for the $j^{\text{th}}$ birth at time $\tau(j-1)$, the conditional hazard at duration $t_j$ is defined to be

$$h_j\{t_j \mid H(\tau(j-1) + t_j)\}. \tag{1}$$

Under conditions specified in Yashin and Arjas (1988), we may integrate (1) to form the survivor function

$$S[t_j \mid H\{\tau(j-1) + t_j\}] = \exp\left[-\int_0^{t_j} h_j[u \mid H\{\tau(j-1) + u\}]\, du\right]. \tag{2}$$

Note that the information contained in $H\{\tau(j-1) + t_j\}$ potentially includes all the information for values of durations less than $t_j$. Their conditions require that

$$\Pr[T_j \leqslant t_j \mid H\{\tau(j-1) + t_j\}] = \Pr\{T_j \leqslant t_j \mid H(\infty)\} \tag{3}$$

i.e., that the information available up to time $\tau(j-1) + t_j$ fully characterizes the conditional distribution of $T_j$ so that new information in the conditioning set arriving after time $\tau(j-1) + t_j$ does not help in predicting the probability that $T_j \leqslant t_j$. Note that this condition does not exclude variables realized after time $\tau(j-1) + t_j$ that are perfectly forecastable at that time (e.g., age, one period in the future).

Assuming that condition (3) holds, we may describe the birth process of a woman by the following recipe. A woman begins menarche at parity zero and continues childless a random length of time, governed by the survivor function

$$\Pr[T_1 > t_1 \mid H\{\tau(0) + t_1\}] = \exp\left[-\int_0^{t_1} h_1\{u \mid H(\tau(0) + u)\}\, du\right]. \tag{4}$$

At calendar time $T(1) = \tau(1)$, the woman conceives and moves to the state where she is at risk for the second birth. The woman resides in that state for a random length of time $T_2$ governed by the conditional survivor function

$$\Pr[T_2 > t_2 \mid H\{\tau(1) + t_2\}] = \exp\left[-\int_0^{t_2} h_2[u \mid H\{\tau(1) + u\}]\, du\right]. \tag{5}$$

By construction, the waiting time for the second birth is $T_2 = \tau(2) - \tau(1)$, i.e., it is the difference between the calendar dates of the second birth and the first birth. At transition time $T(2) = \tau(2)$, the woman conceives again and moves to parity two.

Proceeding in this fashion, $T_3 = \tau(3) - \tau(2)$ is governed by the conditional survivor function

$$\Pr[T_3 > t_3 \mid H\{\tau(2) + t_3\}] = \exp\left[-\int_0^{t_3} h_3[u \mid H\{\tau(1) + u\}]\, du\right]. \tag{6}$$

The conditional density function of duration $T_3 = t_3$ is

$$g[t_3 \mid H\{\tau(2) + t_3\}] = h_3[t_3 \mid H\{\tau(2) + t_3\}] \bullet S[t_3 \mid H\{\tau(2) + t_3\}]. \tag{7}$$

Assuming conditional independence, the conditional joint density of

$$(T_1, T_2, T_3) \quad \text{given} \quad H\left\{\tau(0) + \sum_{i=1}^{3} t_i\right\} \quad \text{is}$$

$$g\left[t_1, \ldots, t_3 \mid H\left\{\tau(0) + \sum_{i=1}^{3} t_i\right\}\right] =$$

$$\prod_{k=1}^{3} h_k[t_k \mid H\{\tau(k-1) + t_k\}] \bullet S[t_k \mid H\{\tau(k-1) + t_k\}] \tag{8}$$

Few Swedish women have more than three births. Accordingly, we do not consider more general models. There is no loss in rigour by focusing solely on the first three birth intervals, integrating out the higher intervals.

If $H\{\tau(j-1)\}$ includes all lagged durations and contains all relevant conditioning information, then conditional independence is a consequence of the laws of conditional probability. See Heckman and Walker (1990*a*; 1990*b*) for more general results.

### Specifying a Model of Demographic Interest: The Relevant Conditioning Set and the Role of Unobserved Heterogeneity

It is natural and, for certain purposes, desirable to equate the relevant conditioning set $H(\tau)$ with the available covariates. An analysis of the relationships between observed covariates and fertility outcomes is the obvious point of departure for any descriptive study of fertility.

The limitations of such empirical relations are well known. It is often the case that analysts and their readers can think of many omitted variables not in the available covariate set that might plausibly affect fertility. The included variables may proxy the omitted variables. The estimated effects of included variables on fertility are inclusive of the effect of the included variables in their own right on fertility and their ability to proxy the omitted variables. These issues are of paramount interest when we wish to use fitted models to evaluate policy interventions that change included variables but not omitted variables. Fitted empirical models may shed little light on the likely effect of such policy interventions.

These issues are central in the analysis of fertility. A long-standing demographic tradition starting with Gini (1924) and continuing with Brass (1958), Sheps (1965), Sheps and Menken (1973), and Menken (1975) postulates temporally persistent female fecundity as an important determinant of fertility. Temporally persistent fecundity differences among women explain declining spell-specific hazards that are a universal feature of fertility data. Despite much careful work (see e.g. Bongaarts and Potter 1983), it is difficult to obtain good measures of fecundity. In most data sets on fertility, there are no measures at all.

The empirical importance of accounting for unobserved fecundity is illustrated in our recent work with Hotz (Heckman, Hotz, and Walker 1985). Models that do not account for unobserved fecundity produce an 'engine of fertility' story: early first births raise the probability of subsequent fertility. Accounting for unobservables, we found that the engine either shuts down or runs in reverse, at least in Swedish data, i.e., early births either have no effect on future fertility or retard future fertility. A naïve reading of the Swedish data suggests that it may be important to prevent teenage pregnancy. Such a conclusion equates a fitted empirical relationship with a valid behavioural relationship. For policy and interpretative analysis, it is sometimes not valid to equate $H(\tau)$ with the available conditioning variables.

It is analytically clarifying to distinguish two different types of unobservables: (*a*) those that are known to the woman being studied and affect her behaviour but are not known to the observing demographer; and (*b*) those that are not known to either the woman being studied or the observer. The latter type of unobservable produces dynamics of its own if the agents being studied learn about their unobservables over the life cycle. It is necessary to account for both types of unobservable to recover the parameters relevant for policy or intervention analysis. We begin our discussion with the first type.

The study of unobservables in multi-state duration models is still in its infancy. The few papers that fit models with unobservables universally assume that unobservables, denoted by $\Theta(\tau)$, can be summarized by a scalar random variable $\Theta$ that is time-invariant with distribution $M(\theta)$. $\Theta$ is often assumed independent of $H(0)$, the initial state of the process. (See, however, Heckman and Singer 1985). The conventional model with unobservables works with densities defined to be conditional on $H(\tau)$ and $\theta$:

$$g[t_k \mid H\{\tau(k-1)+t_k\}, \theta] =$$
$$h_k[t_k \mid H\{\tau(k-1)+t_k\}, \theta] \, S[t_k \mid H\{\tau(k-1)+t_k\}, \theta] \qquad (7a)$$

The conditional density of $T_1, \ldots, T_C$ given $H\left\{\tau(0)+\sum_{i=1}^{C} t_i\right\}$ is obtained from (7a)

by forming an average density, i.e. forming the mean of (7a) with respect to the density of $\theta$:

$$g\left[t_1, t_2, t_3 \mid H\left\{\tau(0) + \sum_{i=1}^{c} t_i\right\}\right] =$$

$$\int_{\underline{\Theta}} \prod_{k=1}^{3} g(t_k \mid H(\tau(k-1) + t_k), \theta) \, dm(\theta) \tag{8a}$$

where $\underline{\Theta}$ is the support of $\Theta$, i.e. its domain of definition.

The two key assumptions in the recent literature—(*a*) that $\Theta(\tau)$ is time-invariant ($= \Theta$) and (*b*) that ($\Theta$) is independent of $H(0)$—are both controversial because it is easy to think of cases where they are false. Assumption (*a*) underlies the classical demographic model of fecundity of Gini (1924), Brass (1958), Sheps (1965), Sheps and Menken (1973), and Menken (1975).

Unobservables unknown to the agent being studied may still be relevant components of model specification. In a study of fertility, it is implausible that individuals know their own $\theta$, at least in making decisions about their first birth. None the less, accounting for $\theta$ is often necessary in order to produce estimates that isolate genuine behavioural effects of covariates on fertility. The existence of unobservables unknown to the woman and the demographer provides a motivation and interpretation for the presence of statistically significant lagged birth intervals in fitted hazard rates for birth parities beyond the first.

A simple example makes this point concrete. Suppose that women deliberately affect their birth probabilities by practising contraception. Let the hazard rate for the $j^{\text{th}}$ birth be

$$h_j[t_j \mid H\{\tau(j-1) + t_j\}, \theta] = c_j(x_j)\theta, \qquad H\{\tau(j-1) + t_j\} = x_j, \tag{9}$$

where $c_j$ is a contraceptive choice component determined by the woman's behaviour as a function of *her* information $x_j$ and $\theta$ is a fecundity component. For parity $j = 0$, it is unreasonable to assume that a woman knows $\theta$. For parity $j > 0$, she may estimate it from her own fertility experience. Specification (9) assumes that fertility densities conditional on $x_j$ and $\theta$ are exponential. Heckman and Walker (1990*c*) find that conditional exponentiality as assumed in this example is a valid description of Hutterite time-to-first-conception data. The relevant conditioning set includes more information than the woman being studied has at her disposal.

Hazard (9) implies that the conditional density of duration $T_j$ is

$$g_j[t_j \mid H\{\tau(j-1) + t_j\}, \theta] = \theta c_j(x_j) \exp\{-t_j c_j(x_j)\theta\}. \tag{10}$$

The goal of policy and interpretative analysis is to recover $c_j(x_j)$ in the presence of $\theta$. To keep the example simple, we assume that the demographer knows $x_j$. In fact, he or she may not, and there may be an additional source of unobservables arising from components of $x_j$ known to the agent but not to the observing demographer. This is the type of unobservable previously discussed.

Assuming that the density of $\Theta$ is $m(\theta)$ and that $\Theta$ is independent of $X_1$, we may write the density of the first-spell duration conditional on $X_1 = x_1$ as

$$g_1(t_1 \mid x_1) = c_1(x_1) \int_\Theta \theta e^{-t_1 \theta c_1(x_1)} m(\theta) d\theta. \tag{11}$$

Elbers and Ridder (1982) present conditions under which $c_1(x_1)$ and the distribution $M(\theta)$ can be identified from duration data even if the functional form of $c_1$ is not known. Failure to control for $\theta$ produces estimated negative duration dependence (i.e., the transition rate to the first birth declines with the length of time a group of women is exposed to the risk of first birth).

Women who experience a first birth may learn something about their $\theta$, and this information might enter their information set and affect contraceptive decisions for the second birth. If women know $m(\theta)$, by Bayes's Theorem

$$m(\theta \mid t_1, x_1) = \frac{m(\theta) g_1(t_1 \mid x_1, \theta)}{g_1(t_1 \mid x_1)} \tag{12}$$

is their revised estimate of the density of $\Theta$. Thus women with short $t_1$ may think they have a large $\Theta$. (For simplicity, we assume that updating occurs only after births are realized. See the more general form of Bayes's Theorem in Shiryayev 1984.) Duration $t_1$ is in the woman's information set for making decisions about $c_2$. So is $m(\theta \mid t_1, x_1)$. Variable $t_1$ may or may not enter $x_2$ in $c_2 = c_2(x_2)$. If $t_1$ is the only new information acquired after one birth, then $x_2 = (x_1, t_1)$ and $c_2 = c_2(x_1, t_1)$. For simplicity, we assume that this is the case.

The density for $t_2$ given $x_1$ and $t_1$ is then

$$g_2(t_2 \mid t_1, x_1) = \int_\Theta g_2(t_2 \mid t_1, x_1, \theta) m(\theta \mid t_1, x_1) d\theta =$$

$$c_2(x_1, t_1) \int_\Theta \theta e^{-t_2 \theta c_2(x_1, t_1)} m(\theta \mid t_1, x_1) d\theta =$$

$$c_1(x_1) \frac{c_2(x_1, t_1)}{g_1(t_1, x_1)} \int_\Theta \theta^2 e^{-\theta \{t_1 c_1(x_1) + t_2 c_2(x_1, t_1)\}} m(\theta) d\theta. \tag{13}$$

The piecemeal empirical approach, which estimates the hazard associated with $g_2(t_2 \mid t_1, x_1)$ without accounting for $\Theta$, cannot isolate the effect of $x_1$ on $c_2$. It does not distinguish the effect of $t_1$ on contraceptive choice in the second interval from the effect of $t_1$ on the conditional distribution of $\Theta$. The latter effect is only a compositional effect, which arises because women with shorter $t_1$ have on average a higher value of $\Theta$. In order to determine if $t_1$ enters $c_2$, ·it is necessary to decompose (13) into its constituent components on the right-hand side.[1] The mathematics that informs us that

$$g(t_1, t_2 \mid x_1) = g_2(t_2 \mid t_1, x_1) g_1(t_1 \mid x_1) = \int_\Theta g_2(t_2 \mid t_1, x_1, \theta) g_1(t_1 \mid x_1, \theta) m(\theta) d\theta \tag{14}$$

does not justify basing policy statements on hazards estimated for the two conditional densities in the middle term of the expression, as has been advocated by

---

[1] Honoré (1987) establishes that $c_1$ and $c_2$ can be non-parametrically identified without any restriction on $E(\Theta)$.

some demographers who feel inconvenienced by having to perform more careful and computationally demanding empirical analyses.

To finish this example, note that (12) is true whether or not the women being studied are Bayesian learners. Values of $t_1$ convey information on $\Theta$, which the women may or may not use. Even if they are not Bayesians, $t_1$ may enter their decision sets because it may affect their resources, states of mind, or reproductive capacities. Even if $t_1$ does not enter $c_2$, it enters (12). Note further that, in formulating the correct likelihood function for the model, it is not necessary to assume that $\Theta$ is independent of the regressors. Obviously, $T_1$ is not independent of $\Theta$. The only requirement is that $\Theta$ is independent of $H(0) = (X_1)$. Note finally that the appropriate density against which to integrate $g(t_2 \mid t_1, x_1, \theta)$ to produce $g(t_2 \mid t_1, x_1)$ is $m(\theta \mid t_1, x_1)$, not $m(\theta)$.

## Dangers of the Piecemeal Approach

For the specification of heterogeneity used in the recent literature—$\Theta$ a time-invariant component distributed independently of $H(0)$—we consider the following question. When can one safely ignore (not estimate) the lower-parity hazard rates and still consistently estimate policy-relevant hazard rates for parities beyond the first? To avoid triviality, we assume that the parameters of the lower-parity hazard rates are not known. Piecemeal estimation strategies that analyse one transition in isolation from other transitions are appealing because they are cheap to implement. Yet, in the presence of unobservables, this strategy generally produces biased and inconsistent estimates of the policy-relevant parameters.

We assume knowledge of the complete history of the process up to the survey date for each woman in our sample. Thus we abstract from biased sampling problems and initial conditions problems that are discussed in Heckman and Singer (1985), Hoem (1985), and Sheps and Menken (1973). We establish the following theorem:

> *Theorem*: Under the stated *sufficient* conditions (beyond the assumptions previously made about heterogeneity), the piecemeal strategy produces a valid likelihood for the estimation of structural third-birth transitions if
> (I) $H(0) = H(\tau)$, all $\tau$
>     (i.e. the covariates are time-invariant)
> (II) The distributions of $T_1$ and $T_2$ given $H(0)$ are non-defective (so $\lim_{t_j \to \infty} S\{t_j \mid H(0)\} = 0, j = 1, 2)$) so eventually all women give birth.
> (III) There is no censoring. ∎

*Proof*:
The joint density of $T_1, T_2, T_3$ is

$$g\{t_1, t_2, t_3 \mid H(0)\} = \int_{\underline{\Theta}} g_1(t_1 \mid H(0), \theta) g_2(t_2 \mid H(0), \theta) g_3(t_3 \mid H(0), \theta) m(\theta) d\theta \quad (15)$$

Integrating out $t_1$ and $t_2$, we obtain

$$g_3\{t_3 \mid H(0)\} = \int_\Theta g_3\{t_3 \mid H(0), \theta\} m(\theta) d\theta \tag{16}$$

Valid inference can be made about the third spell using only data on the third spell. ∎

These conditions are rather severe. Assumptions (II) and (III) imply that we observe all transition times for all women. Assumption (II) implies that all women eventually give birth—i.e., there is no sterility or stopping behaviour. (I) rules out time-dependent environmental or developmental covariates. It also rules out lags affecting behaviour, as is assumed in Rodríguez *et al.* (1984).

These conditions ensure that all women are at risk for a third birth. The implicit sampling frame is assumed to be of sufficient length to ensure that we observe all first and second spells for all women. Thus the distribution of $\Theta$ for women at risk for the first birth is the same as the distribution of women at risk for the third birth. Since the relevant conditioning set does not change with parity $(H(\tau) = H(0)$, for all $\tau)$, the conditioning set for the third birth is independent of $\Theta$. There is thus no selective attrition of women from the sample, and there is no spurious feedback from $\Theta$ to variables in the conditioning set because the conditioning set is fixed and independent of $\Theta$. This rules out any learning by women or any other feedback from previous outcomes to current decisions.

Bayes's Theorem reveals that information about $t_1$ and $t_2$ gives information about $\Theta$. Thus for density $m(\theta)$,

$$m\{\theta \mid t_1, t_2, H(0)\} = \frac{m(\theta) g_1(t_1 \mid H(0), \theta) g_2(t_2 \mid H(0), \theta)}{\int_\Theta g_1(t_1 \mid H(0), \theta) g_2(t_2 \mid H(0), \theta) m(\theta) d\theta}. \tag{17}$$

As previously noted, agents might utilize information about lagged birth intervals in making estimates of $\Theta$ and decisions about third births. Then the information set $H\{\tau(2)\}$ would depend on $t_1$ and $t_2$ and assumption (I) would be false. If $\Theta$ were known to the agent but not to the observing statistician, there would be no such learning, so (I) might still be true.

An instructive alternative derivation of our theorem starts with (17) and $g_3(t_3 \mid H(0), \theta)$ and derives the marginal distribution of $T_3$ by integrating out $t_1$ and $t_2$. Thus

$$g_3\{t_2 \mid H(0)\} =$$

$$\int_0^\infty \int_0^\infty \int_\Theta g_3\{t_3 \mid H(0), \theta\} m\{\theta \mid t_1, t_2, H(0)\} g\{t_1, t_2 \mid H(0)\} d\theta dt_1 dt_2 =$$

$$\int_\Theta g_3\{t_3 \mid H(0), \theta\} m(\theta) d\theta. \tag{18}$$

Note that we use the fact that the denominator of (17) is $g\{t_1, t_2 \mid H(0)\}$. As long as the relevant third-birth conditioning set $H(\tau) = H(0)$ for all $\tau$, and the limits of integration for $t_1$ and $t_2$ are between 0 and $\infty$, the durations of previous spells and their distributions are irrelevant for constructing the density for the third birth.

The theorem fails if these conditions are not satisfied. Thus, if $H(\tau) \neq H(0)$ in the third-birth conditioning set, $t_1$ and $t_2$ enter the conditioning set of $g_3[t_3 \mid H\{\tau(2)\}, \theta]$ since $\tau(2) = \tau(0) + t_1 + t_2$. The distribution no longer separates, and the integration must account for the conditioning arguments. If the data are censored so $t_1 + t_2 + t_3 \leqslant c$, the distributions of the first two spells enter the construction of the marginal density of $t_3$. If the conditional distributions of $T_1$ and $T_2$ are defective, then the third line in equation (18) no longer holds and instead becomes

$$\int_\Theta g_3(t_3 \mid H(0), \theta) \left[ \int_0^\infty \int_0^\infty g_2\{t_2 \mid H(0), \theta\} g_1\{t_1 \mid H(0), \theta\} dt_1 dt_2 \right] m(\theta) d\theta \quad (19)$$

where the term in square brackets does not equal 1 and in general depends on the parameters of $g_2$ and $g_1$. A necessary and sufficient condition for the piecemeal estimation strategy to be based on the correct third-birth spell likelihood is that

$$m\{\theta \mid t_1, t_2, H(\tau_2)\} = m(\theta)$$

so the population density of fecundity $\theta$ ('heterogeneity') for women *at risk* for the third birth is the same as the initial population density $\theta$. If this condition is satisfied, the model may have time-varying variables and defective distributions.

We now make these observations somewhat more precise.

*Defective distributions.* If the densities of either $t_1$ and $t_2$ are defective and either

$$\int_0^\infty g_1\{t_1 \mid H(0), \theta\} dt_1 = K_1\{H(0), \theta\}$$

or                                                                                          (20)

$$\int_0^\infty g_2\{t_2 \mid H(0), \theta\} dt_2 = K_2\{H(0), \theta\}$$

depends on $\theta$, then

$$\int g\{t_1, t_2, t_3 \mid H(0)\} dt_1 dt_2 = \int_\Theta K_1\{H(0), \theta\} K_2\{H(0), \theta\} g_3(t_3 \mid H(0), \theta) m(0) d\theta \quad (21)$$

and the parameters of the $K_i$ functions fundamentally enter the construction of the marginal density of $T_3$.[2]

In the absence of $\theta$ in the first two densities, and in the absence of any restrictions connecting the parameters of $g_3$ with those of $g_1$ and $g_2$, the model separates, and factors $K_1\{H(0)\}$ and $K_2\{H(0)\}$ can be ignored in obtaining consistent estimates of the parameters of $g_3$ using maximum likelihood.

*Censoring.* If the observations are censored so $t_1 + t_2 + t_3 \leqslant c$, then integrating out $t_1$ and $t_2$ in the joint density produces

---

[2] The interchange of integrals is justified by Tonelli's theorem.

$$\int_0^{c-t_3} \int_0^{c-t_2-t_3} g\{t_1, t_2, t_3 \mid H(0)\}\, dt_1 dt_2 =$$

$$\int_\Theta G_1\{c-t_2-t_3 \mid H(0), \theta\}\, G_2\{c-t_3 \mid H(0), \theta\}\, g_3\{t_3 \mid H(0), c, \theta\}\, m(\theta)\, d\theta \quad (22)$$

where $G_i$ is the *cdf* of $T_i$. As in the defective case, the analyst must take account of the parameters of previous spell densities in analysing third-spell data. Now, however, even if $\theta$ does not appear in $G_1$ and $G_2$, and there are no parameter restrictions connecting $G_3$ with $G_1$ and $G_2$, account must be taken of the first two spell densities in constructing the correct likelihood for the marginal third spell.

*Time-dependent conditioning sets.* If attention focuses on estimating $g_3\{t_3 \mid H\{\tau(2) + t_3\}, \theta)$, and if $H\{\tau(2)\}$ is a non-trivial function of $\tau(2)$ (so $\tau(2)$ determines the conditioning set for the third spell), and if $\theta$ determines $g_1$ and/or $g_2$, an additional complication, first noted by Chamberlain (1985), precludes conditioning on $H(\tau(2) + t_3)$ in constructing the marginal third-spell density without adjusting for the effect of the past history on the distribution of $\Theta$. The conditioning set in this case is determined by the outcomes of the preceding spells, which depend, in part, on $\Theta$. The marginal density of $\Theta$ conditional on $H\{\tau(2)\}$

$$m[\theta \mid H\{\tau(2)\}] \quad (23)$$

is not the same as the marginal population density of $\theta$, $m(\theta)$. The third-spell density is

$$g_3[t_3 \mid H\{\tau(2) + t_3\}] =$$

$$\int g_3[t_3 \mid H\{\tau(2) + t_3\}, \theta]\, m[\theta \mid H\{\tau(2)\}\, d\theta] \quad (24)$$

By Bayes's Theorem,

$$m[\theta \mid H\{\tau(2)\}] = \frac{m(\theta)\, g_1[t_1 \mid H\{\tau(0) + t_1\}, \theta]\, g_2[t_2 \mid H\{\tau(1) + t_2\}, \theta]}{\int_\Theta g_1(t_1 \mid H(\tau(0) + t_1), \theta)\, g_2(t_2 \mid H(\tau(0) + t_1 + t_2), \theta)\, m(\theta)\, d\theta} \quad (25)$$

where $\tau(2) = \tau(0) + t_1 + t_2$. The parameters of $g_1$ and $g_2$ enter the construction of the marginal third-spell distribution in a fundamental way. Provided that interest centres on estimating $g_3[t_3 \mid H\{\tau(2) + t_3\}, \theta]$, one must account for the influence of the preceding spells on the sampled distribution.

An alternative consistent estimation strategy to the piecemeal approach is to estimate the model recursively: (*a*) estimate the parameters of $g_1$ from data on $T_1$; (*b*) fixing those parameters, form the correct marginal density of $T_2$, etc. Provided that the first-stage estimators are consistent and estimation error is accounted for in computing standard errors, one can use the constructed marginal density accounting for dependence on the past to estimate the parameters of $g_3$.

In unpublished work, Heckman, Hotz, and Walker have implemented this strategy with mixed success.[3]

## Empirical Specification

In this chapter, we approximate the $j^{th}$ conditional hazard using the following functional form:

$$h_j[t_j \mid H\{\tau(j-1)+t_j\}, \theta] =$$

$$\exp\left\{\gamma_{0j} + \sum_{k=1}^{K} \gamma_{kj}\left(\frac{t^{\lambda_{kj}}-1}{\lambda_{kj}}\right) + \mathbf{Z}(t)\beta_j + c_j\theta\right\} \qquad (26)$$

where $\mathbf{Z}(t)$ includes all observed (by the demographer) covariates, possibly including durations from previous spells and spline functions for current duration. Parity-dependence is incorporated by allowing coefficients to bear parity-specific subscripts.

There are several reasons for incorporating duration-dependence into the hazard even given $\theta$. The waiting time from the onset of menstruation to first conception and the higher-order waiting times are convolutions of underlying component distributions.[4] A conception is followed by a gestation period that is followed by a period of post-partum amenorrhoea before the transition to the next conception. The time to the first birth is a convolution of time from menarche to exposure to pregnancy (marriage or cohabitation) and the waiting time to pregnancy given exposure. Positive duration-dependence is produced when the component processes have non-negative duration-dependence.

Hazard specification (26) encompasses a variety of widely used models. Setting $\beta = 0$, and $K = 1$, and $c_j = 0$ (26) specializes to a Weibull model if $\lambda_{1j} = 0$, to a Gompertz hazard if $\lambda_{1j} = 1$, and to a quadratic model if $K = 2$ and $\lambda_{1j} = 1$ and $\lambda_{2j} = 2$. An exponential model is produced if $K = 0$. Because many conventional duration models are nested within this framework, it is often possible to use likelihood ratio procedures to test competing specifications. Specification (26) also extends previous models by allowing for general time-varying covariates and by introducing unobserved heterogeneity component $\theta$ that is correlated across spells. Permitting the $c_j$ to vary by parity allows the scalar unobservable to play a different role in different transition densities.

In our empirical work, we estimate distribution $M(\theta)$ by the non-parametric maximum-likelihood estimation (NPMLE) procedure described in Heckman and Singer (1984). This procedure approximates any distribution function of unobservables with a finite mixture distribution. Thus we estimate $(p_i, \theta_i)_{i=1}^{I}$ where

---

[3] Note, however, that stronger identifiability conditions are required to implement this piecemeal recursive approach than if joint estimation is performed. Honoré (1987) demonstrates how access to multiple spells of data on the same person weakens the identifiability requirements that must be imposed to identify single-spell models.

[4] We assume the components are independently distributed.

$p_i$ is the weight placed on $\theta_i$, the $\theta_i$ are ordered from lowest to highest, and $\sum_{i=1}^{I} p_i = 1$. $I$ is estimated along with the other parameters of the model. Under conditions specified in Heckman and Singer (1984), the estimated empirical distribution function converges in distribution to $M(\theta)$ at all points of continuity of the latter as the sample size increases. It is the likelihood maximizing approximation to the true distribution.

A useful feature of the Heckman–Singer NPMLE is that it allows for the possibility of point mass at $\theta = -\infty$. For the transition to the first birth, such a value of $\theta$ implies (for $c_1 > 0$) that the proportion of the population having this value is the proportion having no births. A value of $\theta = -\infty$ sets hazard (26) to zero and captures permanent biological or behavioural sterility. In Heckman and Walker (1987) we extend this feature of the NPMLE to a multi-state setting and allow for stopping behaviour at all birth parities.

The survivor function utilized in our empirical work is based on hazard (26). The survivor function for the $j^{th}$ birth is

$$S_j(t_j \mid H(t_j), \theta) = P^{(j-1)}$$
$$+ (1 - P^{(j-1)}) \exp\left[ -\int_0^{t_j} h_j\{u \mid H(u), \theta\} \, du \right], \quad j = 1, 2, 3 \qquad (27)$$

where $P^{(j-1)} = \Pr(\Theta = -\infty)$. The proportion of those at risk for a $j^{th}$ birth who never attain parity $j$, given $\theta$, is

$$\lim_{t \to \infty} S_j(t \mid H(t), \theta) = P^{(j-1)}$$
$$+ (1 - P^{(j-1)}) \exp\left[ -\int_0^{\infty} h_j\{u \mid H(u), \theta\} \, du \right]. \qquad (28)$$

Although it is in principle possible to parameterize $P^{(j-1)}$ to depend on regressors (see Heckman and Walker 1987), we do not do so in this paper.

Collecting all of these ingredients, the contribution to sample likelihood of a woman with fertility history $T_1 = t_1, T_2 = t_2, T_3 = t_3$, sampled with an incomplete $k + 1^{st}$ spell exceeding $\bar{t}_{k+1}$, is

$$\sum_{i=1}^{I} \prod_{j=1}^{k} \left[ \frac{-\partial \ln S_j\{t_j \mid H(t), \theta_i\}}{\partial t_j} \right] S_j(t_j \mid H(t), \theta_i) S_{k+1}(\bar{t}_{k+1} \mid H(t), \theta_i) p_i \qquad (29)$$

using hazard (26) to form survivor function (27). We estimate the parameters $\omega_j = (\gamma_{0j}, \gamma_{kj}(k = 1, \ldots, K), \beta_j, c_j, p_i, \theta_i, I), j = 1, \ldots, C$. We normalize $c_1 = 1$ and observe that for $j = 1, p^{(0)} = \Pr(\Theta = -\infty)$. Estimated model parameters are consistent under conditions specified in Heckman and Singer (1984) and Honoré (1987). A general multi-state computer program, CTM, is used to estimate the model. (See Yi, Walker, and Honoré 1987, and Heckman and Walker 1987). Parametric versions of this model were introduced in Flinn and Heckman (1982; 1983).

## Model Selection Criteria

Hazard (26) produces a variety of models. How should one select among alternative models? Conventional statistical-model selection procedures based on ranking models by their likelihood values require that all competing specifications be nested versions of a general model. Classical likelihood ratio tests cannot be used to select among non-nested models. Many plausible candidate models generated by hazard (26) are not nested. For example, a quadratic hazard model ($K = 2, \lambda_{1j} = 1, \lambda_{2j} = 2$) and a Weibull model ($K = 1, \lambda_{1j} = 0$) are not nested because the Weibull cannot be obtained from the quadratic by 'zeroing out' certain coefficients of variables in the quadratic specification.

Unfortunately, little is known about non-nested model selection. What is known is that ranking non-nested models on the basis of likelihood values rewards complex models with many parameters that may do very poorly when measured by predictive criteria such as out-of-sample forecasts. Based on this observation, several procedures have been advocated in the recent literature. Schwarz (1978) presents a large sample model selection criterion for selecting the best member of an exponential model that penalizes models with many parameters. His procedure is not applicable here because hazard (26) generates models outside the exponential family. However, we use the Schwartz metric as one widely used criterion of model selection that has the virtue of penalizing complex models.

An *ad hoc* model selection criterion uses computational cost or computational complexity as the metric by which to evaluate competing model specifications, ignoring fit altogether. This criterion is more often applied across studies than within a given study. Judgements about computational complexity are based on the availability of computing resources as well as on previous computing experience. It is a myopic criterion in light of the steady advance of computing power.

We also follow demographic tradition (e.g. Majumdar and Sheps 1970) and use $\chi^2$ goodness-of-fit tests to examine how well alternative models predict fertility attained at various ages (20, 25, 30, 35). $\chi^2$ can be defended as a conventional metric that provides cell-by-cell information about the empirical success of any candidate specification. To define the test statistic, let $\hat{P}_j(\tau)$ denote the predicted proportion at parity $j$ ($j = 0, 1 \ldots, C$) by exposure length $\tau$; and let $P_j(\tau)$ denote its observed sample counterpart. The test statistic is

$$R(\tau) = N \sum_{j=0}^{C} \frac{\{\hat{P}_j(\tau) - P_j(\tau)\}^2}{\hat{P}_j(\tau)}$$

where $N$ is the sample size. Under conditions specified in Heckman (1984), $R(\tau)$ has an asymptotic $\chi^2$ distribution with $C - 1$ degrees of freedom. Single-cell tests are asymptotically distributed as $\chi^2$ with one degree of freedom. In large samples the true model is the best-fitting one, provided that proper account is taken of the effect of parameter estimation on the distribution of $\chi^2$ and the regressors are exogenous. Using each of our fitted models, we predict the expected number of conceptions for each woman with exposure to pregnancy of time $\tau$. By evaluating alternative models by their ability to predict births at a given age, we use a different dependent variable (counts or parity) than is used to fit the model (durations). In a parametric model that does not fully saturate the data, this evaluation strategy is a more stringent test of competing models than would be obtained by using the same dependent variable both to fit and to evaluate competing specifications of the underlying stochastic process.

We employ three additional model selection criteria: (*a*) stability of estimated parameters across cohorts, (*b*) evaluation of the aggregate time-series properties of a fitted micro-model, and (*c*) the Schwarz (1978) criterion, to rank models.

Parameter stability is evidence of the explanatory power of a model. Tests based on the aggregate time-series properties of fertility rates generated by an aggregated micro-model provide an independent check on the adequacy of a fitted micro-duration model. Like the $\chi^2$ test, tests of the time-series properties of an aggregated micro-model offer evidence on the fit of a model in a metric other than the one used to estimate the model. We test if the differences between sample and predicted annual birth rates are serially correlated. Evidence that they are indicates model misspecification. The Schwartz criterion penalizes models with many parameters. It favours parsimony over fit and can be shown to produce a 'correct' model under certain conditions.

To obtain predicted annual birth rates for a cohort to perform the time series tests, we integrate the estimated birth-process model over the sample period using each individual's observed regressor path. We produce calendar year rates for each woman using the date of onset of the process, her previous birth intervals, and incomplete current spells to bring her to the current year. We sum these individual rates over all members of the cohort to produce an estimated aggregate rate.

Let $\tau[k]$ denote the calendar date of the $k^{\text{th}}$ birth, with $\tau[0]$ equal to the calendar date of the initiation of the process. For expositional convenience, assume that the process starts at calendar time zero ($\tau[0] = 0$). The probability that woman $i$, with observed covariate path $\mathbf{Z}$, will have a birth at calendar time $\mathbf{Z}$ is

$$\bar{B}_i(\tau) = P(\text{woman } i \text{ has a birth at calendar time } \tau \mid \mathbf{Z}) =$$

$$\sum_{k=1}^{3} h_k(\tau - \tau[k-1] \mid \mathbf{Z}) \bullet P_{k-1}(\tau \mid \mathbf{Z}) \tag{30}$$

where $h_k(\tau - \tau[k-1] \mid \bullet)$ is the occurrence rate of a birth of order $k$ at duration $\tau - \tau[k-1]$ and $P_{k-1}(\tau \mid \bullet)$ is the probability that the woman is at risk of a birth of order $k$ at calendar time $\tau$ conditional on the observed covariate path. We use the identity that calendar time at age $\tau = 0$ plus the sum of previous birth intervals and the current incomplete interval gives the current calendar year at which we evaluate the birth rate. We also assume that few women have more than three births.

Aggregate birth rates are reported on an annual basis. The hazard rate is defined at a point in time for each individual in a cohort. For each person we aggregate the predicted instantaneous rates into annual rates. Summation of the individual predicted birth rates yields the predicted annual birth rate for the cohort.

Evaluating the probability that a woman is at risk for the $k^{th}$ birth is computationally demanding but is required for both the $\chi^2$ and time-series specification tests. Knowledge of this probability enables us to compute expected durations in states and all the other summary statistics of the fitted life cycle model that are reported below. The probability at time $\tau$ that a woman is at risk for the $k^{th}$ birth is:

$$P_k(\tau \mid \bullet) = \int_0^\tau \cdots \int_0^{\tau - \sum_{l=1}^{k-3} u_l} \int_0^{\tau - \sum_{l=1}^{k-2} u_l} \left[ \prod_{l=1}^{k-1} g(u_l \mid \bullet) \right] S_k \left( \tau - \sum_{l=1}^{k-1} u_l \mid \bullet \right) \left( \prod_{l=1}^{k-1} du_l \right) \quad (31)$$

where $g(t_j)$ is the conditional density function for the waiting time for the $j^{th}$ birth and $S_k(t)$ is the conditional survivor function for parity $k$.

Direct numerical integration of expressions such as equation (31) is prohibitively costly. We use Monte Carlo procedures to replicate each individual's fertility history using the estimated birth process model and the individual's observed covariate path. Lagged durations are integrated out. The replications are then averaged to obtain the individual's predicted period-specific birth rates. We determined that, after 100 replications per individual, the first three decimal places do not change in estimating the cohort's parity probabilities $P_k(\tau \mid \bullet)$, $k = 0, 1, 2, 3$ for ages 20, 25, 30, and 35. For additional details on the Monte Carlo procedure, see Heckman and Walker (1990a).[5]

## The 1981 Swedish Fertility Survey and Institutional Background

In this section we describe the data we analyse. We then present recent policy and demographic trends in Sweden. This discussion provides the context for interpreting the empirical analysis presented in the next section.

---

[5] In the $\chi^2$ test, the predicted parity distribution depends on estimated parameters. Thus we should adjust the test statistics to account for parameter estimation error. Computational costs required to produce numerically stable versions of the estimation error-adjusted test proved to be prohibitive. All the $\chi^2$ statistics reported below do not adjust for parameter estimation error in the fashion described in Heckman and Walker (1987). Using the same data to estimate and test the model biases the conventional $\chi^2$ test towards acceptance (Heckman 1984). Our experience in simpler models suggests, however, that correcting our test statistics for estimation error will not reverse inferences reported below. Similar findings are reported by Heckman and Sedlacek (1985) and Feinstone (1984). An alternative procedure splits the original sample into estimation and testing samples. This procedure avoids the bias towards acceptance induced by using the same data to estimate and test a model. When this procedure is applied to the data analysed in the 3rd section of this chapter, we find no reversal of inference from the $\chi^2$ tests, which do not account for estimation error.

## The 1981 Swedish Fertility Survey

The data used in this study are from the 1981 Swedish Fertility Survey. It is a retrospective survey conducted by Statistics Sweden of native-born Swedish women from the birth cohorts 1936–60. Women are drawn from the Central Population Register by a random sample from five five-year birth cohorts (1936–40, 1941–5 ... 1956–60). The survey instrument administered was a World Fertility Survey questionnaire modified to fit the Swedish context. It contains over 100 questions on life cycle fertility, employment, education, and marital and cohabitational events (consensual unions) as well as social background, current life style, and future fertility plans. The quality of the survey data is generally considered to be good (Hoem and Rennermalm 1985). The number of cases analysed in this chapter and the distribution of births for the first four cohorts (1936–55) are reported in Table 7.1. Less than a third of the members of the youngest cohort (1956–60) have a first birth, and accordingly data from this cohort are not analysed. We include the fourth cohort in our analysis even though it contains few third births.

TABLE 7.1. *Cases analysed and parity distribution at survey date, by cohort.*

| Parity | Parity distribution at survey date | | | |
| --- | --- | --- | --- | --- |
| | Cohort 1 (b. 1936–40) (N = 486) | Cohort 2 (b. 1941–5) (N = 997) | Cohort 3 (b. 1946-50) (N = 1006) | Cohort 4 (b. 1951–5) (N = 1034) |
| 0 | 60 | 114 | 161 | 385 |
| 1 | 74 | 179 | 200 | 280 |
| 2 | 207 | 449 | 474 | 304 |
| 3 | 104 | 207 | 148 | 60 |
| 4 | 29 | 43 | 17 | 3 |
| 5 | 8 | 3 | 6 | 2 |
| 6 | 3 | 2 | | |
| 7 | 1 | | | |

The survey did not gather individual wage and income information. To circumvent this problem, two time-series on wages and income were constructed. The first series uses the real average annual manufacturing male and female wage rates to proxy male income and female wages. Wilkinson (1973) uses these wages in his study of Swedish fertility. The manufacturing wage series is the only gender-specific wage series available from published sources for the entire period under consideration (1948–81). We also constructed a time-series of wages using summary measures of personal tax returns by age and sex for selected years published by Statistics Sweden. Using some interpolation, it is possible to generate a complete age- and gender-specific income series.

## Institutional Background and Recent Demographic and Economic Trends

During the post-war period the trend of the female–male wage ratio in Sweden has been very different from its counterpart in the USA. Real wages in Sweden increased during the post-war period. Over 1950–80, the manufacturing sector real male wages increased by 96% while real female wages rose by 120%. Most of the gain occurred before 1977. Fig. 7.1 plots the female wage as a percent of the male wage for manufacturing wages. By 1980, female wages were 90% of male wages. In contrast, over the same period in the USA, female wages as a percentage of male wages remained roughly constant at 65%. To the extent that child care is a female, time-intensive activity, an exogenously imposed narrowing of wages should lead to a reduction of fertility if the neoclassical economic theory of fertility is correct.

It is plausible that in Sweden the wage process is exogenous to the fertility process. Sweden uses centralised collective-bargaining agreements to set wages

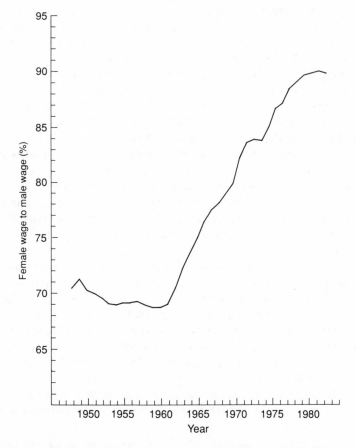

Fig. 7.1 Wages of females relative to wages of males, Sweden, 1948–1982.

and salaries. From the mid-1950s until 1983, industrial wages were set by collective bargaining agreements between the national trade union and the national employers' association. A basic principle of the national collective-bargaining agreements that reflects Swedish egalitarian beliefs is the 'solidaristic wage policy'. Developed by the national trade union, it became part of the national agreement in the late 1950s. The essence of wage solidarity is 'equal pay for equal work—workers performing the same job are expected to receive the same wage, irrespective of interfirm or interindustry differences in productivity and profitability' (Flanagan 1987). Operationally, this has meant increasing the wage of low-productivity workers (primarily women) while moderating wage increases for high-productivity workers in profitable industries.

The implementation of the solidaristic wage policy into national collective-bargaining agreements accounts for the increasing relative wage rates of women in Sweden. Note in Fig. 7.1 that the gain in relative female wages occurs after 1960. Bjorklund (1986) and Flanagan (1987) argue that the solidaristic wage policy has been effective in compressing all aspects of the wage structure (e.g. age, experience, gender, education, and industry differentials) since the mid-1960s. These studies have two important implications for the empirical work presented here. First, they imply that the change in relative female wages was due to an exogenous, institutional force. Second, they lend credibility to our use of aggregate wages in an analysis of individual fertility histories, since aggregate wage policy, uniformly applied, accounts for much of the wage growth of individuals.

In addition to the changing relative wage trend since the Second World War, Sweden has been active in implementing a broad range of social policies. For example, it has been at the forefront of providing child care benefits to allow women equal opportunity in the labour market. These programmes have been explicitly work-conditioned, with benefits replacing labour earnings for a considerable period of time following the birth of a child. Such programmes apply to women at all parities considered in this chapter. An important feature of Sweden's other social programmes is that, with few exceptions, they are not means-tested.

Concurrent with the increasing level of real wages are several demographic trends. The female labour force participation rate has risen dramatically, especially since 1960. For women in the prime child-bearing ages (25–34), female labour force participation rose from 55.2% in 1963 to 81.3% in 1980.[6] Only teenagers and 'retirees' (those aged 65–75) exhibited lower female participation rates in 1980 than in 1963. Male labour force participation rates decreased for teenagers and for men near retirement (aged 55–64). Rates for other male age groups remained constant.

Family formation patterns have also changed as women in successively later cohorts delay entry into their first marriage. An interesting phenomenon is that

---

[6] See Table 14(*c*) of Gladh and Gustafsson (1981). For the same period, married female participation rates increased from 48.7% to 78.1%.

young women are substituting consensual unions for marriage (Hoem and Rennermalm 1985). Moreover, women of the younger cohorts form these unions at younger ages than did their counterparts in earlier cohorts.[7]

TABLE 7.2. *Proportion achieving parties two and three by age and cohort.*

| Age | Cohort 1 (b. 1936–40) | Cohort 2 (b. 1941–5) | Cohort 3 (b. 1946–50) | Cohort 4 (b. 1951–5) |
|-----|-----|-----|-----|-----|
| | I. *Proportion achieving parity two* | | | |
| 25 | 0.260 | 0.282 | 0.275 | 0.213 |
| 30 | 0.568 | 0.564 | 0.562 | |
| | II. *Proportion achieving parity three* | | | |
| 25 | 0.057 | 0.049 | 0.047 | 0.025 |
| 30 | 0.181 | 0.151 | 0.131 | |

Changes in fertility behaviour are summarized in Table 7.2. Section I reports the proportion of women of at least parity two by age and cohort. Section II reports the same information for parity three. From Section I, the time to the second birth is stable for the first three cohorts (women born 1936–50). This evidence suggests that women in Cohorts 2 and 3 have their first two children earlier than women in Cohort 1 (compare proportions at age 25). There is a noticeable decline in the proportion having the first two births for the youngest cohort.

From Section II of Table 7.2, it can be seen that the incidence of third births declines across cohorts. At age 30, a smaller proportion of women in each subsequent cohort have a third birth. The decline is most pronounced for the fourth cohort. The proportion of women with a third birth at age 25 is roughly half that of the previous cohorts. A broad characterization of recent Swedish fertility behaviour is one of earlier but fewer births for women born between 1936 and 1950. For women in the youngest cohort, there is evidence of delayed fertility and a hint that there will be fewer third births.

## The Evidence

This section presents results from an extensive empirical analysis reported more fully in Heckman and Walker (1990*a*). We first summarize robust features found in virtually all fitted models, and then present the neoclassical model that satisfies all of our model selection criteria except that of estimated parameter stability

---

[7] Of the 1936–40 cohort, 34% experienced a union by age 20, versus 53% for the 1951–5 cohort. Only 5% of the 1951–5 cohort are married by age 20, versus 17% for the 1936–40 cohort.

across cohorts. We compare these results with those obtained from a conventional demographic model, patterned after Rodríguez *et al.* (1984), that is successful in predicting fertility attained at different ages but is less successful when measured by the other model selection criteria. We then explore the implications of wage and income change for the best-fitting neoclassical model. We estimate models for *times to conception* for four birth cohorts of Swedish women born in 1936–40, 1941–5, 1946–50, and 1951–5. The regressors used in the models reported here are presented in Table 7.3.

TABLE 7.3. *Definition of variables utilized in analysis.*

| | |
|---|---|
| Duration | No. of months/100 spent in the current spell. |
| Male income | Age-specific average annual income in 1970 kronor for males based on Swedish personal income tax returns data. This variable is zero if the woman is single (not married and not cohabiting with a male). Expressed in thousands of kronor. |
| Female wage | Age-specific average nourly wage rates in 1970 kronor for females based on Swedish personal income tax returns data. Expressed in tens of kronor. |
| Urban | A dummy variable = 1 if the woman grew up in an urban area (Stockholm, Gothenburg, or Malmö) of Sweden and 0 otherwise. |
| White-collar | A dummy variable = 1 if the woman's father was in a white-collar occupation when she was growing up and 0 otherwise. |
| Bdur1 | The length of the first conception interval, measured in months/100. |
| Bdur2 | The length of the second conception interval, measured in months/100. |

## Evidence of Wage Effects and Duration Dependence

We fit 148 different models differing in their specification of duration dependence (the $\lambda_{kj}$ in equation (26)), including models with time trends, dummy variables for policy epochs, age variables, and variables measuring marital status. Models are estimated based on each of the female wage and male income variables defined in the second section of this chapter as well as the other variables presented in Table 7.3. In Heckman and Walker (1990a) we present the estimated male income and female wage coefficients for each of these models.

We use current values of female wages and male income, and do not include measures of expected future wages and income despite the importance of such variables in life cycle theory in economics. Our reason for excluding future wages and earnings is a practical one: future female wages and male earnings are highly correlated with current values. Models that include current and future values are numerically unstable and cannot be estimated.

Holding current wages constant, higher future female wages likely increase fertility transition rates (Ward and Butz 1980). Thus our estimated female wage effects probably *understate* in absolute value the effect of higher current wages on fertility transitions, holding future wages constant. Holding current male income constant, higher future male income likely increases fertility transition rates. Thus our estimates of male income effects probably overstate the effect of higher current male income on fertility transitions, holding future income fixed. From a general life cycle perspective, tests (against zero as a null hypothesis) of current female wage effects are biased toward acceptance of the null hypothesis, and tests (against zero as a null hypothesis) of current male wage effects are biased toward rejection of the null hypothesis. Evidence of statistically significant female wage or male income effects contradicts the null hypothesis that the neoclassical model is false.

Since the labour force participation rate of women in Sweden exceeded 85% in 1980 for women in our survey, and since virtually all Swedish women work sometime in their life, we do not interact male income with a dummy variable indicating a woman's labour force status as is suggested by the static Willis (1973) model. (Non-working women are at a corner in their time allocation budget, and male income effects are predicted to be weaker in constrained households.) From a life cycle perspective, Swedish women are interior solutions in the sense of the Willis model because all women work at some time in their life.

In virtually all the 148 specifications we have fitted, we find a negative effect of the woman's wage on the first three transition rates.[8] The negative estimates are statistically significant. Estimated male income effects are generally positive. The estimated male income effect is weakened when marital status is entered as a separate regressor. (Recall that male income is set to zero if the woman is single.) Except for models that include a separate measure of marital status, male income positively affects all transitions, usually statistically significantly so. This evidence from a diversity of models suggests a statistically important role for female wages and male income. An important empirical regularity found in all models with wages and incomes in which parity-specific stopping probability (the $P^{(j)}$) is introduced is that the non-parametric maximum-likelihood estimator converges to a degenerate (one point) distribution. Unobservables correlated across birth orders are not an important feature of modern Swedish fertility data. This finding vindicates the low-cost, piecemeal estimation approach discussed above, and stands in sharp contrast to our evidence for the agrarian communist Hutterite population, in which there is no inequality in resources among families (Heckman and Walker 1987). In advanced economies, socioeconomic variability apparently swamps biological variability. In all models in which non-zero duration-dependence is permitted, we find positive duration-dependence as implied by demographic models that interpret waiting times as convolutions of independent components with non-negative duration dependence.

### The Best-Fitting Neoclassical Model

Table 7.4 presents estimates of a Weibull model ($K_j = 1, \lambda_{kj} = 0$ in (26)) with mover–stayer heterogeneity controls (parity-specific stopping probabilities $P^{(j)}$

[8] Fewer than 3.3% of Swedish women have more than 3 births. Estimates of transition rates to 4th births were numerically unstable. Accordingly, we define the likelihood to apply to 3 or fewer births by estimating transitions through the 3rd birth.

TABLE 7.4. Weibull birth process model with wage and income variable derived from tax tables and only parity-specific stopping as the unobserved heterogeneity control ($K_j = 1$, $\lambda_{ij} = 0$, $j = 1, 2, 3$).

| Variable/Transition | Cohort 1 (b. 1936–40) | | Cohort 2 (b. 1941–5) | | Cohort 3 (b. 1946–50) | | Cohort 4 (b. 1951–5) | |
|---|---|---|---|---|---|---|---|---|
| | Estimate | Std. Err. | Estimate | Std. Err. | Estimate | Std. Err. | Estimate | Std. Err. |
| *1st conception* | | | | | | | | |
| Intercept | 1.0440 | 0.1941 | 1.3680 | 0.1440 | 1.5668 | 0.1625 | 1.4911 | 0.2201 |
| *Ln* duration | 1.9203 | 0.2521 | 2.3907 | 0.1980 | 2.0380 | 0.1905 | 2.3097 | 0.2496 |
| Male income II | 1.0850 | 0.0723 | 0.8242 | 0.0467 | 0.9926 | 0.0590 | 0.8809 | 0.0589 |
| Female wage II | −4.7380 | 0.5740 | −3.9623 | 0.3070 | −3.3834 | 0.2729 | −2.6895 | 0.2576 |
| Urban | −0.0361 | 0.0947 | 0.0865 | 0.0657 | −0.0482 | 0.0700 | 0.0178 | 0.0922 |
| White-collar | −0.2575 | 0.1015 | −0.1878 | 0.0685 | −0.4230 | 0.0797 | −0.4225 | 0.0939 |
| *2nd conception* | | | | | | | | |
| Intercept | 2.1088 | 0.1852 | 2.3618 | 0.1506 | 2.2872 | 0.1628 | 2.4284 | 0.2447 |
| *Ln* duration | 0.4586 | 0.0701 | 0.6205 | 0.0537 | 0.6177 | 0.0526 | 0.7735 | 0.0810 |
| Male income II | 0.5765 | 0.0961 | 0.6558 | 0.0778 | 0.7708 | 0.0930 | 0.8480 | 0.1229 |
| Female wage II | −3.0311 | 0.4429 | −2.6007 | 0.2650 | −1.9492 | 0.2474 | −1.8167 | 0.2976 |
| Urban | 0.1760 | 0.1123 | 0.2348 | 0.0716 | 0.1830 | 0.0779 | 0.2022 | 0.1231 |
| White-collar | 0.1119 | 0.1170 | −0.0929 | 0.0761 | 0.0546 | 0.0801 | −0.1546 | 0.1316 |
| *3rd conception* | | | | | | | | |
| Intercept | 2.4871 | 0.4181 | 2.5754 | 0.3897 | 2.0369 | 0.5804 | 4.5067 | 0.9231 |
| *Ln* duration | 0.4808 | 0.1377 | 0.4566 | 0.1177 | 0.3796 | 0.1360 | 1.1799 | 0.2415 |
| Male income II | 0.5059 | 0.2705 | 0.2355 | 0.1111 | 0.0623 | 0.1182 | 0.8124 | 0.3116 |
| Female wage II | −4.8733 | 0.9947 | −3.0653 | 0.3752 | −1.9892 | 0.3702 | −2.9032 | 0.8660 |
| Urban | 0.4753 | 0.2108 | 0.0732 | 0.1612 | −0.4042 | 0.1607 | −0.9104 | 0.3647 |
| White-collar | 0.0301 | 0.2218 | 0.1570 | 0.1698 | 0.1357 | 0.1696 | 0.2099 | 0.3523 |

TABLE 7.4. (contd.)

| | Cohort 1 (b. 1936–40) | | Cohort 2 (b. 1941–5) | | Cohort 3 (b. 1946–50) | | Cohort 4 (b. 1951–5) | |
|---|---|---|---|---|---|---|---|---|
| | Estimate | Std. Err. | Estimate | Std. Err. | Estimate | Std. Err. | Estimate | Std. Err. |
| *Estimates*[a] | | | | | | | | |
| $\mu_0$ | *Parity 0* | | *Parity 0* | | *Parity 0* | | *Parity 0* | |
| | −2.3801 | 0.1820 | −2.6004 | 0.1499 | −2.6132 | 0.1811 | −2.0172 | 0.2760 |
| Implied Probabilities | 0.0847 | | 0.0691 | | 0.0683 | | 0.1174 | |
| $\mu_1$ | *Parity 1* | | *Parity 1* | | *Parity 1* | | *Parity 1* | |
| | −1.8403 | 0.1620 | −1.817 | 0.1174 | −1.9005 | 0.1297 | −1.6755 | 0.1854 |
| Implied Probabilities | 0.1370 | | 0.1322 | | 0.1301 | | 0.1577 | |
| $\mu_2$ | *Parity 2* | | *Parity 2* | | *Parity 2* | | *Parity 2* | |
| | −0.4540 | 0.2163 | −0.6603 | 0.2612 | −2.9326 | 3.9330 | 0.1205 | 0.3107 |
| Implied Probabilities | 0.3884 | | 0.3407 | | 0.0506 | | 0.5301 | |
| Log-likelihood | −707.8 | | −1417.8 | | −1189.7 | | −956.6 | |

[a] Stayer probabilities $P^{(j)} = \{1 + \exp(-\mu_j)\}^{-1}$.

TABLE 7.5. Tests of the model in Table 8.4 ($K_j = 1, \lambda_{ij} = 0, j = 1, 2, 3$).

| No. of conceptions | Cohort 1 (b. 1936–40) | | | Cohort 2 (b. 1941–5) | | | Cohort 3 (b. 1946–50) | | | Cohort 4 (b. 1951–5) | | |
|---|---|---|---|---|---|---|---|---|---|---|---|---|
| | Sample[a] | Pred[b] | Test | Sample | Pred | Test | Sample | Pred | Test | Sample | Pred | Test |
| By age 20 | | | | | | | | | | | | |
| $n = 0$ | 0.776 | 0.760 | 0.67 | 0.771 | 0.743 | 4.23 | 0.744 | 0.721 | 2.74 | 0.814 | 0.800 | 1.41 |
| $n = 1$ | 0.161 | 0.163 | 0.03 | 0.170 | 0.189 | 2.51 | 0.178 | 0.208 | 5.49 | 0.141 | 0.160 | 2.77 |
| $n = 2$ | 0.051 | 0.062 | 0.87 | 0.052 | 0.054 | 0.07 | 0.067 | 0.058 | 1.46 | 0.041 | 0.037 | 0.43 |
| $n = 3$ | 0.012 | 0.015 | 0.25 | 0.007 | 0.014 | 3.45 | 0.011 | 0.013 | 0.38 | 0.004 | 0.003 | 0.05 |
| Joint | | | 1.25 | | | 6.60 | | | 6.82 | | | 3.06 |
| By age 25 | | | | | | | | | | | | |
| $n = 0$ | 0.399 | 0.395 | 0.05 | 0.367 | 0.380 | 0.74 | 0.375 | 0.376 | 0.01 | 0.484 | 0.483 | 0.00 |
| $n = 1$ | 0.268 | 0.299 | 2.40 | 0.288 | 0.310 | 2.26 | 0.267 | 0.293 | 3.25 | 0.252 | 0.276 | 2.87 |
| $n = 2$ | 0.247 | 0.230 | 0.80 | 0.259 | 0.234 | 3.56 | 0.285 | 0.258 | 4.10 | 0.222 | 0.203 | 2.66 |
| $n = 3$ | 0.086 | 0.076 | 0.71 | 0.086 | 0.076 | 1.38 | 0.073 | 0.073 | 0.00 | 0.042 | 0.038 | 0.42 |
| Joint | | | 2.94 | | | 6.07 | | | 5.25 | | | 4.54 |
| By age 30 | | | | | | | | | | | | |
| $n = 0$ | 0.183 | 0.149 | 5.05 | 0.173 | 0.147 | 5.44 | 0.183 | 0.181 | 0.03 | | | |
| $n = 1$ | 0.216 | 0.246 | 2.35 | 0.215 | 0.254 | 8.36 | 0.210 | 0.225 | 1.39 | | | |
| $n = 2$ | 0.383 | 0.407 | 1.25 | 0.425 | 0.418 | 0.24 | 0.451 | 0.437 | 0.85 | | | |
| $n = 3$ | 0.218 | 0.198 | 1.24 | 0.187 | 0.181 | 0.34 | 0.156 | 0.157 | 0.00 | | | |
| Joint | | | 7.68 | | | 11.00 | | | 1.56 | | | |

TABLE 7.5. (contd.)

| No. of conceptions | Cohort 1 (b. 1936–40) | | | Cohort 2 (b. 1941–5) | | | Cohort 3 (b. 1946–50) | | | Cohort 4 (b. 1951–5) | | |
|---|---|---|---|---|---|---|---|---|---|---|---|---|
| | Sample[a] | Pred[b] | Test | Sample | Pred | Test | Sample | Pred | Test | Sample | Pred | Test |
| By age 35 | | | | | | | | | | | | |
| $n=0$ | 0.134 | 0.113 | 2.24 | 0.123 | 0.109 | 2.23 | | | | | | |
| $n=1$ | 0.165 | 0.176 | 0.42 | 0.174 | 0.189 | 1.67 | | | | | | |
| $n=2$ | 0.416 | 0.435 | 0.79 | 0.450 | 0.461 | 0.40 | | | | | | |
| $n=3$ | 0.285 | 0.276 | 0.26 | 0.253 | 0.241 | 0.74 | | | | | | |
| Joint | | | 2.94 | | | 4.01 | | | | | | |

[a] Sample probability.    [b] Predicted probability.

$\chi^2$ critical values:

| df | 10% | 5% | 1% |
|---|---|---|---|
| 3 | 6.25 | 7.81 | 11.35 |
| 1 | 1.64 | 2.74 | 5.41 |

Bonferroni statistics:

| 2.5% | 1.67% | 1.25% |
|---|---|---|
| 9.35 | 10.25 | 10.88 |

in the model but no unobservables correlated across fertility spells). Estimated female wage coefficients are negative and statistically significant for all transitions and for all cohorts. The estimated male income coefficients are all positive, and are generally statistically significant. These estimates indicate that higher female wages lengthen birth intervals and reduce fertility. Higher male income increases the rate of arrival of conceptions for all three transitions.

The model exhibits positive duration-dependence in each transition. There is also evidence that women from white-collar backgrounds tend to delay their first birth. For the first transition, the estimated white-collar coefficients are negative and statistically significant. No stable pattern is found in the higher-order transitions. There is little effect of urban background on fertility.

To evaluate the power of this model in predicting fertility, we compute goodness-of-fit tests comparing observed with predicted conceptions attained by various ages. Table 7.5 reports $\chi^2$ tests for selected ages for each of the four cohorts. The first column for each cohort is the observed fertility attainment distribution in the sample. The second column for each cohort lists the predicted fertility attainment distribution. It is followed by the single-cell $\chi^2$ test statistic in Column 3. The joint $\chi^2$ test statistic is listed beneath the single-cell statistics for each age. At the bottom of the table are 5% critical values for one and three degrees of freedom. Because tests within a cohort are not independent, a Bonferroni test is used to evaluate the joint hypothesis that predicted parity distributions fit at each of the selected ages. This test is based on the maximum $\chi^2$ statistic over all age groups for each cohort. The size of the test depends on the number of age groups tested. Four age groups are used for cohorts one and two. Three are used for the third cohort. Two are used for the fourth cohort. To achieve an overall $\alpha\%$ significance level for a group with j age cells requires a significance level of $\alpha/j$ for the maximum test statistic. Thus we require a 1.24% significance level for the maximum for Cohort 4, 1.67% for Cohort 3, and 2.5% for Cohorts 1 and 2.

The models pass the tests at a 5% significance level for all cohorts and at all ages except for Cohort 2 at age 30. In that case, the model under-predicts the number of childless women. For all other ages and cohorts, the test statistics indicate that the models are consistent with the data. Moreover, 5% Bonferroni tests are passed by the estimated models for Cohorts 1, 3, and 4. The model for the Cohort 2 is barely rejected; the test statistic at age 30 is 11.0; the critical value is 10.9. The neoclassical model presented in Table 7.5 is the only model with female wages and male incomes of all those summarized in Heckman and Walker (1990*a*) that passes the goodness-of-fit tests for all but Cohort 2.

The upper panel of Table 7.6 (labelled the 'Neoclassical model') presents an analysis of the residuals formed by subtracting predicted annual birth rates from sample annual birth rates. (Birth rates are obtained by shifting conception rates 9 months forward.) Serial dependence in these residuals is evidence of model misspecification. We regress estimated residuals on once-lagged residuals. MaCurdy (1986) establishes that, under the null hypothesis of no serial dependence, valid large-sample tests of serial dependence in the residuals can be conducted ignoring the contribution of estimation error to the fitted residuals.[9] Except for the Cohort 2, there is strong evidence that the best-fitting model predicts the level of fertility, since the estimated intercept terms are not statistically significantly different from zero. The estimation metric does not force the residuals to have a zero mean. Only the model for Cohort 2 exhibits first-order serial correlation in the residuals. In other work (Heckman and Walker 1989), we find that aggregating the nonlinear micro-model of fertility to produce aggregate birth rates produces a much better forecasting equation than one fitted on aggregate data.

TABLE 7.6. *Autoregressions of the differences between calendar-year sample and predicted birth probabilities by cohort (standard errors in parentheses)* ($e_t = \alpha + \rho\, e_{t-1} + u_t$).

| | Cohort 1 (b. 1936–40) | Cohort 2 (b. 1941–5) | Cohort 3 (b. 1946–50) | Cohort 4 (b. 1951–5) |
|---|---|---|---|---|
| *Neoclassical model* | | | | |
| $\alpha$ | − 0.001 (0.002) | − 0.118 (0.002) | − 0.001 (0.002) | − 0.001 (0.002) |
| $\rho$ | 0.049 (0.189) | 0.464 (0.185) | − 0.385 (0.218) | − 0.151 (0.277) |
| DW[a] | 2.00 | 1.92 | 1.95 | 2.05 |
| $\sigma$ | 0.009 | 0.01 | 0.009 | 0.007 |
| N | 30 | 25 | 20 | 15 |
| *Demographic model* | | | | |
| $\alpha$ | − 0.002 (0.002) | − 0.001 (0.002) | − 0.001 (0.003) | 0.005 (0.006) |
| $\rho$ | 0.366 (0.181) | 0.655 (0.175) | − 0.057 (0.256) | 1.036 (0.151) |
| DW[a] | 2.07 | 2.00 | 2.00 | 1.34 |
| $\sigma$ | 0.001 | 0.011 | 0.013 | 0.020 |

[a] DW = Durbin–Watson Statistic.    [b] $\sigma = \sqrt{\mathrm{Var}\, u_t}$.

Table 7.7 presents Wald tests of equality of male income and female wage coefficients across the four cohorts. This hypothesis is decisively rejected. We explore this failure of the model in the subsection below on parameter instability across cohorts.

## Comparison with a Demographic Model

Table 7.8 reports estimates of a model with Weibull duration-dependence and parity-specific stopping behaviour ($P^{(j-1)}$ present in the model) but without unobservables correlated across spells. In addition, background covariates and lagged birth intervals are included. The four columns of Table 7.8 correspond to the first four Swedish Fertility Survey cohorts, with the oldest cohort reported in the leftmost column. For each cohort we report the estimated parameters of the

[9] Because our estimated parameters are $\sqrt{N}$ consistent, his results apply. This is true conditional on our maintaining the specification of a degenerate mixing distribution.

hazard for the first three conception intervals. The estimated parity-specific stopping proportions are reported below the estimates of the hazard parameters.

TABLE 7.7. *Wald tests of equality of male income and female wage coefficients across cohorts for each transition*[a].

| Weibull model | $(K_j = 1, \lambda_{1j} = 0, j = 1, 2, 3)$ | | |
|---|---|---|---|
| | Test statistics | Degrees of freedom | Probability |
| *Male income* | | | |
| Transition | | | |
| First | 11.37 | 3 | 0.010 |
| Second | 3.99 | 3 | 0.263 |
| Third | 6.53 | 3 | 0.088 |
| *Female wage* | | | |
| Transition | | | |
| First | 16.38 | 3 | 0.001 |
| Second | 8.45 | 3 | 0.038 |
| Third | 9.46 | 3 | 0.024 |

[a] The Wald tests reported in this chapter are based on the unrestricted estimates and are reported separately for each transition.

All transitions exhibit positive duration-dependence. The estimated slope coefficients are statistically significant at conventional levels for all cohorts in transitions 1 and 2 and for the youngest cohort in the third transition. The background covariates (urban and white-collar), which are included to control for the initial conditions of the process, exhibit little algebraic sign regularity or statistical significance except for the white-collar coefficients in the first transition. For that transition, white-collar background has an estimated negative and statistically significant effect across all cohorts: growing up in a white-collar family lowers the probability of a first birth and increases the waiting time to the first birth.

Lagged birth durations are frequently used as proxies for serially correlated unobservable heterogeneity (see Heckman and Walker 1987). This justification for incorporating lags suggests that the estimated coefficients on the previous spells should be negative. For example, if the unobservable is fecundity, then women with low fecundity will have longer than average spells. A long first spell should be followed by long subsequent spells, and hence a negative coefficient should be estimated in the hazard function. Only in the third transition are estimated coefficients of the previous spell lengths negative. In the second transition, the estimated coefficients for the first spell are positive. These estimated effects are statistically significant for Cohorts 1 and 3. Since all women are assumed to start the fertility process at the same age, the length of the first spell measures the age at the start of the second spell. The estimated positive coefficient in the second transition on the lagged birth variables suggests catching-up

TABLE 7.8. *Demographic birth process model with Weibull duration-dependence, background covariates, lagged duration-dependence, and only parity-specific stopping as the unobserved heterogeneity control* ($K_j = 1, \lambda_{ij} = 0, j = 1, 2, 3$).

| Variable/Transition | Cohort 1 (b. 1936–40) | | Cohort 2 (b. 1941–5) | | Cohort 3 (b. 1946–50) | | Cohort 4 (b. 1951–5) | |
|---|---|---|---|---|---|---|---|---|
| | Estimate | Std. Err. | Estimate | Std. Err. | Estimate | Std. Err. | Estimate | Std. Err. |
| *1st conception* | | | | | | | | |
| Intercept | 0.2219 | 0.0745 | 0.1704 | 0.0529 | 0.4261 | 0.0552 | 0.4927 | 0.0920 |
| *ln* duration | 1.6270 | 0.0983 | 1.5900 | 0.0794 | 1.5762 | 0.0833 | 1.8948 | 0.1353 |
| Urban | −0.0734 | 0.0918 | 0.0807 | 0.0634 | −0.0108 | 0.0772 | −0.0205 | 0.1018 |
| White-collar | −0.2397 | 0.0970 | −0.2145 | 0.0679 | −0.4601 | 0.0893 | −0.5447 | 0.1067 |
| *2nd conception* | | | | | | | | |
| Intercept | 1.2561 | 0.1247 | 1.7142 | 0.1074 | 1.6860 | 0.1209 | 1.9322 | 0.1783 |
| *ln* duration | 0.3732 | 0.0582 | 0.5584 | 0.0523 | 0.6111 | 0.0532 | 0.8075 | 0.0897 |
| Urban | 0.1921 | 0.0992 | 0.2152 | 0.0685 | −0.1307 | 0.0776 | 0.2624 | 0.1213 |
| White-collar | 0.0147 | 0.0994 | −0.0570 | 0.0733 | 0.0591 | 0.0801 | −0.0828 | 0.1322 |
| Bdur1 | 0.2124 | 0.1051 | 0.0182 | 0.0979 | 0.2992 | 0.1069 | 0.2740 | 0.2055 |
| *3rd conception* | | | | | | | | |
| Intercept | 1.4839 | 0.2681 | 2.0301 | 0.2890 | 1.6148 | 0.3933 | 3.4050 | 0.7111 |
| *ln* duration | 0.2735 | 0.1074 | 0.1989 | 0.0955 | 0.1805 | 0.1203 | 0.9456 | 0.2556 |
| Urban | 0.5911 | 0.1914 | 0.0240 | 0.1610 | −0.4028 | 0.1904 | −0.7267 | 0.3486 |
| White-collar | −0.1529 | 0.1934 | 0.2818 | 0.1807 | 0.2006 | 0.2035 | 0.2895 | 0.3832 |
| Bdur1 | −0.1353 | 0.2453 | −1.0541 | 0.2121 | −1.2686 | 0.2570 | −0.8221 | 0.6720 |
| Bdur2 | −0.2427 | 0.0571 | −0.1759 | 0.0340 | −0.0670 | 0.0417 | −0.1408 | 0.0982 |

TABLE 7.8. (contd.)

| | Cohort 1 (b. 1936–40) | | Cohort 2 (b. 1941–5) | | Cohort 3 (b. 1946–50) | | Cohort 4 (b. 1951–5) | |
|---|---|---|---|---|---|---|---|---|
| | Estimate | Std. Err. | Estimate | Std. Err. | Estimate | Std. Err. | Estimate | Std. Err. |
| μ estimates[a] | | | | | | | | |
| $\mu_0$ | *Parity 0* −1.9603 | 0.1379 | *Parity 0* −2.0619 | 0.1009 | *Parity 0* −1.8069 | 0.1033 | *Parity 0* −0.9483 | 0.1109 |
| Implied probability | 0.1234 | | 0.1129 | | 0.1410 | | 0.2792 | |
| $\mu_1$ | *Parity 1* −1.5825 | 0.1330 | *Parity 1* −1.5694 | 0.0967 | *Parity 1* −1.5741 | 0.1061 | *Parity 1* −1.2244 | 0.1383 |
| Implied probability | 0.1704 | | 0.1723 | | 0.1716 | | 0.2272 | |
| $\mu_2$ | *Parity 2* 0.0968 | 0.1467 | *Parity 2* −0.1110 | 0.1364 | *Parity 2* −0.5028 | 0.3091 | *Parity 2* 0.3406 | 0.2493 |
| Implied probability | 0.5242 | | 0.4723 | | 0.3769 | | 0.5843 | |
| Log-likelihood | −860.0 | | −1677.8 | | −1454.1 | | −1118.4 | |

[a] Stayer probability $P^{(j)} = \{1 + \exp(-\mu_j)\}^{-1}$

behaviour. In the third transition, coefficients on previous spell lengths are negative and statistically significant for all cohorts.

The estimated stopping proportions are stable across the first three cohorts for the first two parities (0 and 1). The estimated stayer proportion for the highest parity and third cohort is anomalously low. The long-run proportion of childless women in the Cohort 4 is estimated to be about twice that of the previous cohorts. Delayed first births for this cohort may signal fewer completed births.

To evaluate the predictive power of this model, we compute goodness-of-fit tests comparing observed with predicted parity distributions at various ages. Table 7.9 reports $\chi^2$ tests for selected ages for each of the four cohorts. The first column for each cohort is the observed parity distribution in the sample. The second column lists the predicted parity distribution. It is followed by the single-cell $\chi^2$ test statistic in Column 3. The joint $\chi^2$ test statistic is listed beneath the single-cell statistics for each age. At the bottom of the table are 5% critical values for one and three degrees of freedom. Because tests within a cohort are not independent, a Bonferroni test is used to evaluate the joint hypothesis that the predicted parity distributions fit at each of the selected ages. Critical values are reported at the base of the table.

For Cohorts 1, 3, and 4, the joint test statistics at each age are well under the 5% critical value of 7.81. The joint test statistics indicate that the model does not explain the fertility of Cohort 2 at ages 25 and 30. The model passes these tests at these ages at the 1% level, however. The model fits the third transition rather well; the individual cell tests for parity three reject only at age 20 for Cohort 2 (where there are few births to explain) and at age 30 for Cohort 1.

In results reported in Heckman and Walker (1990*a*), we find that changing any one of the aspects of the fitted specification (deleting previous birth intervals, using other duration-dependence specifications, or dropping the mover–stayer model) produces a model at odds with the data. Models with unobservables correlated across spells are not the best-fitting ones. The demographic specification (excluding wages), with estimates. reported in Table 7.8, is the simplest model that fits the Swedish data in the sense of passing classical $\chi^2$ goodness-of-fit tests. However, Wald tests reject the hypothesis that the parameters are stable across cohorts for each transition, reported in Table 7.10.

The demographic model fails the time-series test of predicting aggregate birth probabilities for more cohorts than does the neoclassical model. The lower panel of Table 7.6 displays the regression coefficients from the regression of residuals from the demographic model on lagged residuals. For three of the four cohorts of Swedish women, there is evidence of statistically significant serial correlation ($\rho > 0$). The residuals from the neoclassical model are serially correlated only for one cohort of women, and the associated P values are much higher for the neoclassical model than the demographic model.

TABLE 7.9. $\chi^2$ Goodness-of-fit tests of the model in Table 7.8.

| No. of conceptions | Cohort 1 (b. 1936–40) | | | Cohort 2 (b. 1941–5) | | | Cohort 3 (b. 1946–50) | | | Cohort 4 (b. 1951–5) | | |
|---|---|---|---|---|---|---|---|---|---|---|---|---|
| | Sample[a] | Pred[b] | Test | Sample | Pred | Test | Sample | Pred | Test | Sample | Pred | Test |
| **By age 20** | | | | | | | | | | | | |
| $n=0$ | 0.776 | 0.795 | 1.15 | 0.771 | 0.784 | 0.99 | 0.744 | 0.764 | 2.08 | 0.814 | 0.826 | 1.00 |
| $n=1$ | 0.161 | 0.146 | 0.86 | 0.170 | 0.154 | 1.84 | 0.178 | 0.175 | 0.06 | 0.141 | 0.133 | 0.54 |
| $n=2$ | 0.051 | 0.046 | 0.31 | 0.052 | 0.048 | 0.42 | 0.067 | 0.051 | 5.36 | 0.041 | 0.036 | 0.68 |
| $n=3+$ | 0.012 | 0.013 | 0.01 | 0.007 | 0.014 | 3.46 | 0.011 | 0.010 | 0.02 | 0.004 | 0.005 | 0.12 |
| Joint | | | 1.28 | | | 5.59 | | | 5.65 | | | 1.43 |
| **By age 25** | | | | | | | | | | | | |
| $n=0$ | 0.399 | 0.416 | 0.59 | 0.367 | 0.401 | 4.83 | 0.375 | 0.384 | 0.34 | 0.484 | 0.484 | 0.00 |
| $n=1$ | 0.268 | 0.289 | 1.14 | 0.288 | 0.294 | 0.17 | 0.267 | 0.293 | 3.21 | 0.252 | 0.267 | 1.06 |
| $n=2$ | 0.247 | 0.216 | 2.82 | 0.259 | 0.224 | 6.80 | 0.285 | 0.252 | 5.81 | 0.222 | 0.204 | 2.28 |
| $n=3+$ | 0.086 | 0.079 | 0.40 | 0.086 | 0.081 | 0.41 | 0.073 | 0.071 | 0.04 | 0.042 | 0.046 | 0.38 |
| Joint | | | 3.73 | | | 8.68 | | | 6.85 | | | 2.44 |
| **By age 30** | | | | | | | | | | | | |
| $n=0$ | 0.183 | 0.181 | 0.01 | 0.173 | 0.169 | 0.08 | 0.183 | 0.186 | 0.08 | | | |
| $n=1$ | 0.216 | 0.244 | 2.02 | 0.215 | 0.254 | 8.18 | 0.210 | 0.221 | 0.74 | | | |
| $n=2$ | 0.383 | 0.395 | 0.33 | 0.425 | 0.399 | 2.90 | 0.451 | 0.430 | 1.83 | | | |
| $n=3+$ | 0.218 | 0.179 | 4.94 | 0.187 | 0.178 | 0.64 | 0.156 | 0.162 | 0.30 | | | |
| Joint | | | 5.79 | | | 8.43 | | | 1.94 | | | |

TABLE 7.9. (contd.)

| | Cohort 1 (b. 1936–40) | | | Cohort 2 (b. 1941–5) | | | Cohort 3 (b. 1946–50) | | | Cohort 4 (b. 1951–5) | | |
|---|---|---|---|---|---|---|---|---|---|---|---|---|
| | Sample[a] | Pred[b] | Test | Sample | Pred | Test | Sample | Pred | Test | Sample | Pred | Test |
| By age 35 | | | | | | | | | | | | |
| $n = 0$ | 0.134 | 0.129 | 0.10 | 0.123 | 0.118 | 0.24 | | | | | | |
| $n = 1$ | 0.165 | 0.170 | 0.09 | 0.174 | 0.180 | 0.27 | | | | | | |
| $n = 2$ | 0.416 | 0.441 | 1.29 | 0.450 | 0.446 | 0.08 | | | | | | |
| $n = 3+$ | 0.285 | 0.260 | 1.69 | 0.253 | 0.256 | 0.05 | | | | | | |
| Joint | | | 2.14 | | | 0.51 | | | | | | |

[a] Sample probability.  [b] Predicted probability.

$\chi^2$ critical values:

| df | 10% | 5% | 1% |
|---|---|---|---|
| 3 | 6.25 | 7.81 | 11.35 |
| 1 | 1.64 | 2.74 | 5.41 |

Bonferroni statistics:

| 2.5% | 1.67% | 1.25% |
|---|---|---|
| 9.35 | 10.25 | 10.88 |

TABLE 7.10. *Wald tests of parameter stability across cohorts 1–4 for estimates reported in Table 7.8.*

|  | Transition | Degree of freedom | Test statistic | Probability |
|---|---|---|---|---|
| All coefficients of | 1 | 12 | 28.44 | 0.0048 |
| parity-specific hazard restricted | 2 | 15 | 51.41 | 0.0000 |
| to be equal across cohorts | 3 | 18 | 102.89 | 0.0000 |
| Tests on lagged birth | 2 | 3 | 4.35 | 0.2264 |
| variable coefficients restricted | 3 | 6 | 18.82 | 0.0045 |
| to be equal across cohorts |  |  |  |  |

The Schwarz criterion penalizes the likelihood for the number of fitted parameters (see the definition at the base of Table 7.11). The neoclassical model dominates the demographic model in terms of parsimony of parameters relative to fit.

TABLE 7.11. *Schwarz criterion of model fit*[a].

| Model | Cohort 1 | Cohort 2 | Cohort 3 | Cohort 4 |
|---|---|---|---|---|
| Neoclassical | − 767.8 | − 1490.3 | − 1262.4 | − 1029.5 |
| Demographic | − 915.7 | − 1739.3 | − 1516.4 | − 1180.9 |

[a] = log-likelihood − $(ln N)/2$ (no. of estimated parameters).

In summary, the neoclassical model fits the data as well as the demographic model in terms of $\chi^2$ measures of fit. Both models exhibit instability of estimated parameters across cohorts. In terms of the Schwarz criterion that penalizes complex models, and in terms of the time-series properties of the estimated residuals, the neoclassical model dominates the demographic model that excludes wages and income.

### Lagged Birth Intervals and Wages: Combining the Best-Fitting Models

The class of best-fitting models contains two members. The models differ only in terms of their regressors. It is natural to ask whether an extended model that nests both is superior in terms of goodness of fit. Somewhat surprisingly, the answer is no.

Estimates for the extended model are reported in Table 7.12. First-transition estimates are identical, as they must be, to those reported in Table 7.4. For the second and third transitions, the estimated coefficients for the economic covariates exhibit the same sign pattern as previously reported. Most estimated male income coefficients are reduced slightly in absolute value, as are the female wage coefficients for the third transition. Introduction of lagged birth variables increases (in absolute value) the estimated female wage coefficients for the second

TABLE 7.12. *Birth-process model with Weibull duration-dependence background covariates, lagged duration-dependence, age-specific wages, and only parity-specific stopping as the unobserved heterogeneity control ($K_j = 1, \lambda_{1ij} = 0, j = 1, 2, 3$).*

| Variable/Transition | Cohort 1 (b. 1936–40) | | Cohort 2 (b. 1941–5) | | Cohort 3 (b. 1946–50) | | Cohort 4 (b. 1951–5) | |
|---|---|---|---|---|---|---|---|---|
| | Estimate | Std. Err. | Estimate | Std. Err. | Estimate | Std. Err. | Estimate | Std. Err. |
| | *1st conception* | | *1st conception* | | *1st conception* | | *1st conception* | |
| Intercept | 1.0441 | 0.1950 | 1.3685 | 0.1444 | 1.5664 | 0.1627 | 1.4915 | 0.2212 |
| *ln* duration | 1.9204 | 0.2512 | 2.3917 | 0.1985 | 2.0372 | 0.1903 | 2.3103 | 0.2513 |
| Male income | 1.0851 | 0.0725 | 0.8248 | 0.0468 | 0.9926 | 0.0593 | 0.8809 | 0.0590 |
| Female wage | -4.7382 | 0.5754 | -3.9630 | 0.3078 | -3.3827 | 0.2731 | -2.6899 | 0.2584 |
| Urban | -0.0361 | 0.0954 | 0.0857 | 0.0657 | -0.0482 | 0.0712 | 0.0178 | 0.0923 |
| White-collar | -0.2576 | 0.1019 | -0.1873 | 0.0684 | -0.4230 | 0.0798 | -0.4225 | 0.0940 |
| Bdur1 | 0.0000 | 0.0000 | 0.0000 | 0.0000 | 0.0000 | 0.0000 | 0.0000 | 0.0000 |
| Bdur2 | 0.0000 | 0.0000 | 0.0000 | 0.0000 | 0.0000 | 0.0000 | 0.0000 | 0.0000 |
| | *2nd conception* | | *2nd conception* | | *2nd conception* | | *2nd conception* | |
| Intercept | 2.2025 | 0.2017 | 2.5379 | 0.1629 | 2.5067 | 0.1843 | 2.5857 | 0.2633 |
| *ln* duration | 0.6506 | 0.0953 | 0.8409 | 0.0823 | 0.8645 | 0.0852 | 0.9824 | 0.1174 |
| Male income | 0.4244 | 0.1109 | 0.5426 | 0.0825 | 0.6927 | 0.0936 | 0.8062 | 0.1236 |
| Female wage | -4.3147 | 0.6229 | -3.6444 | 0.3580 | -2.8944 | 0.3410 | -2.6655 | 0.3992 |
| Urban | 0.1662 | 0.1163 | 0.2079 | 0.0761 | -0.1837 | 0.0825 | 0.1534 | 0.1263 |
| White-collar | 0.0565 | 0.1239 | -0.1122 | 0.0806 | 0.0597 | 0.0864 | -0.1712 | 0.1328 |
| Bdur1 | 0.8722 | 0.2587 | 0.9163 | 0.2247 | 1.0366 | 0.2461 | 1.1680 | 0.3897 |
| Bdur2 | 0.0000 | 0.0000 | 0.0000 | 0.0000 | 0.0000 | 0.0000 | 0.0000 | 0.0000 |
| | *3rd conception* | | *3rd conception* | | *3rd conception* | | *3rd conception* | |
| Intercept | 3.0067 | 0.4706 | -2.5793 | 0.4163 | 2.0603 | 0.5974 | 4.8728 | 0.9617 |
| *ln* duration | 0.4367 | 0.1880 | 0.3609 | 0.1390 | 0.3432 | 0.1607 | 1.0349 | 0.3009 |
| Male income | 0.3709 | 0.3407 | 0.1717 | 0.1195 | 0.0680 | 0.1251 | 0.9042 | 0.3409 |
| Female wage | -4.4546 | 1.0784 | -2.7280 | 0.4970 | -1.8425 | 0.5481 | -2.1571 | 1.2074 |

TABLE 7.12. (contd.)

| | Cohort 1 (b. 1936–40) | | Cohort 2 (b. 1941–5) | | Cohort 3 (b. 1946–50) | | Cohort 4 (b. 1951–5) | |
|---|---|---|---|---|---|---|---|---|
| | Estimate | Std. Err. | Estimate | Std. Err. | Estimate | Std. Err. | Estimate | Std. Err. |
| Urban | 0.4956 | 0.2063 | 0.0140 | 0.1516 | −0.4001 | 0.1601 | −0.9155 | 0.3589 |
| White-collar | 0.0634 | 0.2183 | 0.1305 | 0.1610 | 0.1286 | 0.1703 | 0.1569 | 0.3486 |
| Bdur1 | 0.2663 | 0.5424 | 0.1544 | 0.3610 | −0.0882 | 0.5053 | −0.7708 | 1.0825 |
| Bdur2 | −3.1479 | 0.8375 | −1.5724 | 0.5081 | −0.4852 | 0.6498 | −3.3132 | 1.5610 |
| μ estimates[a] | | | | | | | | |
| | *Parity 0* | | *Parity 0* | | *Parity 0* | | *Parity 0* | |
| μ | −2.3801 | 0.1821 | −2.5996 | 0.1498 | −2.6133 | 0.1812 | −2.0172 | 0.2762 |
| Implied probability | 0.0847 | | 0.0692 | | 0.0683 | | 0.1174 | |
| | *Parity 1* | | *Parity 1* | | *Parity 1* | | *Parity 1* | |
| μ | −1.8692 | 0.1708 | −1.9009 | 0.1217 | −1.9112 | 0.1336 | −1.7814 | 0.2144 |
| Implied probability | 0.1336 | | 0.1300 | | 0.1288 | | 0.1441 | |
| | *Parity 2* | | Parity 2 | | *Parity 2* | | *Parity 2* | |
| μ | −0.8348 | 0.2747 | −1.0608 | 0.4123 | −3.1455 | 5.3881 | 0.0749 | 0.2952 |
| Implied probability | 0.3026 | | 0.2572 | | 0.413 | | 0.5187 | |
| Log-likelihood | −691.4 | | −1402.1 | | −1179.8 | | −949.8 | |

[a] Stayer probability $P(j) = \{1 + \exp(-\mu_j)\}^{-1}$.

TABLE 7.13. $\chi^2$ Goodness-of-fit tests for the model of Table 7.12.

| No. of conceptions | Cohort 1 (b. 1936–40) | | | Cohort 2 (b. 1941–5) | | | Cohort 3 (b. 1946–50) | | | Cohort 4 (b. 1951–5) | | |
|---|---|---|---|---|---|---|---|---|---|---|---|---|
| | Sample[a] | Pred[b] | Test | Sample | Pred | Test | Sample | Pred | Test | Sample | Pred | Test |
| **By age 20** | | | | | | | | | | | | |
| $n=0$ | 0.776 | 0.795 | 1.15 | 0.771 | 0.784 | 0.99 | 0.744 | 0.764 | 2.08 | 0.814 | 0.826 | 1.00 |
| $n=1$ | 0.161 | 0.146 | 0.86 | 0.170 | 0.154 | 1.84 | 0.178 | 0.175 | 0.06 | 0.141 | 0.133 | 0.54 |
| $n=2$ | 0.051 | 0.046 | 0.31 | 0.052 | 0.048 | 0.42 | 0.067 | 0.051 | 5.36 | 0.041 | 0.036 | 0.68 |
| $n=3+$ | 0.012 | 0.013 | 0.01 | 0.007 | 0.014 | 3.46 | 0.011 | 0.010 | 0.02 | 0.004 | 0.005 | 0.12 |
| Joint | | | 1.28 | | | 5.59 | | | 5.65 | | | 1.43 |
| **By age 25** | | | | | | | | | | | | |
| $n=0$ | 0.399 | 0.416 | 0.59 | 0.367 | 0.401 | 4.83 | 0.375 | 0.384 | 0.34 | 0.484 | 0.484 | 0.00 |
| $n=1$ | 0.268 | 0.289 | 1.14 | 0.288 | 0.294 | 0.17 | 0.267 | 0.293 | 3.21 | 0.252 | 0.267 | 1.06 |
| $n=2$ | 0.247 | 0.216 | 2.82 | 0.259 | 0.224 | 6.80 | 0.285 | 0.252 | 5.81 | 0.222 | 0.204 | 2.28 |
| $n=3+$ | 0.086 | 0.079 | 0.40 | 0.086 | 0.081 | 0.41 | 0.073 | 0.071 | 0.04 | 0.042 | 0.046 | 0.38 |
| Joint | | | 3.73 | | | 8.68 | | | 6.85 | | | 2.44 |
| **By age 30** | | | | | | | | | | | | |
| $n=0$ | 0.183 | 0.181 | 0.01 | 0.173 | 0.169 | 0.08 | 0.183 | 0.186 | 0.08 | | | |
| $n=1$ | 0.216 | 0.244 | 2.02 | 0.215 | 0.254 | 8.18 | 0.210 | 0.221 | 0.74 | | | |
| $n=2$ | 0.383 | 0.395 | 0.33 | 0.425 | 0.399 | 2.90 | 0.451 | 0.430 | 1.83 | | | |
| $n=3+$ | 0.218 | 0.179 | 4.94 | 0.187 | 0.178 | 0.64 | 0.156 | 0.162 | 0.30 | | | |
| Joint | | | 5.79 | | | 8.43 | | | 1.94 | | | |

TABLE 7.13. (contd.)

| No. of conceptions | Cohort 1 (b. 1936–40) | | | Cohort 2 (b. 1941–5) | | | Cohort 3 (b. 1946–50) | | | Cohort 4 (b. 1951–5) | | |
|---|---|---|---|---|---|---|---|---|---|---|---|---|
| | Sample[a] | Pred[b] | Test | Sample | Pred | Test | Sample | Pred | Test | Sample | Pred | Test |
| By age 35 | | | | | | | | | | | | |
| $n = 0$ | 0.134 | 0.129 | 0.10 | 0.123 | 0.118 | 0.24 | | | | | | |
| $n = 1$ | 0.165 | 0.170 | 0.09 | 0.174 | 0.180 | 0.27 | | | | | | |
| $n = 2$ | 0.415 | 0.441 | 1.29 | 0.450 | 0.446 | 0.08 | | | | | | |
| $n = 3 +$ | 0.285 | 0.260 | 1.69 | 0.253 | 0.256 | 0.05 | | | | | | |
| Joint | | | 2.14 | | | 0.51 | | | | | | |

[a] Sample probability.   [b] Predicted probability.

$\chi^2$ critical values:

| df | 10% | 5% | 1% |
|---|---|---|---|
| 3 | 6.25 | 7.81 | 11.35 |
| 1 | 1.64 | 2.74 | 5.41 |

Bonferroni statistics:

| 2.5% | 1.67% | 1.25% |
|---|---|---|
| 9.35 | 10.25 | 10.88 |

transition. With wages added to the model, estimated coefficients of the lagged birth variables for the second transition increase and become statistically significant. In the third transition, the inclusion of wages weakens the estimated effect of lagged births, and there are some sign reversals. The estimated wage effects are robust to the inclusion of lagged birth intervals.

Table 7.13 reports $\chi^2$ goodness-of-fit tests for the extended model with both wages and lagged birth variables in the regressor set. The extended model, like its demographic predecessor, fails the joint tests for Cohort 2 at ages 25 and 30. Unlike the best-fitting models, the combined model fails at age 25 for Cohort 3. The combined model fits the third-parity cell at ages 25 and above. Strict application of the $\chi^2$ model selection criteria rejects the combined model as a member of the best-fitting class. The extended model overfits the intra-cohort fertility processes. While the combined model is best in terms of the Schwarz criterion, it fails the time-series goodness-of-fit tests.

## Parameter Instability across Cohorts: Indirect Evidence on Policy Effects

Given the robustness of the sign and significance of the estimated economic coefficients across virtually all specifications, it is natural to ask if the estimated coefficients of the economic variables are stable across cohorts. The coefficients of the estimated birth process measure the total effect, directly through contraceptive choice and indirectly through labour force participations and household formation, of changes in wages incomes and variables on fertility. If the policy environment in which individuals are operating is stable and tastes do not change, the reduced-form coefficients will be stable over time. Evidence of parameter drift can be interpreted as evidence of structural change due to policy or taste change. Wald tests for parameter stability are reported in Table 7.14. Using the tax-table-derived wages and income estimates used to estimate the model of Table 7.4, the estimated male-income coefficients are significantly different across cohorts only for the first transition. Female-wage coefficients are different across all transitions for all four cohorts.[10]

Inter-cohort patterns of estimated coefficients provide indirect evidence in support of policy effects. The pattern of declining coefficients for male income in the first transition across successive cohorts is consistent with the interpretation that women in later cohorts are less dependent on the male's income in initiating the fertility process. Increasing child care benefits, greater female market participation, and later age at first marriage all reduce the dependency of women on male income. These factors may also account for the observed rise in the fraction of women in consensual unions who have lower fertility rates.

---

[10] Inferences about the stability of estimated female-wage coefficients are sensitive to the assumed functional form of the duration-dependence and wage-series used. When manufacturing wages are used in a Weibull model, the female-wage coefficients are not significantly different across cohorts. Similarly, in a model with quadratic duration-dependence and tax-table-derived wages, estimated female-wage coefficients are not significantly different across cohorts. However, neither model passes our goodness-of-fit tests. See Heckman and Walker (1990a).

TABLE 7.14. *Wald tests of equality of economic coefficients across cohorts for each transition: age-specific incomes derived from tax-tables*[a].

| Weibull model | $(K = 1, \lambda_{1j} = 0, j = 1, 2, 3)$ | | |
|---|---|---|---|
| | Test statistic | Degree of freedom | Probability |
| *Male income II* | | | |
| Transition | | | |
| First | 11.37 | 3 | 0.010 |
| Second | 3.99 | 3 | 0.263 |
| Third | 6.53 | 3 | 0.088 |
| *Female wage II* | | | |
| Transition | | | |
| First | 16.38 | 3 | 0.001 |
| Second | 8.45 | 3 | 0.038 |
| Third | 9.46 | 3 | 0.024 |

[a] The Wald tests reported in this chapter are based on the unrestricted estimates and are given for each transition density.

The pattern of declining female-wage coefficients across cohorts is also consistent with the hypothesis of reduced female attachment to the household. During the period of our sample, female labour force participation rates increased, as did work-conditioned child care benefits. Increasing the female wage rate increases the price of child services. The growth in work-conditioned child care benefits makes the measured female wage an increasingly less accurate proxy for the price of time in later cohorts. Concomitant with the rising female wage has been the growth in free day-care centres and public child care benefits, which reduce the cost of child care and offset the increasing cost of the woman's time. These programmes offset the negative effect of the rise in female wages on fertility.

It is useful to perform the counterfactual experiment of predicting the expected number of conceptions for a cohort using the preceding cohort's estimated coefficients and the cohort's own regressors. The best-fitting economic model with coefficients estimates, reported in Table 7.4, is simulated. The second column of Table 7.15 reports the expected number of conceptions by cohort for ages 25–35. The agreement between predicted and sample conceptions (Column 1) is rather close. The predicted numbers of conceptions from the counterfactual simulation are reported in the third column of Table 7.15. Column 4 reports the change in predicted conceptions across cohorts (i.e., Column 4 is the change in predicted fertility from that of the preceding cohort). The last two columns of Table 7.15 present one decomposition of the net changes listed in Column 4. Column 5 reports the net change attributable to the change in coefficients across different cohorts. Assuming that cohort $j$ has the same coefficients as cohort $j-1$, but allowing regressors to differ in the manner found in our sample, we under-predict the number of conceptions experienced by each cohort. The positive net effects reported in Column 4 suggest that behaviour across successive cohorts is becoming increasingly pronatalist. This evidence is consistent with the notion that omitted policy variables have stimulated fertility.

TABLE 7.15. *Counterfactual simulation of expected number of conceptions at the indicated age using cohort-specific birth process estimates of best-fitting economic model.*

| Cohort | Sample values | Predicted using own covariates and estimated parameters | Predicted using own covariates and estimates from preceding cohort | Observed net change between successive cohorts | Net change due to changes in coefficients | Net change due to changes in covariates |
|---|---|---|---|---|---|---|
| | (1) | (2) | (3) | (4) | (5) | (6) |
| Age 25 | | | | | | |
| 1 | 1.040 | 1.061 | — | — | — | — |
| 2 | 1.064 | 1.068 | 0.686 | 0.007 | 0.382 | − 0.375 |
| 3 | 1.056 | 1.073 | 0.662 | 0.005 | 0.411 | − 0.406 |
| 4 | 0.820 | 0.826 | 0.624 | − 0.247 | 0.202 | − 0.449 |
| Age 30 | | | | | | |
| 1 | 1.636 | 1.741 | — | — | — | — |
| 2 | 1.626 | 1.708 | 1.175 | − 0.033 | 0.533 | − 0.566 |
| 3 | 1.580 | 1.617 | 1.042 | − 0.091 | 0.575 | − 0.666 |
| Age 35 | | | | | | |
| 1 | 1.852 | 1.931 | — | — | — | — |
| 2 | 1.833 | 1.879 | 1.366 | − 0.052 | 0.513 | − 0.565 |

The last column of Table 7.15 shows the net effect of wage change across cohorts. Using cohort estimated coefficients from cohort $j$ with the covariate path from cohort $j-1$ greatly reduces predicted fertility. The inter-cohort change in estimated parameters mitigates the negative effect of increased wages. The pattern of cohort drift suggests that the changing policy environment in Sweden has increased Swedish fertility.

## Implications of the Estimates for the Effects of Wage Change on Life Cycle Fertility

Table 7.16 summarizes the effect of changes in tax-table male and female wages on the pattern of life cycle fertility for women in the first cohort. The simulations increase the wage paths facing women and men by 12.2% at all ages. Aggregating the implied life cycle fertility paths across all women and using the coefficients reported in Table 7.4 produces the results shown in Table 7.16. The results reported for women in the first cohort are typical of those found for all cohorts of women when wages are changed in a similar fashion.

TABLE 7.16. *The impact of wage and income change on life cycle fertility.*

|  | Base | Change due to a 12.2% rise in male wage | Change due to a 12.2% rise in female wage |
|---|---|---|---|
| **I** | | | |
| % childless | 10.9 | − 0.40 | 1.5 |
| % having exactly 1 child by age 40 | 15.4 | − 1.10 | 2.8 |
| % having exactly 2 children by age 40 | 44.4 | − 1.70 | 3.4 |
| % having exactly 3 children by age 40 | 29.3 | 3.20 | − 7.7 |
| **II** | | | |
| Predicted no. of children by age 40 | 1.92 | 0.05 | − 0.13 |
| Implied elasticity | — | 0.21 | − 0.55 |
| **III** | | | |
| Mean time in months[a] to | | | |
| First conception (measured from age 13) | 120 | − 3 | 5 |
| Second conception (measured from first birth) | 38 | − 2 | 3 |
| Third conception (measured from second birth) | 44 | − 2 | 1 |

[a]  Evaluated at age 40 for those who experienced the event.

Panel I presents the impact of wage change on the distribution of fertility completed at age 40. This age is near the end of the child-bearing years, and is within the range of data on fertility histories available for the first cohort. There is little effect of wage change on the percentage of women who are childless.[11] The principal effect of wage change is on the third birth. Higher wages for women substantially reduce third births. Higher wages for men substantially increase the proportion of women having a third birth. (Few Swedish women have more than three children, so it is not possible to estimate transition functions to higher parities.) Panel II summarizes Panel I by presenting the impact of wage change on the predicted number of children at age 40. The female wage elasticity is more than twice the male wage elasticity. This finding highlights the central role of female wages on fertility.

Panel III reports the effect of wage change on inter-birth intervals. The strongest impact of wages is on the time to the first birth. This is an effect conditioned on observed marriage or cohabitation patterns, and probably understates (in absolute value) the net effect (allowing marital status to adjust). The effect of the female wage on the time to first birth is especially strong. Higher female wages lead to longer inter-birth intervals, although the effect on the transition time to the third birth is quite weak. These results indicate that the strongest effect of

[11]  The best-fitting Weibull model is not well suited to investigate the effect of wage change on childlessness. This is so because the Weibull model is non-defective—asymptotically the predicted proportion childless is $P^{(t)}$, and we do not parameterize $P^{(t)}$ to depend on wages.

wages is on the postponement of the first birth. However, the simulations reveal some effects of wages on transition times to higher-order birth intervals. Wages affect both the level of births and the rate at which they are achieved.

It is of interest to examine the effect of wage change on third-birth rates by age. Using a discrete approximation to the hazard and survivor functions, the third-birth rate at age $a$, $r(a)$, is

$$r(a) = \bar{h}_3(a)\,\bar{S}(a) \times 1000 \tag{31}$$

where $\bar{h}_3(a)$ is the probability of having a third birth at age $a$ given that the woman has had two births, and $\bar{S}_3(a)$ is the probability that the woman is at risk of a third birth.

TABLE 7.17. *Impact of wage changes on third-birth rates by age.*

| Age | Base third-birth rate per 1 000 | Change due to 12% rise in male wage | | Change due to 12% rise in female wage | |
|---|---|---|---|---|---|
| | | Partial effect | Total effect | Partial effect | Total effect |
| 20 | 0.0 | 0.0 | 0.0 | 0.0 | 0.0 |
| 21 | 0.1 | 0.0 | 0.0 | 0.0 | 0.0 |
| 22 | 0.1 | 0.0 | 0.0 | 0.0 | 0.0 |
| 23 | 0.3 | 0.0 | 0.0 | − 0.2 | − 0.3 |
| 24 | 0.4 | 0.0 | 0.0 | − 0.1 | − 0.2 |
| 25 | 0.5 | 0.1 | 0.2 | 0.0 | − 0.2 |
| 26 | 0.7 | 0.1 | 0.0 | − 0.3 | − 0.5 |
| 27 | 1.6 | 0.3 | 0.7 | − 0.8 | − 1.2 |
| 28 | 2.2 | 0.5 | 1.1 | − 0.6 | − 1.4 |
| 29 | 4.1 | 0.0 | 1.1 | − 1.4 | − 2.8 |
| 30 | 5.1 | 0.7 | 2.2 | − 1.6 | − 3.3 |
| 31 | 7.1 | 1.0 | 2.9 | − 1.3 | − 3.8 |
| 32 | 9.1 | 2.9 | 5.4 | − 3.1 | − 6.0 |
| 33 | 14.0 | 3.9 | 7.1 | − 5.4 | − 8.9 |
| 34 | 16.4 | 4.2 | 7.0 | − 6.5 | − 10.1 |
| 35 | 19.0 | 4.0 | 6.3 | − 7.7 | − 11.3 |
| 36 | 20.7 | 6.3 | 8.0 | − 8.4 | − 11.6 |
| 37 | 23.0 | 3.5 | 4.0 | − 9.1 | − 11.8 |
| 38 | 23.5 | 4.7 | 4.5 | − 9.3 | − 11.1 |
| 39 | 23.9 | 5.6 | 4.7 | − 9.6 | − 10.4 |
| 40 | 22.9 | 6.5 | 5.0 | − 9.3 | − 9.0 |
| TOTAL | | 24.6 | 59.0 | − 74.7 | − 103.9 |

Table 7.17 presents the impact of the wage changes considered in Table 7.16 on age-specific third-birth rates. We decompose the effect of the wage change into a partial effect and a total effect. The partial effect is defined as

$$\Delta_P r(a) = \{\Delta\bar{h}_3(a)\}\,\bar{S}_3(a) \times 1000 \tag{32}$$

i.e., the effect of wage change on the age-specific rates holding constant the population at risk for a third birth. The total effect is defined as

$$\Delta r(a) = \{\Delta \bar{h}_3(a)\} \bar{S}_3(a) + \bar{h}_3(a) \{\Delta \bar{S}_3(a)\} \tag{33}$$

and is inclusive of the effect of the wage change on changing the population at risk for pregnancy. The variations are taken with respect to changes in the wage paths.

The total effect measures the change in age-specific birth rates that results when women of all ages are confronted with a new lifetime profile of wages and adjust their lifetime fertility accordingly. The partial effect measures the short-run change in birth rates at age $a$ when women have responded to baseline wages up to age $a$ and modify only their age-specific fertility at age $a$. It measures the effect of the new wage path conditional on the distribution of people at risk generated by the baseline wage path. The partial effect approximates short-run responses to wage change of the sort observed over business cycles.[12]

The total effect of an increase in male wages is to increase third births and to concentrate age-specific third-birth rates into the age interval 30–40. The partial effect of male wage change is to increase third births at virtually all ages. Note that the relative magnitude of a female wage change on third-birth rates is approximately twice that of a comparable male wage increase. Moreover, for almost every age, long-run impacts are larger (in absolute value) than partial or short-run effects. This is a consequence of the net impact on the lower-order parities; allowing the stock of women at risk for a third birth to adjust considerably augments the short-run effect.[13] These accumulated-stock effects account for 28% of the total impact of female wages on third births by age 40. In order to determine the full impact of economic variables on age-specific third-birth rates, it is important to account for their effect of placing women at risk for a third birth as well as their effect on causing women at risk to have a third birth.

Figs. 7.2 and 7.3 decompose the simulated change in age-specific third-birth rates into components attributable to wage change operating on each of the three parity-specific hazard rates: the hazard rate for time to the first birth, the hazard rate for time to the second birth, and the hazard rate for time to the third birth. Fig. 7.2—for the female wage change—charts the base age-specific third-birth rate ('Base'). The curve labelled '1' displays the effect on the age-specific third-birth rate of changing the female wage profile in the first-birth hazard rate only.

---

[12] The partial effect captures short-run business cycle movements in fertility exactly if agents use stationary (static) expectations to forecast future wages or if wages follow a random walk. Since we cannot estimate a model that distinguishes the impact of changes in current and future wages on fertility decisions, we cannot estimate the full business cycle response. If the female wage is transitorily higher today, it is likely that the decline in current fertility is higher than measured in Table 7.17, since it is plausible that female time is substitutable over time. If the male wage is transitorily higher, it is likely that the partial effect of male wages reported in Table 7.17 overstates the effect of male income on age-specific birth rates because the true wealth effect of a male wage change is small.

[13] Recall that we condition on marital status. A higher male wage is likely to accelerate family formation and shift the unconditional birth rate schedule toward younger ages. A higher female wage is likely to postpone family formation and shift the unconditional birth rate schedule toward later ages.

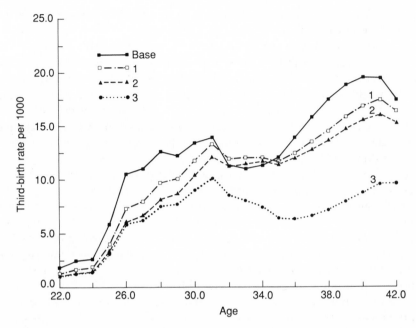

Fig. 7.2 Female wage change.

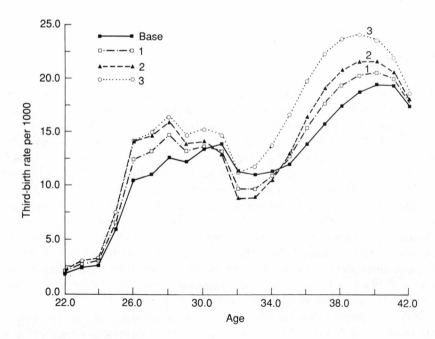

Fig. 7.3 Male wage change.

The curve labelled '2' displays the effect on age-specific third-birth rates of changing the female wage in the first two hazard rates. The curve labelled '3' displays the total effect of the female wage change on age-specific third-birth rates. At later ages, most of the effect of the female wage change is due to the direct effect of the increased female wage operating through the hazard for the third birth, although there is still a non-negligible effect of wage change on the first two hazard rates. At the early ages, a substantial fraction of the total simulated change comes from the effect of female wage change operating through the hazard rate to the first birth and changing the proportion of women who are at risk for a third birth.

Fig. 7.3 records a parallel decomposition for the simulated male wage change. At the early ages, most of the effect of male wage change comes through the effect of male wages on the hazard rate for the first birth. Higher male wages place more women at risk of a third birth. Around age 32, increased male income, operating through the hazard rate for the time to the second birth, actually decreases age-specific third-birth rates. At later ages, wages, operating through the first two hazard rates and affecting the risk, still account for a substantial portion of the increase in age-specific third-birth rates.

These simulations demonstrate the importance of accounting for the history of a birth process in evaluating the impact of changes in socioeconomic variables on third births. Changes that affect a woman's risk of a third birth are an important component of the total effect of changes in socioeconomic variables on third births.

## Conclusions

This chapter considers the formulation, estimation, and evaluation of multi-state models of fertility dynamics. We discuss the role of unobservables in fertility models and the importance of accounting for unobservables in estimating dynamic fertility models that can be used in policy or intervention analysis. We discuss the dangers of piecemeal estimation strategies when serially correlated, person-specific unobservables are present. We investigate the decline in third births for four cohorts of Swedish women. We estimate multi-state birth-process models using a robust semiparametric estimator that enables us to control for time-varying variables, serially correlated unobservables, and general forms of duration-dependence. We find that the piecemeal approach can be applied without danger to the Swedish data. We fit a variety of models to the data, and to evaluate those models we use $\chi^2$ goodness-of-fit tests, parameter stability tests, tests that penalize models with many parameters, and tests based on the time-series properties of the residuals of predicted birth rates.

A demographic model that excludes wages and incomes but includes lagged birth durations, Weibull duration-dependence, and mover–stayer heterogeneity passes $\chi^2$ tests but fails the other tests. A neoclassical model that uses aggregate age-specific male- and female-wage variables in place of the lagged birth variables to fit the cohort-specific birth process performs much better. In Heckman and Walker (1990*a*) we consider a variety of additional tests of the main findings presented here. We find that our estimated wage and income effects are robust to a variety of model perturbations. Of special interest is the robustness to the inclusion of age and time trend variables, and to the introduction of alternative specifications of marital status.

For the model with wages, we find that the estimated wage effects on fertility are statistically significant and economically plausible. Estimated female-wage effects are robust to the inclusion or exclusion of variables measuring the woman's education, marital status, time trends, and policy impacts. We find similar robustness for the estimated impact of male wages on fertility. The strength of the estimated male-income effect is attenuated when marital-status variables are entered as regressors. The best-fitting models exclude marital-status variables. Our results lend support to the claim of economists that wages, especially female wages, play a central role in determining fertility dynamics.

The best-fitting model with wages and income exhibits drift in estimated wage coefficients across cohorts that is consistent with the introduction and enhancement of social programmes designed to promote equality between men and women and programmes that offer work-conditioned child care benefits. The estimated positive effect of male income on fertility diminishes in size in more recent cohorts. This result is consistent with growth in general benefits to women independent of marital status. The estimated negative effect of female wage rates on fertility also declines in more recent cohorts. This trend is consistent with the growth in work-conditioned child care and maternity benefits that offset the impact of wages on fertility.

Simulating alternative male and female wage profiles, we separate the effect of wages on the entry into the risk set of women eligible for the third birth from the effect of wages on the age-specific rate of third births conditional on women being at risk. We find that higher wages for women delay the onset of pregnancy and increase inter-birth intervals. Higher female wages barely affect childlessness, and have their primary effect on reducing third births. When wages are higher, pregnancy tends to be concentrated in a shorter span of the life cycle that starts later in life.

Wages for men have quantitatively weaker effects on fertility than do the wages of women. Higher male wages reduce a woman's time to first birth, reduce inter-birth intervals, and barely affect the proportion of childless women in the population. The impact of higher male wages is to increase the proportion of families with three children and expand the span of years during which women engage in child-bearing.

The direct effect of wages on third births, holding constant the stock of women at risk of a third birth, accounts for 72% of the total impact of a permanent wage change on completed births at age 40. The indirect effect of wages on placing women at risk for a third birth (the stock effect) accounts for the remaining 28%.

An empirical analysis that restricts attention only to third-birth transition rates considerably underestimates the impact of wages on third births.

The robustness of the estimated wage effects on fertility and their interpretative plausibility provide encouraging evidence that improved longitudinal measures of household income and programme benefits will be of great value in predicting Swedish fertility and accounting for cohort drift.

The unimportance of serially correlated unobservables indicates that computationally less demanding piecemeal estimation schemes that ignore the history of the process will yield consistent estimates. Unlike the situation in primitive economic societies like the Hutterites, where serially correlated fecundity differences play a central role in accounting for fertility, in modern Sweden serially correlated unobservables play a negligible role.

This finding is consistent with the greater variability across people in wealth, status, and economic resources in modern societies than is the case for primitive economic societies, where inequality in wealth and resources is much less pronounced. Our suggestion is that, in modern societies, variation in socioeconomic variables may swamp the variation in fecundity in accounting for fertility dynamics.

## References

Bjorklund, A. (1986), *Assessing the Decline of Wage Dispersion in Sweden* (IUI, Stockholm).

Bongaarts, J., and Potter, R. G. (1983), *Fertility, Biology and Behavior* (Academic Press, New York).

Brass, W. (1958), 'The Distribution of Births in Human Populations', *Population Studies*, 12. 1: 51–72.

Chamberlain, G. (1985), 'Heterogeneity, Omitted Variables Bias and Duration Dependence', in J. Heckman and B. Singer (eds.), *Longitudinal Analysis of Labour Market Data* (CUP, Cambridge).

Elbers, C., and Ridder, G. (1982), 'True and Spurious Duration Dependence: The Identifiability of the Proportional Hazard Model', *Review of Economic Studies*, 49: 403–10.

Feinstone, L. (1984), 'Intra-Daily Market Efficiency and Price Processes in the Future Market in Foreign Exchange', Ph.D. dissertation, Univ. of Chicago.

Flanagan, R. (1987), 'Efficiency and Equality in Swedish Labor Markets', in B. P. Bosworth and A. M. Rivlin (eds.), *The Swedish Economy* (The Brookings Institution, Washington, DC).

Flinn, C., and Heckman, J. (1982), 'Models for the Analysis of Labor Force Dynamics', in G. Rhodes and R. Basmann (eds.), *Advances in Econometrics*, iii (JAI Press, Greenwich, Conn.).

—— (1983), 'The Likelihood Function for the Multistate-Multiepisode Model in Models for the Analysis of Labor Force Dynamics', in R. Basmann and G. Rhodes (eds.), *Advances in Econometrics*, iii (JAI Press, Greenwich, Conn.).

Gini, C. (1924), 'Premiers Recherches sur la Fécondabilité de la Femme', *Proceedings of International Mathematics Congress*, 2: 889–992.

Gladh, L., and Gustafsson, S. (1981), 'Labor Market Policy Related to Women and Employment in Sweden, *Swedish Country Report to the Conference on Regulation Theory of the Labor Market Related to Women: International Comparison of Labor Market Policy Related to Women*, IIMVP/LMP, 8–9 Dec., Berlin.

Heckman, J. (1984), 'The $\chi^2$ Goodness of Fit Statistics for Models with Parameters Estimated from Microdata', *Econometrica*, 52. 6: 1543–7.

—— Hotz, J., and Walker, J. (1985), 'New Evidence on the Timing and Spacing of Births', *American Economic Review*, 75. 2: 179–84.

—— and Sedlacek, G. (1985), 'Heterogeneity, Aggregation, and Market Wage Functions: An Empirical Analysis of Self-Selection in the Labor Market', *Journal of Political Economy*, 93: 1077–1125.

—— and Singer, B. (1984), 'A Method for Minimizing the Impact of Distributional Assumptions in Econometric Models for Duration Data', *Econometrica*, 52: 271–320.

—— —— (1985), 'Social Science Duration Analysis', in J. Heckman and B. Singer (eds.), *Longitudinal Analysis of Labour Market Data* (CUP, Cambridge).

—— and Walker, J. (1987), 'Using Goodness of Fit and Other Criteria to Choose among Competing Duration Models: A Case Study of Hutterite Data', in C. Clogg (ed.), *Sociological Methodology, 1987* (American Sociological Association, Washington, DC).

—— —— (1989), 'Forecasting Aggregate Period-Specific Birth Rates: The Time Series Properties of a Microdynamic Neoclassical Model of Fertility', *Journal of the American Statistical Association*, 84: 958–65.

—— —— (1990*a*), 'Economic Models of Fertility Dynamics: A Study of Swedish Fertility', in P. Schultz (ed.), *Research in Population Economics*, vii (JAI Press, Greenwich, Conn.).

—— —— (1990*b*), 'The Relationship between Wages and Income and the Timing and Spacing of Births: Evidence from Swedish Longitudinal Data', *Econometrica*, 58 (Nov.): 1411–41.

—— —— (1990*c*), 'Estimating Fecundability from Data on Waiting Time to First Conception', *Journal of the American Statistical Association*, 3: 283–94.

Hoem, J. (1985), 'Weighting, Misclassification and Other Issues in the Analysis of Survey Samples of Life Histories', in J. Heckman and B. Singer (eds.), *Longitudinal Analysis of Labour Market Data* (CUP, Cambridge).

—— and Rennermalm, B. (1985), 'Modern Family Initiation in Sweden: Experience of Women Born between 1936 and 1960', *European Journal of Population*, 1. 1: 81–112.

Honoré, B. (1987), 'Identification and Estimation of Econometric Duration Models', Ph.D. dissertation, Univ. of Chicago.

MaCurdy, T. (1986), *A Guide To Applying Time Series Models to Panel Data*, Stanford Univ. Working Paper.

Majumdar, H., and Sheps, M. (1970), 'Estimators of Type 1 Geometric Distribution from Observations on Conception Times', *Demography*, 7: 349–60.

Menken, J. (1975), 'Estimating Fecundability', Ph.D. dissertation, Princeton Univ.

Rodríguez, G., Hobcraft, J., McDonald, J., Menken, J., and Trussell, J. (1984), 'A Comparative Analysis of the Determinants of Birth Intervals', *Comparative Studies*, 30 (May), World Fertility Survey (London).

Schwarz, G. (1978), 'Estimating the Dimension of a Model', *Annals of Statistics*, 6. 2: 461–4.

Sheps, M. (1965), 'An Analysis of Reproductive Patterns in an American Isolate', *Population Studies*, 19. 1: 65–80.

—— and Menken, J. (1973), *Mathematical Models of Conception and Birth* (University of Chicago Press, Chicago).

Shiryayev, A. (1984), *Probability* (Springer-Verlag, Berlin).

Ward, M., and Butz, W. (1980), 'Completed Fertility and Its Timing', *Journal of Political Economy*, 88: 917–40.

Walker, J. (1986), 'The Timing and Spacing of Births in Sweden', Ph.D. dissertation, Univ. of Chicago.

Wilkinson, M. (1973), 'An Econometric Analysis of Fertility in Sweden, 1870–1965', *Econometrica*, 41. 4: 633–42.

Willis, R. (1973), 'Economic Theory of Fertility Behavior', in T. W. Schultz (ed.), *The Economics of the Family* (University of Chicago Press, Chicago).

Yashin, A., and Arjas, E. (1988), 'A Note on Random Intensities and Conditional Survivor Functions', *Journal of Applied Probability*, 25: 630–5.

Yi, K. M., Walker, J., and Honoré, B. (1987), 'CTM: A User's Guide', unpublished, Univ. of Chicago.

# 8 Incomplete Data in Event History Analysis

RODERICK J. A. LITTLE

Longitudinal studies are an increasingly popular method of data collection in a wide range of disciplines, including medicine, public health, sociology, economics, and demography. Many of these studies produce data in the form of event histories (Tuma and Hannan 1978), where individuals are followed over a period of time and dates of events are recorded; for example, births or marital changes in a demographic survey, progression of disease in a clinical trial, changes of employment status in an income survey, or pollution episodes in an environmental study. It is now widely recognized that the analysis of data in this form requires the methodology of survival analysis (see e.g. Kalbfleisch and Prentice 1980), and extensions of that methodology to handle recurring events. This chapter discusses problems arising from incomplete data in the analysis of event histories.

The chapter is organized as follows. The next two sections give an overview of general strategies for handling incomplete data, and review analytic approaches to event histories with complete data. The remainder of the chapter is devoted to incomplete data analyses that relate $y$, an outcome variable measuring the rate of occurrence of an event, to a set of covariates $x$.

Two generic missing-data problems are considered. I first discuss incompleteness on the outcome variable arising because, for individual $i$, the time to an event is known only to lie in an interval $(l_i, r_i)$, where $-\infty \leq l_i \leq r_i \leq \infty$; in particular, for complete data, $l_i = r_i$ for *right-censored* data $l_i$ is finite and $r_i = \infty$, and for *interval-censored* or *grouped* data $l_i$ and $r_i$ are finite and $l_i \leq r_i$. Right-censored data have an extensive literature and occur commonly, for example, when a study is terminated before an event occurred, or when an individual drops out of a study prematurely. Interval-censoring has received less attention. It occurs in demographic surveys based on retrospective event histories, when some individuals may not recall the exact dates of events but may recall the year or the number of years between successive events such as the birth of two children. This information leads to an interval for each event, which may be refined to take into account logical constraints (such as a requirement that births are at least nine months apart). For data from the World Fertility Survey, Otto (1980) describes a complex program for defining these ranges in the presence of information given in a variety of reporting modes.

Wave non-response in panel surveys yields gaps in an event history that can result in interval-censored data for certain spells. For example, the Survey of

Income and Program Participation (SIPP) conducted by the US Bureau of the Census interviews at four-month intervals, and at each interview asks about receipt of a large set of income types for each of the previous four months. Consider an individual present in waves 1 and 3 but missing in wave 2, reporting receipt of an income type for each month at the wave 1 interview, and non-receipt for each month at the wave 3 interview. Assuming one transition from receipt to non-receipt, the date of transition from receipt to non-receipt (and hence the spell length) is bounded within a four-month period that would have been covered by the missing wave interview. Even with complete data, response errors yield greater rates of transition between waves than within waves (Weidman 1986; Hill 1987). One possible way of reflecting response error would be to replace precisely reported dates of events by intervals that reflect the extent of response error suggested by the data.

The second generic missing-data problem reviewed here, event history analysis with missing data on the covariates, seems to have received very little attention; Whittemore and Grosser (1986) present a general maximum-likelihood (ML) framework for handling the problem, with examples that focus more on response errors in the covariates than on missing data; I discuss an approach of Schluchter and Jackson (1989) for categorical predictors, and propose some other treatments of the problem.

## Strategies for Handling Incomplete Data

### Introduction

In survey settings, two forms of missing data are commonly distinguished; *unit non-response*, where entire questionnaires are missing because of inability to contact or interview a sampled individual, and *item non-response*, where an interview is conducted but particular questions are missing, through refusal to answer, interviewer errors, or deletion of inconsistent responses in the editing process. Both these problems affect the analysis of event histories, but attention has been focused on another form of incompleteness, arising because some histories are recorded only for a segment of the time-window of interest. This longitudinal incompleteness may be an inherent feature of the study design, as when a study of fixed length captures subsets of experience of different age cohorts, or it may arise from attrition from the study, or from wave non-response, when one wave of data from a panel survey is omitted through inability to contact the respondent at one time-point. Longitudinal incompleteness leads to some degree of item non-response, but also leads to censoring effects where partial knowledge about the time to an event is available (for example, that the time is greater than some known value).

It is useful to distinguish three broad strategies for dealing with missing data: *weighting*, *imputation*, and *direct analysis of the incomplete data*. Weighting methods, which are usually used to handle unit non-response, discard the non-responding units and assign weights to the responding units that attempt to compensate for bias entailed by restriction to the respondent sample. These weights are often combined with weights for unequal probability sampling, and may entail post-stratification to control totals, for example from a suitable census. Descriptive analyses of the sample, such as cross-tabulations, generally should use these weights to provide better estimates of population quantities; thus, in the context of event history analysis, a better estimate of the population distribution of times to an event might be based on a sample histogram that weights the contribution from each respondent. In more analytic model-based procedures, the role of sampling and non-response weights is more contentious, particularly when the question of the appropriate choice of standard errors arises. Since weighting for unit non-response is a general issue that extends beyond the analysis of event histories, and I cannot do it justice here, I do not propose to discuss it further.

## Imputation

Imputation creates a rectangular data set convenient for subsequent analysis by replacing missing values by estimates based on the recorded information in the incomplete questionnaire. For reviews of imputation methods, see Kalton and Kasprzyk (1982; 1986), Sande (1982), Madow *et al.* (1983: vol. ii), Little and Rubin (1987: ch. 4, 12), and Little (1988*a*). In the latter paper, I argue that a good imputation scheme should have the following characteristics:

C1. Imputations should be based on the predictive distribution of the missing values, given the values of observed variables for the case. The conditioning on observed data is particularly important.

C2. Imputations should be drawn from the predictive distribution, not means. Means can be somewhat more efficient for inferences about means or totals, but yield distorted estimates of distribution and of association; thus their use as all-purpose imputations is questionable.

C3. A method should be provided for computing appropriate sampling errors of estimates from the filled-in data. Methods that supply a single imputation are usually deficient in this regard, since a single value cannot reflect imputation error; standard errors from the filled-in data are too optimistic. Rubin (1978; 1987) proposes *multiple imputation* as a solution for this problem. Two or more (say $I$) values are drawn from the predictive distribution of each missing value, and then complete-data analyses are repeated $I$ times, once with each imputation substituted. Let $\hat{\theta}_m$ be the estimate of a particular parameter $\theta$ from the mth analysis, and let $\hat{v}_m$ be the estimated variance. The final estimate of $\theta$ is $\hat{\theta} = \Sigma\hat{\theta}_m/I$, with estimated variance

$$\hat{v}^2 = s_W^2 + (1 + I^{-1})s_b^2 \tag{1}$$

where $s_W^2 = \Sigma\hat{v}_m/I$ is the average variance within imputed data sets and $s_b^2 = \Sigma(\hat{\theta}_m - \hat{\theta})^2/(I - 1)$ is the between-imputation variance, and reflects uncertainty in the imputation process. Large-sample inference for $\theta$ is based on treating $(\hat{\theta} - \theta)/\hat{v}$ as $t$ distributed with $v = (I - 1)[1 + \{I/(I + 1)\} s_W^2/s_b^2]$ degrees of freedom. For theory underlying the method and practical examples, see Rubin and Schenker (1986) and Rubin (1987).

As an application of multiple imputation to event histories, consider the problem of interval censoring of birth events, where information in the data yields an interval $(l, r)$ of possible values for the length of a spell. A minimal application of C1 dictates that an imputed value should lie in the interval $(l, r)$. A naïve approach imputes values at the midpoint of this interval. However, C2 and C3 suggest instead drawing imputes randomly in the interval, supplying two or more draws for each missing value, and deriving estimates using the multiple-imputation method described above. A simple approach might choose draws from the uniform distribution between $l$ and $r$, which would be adequate if the intervals are small compared to the variance of the distribution of spell lengths. (This is in fact the approach adopted in the WFS example mentioned in the introductory section.) More sophisticated approaches base the draws on a suitable model for the distribution of the spell length, which is conditional on known information available for each case. A comparison of these two approaches is given below.

### Maximum Likelihood (ML) and the EM Algorithm

In direct analysis of incomplete data the missing values are left as gaps in the data set, identified by special missing data codes, and the treatment of missing data is deferred to the analysis stage. Given data in this form, most statistical-analysis packages discard cases that contain incomplete information (complete-case analysis) or restrict attention to cases where the variable of interest is observed (available-case analysis). More elaborate approaches model the incomplete data and apply likelihood-based methods such as maximum likelihood (ML) (see e.g. Little and Rubin 1987: pt. 2). In the event history context, complete-case and available-case methods that discard censored cases usually lead to bias, and ML approaches are more successful (Tuma and Hannan 1978).

Let $\mathbf{Y}$ represent the data matrix in the absence on incomplete data, and let $\mathbf{R}$ be the missing-data indicator matrix, with $(i, j)$th entry taking the value 1 if $y_{ij}$ is observed and 0 if $y_{ij}$ is missing. ML is based on a model consisting of a density $f(\mathbf{Y} \mid \theta)$ for $\mathbf{Y}$ indexed by unknown parameters $\theta$, and a distribution $f(\mathbf{R} \mid \mathbf{Y}, \psi)$ for $\mathbf{R}$ given $\mathbf{Y}$ indexed by unknown parameters $\psi$, which models the missing-data mechanism. The complete-data likelihood is then

$$L(\theta, \psi \mid \mathbf{R}, \mathbf{Y}) = k f(\mathbf{Y} \mid \theta) f(\mathbf{R} \mid \mathbf{Y}, \psi) \qquad (2)$$

treated as a function of $\theta$ and $\psi$, where $k$ is a constant with respect to these parameters. Let $\mathbf{Y}_{obs}$ represent the values of $\mathbf{Y}$ in fact observed, and $\mathbf{Y}_{mis}$ the values that are missing. The likelihood given the data observed is then

$$L(\theta, \psi \mid \mathbf{R}, \mathbf{Y}_{obs}) = k \int f(\mathbf{Y} \mid \theta) f(\mathbf{R} \mid \mathbf{Y}, \psi) \, d\mathbf{Y}_{mis} \qquad (3)$$

where the integration is over the missing entries in $\mathbf{Y}$. ML finds estimates $\theta$ and $\psi$ to maximize (3).

A simpler analysis bases inference on the likelihood *ignoring the missing-data mechanism*: $L(\theta \mid \mathbf{Y}_{obs}) = k \int f(\mathbf{Y} \mid \theta) \, d\mathbf{Y}_{mis}$, which does not include a term from the distribution of the missing-data mechanism, $f(\mathbf{R} \mid \mathbf{Y}, \psi)$. Rubin (1976) presents assumptions under which inference for $\theta$ based on this simpler likelihood is equivalent to inference based on the full likelihood (3), that is, the missing-data mechanism is ignorable. The key condition is that the missing data are *missing at random* (MAR), which Rubin defines as meaning that the conditional distribution of $\mathbf{R}$ given $\mathbf{Y}$ and $\psi$ does not depend on the values of missing variables $\mathbf{Y}_{mis}$ (although it may depend on the observed variables $\mathbf{Y}_{obs}$). For censored data, missingness depends on the time to the event itself, which is missing when it is censored; thus censoring is not an ignorable mechanism, and likelihood inferences need to be based on the full likelihood (3).

ML methods have important advantages over other methods for handling missing data. Assumptions are clearly articulated in the model for the data and the missing-data mechanism. The estimates enjoy the usual optimal large-sample properties of ML, and inversion of the information matrix yields large-sample standard errors for estimates that take into account incompleteness in the data (unlike most single-imputation methods). Drawbacks of ML include the need to specify a full model for the data, which may be difficult in the event history context where the data are multivariate and non-normal, and the fact that estimation often requires an iterative algorithm that is not available in standard statistical software, and may involve intensive computation for large data sets.

When an iterative algorithm is needed, standard methods such as Newton–Raphson and scoring can be used to maximize the likelihood. However, the ubiquitous EM (expectation-maximization) algorithm (Dempster, Laird, and Rubin 1977; Little and Rubin 1987: ch. 7, 11) is an alternative approach that can be easier to program, and provides insights into simpler incomplete-data methods based on imputation.

The EM algorithm maximizes the likelihood in equation (3) by the following procedure. (i) Find initial estimates $\theta^{(0)}$ and $\psi^{(0)}$ of $\theta$ and $\psi$, for example from the complete cases. (ii) At iteration $b$, given current estimates $\theta^{(b)}$ and $\psi^{(b)}$, compute the expected value of the complete-data log-likelihood given the observed data, $\theta^{(b)}$ and $\psi^{(b)}$; that is, in symbols,

$$Q(\theta, \psi \mid \theta^{(b)}, \psi^{(b)}) =$$

$$\int \log L(\theta, \psi \mid \mathbf{R}, \mathbf{Y}) f(\mathbf{Y}_{mis} \mid \mathbf{Y}_{obs}, \mathbf{R}, \theta = \theta^{(b)}, \psi = \psi^{(b)}) \, d\mathbf{Y}_{mis}. \tag{4}$$

This is the expectation or E-step of the algorithm. (iii) Find $\theta^{(b+1)}$, $\psi^{(b+1)}$ to maximize $Q$ with respect to $\theta$ and $\psi$; this is the maximization or M-step. (iv) Replace $\theta^{(b)}$ and $\psi^{(b)}$ by $\theta^{(b+1)}$ and $\psi^{(b+1)}$ in the next iteration, and proceed until convergence.

The M-step in this algorithm is closely related to complete-data ML, and hence is straightforward if complete-data ML is non-iterative or available using standard software. Also, if the complete-data log-likelihood is linear in $\mathbf{Y}_{mis}$, then the E-step amounts to imputing $\mathbf{Y}_{mis}$, thus establishing a link with imputation methods. A strength and weakness of EM is that it does not involve computation of an information matrix for the parameters at each iteration. This is good because potentially lengthy computations are avoided, bad because the information matrix provides estimates of standard errors of the parameters, which are not an output of the EM iterations. The last two sections of this chapter give some examples of EM for event history analysis.

## Event History Analysis with Complete Data

### Definition of Event History

In any incomplete-data problem, an important initial step is to consider what analysis would be appropriate if the data were complete. Thus I begin by outlining procedures for analysing complete event history data. Since the field is broad, my review will be incomplete and restrictive; nevertheless, it will set the stage for my remarks on incomplete data.

One way of defining a complete event history is as a sequence of variables

$$(T_{ij}, E_{ij}, \ j = 1, \ldots, v_i) \tag{5}$$

recorded for individual $i$, where $T_{i1} < T_{i2} < \ldots < T_{iv_i}$ is an ordered sequence of time points at which events occur, and $E_{ij}$ is a categorical variable defining the event at time $T_{ij}$. Several notes are in order:

(i) An origin for defining time (say $T_{i0}$) is implicit in this definition; in some circumstances this may be a calendar date that is constant for all $i$ (for example, when period-specific rates of an event are the ultimate objective). In other cases the origin may be specific to each individual; for example, date of birth if age-specific events are of interest.

(ii) In (5) the $E_{ij}$ often define *changes* in state or *transitions* (birth, marriage, change in disease stage, entry into the labour force), not states themselves. An alternative approach is to have a set of variables defining states at each point in time (as in Tuma 1982). For example, instead of denoting the date at which a job commences, one might record presence or absence of a job every month. I prefer (5) for conceptual purposes, although it may or may not be preferable as a method for storing information.

(iii) Often interest focuses on relating summary measures of the event history to a set of covariates $\mathbf{X}_i$, which may be fixed or changing over time ('time-varying').

(iv) Each event $E_{ij}$ may have associated with it quantitative information $A_{ij}$ (such as dollar amount of an income type, or multiplicity of a birth). Although these amounts may be very important as outcomes, event history analysis as defined by Tuma and Hannan (1978) appears to restrict their role to that of covariates; times of events and functions of these times serve as outcomes.

(v) Outcomes derived from the times of events include *spells*, which are differences between times of events, and counts of events in a fixed period. In survival analysis, survival time is a spell and five-year survival is a count (0 or 1) in a fixed interval. If the event is birth to a mother, then age at first birth is the spell from birth of mother to birth of first child; a count of events that also measures fertility is number of births in the first five years of marriage (which, since fertility is a recurrent event, may be more than one). If a single recurring event (such as births) is under consideration, the event history can be described equivalently in terms of spells, which are just differences in times between successive events ($S_{ij} = T_{ij} - T_{i,j-1}$); if more than one event type is woven into the event history, however, it seems to me simpler to view the series as a chronology of events, with spells as derived quantities.

## Methods for Analysing Complete Event Histories: Analysis of Spell Length

Since spell length is a continuous variable, an obvious analytic approach is to apply standard regression techniques of the normal linear model, for example regressing spell length on covariates characterizing the sample (cohort, educational group, treatment, and so on). This strategy merits discussion in the missing-data context, since considerable literature exists on ML estimation for normal linear models with missing values (see e.g. Little and Rubin 1987: ch. 6, 8, 11). Three problems can be cited:

(i) The distribution of spells is usually not normal, typically being skewed to the right. This can usually be fixed by transformation, for example by taking logarithms of the spell lengths.

(ii) More seriously, conceptual problems arise when the state is not absorbing, that is, not all individuals ultimately experience the event under study. For example, in a study of age at marriage, how does one handle individuals who never marry? A reasonable approach is to restrict the normal model to individuals who eventually experience the event (individuals who do marry) and to supplement this with an analysis of the binary variable indicating whether or not the event is ever experienced. Although this approach seems reasonable given complete histories, it is hard to implement when the event histories are incomplete, as when histories are censored.

(iii) A third defect is the inability of a regression on spell length to model adequately the effects of covariates that change within the spell, and hence cause variation in the risk of the event.

*Hazard* models are superior to standard linear models for the analysis of spells, since they are relatively successful in handling censored data and time-varying covariates. Rather than modelling mean spell length, as in regression, these models assess systematic variation in the hazard function

$$\lambda_i(t, \mathbf{x}_i) = \lim_{\Delta \to 0} \frac{\text{pr}(t < S_i < t + \Delta \mid S_i \geq t, \mathbf{x}_i)}{\Delta} \tag{6}$$

where $S_i$ is the spell length for individual $i$, $\mathbf{x}_i$ is a set of covariates (possibly functions of $t$ if time-varying), and time $t$ is measured from a suitable origin. Modelling the *incremental* probability of experiencing an event in $(t, t + \Delta)$ given no event up to $t$ allows censored cases to be included in the analysis, and also allows the effect of time-varying covariates to be modelled. *Proportional-hazards* models are based on the equation

$$\lambda_i(t, \mathbf{x}_i) = \lambda(t) \exp(\mathbf{x}_i \boldsymbol{\beta}), \tag{7}$$

where $\lambda(t)$ is a baseline hazard function and $\boldsymbol{\beta}$ characterizes the effects of covariates $\mathbf{x}_i$. A variety of assumptions are made about $\lambda(t)$:

(i) $\lambda(t)$ can be treated as an arbitrary function (the Cox model, as in Cox 1972), and parameters $\boldsymbol{\beta}$ estimated by partial-likelihood methods (Cox 1972; 1975).

(ii) $\lambda(t)$ can be modelled using a specific parametric form. The simplest choice is to assume $\lambda(t)$ is constant, leading to spells that have an exponential distribution (Glasser 1967). Other common choices for $\lambda(t)$ are

(a) $\alpha t^{\gamma - 1}$, yielding Weibull-distributed spells (Prentice 1973);

(b) a polynomial in $t$ (Tuma 1982);

(c) $\lambda(t) = \dfrac{\lambda(\lambda t)^{k-1} \Gamma(k)^{-1}}{1 - I_k(\lambda t)}$, $I_k(s) = \dfrac{\int_0^s u^{k-1} e^{-u} du}{\Gamma(k)}$, where $\Gamma()$ is the gamma func-

tion, yielding gamma-distributed spells; and

(d) $\lambda(t) = \lambda_k, t_{k-1} < t \leq t_k, 1 \leq k \leq K$, a step-function over a set of $K$ time-intervals. (I shall call this a *grouped-hazard* function). This choice yields a grouped version of the Cox model (Holford 1976; 1980; Allison 1982). These models can be fitted by simultaneously maximizing the likelihood over $\boldsymbol{\beta}$ and the parameters of the baseline hazard function.

Extensions of these models allow for non-proportional hazards by including interactions between the baseline hazards and the covariates, and include random effects for individuals to model heterogeneity (Flynn and Heckman 1982).

## Methods for Analysing Complete Event Histories: Counting Events in a Fixed Interval

An alternative to analyses of spell length is to count the number of events in a fixed interval, and then regress this count on covariates. A simple analysis would apply standard linear regression, relying on the central-limit theorem to overcome the evident lack of normality of the event count. A more sophisticated approach is to fit a nonlinear model more appropriate for counts. If the event is non-recurrent, the outcome is binary, so a logistic or probit model is suggested. For recurrent events where counts greater than one are possible, one might fit the following rate model:

$$E(c_i) = \mu_i; \quad \text{Var}(c_i) = \sigma^2\mu_i; \quad \log(\mu_i) = \beta x_i, \tag{8}$$

where $c_i$ is the count of events in the fixed interval. Observe that the variance of $c_i$ is assumed proportional to the mean $\mu_i$, reflecting increasing variation with the mean. Also, the logarithm of the mean is assumed linear in the covariates $x_i$, which constrains the expected counts to be greater than zero. However, this model allows values of zero for observed counts. In contrast, the simpler tactic of applying a linear model to $\log(c_i)$ is less satisfying, since an *ad hoc* procedure is needed to deal with zero counts, such as adding an arbitrary constant. The rate model can be fitted using a nonlinear regression program. Alternatively, it can be fitted as a generalized linear model (Baker and Nelder 1978) by specifying a log link and a Poisson error structure. The Poisson error assumption is justified when times to events follow a Poisson process, and yields a model analogous to an exponential log-linear model for spell length (Holford 1980). It implies that $\sigma^2 = 1$; however, the fitting method allows $\sigma^2$ to be treated as a parameter to be estimated, thus allowing over-dispersion from the basic Poisson model. The following notes are in order:

(i) Analysis of counts in an interval rather than spells entails a loss of information if an individual's hazard function is not constant within the interval. The loss of information increases as the interval is widened.

(ii) A more serious limitation of modelling counts of events in an interval is that the effects of time-varying covariates can be readily assessed only when the effects occur before the start of the interval. For example, if the outcome is the number of births over a five-year period, the effects of contraceptive use within that period on this outcome cannot be estimated without instrumental variables to disentangle bidirectional causality between the variables; on the other hand, the effects of contraceptive use before the five-year interval can be assessed by straightforward regression techniques.

(iii) The analysis of counts in an interval does have some advantages over analysis of spells. It does not require specialized software for survival analysis, and does not require assumptions about the distribution of spell lengths. Also, in the context of demographic surveys, the outcome variable has a more direct correspondence with standard demographic measures such as fertility rates. If events are recurrent and relatively frequent, the information in a single spell may be small, and analysis of counts in an interval may be more powerful. Finally, counts in an interval may be less sensitive to errors in the timing of spells, caused by heaping on particular spell lengths, or 'seam' effects in panel surveys (e.g. Hill 1987).

(iv) Models for counts in an interval can be extended to handle varying interval sizes between individuals. If the count $c_i$ occurs within an interval of length $d_i$, then a useful extension of the linear regression model is to assume

$$c_i/d_i \sim_{\text{ind}} N(\beta x_i, \sigma^2/d_i), \tag{9}$$

the normal distribution with mean $\beta x_i$ and variance $\sigma^2/d_i$; Little (1988b) calls (9) the *extended-ratio model*; for applications to fertility data see Little and Perera (1981) or Hobcraft and Little (1984). The covariates $x_i$ may include $d_i$; note that the variance of $c_i/d_i$ in (9) declines as $d_i$ increases. The rate model (8) can be modified to handle varying interval lengths by including $\log(d_i)$ as a covariate.

## Event Histories with Incomplete Data on Spell Length

### Censored Data

It has long been recognized that when some cases are right-censored, analysis of the complete cases leads to bias toward shorter spells; from the general perspective of Rubin's (1976) theory of missing-data mechanisms, right-censoring is a *non-ignorable* missing-data mechanism, in that missingness depends on the value of the missing variable (see e.g. Little and Rubin 1987: ch. 5, 11). An important element of life-table methods is their ability to handle censored data.

The *product-limit* estimator deals with censoring for the single-sample problem, that is, with no covariates. Similar estimators were used extensively by actuaries before the formal statistical properties of the product-limit estimator were studied in the fundamental paper by Kaplan and Meier (1958). The probability of survival to time $t$ is estimated as

$$\hat{G}(t) = \prod_{j:\,t_j < t} \frac{n_j - e_j}{n_j} \tag{10}$$

where the product is over times $t_j$ when events occur, $n_j$ is the number of individuals in the sample just before $t_j$, and $e_j$ is the number of events that occur at $t_j$. Censored individuals are included in the counts $n_j$ until they drop out, thus inflating the argument in the product and removing the downward bias in the survival function computed from complete cases. The likelihood for a general survivor function $G(t)$ can be written as

$$l = \prod_{\substack{\text{events} \\ i}} \{G(t_i - 0) - G(t_i + 0)\}^{e_i} \prod_{\substack{\text{censored} \\ k}} G(c_k) \tag{11}$$

where $G(t_i - 0)$ and $G(t_i + 0)$ is the survivor function just before and just after the event at $t_i$. Kaplan and Meier (1958) show that $\hat{G}(t)$ maximizes $l$ in the absence of constraints on the form of $G(t)$, that is, it is the non-parametric ML estimate of $G(t)$. If covariates $x$ are present, a simple approach is to form strata and apply the product-limit estimator separately within each stratum. Alternatively, the proportional-hazards model (7) can be fitted by partial-likelihood methods.

Parametric-hazard models with censored data are extensively treated in the life-testing literature. We sketch here ML methods. Note that the density $f(t)$ and the survivor function $G(t)$ are related to the hazard function $\lambda(t)$ by the expressions

$$f(t) = \lambda(t) \exp - \left( \int_0^t \lambda(u) \, du \right); \qquad G(t) = \exp - \left( \int_0^t \lambda(u) \, du \right). \qquad (12)$$

Hence the log-likelihood of a censored sample is

$$l = \sum_{\substack{\text{events} \\ i=1}}^{I} \left( \ln \lambda(t_i) - \int_0^{t_i} \lambda(u) \, du \right) - \sum_{\substack{\text{censored} \\ k=1}}^{K} \left( \int_0^{c_k} \lambda(u) \, du \right) \qquad (13)$$

where $t_1, \ldots, t_I$ are the lengths of completed spells, $c_1, \ldots, c_K$ are the censoring times for censored cases. ML estimates are obtained by substituting the assumed form for the hazard function in (13) and maximizing the resulting function. For example, if the hazard is a constant $\lambda$, so that spell length has an exponential distribution, (13) becomes

$$l(\lambda) = \sum_{\substack{\text{events} \\ i=1}}^{I} \{ \ln \lambda - \lambda t_i \} - \sum_{\substack{\text{censored} \\ k=1}}^{K} \lambda c_k. \qquad (14)$$

Setting the derivative of $l$ to zero and solving yields the ML estimate

$$\hat{\lambda} = \frac{I}{\sum t_i + \sum c_k}, \qquad (15)$$

which is simply the number of events divided by total exposure. If a grouped hazard function is assumed, the ML estimate of the hazard $\lambda_j$ in time interval $j$ is simply the ratio of events to exposure within interval $j$. For the Weibull or polynomial hazard models, the integrals in (13) have simple analytic solutions, so the log-likelihood has a relatively simple form, although ML estimation requires iterative methods.

Covariates can be included in these models by replacing the hazard function $\lambda(t_i)$ in (13) by a function $\lambda(t_i, \mathbf{x}_i)$ such as that in equation (7), and maximizing with respect to both the hazard parameters and $\beta$; time-varying covariates are allowed. For all these models, asymptotic standard errors can be found in the usual way from the inverse of the information matrix.

## Analysis of Spell Lengths from Partially Grouped Data

Now suppose more generally that the spell length $s_i$ for individual $i$ is known to lie in the interval $(l_i, r_i)$, $-\infty \leqslant l_i \leqslant r_i \leqslant \infty$. The form of the likelihood for a single sample with general survivor function $G(t)$ is the following generalization of (11):

$$l = \prod_{\substack{\text{cases} \\ i}} \{ G(l_i - 0) - G(r_i - 0) \}. \qquad (16)$$

Peto (1973) discusses ML estimation of $G$. From the sets $(l_i)$ and $(r_i)$, we can derive all the distinct closed intervals whose left and right endpoints lie in the sets $(l_i)$ and $(r_i)$ respectively, that contain no members of $(l_i)$ and $(r_i)$ other than at their left and right endpoints, respectively, and that are known to include at least one event. If these intervals are written in order as $(p_1, q_1)$, $(p_2, q_2)$, ..., $(p_m, q_m)$ then Peto shows that a non-parametric ML estimate of $G$ is flat between the intervals, and drops an amount $s_j$ between $p_j$ and $q_j$, where $\Sigma_{j=1}^m s_j = 1$. Moreover, the maximized value of the likelihood is the same irrespective of how the decreases in $(p_j, q_j)$ occur, so indeterminacy in $\hat{G}$ exists in intervals where $s_j > 0$ and $p_j \neq q_j$.

Iteration is generally needed to compute the drops $s_j$. Peto discusses a search algorithm; Turnbull (1976), extending Peto's work to include truncated data, provides a 'self-consistency' algorithm which is an interesting example of an EM algorithm. The E-step at iteration $b$ allocates each incomplete case fractionally over the intervals $(l_j, u_j)$ in which the spell length may occur, with fractions proportional to current estimates of the drops $\{s_j^{(b)}\}$. The M-step computes new drops

$$s_j^{(b+1)} = c_j^{(b)}/n \tag{17}$$

where $c_j^{(b)}$ is the sum of complete and fractional cases allocated to interval $j$. E and M-steps are repeated until convergence. This algorithm is illustrated on a small artificial data set in Table 8.1.

For partially grouped data with covariates, the partial-likelihood methods of Cox (1972) do not appear to generalize easily to an interval-censored outcome, as noted by Finkelstein (1986). Instead, the latter paper and Finkelstein and Wolfe (1985) develop full ML extensions of $\hat{G}$ that simultaneously estimate the set of drops and the regression coefficients on covariates. The earlier paper considers a non-standard model that factors the joint distribution of covariates $\mathbf{X}$ and spell length $S$ in the form

$$f(\mathbf{x}, s \mid \theta, \varphi) = f(\mathbf{x} \mid s, \theta) f(s \mid \varphi). \tag{18}$$

This model can be fitted using an appealing extension of the EM algorithm for the single sample problem. However, it does not usually yield the standard proportional-hazards model for the conditional distribution of $S$ given $\mathbf{X}$. Finkelstein (1986) considers ML estimation for this more standard model; however, EM is not useful, and ML estimation is achieved using a scoring algorithm, which is only practical if the number of parameters (and, in particular, the number of drops) is small enough for the inversion of the information matrix to be manageable. Asymptotic properties of estimates from these models seem uncertain, since the number of parameters increases with the number of observations.

For the parametric-hazard models of the previous section, the log-likelihood is

$$l = \sum_{i:\, l_i = r_i = t_i} \left\{ ln\, \lambda(t) - \int_0^{t_i} \lambda(u)\, du \right\}$$

$$+ \sum_{i:\, l_i < r_i} ln \left[ \exp\left\{ -\int_0^{l_i} \lambda(u)\, du \right\} - \exp\left\{ -\int_0^{r_i} \lambda(u)\, du \right\} \right] \tag{19}$$

TABLE 8.1.   *Illustration of EM algorithm for estimating the empirical survivor function from data with right- and interval-censoring*

(a) *Data, time-ordered* (subscript = observation number, $x$ = event, $c$ = right-censored, $(l, r)$ = interval-censored)

$$x_1 < c_2 < l_3 < r_3 < l_4 < x_5 < c_6 < x_7 < r_4 < x_8 < c_9$$

(b) *EM algorithm for computing the vector of drops, s*

| Interval | Initial estimate of drops $s^{(0)}$ | Iteration 1 E-step Allocation of unclassified cases 2 | 4 | 6 | M-step $s^{(1)}$ | Iteration 2 E-step Allocation of unclassified cases 2 | 4 | 6 | M-step $s^{(2)}$ |
|---|---|---|---|---|---|---|---|---|---|
| $I_1 = [x_1, x_1]$ | 1/6 | | | | 0.111 | | | | 0.111 |
| $I_3 = [l_3, r_3]$ | 1/6 | 0.200 | | | 0.133 | 0.150 | | | 0.128 |
| $I_5 = [x_5, x_5]$ | 1/6 | 0.200 | 0.500 | | 0.189 | 0.213 | 0.456 | | 0.185 |
| $I_7 = [x_7, x_7]$ | 1/6 | 0.200 | 0.500 | 0.333 | 0.226 | 0.254 | 0.544 | 0.399 | 0.244 |
| $I_8 = [x_8, x_8]$ | 1/6 | 0.200 | | 0.333 | 0.170 | 0.191 | | 0.300 | 0.164 |
| $I_9 = [c_9, \infty]$ | 1/6 | 0.200 | | 0.333 | 0.170 | 0.191 | | 0.300 | 0.164 |

| Interval | Current estimate of drops $s^{(2)}$ | Iteration 3 E-step Allocation of unclassified cases 2 | 4 | 6 | M-step $s^{(3)}$ | Iteration 4 E-step Allocation of unclassified cases 2 | 4 | 6 | M-step $s^{(4)}$ |
|---|---|---|---|---|---|---|---|---|---|
| $I_1 = [x_1, x_1]$ | 0.111 | | | | 0.111 | | | | 0.111 |
| $I_3 = [l_3, r_3]$ | 0.128 | 0.144 | | | 0.127 | 0.143 | | | 0.127 |
| $I_5 = [x_5, x_5]$ | 0.185 | 0.208 | 0.431 | | 0.182 | 0.205 | 0.419 | | 0.180 |
| $I_7 = [x_7, x_7]$ | 0.244 | 0.275 | 0.569 | 0.424 | 0.252 | 0.284 | 0.581 | 0.435 | 0.256 |
| $I_8 = [x_8, x_8]$ | 0.164 | 0.187 | | 0.288 | 0.164 | 0.185 | | 0.283 | 0.163 |
| $I_9 = [c_9, \infty]$ | 0.164 | 0.187 | | 0.288 | 0.164 | 0.185 | | 0.283 | 0.163 |

TABLE 8.1. (contd.)

| Interval | Current estimate of drops $s^{(4)}$ | Iteration 5 E-step Allocation of unclassified cases | | | M-step $s^{(5)}$ | Iteration 6 E-step Allocation of unclassified cases | | | M-step $s^{(6)}$ |
|---|---|---|---|---|---|---|---|---|---|
| | | 2 | 4 | 6 | | 2 | 4 | 6 | |
| $I_1 = [x_1, x_1]$ | 0.111 | | | | 0.111 | | | | 0.111 |
| $I_3 = [l_3, r_3]$ | 0.127 | 0.143 | | | 0.127 | 0.143 | | | 0.127 |
| $I_5 = [x_5, x_5]$ | 0.180 | 0.203 | 0.413 | | 0.180 | 0.203 | 0.412 | | 0.179 |
| $I_7 = [x_7, x_7]$ | 0.256 | 0.288 | 0.587 | 0.440 | 0.257 | 0.289 | 0.588 | 0.441 | 0.258 |
| $I_8 = [x_8, x_8]$ | 0.163 | 0.183 | | 0.280 | 0.163 | 0.183 | | 0.280 | 0.163 |
| $I_9 = [c_9, \infty]$ | 0.163 | 0.183 | | 0.280 | 0.163 | 0.183 | | 0.280 | 0.163 |

*Notes*: The 6 listed intervals $I_1, I_3, I_5, I_7, I_8, I_9$ are known from the data to contain events 1, 3, 5, 7, 8, and 9 respectively; the ML estimate of the distribution function changes only in these intervals (see text), and the algorithm computes ML estimates of the drops $s = (s_1, s_3, s_5, s_7, s_8, s_9)$, which are the probabilities of falling in these intervals. Initially, $s$ is set to $s_0 = (1/6, 1/6, 1/6, 1/6, 1/6, 1/6)$. The E-step of Iteration 1 allocates the 3 unclassified cases (2, 4, 6) fractionally over the intervals $I_j$ in which they may belong. The M-step estimates $s_j^{(1)} =$ fraction of cases allocated to $I_j$ (e.g. $s_5^{(1)} = (1 + 0.2 + 0.5)/9 = 0.189$). The E-step for Iteration 2 reallocates the 3 unclassified cases according to their conditional probabilities based on $s^{(1)}$. E.g. the fraction of case 2 allocated to $I_5$ is $0.189/(0.133 + 0.189 + 0.226 + 0.170 + 0.170) = 0.213$, and so on. The M-step is as before. The estimates from Iteration 6, $s^{(6)} = (0.111, 0.127, 0.179, 0.258, 0.163, 0.163)$, are close to convergence.

which tends to be harder to maximize than its analog for censored data, equation (13). In particular, the single-sample exponential model with constant hazard $\lambda$ yields

$$l = \sum_{i: l_i = r_i = t_i} (ln\,\lambda - \lambda t_i) + \sum_{i: l_i < r_i} ln\,\{\exp(-\lambda l_i) - \exp(-\lambda r_i)\} \qquad (20)$$

which differs from the censored case in not having an explicit solution. The EM algorithm for this problem is relatively easy, since the complete-data log-likelihood is linear in the spell times: at iteration $b$ with current estimate $\lambda^{(b)}$, the E-step estimates the time for grouped spell $i$ as

$$s_i^{(b)} = E(s_i \mid l_i \leq s_i \leq r_i, \lambda^{(b)}) = \frac{1}{\lambda^{(b)}} + \frac{l_i e^{-\lambda^{(b)}l_i} - r_i e^{-\lambda^{(b)}r_i}}{e^{-\lambda^{(b)}l_i} - e^{-\lambda^{(b)}r_i}} \qquad (21)$$

obtained by integration of the exponential density. The M-step computes $\lambda^{(b+1)}$ as the number of events divided by the total exposure, observed or imputed using (21).

The introduction of covariates into this exponential model via (7) produces a similarly simple E-step; the current estimated hazard $\lambda^{(b)}$ in (21) is replaced by

$$\lambda_i^{(b)}(t, \mathbf{x}_i) = \lambda^{(b)} \exp(\mathbf{x}_i \beta^{(b)}) \qquad (22)$$

where $\lambda^{(b)}$ and $\beta^{(b)}$ are current estimates of the parameters. The M-step consists of complete-data ML with incomplete spell lengths replaced by estimates from the E-step. This maximization itself involves iteration, but it can be carried out using a non-linear regression program, or the GLIM statistical package (Baker and Nelder 1978).

With regard to other parametric-hazard models, the grouped exponential hazard model has the useful feature that the complete-data log-likelihood remains linear in the spell lengths, so the E-step of EM still consists in computing the expected spell length given that it lies in the interval $(l, r)$. This takes the form of (21) if the hazard rate is constant in the interval $(l, r)$, but if the hazard rate changes in the interval the computations become messy, although not intractable. For the Weibull, polynomial, and gamma hazard models, the complete-data log-likelihood is not linear in the spell lengths, and the E-step of EM becomes even more complicated. Direct maximization of the likelihood may be just as easy (or hard) as EM for these models.

## Simpler Imputation-Based Approaches

Given the complexity of the ML approach (particularly when the distribution of spell length deviates from the exponential), simpler approaches to the interval-censoring problem seem worth considering. As mentioned above, one approach is to impute multiply two or more draws from an appropriate conditional distribution of spell length, given that it falls in the recorded interval. For an incomplete case with spell $S$ lying in the range $(l, r)$, the simplest approach would assume a uniform distribution of $S$ in the interval, and draw for the $m^{\text{th}}$ impute

$$\hat{S}_{um} = l + u_m(r - l), \tag{23}$$

where $u_m$ is a uniform random deviate. A refinement would draw from a more appropriate conditional distribution of $S$ given $S \in (l, r)$. If $S$ is considered exponentially distributed, then the conditional distribution of $S - l$ given that $S > l$ is also exponential, so one could draw

$$\hat{S}_{em} = l + v_m \tag{24}$$

where $v_m$ is drawn from the exponential distribution truncated at $r - l$. Note that this impute, unlike (23), depends on the exponential hazard rate, which requires estimation from similar individuals, or from a formal analysis of the complete and right-censored cases. (Right-censored cases could also be imputed with draws $v$ from the full exponential distribution, but since these imputes involve extrapolation rather than interpolation they appear more sensitive to the distributional assumption. Also, since methods for handling right-censoring are well developed, the argument for imputing these cases seems weaker.) A refinement of (24) propagates uncertainty in estimating $\lambda$ by drawing a different hazard $\hat{\lambda}_m$ for each value of $m$ from its posterior distribution; see Rubin (1987) for details.

The assumptions of uniform or exponential spell length within the interval may seem restrictive, but may produce useful approximate analyses if the intervals are small or if the number of cases requiring imputation is small. To compare (23) and (24), we consider the first two moments of the uniform and censored exponential distributions in an interval. For the impute (23), we have

$$E(\hat{S}_{um}) = (l + r)/2, \quad \text{Var}(\hat{S}_{um}) = (r - l)/12 \tag{25}$$

by properties of the uniform distribution. For the impute (24), straightforward calculations based on the exponential distribution yield

$$E(\hat{S}_{em}) = \{1 - w(d)\} l + w(d) r, \quad \text{Var}(\hat{S}_{um}) = v(d)/\lambda^2 \tag{26}$$

where $\lambda$ is the exponential hazard

$$w(d) = \frac{1}{d} - \frac{1}{e^{d-1}} \quad v(d) = 1 - \frac{d^2 e^d}{(e^d - 1)^2} \tag{27}$$

and $d = \lambda(r - l)$, that is, the width of interval in units of the mean spell length $1/\lambda$; we call $d$ the standardized interval width. Table 8.2 displays $w(d)$ and $1200 v(d)/d^2$, the exponential variance expressed as a percentage of the uniform variance, as a function of $d$: The uniform imputation assigns a constant weight of $1/2$ to $l$ and $r$; comparing with the exponential weight in the second row, we see that this is correct if $d$ is small, but gives too much weight to $r$ (that is, tends to overestimate the spell length) if $d$ is large. The bias is not too serious unless the standardized interval width is greater than 1. From the third row of Table 8.2 we see that the uniform imputes have variances that are too high relative to the exponential imputes, with a modest degree of over-dispersion for $d < 2$; for $d > 2$ the problem becomes rapidly more serious as $d$ increases.

TABLE 8.2

| $d$ | $\downarrow 0$ | 0.1 | 0.2 | 0.5 | 1 | 1.5 | 2 | 3 | 4 | 5 | $\uparrow \infty$ |
|---|---|---|---|---|---|---|---|---|---|---|---|
| $w(d)$ | 1/2 | 0.49 | 0.48 | 0.46 | 0.42 | 0.38 | 0.34 | 0.28 | 0.23 | 0.19 | $1/d$ |
| $1200v(d)/d^2$ | 100 | 100 | 100 | 99 | 95 | 90 | 83 | 67 | 52 | 40 | $12/d^2$ |

These results suggest that, if the interval widths are generally smaller than the mean spell length, then bias from the uniform draws is small. If the widths are much greater than the mean, then draws from a more appropriate distribution, such as the exponential, may yield noticeably better answers.

## Missing Data in the Covariates

So far we have treated grouped or censored data on the length of spell $s$, assuming that covariates $\mathbf{x}$, if present, are completely observed. Missing values on the covariates create new analytic problems. As in the previous section, our preferred strategy is to model the data and use ML to estimate the parameters. An important issue in this approach is to find a practically useful formulation of the model that leads to tractable likelihoods, which can be maximized without extensive numerical integration or other lengthy calculations.

Standard survival models for spell length treat covariates as fixed. If the covariates have missing values, then the likelihood approach requires that they are also treated as random variables with a distribution. (The alternative of treating missing values of covariates as parameters is not recommended, for reasons discussed in Little and Rubin (1987: s. 5.4).) Strictly speaking, covariates that are fully observed might be fixed in the model, but in this discussion I shall consider models for the full distribution of $S$ and $\mathbf{X}$.

Schluchter and Jackson (1989) present ML estimation for data with right-censored spells and incomplete categorical covariates $\mathbf{X}$, based on a model that factors the joint distribution of $S$ and $\mathbf{X}$ as the product of the conditional distribution of $S$ given $\mathbf{X}$ and the marginal distribution of $\mathbf{X}$. Specifically, they assume (a) categorical covariates $\mathbf{X}$ forming a multi-way contingency table with (say) $M$ cells, with a multinomial distribution with probability $\theta_m$ associated with cell $m$, and (b) a model for $S \mid \mathbf{X}$ with a grouped hazard function, that is, a step-function over a set of fixed time intervals, and a log-linear model relating the hazard to the covariates $\mathbf{X}$. For example, suppose there are two categorical covariates $X_1$ and $X_2$ with $I$ and $J$ levels, and the hazard is grouped in $K$ time intervals. Let $\lambda_{ijk}$ denote the hazard function in the $k^{\text{th}}$ time interval given $X_1 = i$, $X_2 = i$ and write

$$\log \lambda_{ijk} = \lambda + \beta_{1i} + \beta_{2j} + \beta_{3k} + \beta_{12ij} + \beta_{13ik} + \beta_{23jk} + \beta_{123ijk} \tag{28}$$

for $i = 1, \ldots, I$, $j = 1, \ldots, J$, and $k = 1, \ldots, K$. This saturated model allows a distinct hazard for each value of $i$, $j$, and $k$. Other models are obtained by setting terms in the model to zero. In particular setting $\beta_{13ik} = \beta_{23jk} = \beta_{123ijk} = 0$ for all $i$, $j$, and $k$ yields a proportional-hazards model of the form (7).

In general, for each subject $i$ define the vector $\mathbf{W}_i = (W_{i1}, \ldots, W_{iM})$, where $W_{im} = 1$ if the observed covariates imply that subject $i$ can fall in cell $m$ of the contingency table formed by the covariates, and $W_{im} = 0$ otherwise. In particular, if the covariates are fully observed, $W_i$ contains 1 one and $M - 1$ zeros. Also let $T_i$ be the survival time for subject $i$, $\delta_i = 1$ if $T_i$ is an event and $\delta_i = 0$ if $T_i$ is a censoring time, and let $b_{ki}$ be the exposure contributed by $i$ to the $k^{\text{th}}$ time interval. The log likelihood of the observed data is then

$$l = \sum_{i=1}^{n} \sum_{m=1}^{M} W_{im} \, \theta_m \, S_{im} \, \lambda_{km}^{\delta_i} \tag{29}$$

where $S_{im} = \exp\left\{-\sum_{k=1}^{K} \lambda_{km} b_{ki}\right\}$ is the probability that a subject in cell $m$ survives to time $T_i$. Schluchter and Jackson suggest maximizing this function by a Newton–Raphson algorithm if the number of parameters is modest. If not, they propose a generalized EM algorithm (Dempster, Laird, and Rubin 1977), where the E-step involves fractional allocation of failures, exposure time, and persons into cells of the table defined by the covariates, and the M-step increases the likelihood by one step of an iterative proportional fitting algorithm.

Note that, although (28) is a log-linear model, it does not correspond to a standard log-linear model for the full $I \times J \times K$ contingency table in the absence of censoring or missing covariates. That would set the logarithm of the probability that $X_1 = i$, $X_2 = j$, and an event occurs in interval $k$ equal to the right side of (28), rather than the logarithm of the hazard of an event. An alternative approach would be to record only the time category in which events occurred, and to fit a standard log-linear contingency table model to the incomplete $I \times J \times K$ table, using the EM algorithm (see Fuchs 1982; Little and Rubin 1987: ch. 9). Censored cases would be fractionally allocated over time categories that include or extend beyond the censoring point. The resulting algorithm is simpler than that of Schluchter and Jackson, and interactions with the time variable capture the effects of the covariates on the spell length. However, the Schluchter and Jackson approach has the advantage that it corresponds to a more standard model for survival analysis.

The standard log-linear-model approach is natural when the outcome is changed to a binary variables $S^*$ indicating whether the spell is greater than a fixed period (as in a five-year survival rate). The log-linear model for the joint distribution then corresponds to a logistic model for the conditional distribution of $S^*$ given $\mathbf{X}$. In the above example, the data then reduce to an $I \times J \times 2$ table with supplemental margins from cases with $X_1$ or $X_2$ missing. The E-step of EM classifies the supplemental margins fractionally into the full table using current estimates of the cell probabilities; the M-step fits the log-linear model to the filled-in data, and can be accomplished with existing software for complete data.

So far we have considered methods appropriate for categorical covariates. Continuous covariates can be handled by categorization, but a more satisfying approach would allow both continuous and categorical covariates in the model. The Schluchter and Jackson approach does not appear to extend easily to this situation; for example, if the proportional-hazards model for $S$ given $\mathbf{X}$ is coupled with a multivariate normal distribution for a set of continuous covariates $\mathbf{X}$, the marginal distribution of $S$ and observed components of $\mathbf{X}$ does not have a explicit form, so the likelihood becomes difficult to maximize; EM does not appear to help.

If the requirement of obtaining a standard hazard rate model for $S$ given $\mathbf{X}$ is relaxed, more tractable ML algorithms can be found that allow continuous covariates. For example, suppose survival $S$ is grouped into $K$ categories, and the covariates consist of $V$ categorical variables $Y_1, \ldots, Y_V$, forming a $V$-way contingency table with $M$ cells, and $K$ continuous variables $X_1, \ldots, X_K$. The data then consist of incomplete information from $V + 1$ categorical variables $S, Y_1, \ldots, Y_V$, and $K$ continuous variables. Little and Schluchter (1985) discuss ML estimation for data of this form, under the following general location model of Olkin and Tate (1961):

(a) The joint distribution of $S, Y_1, \ldots, Y_V$ is multinomial, with cell probabilities constrained by a log-linear model;

(b) the joint distribution of $X_1, \ldots, X_K$ given $S, Y_1, \ldots, Y_V$ is multivariate normal with mean that has a linear (multivariate analysis of variance) model over the categorical variables, and constant covariance matrix.

The parameters of this model can be estimated using EM, and involve standard tools like discriminant analysis and the sweep operator. If $S$ has just two categories, the model implies a logistic model for the probability of survival given the covariates; thus it extends the contingency table approach noted above to handle continuous covariates. With more than two categories a multiple logistic model is obtained. This model is also discussed in Little and Rubin (1987: ch. 10), and is applied to longitudinal income data in Little and Su (1987).

The approaches discussed here are computationally tractable, but they are also complex and iterative, and thus are difficult to apply to large data sets unless considerable computing power is available. Less powerful but easier approaches that make some use of the incomplete cases merit study; one such approach is the *hot deck*, where each incomplete case is matched to a complete case that is similar with respect to observed variables, and then missing values imputed using recorded values from the matched complete case. Multiple imputation can be achieved by supplying two or more matches for each incomplete case. A good general choice of metric is the predictive mean metric first proposed by Rubin (see Little 1988b). An issue requiring further work is a good choice of metric when the ultimate objective is a form of event history analysis.

## Conclusion

I have considered some general tools for handling incomplete data, methods for analysing event history data when data are complete, and ways these methods can be modified when incomplete information is available on the times to events or when covariates are missing. My preference is for an explicit model-based approach, with parameters estimated by maximum likelihood. However, these techniques often result in complex iterative algorithms and may be impractical in some settings. Thus, simpler, imputation-based methods also deserve study, particularly if multiple imputation is applied to reflect uncertainty in the imputation process.

## References

Allison, P. D. (1982), 'Discrete-Time Methods for the Analysis of Event Histories', *Sociological Methodology 1982* (San Francisco), 61–98.

Baker, R., and Nelder, J. (1978), *The GLIM System, Release 3* (Oxford).

Cox, D. R. (1972), 'Regression Models and Life Tables', *Journal of the Royal Statistical Society*, ser. B, 34. 2: 187–220.

—— (1975), 'Partial Likelihood', *Biometrika*, 62. 2: 269–76.

Dempster, A. P., Laird, N. M., and Rubin, D. B. (1977), 'Maximum Likelihood from Incomplete Data via the EM Algorithm', *Journal of the Royal Statistical Society*, ser. B, 39. 1: 1–38.

Finkelstein, D. M. (1986), 'A Proportional Hazards Model for Interval-Censored Failure Time Data', *Biometrics*, 42. 4: 845–54.

—— and Wolfe, R. A. (1985), 'A Semiparametric Model for Regression Analysis of Interval-Censored Failure Time Data', *Biometrics*, 41. 4: 933–45.

Flynn, C. J., and Heckman, J. J. (1982), 'New Methods for Analyzing Individual Event Histories', *Sociological Methodology 1982* (San Francisco), 99–140.

Fuchs, C. (1982), 'Maximum Likelihood Estimation and Model Selection in Contingency Tables with Missing Data', *Journal of the American Statistical Association*, 77. 378: 270–8.

Glasser, M. (1967), 'Exponential Survival with Covariance', *Journal of the American Statistical Association*, 62. 318: 561–8.

Hill, D. H. (1987), 'Response Errors around the Seam: Analysis of Change in a Panel with Overlapping Reference Periods', *Proceedings of the Survey Research Methods Section, American Statistical Association 1987* (Alexandria, Va.), 210–15.

Hobcraft, J., and Little, R. J. A. (1984), 'Fertility Exposure Analysis: a New Method for Assessing the Contribution of Proximate Determinants to Fertility Differentials', *Population Studies*, 38. 1: 21–45.

Holford, T. R. (1976), 'Life Tables with Concomitant Information', *Biometrics*, 32. 3: 587–97.

—— (1980), 'The Analysis of Rates and Survivorship Using Log-Linear Models', *Biometrics*, 36. 2: 299–305.

Kalbfleisch, J. D., and Prentice, R. L. (1980), *The Statistical Analysis of Failure Time Data* (John Wiley, New York).

Kalton, G., and Kasprzyk, D. (1982), 'Imputing for Missing Survey Responses', *Proceedings of the Survey Research Methods Section, American Statistical Association 1982* (Alexandria, Va.), 22–31.

—— —— (1986), 'The Treatment of Missing Survey Data', *Survey Methodology*, 12. 1: 1–16.

Kaplan, E. L., and Meier, P. (1958), 'Nonparametric Estimation from Incomplete Observations', *Journal of the American Statistical Association*, 53. 282: 457–81.

Little, R. J. A. (1988a), 'Missing Data in Large Surveys' (with discussion), *Journal of Business and Economic Statistics*, 6. 3: 287–301.

—— (1988b), 'Statistics at the World Fertility Survey', *American Statistician*, 42. 1: 31–6.

—— and Perera, S. (1981), 'Illustrative Analysis: Socioeconomic Differentials in Cumulative Fertility in Sri Lanka—A Marriage Cohort Approach', WFS Scientific Report No. 12 (International Statistical Institute, Voorburg).

—— and Rubin, D. B. (1987), *Statistical Analysis with Missing Data* (John Wiley, New York).

—— and Schluchter, M. D. (1985), 'Maximum Likelihood Estimation for Mixed Continuous and Categorical Data with Missing Values', *Biometrika*, 72. 3: 497–512.

—— and Su, H.-L. (1987), 'Missing-Data Adjustments for Partially-Scaled Variables', *Proceedings of the Survey Research Methods Section, American Statistical Association 1987* (Alexandria, Va.), 644–9.

Madow, W. G., Nisselson, H., Olkin, I., and Rubin, D. B. (1983) (eds.), *Incomplete Data in Sample Surveys*, i–iii (Academic Press, New York).

Olkin, I., and Tate, R. F. (1961), 'Multivariate Correlation Models with Mixed Discrete and Continuous Variables', *Annals of Mathematical Statistics*, 32. 2: 448–65.

Otto, J. (1980), 'DEIR (Date Imputation and Recode Program), User's Manual', WFS Technical Report No. 1430 (International Statistical Institute, Voorburg).

Peto, R. (1973), 'Experimental Survival Curves for Interval-Censored Data', *Applied Statistics*, 22. 1: 86–91.

Prentice, R. L. (1973), 'Exponential Survivals with Censoring and Explanatory Variables', *Biometrika*, 60. 2: 279–84.

Rubin, D. B. (1976), 'Inference and Missing Data' (with discussion), *Biometrika*, 63. 3: 581–92.

—— (1978), 'Multiple Imputations in Sample Surveys: A Phenomenological Bayesian Approach to Nonresponse', *Proceedings of the Survey Research Methods Section, American Statistical Association 1978* (Alexandria, Va.), 20–34.

—— (1987), *Multiple Imputation in Sample Surveys and Censuses* (John Wiley, New York).

—— and Schenker, N. (1986), 'Multiple Imputation for Interval Estimation from Simple Random Samples with Ignorable Nonresponse', *Journal of the American Statistical Association*, 81. 394: 366–74.

Sande, I. G. (1982), 'Imputation in Surveys: Coping with Reality', *American Statistician*, 36. 3: 145–52.

Schluchter, M. D., and Jackson, K. L. (1989), 'Log-Linear Analysis of Censored Survival Data with Partially Observed Covariates', *Journal of the American Statistical Association*, 84. 405: 42–52.

Tuma, N. B. (1982), 'Nonparametric and Partially Parametric Approaches to Event-History Analysis', *Sociological Methodology 1982* (San Francisco), 1–60.

Tuma, N. B. and Hannan, M. T. (1978), 'Approaches to the Censoring Problem in Analysis of Event Histories', *Sociological Methodology 1979* (San Francisco), 209–40.

Turnbull, B. W. (1976), 'The Empirical Distribution Function with Arbitrarily Grouped, Censored and Truncated Data', *Journal of the Royal Statistical Society*, Ser. B, 38. 3: 290–5.

Weidman, L. (1986), 'Investigation of Gross Changes in Income Recipiency from the Survey of Income and Program Participation', *Proceedings of the Survey Research Methods Section, American Statistical Association 1986* (Alexandria, Va.), 231–6.

Whittemore, A. S., and Grosser, S. (1986), 'Regression Methods for Data with Incomplete Covariates', in S. H. Moolgavkar and R. L. Prentice (eds.), *Modern Statistical Methods in Chronic Disease Epidemiology* (John Wiley, New York).

# 9 Analysis of Current-Status Data

IAN D. DIAMOND, JOHN W. MCDONALD

The methods of survival analysis can be used to study the relationship between explanatory variables and the length of time or duration between one event and a subsequent event. In many areas of research, one variable of common interest is the age at which a certain event or 'milestone' occurs. In demography, age at weaning, menarche, first intercourse, first marriage, first birth, sterilization, menopause, and death are studied. There are many examples in other fields where age at which a milestone occurs is studied. For the purposes of exposition we confine ourselves only to situations where the variable of interest is the age at some milestone.

In survival analysis, the regression effects of explanatory variables on survival times (age at milestone) are of prime interest. These regression effects are usually studied using two classes of models: the proportional-hazards (PH) model and the accelerated-life (AL) model. The PH model assumes that hazard rates for individuals are in constant ratio over time. The AL model assumes that survival distributions for individuals have the same 'shape' but that differences between individual survival distributions are the result of a time-scale change. In other words, individuals proceed across the time axis at potentially different speeds so that one individual has an accelerated life relative to another, slower individual. Usually, a parametric model is assumed for the underlying survival distribution in an AL model. AL models are usually expressed as a linear regression model for the logarithm of the lifetime $T$. The common parametric models are of the form $Y = \mathbf{x}'\beta + \sigma\varepsilon$, where $Y = \log T$ represents log lifetime, $\sigma$ is a scale parameter, and $\varepsilon$ has a known error distribution, e.g. standard normal so that lifetime $T$ has a log-normal distribution.

One method of studying the relationship between the age at a particular milestone and some explanatory variables is to use 'current-status' data. These data comprise information on whether the milestone has or has not been reached at the time of a survey and information on age at the time of the survey. If the milestone has been reached, we have incomplete information on when this occurred. On the other hand, we do not know when it will be reached (if ever) for those respondents who have not achieved the milestone at the time of the survey. Current-status data thus correspond to the extreme situation where all the survival time data are either right-censored or left-censored. While these data constraints are restrictive, it is still possible to estimate the distribution using parametric models (Nelson 1978; 1982), to fit parametric models that include explanatory variables, and to estimate some non-parametric models. This chapter first discusses the advantages and disadvantages of current-status data and then reviews the fitting of PH and AL models to such data.

## Methods of Data Collection (or Types of Data)

### Retrospective Data

Data on the timing or date of events are often collected retrospectively by interview, usually by conducting a survey or census. Respondents can answer only that the milestone (1) occurred at a certain age or (2) has not yet occurred, i.e. right-censored data (age at milestone > age at survey).

### Advantages

The major attraction of retrospectively reported data is the obvious ease of collection, despite the fact that, unless a proxy respondent is reliable, the respondent must survive to the time of the survey or census. However, in many demographic situations this is not too restrictive an assumption. In many countries, for example, relatively few women now die before they reach puberty, so this method would be feasible for studying age at menarche if women can reliably report this date and are interviewed 'soon' thereafter.

### Disadvantages

Unfortunately, retrospective data may contain serious reporting errors of unknown size and direction resulting from recall errors or misreporting. People are notoriously poor at recalling events and the timing of events (see Bernard *et al.* 1984 and Moss and Goldstein 1985 for a review). Several factors are known to influence recall accuracy. In general, more errors occur the greater the time-lag between an event and its recall. A variety of studies have found that more recent events were more accurately recalled than those in the more distant past (Cannell *et al.* 1977). A second factor known to influence recall accuracy is the relative salience of the event. For example, many women believe that menstruation is an essential characteristic of femininity and that menarche is the time when one 'becomes a woman' (WHO 1981*a*). The importance of this event may account for some women's greater-than-expected accuracy in remembering facts such as age at menarche.

How do we know when the information reported is accurate? This is usually determined by cross-checking with other sources such as administrative records or by reinterview at a later date. Research into the recall accuracy of dates is limited. A Swedish longitudinal study of 339 girls (Bergsten-Brucefors 1976) found a correlation of .81 between actual and recalled age at menarche some four years after the event. Damon *et al.* (1969) reported a correlation of .78 between actual and recalled age of menarche some 19 years after the event ($n = 60$), and Damon and Bajema (1974) found a correlation of 0.60 after 39 years. As expected, recall accuracy declines with the length of the recall period.

Alternatively, the occurrence of such factors as digit preference or age heaping also casts doubt on the accuracy of the reports. For example, MacMahon and Worcester (1966) found that there was 'marked terminal digit clustering' of reported age at menopause around ages ending in zero and five. They concluded that standard life-table methods (to handle right-censored data) would give erroneous results, and decided to ignore the reported age at menopause and to estimate the distribution of age at natural menopause using only the current-status answers.

### Prospective or Longitudinal Data

Marshall and Tanner (1986) discuss methods of data collection on age at menarche and conclude that 'the method of data collection by recollection is clearly unsatisfactory, but it was used in nearly all the older surveys'. They then discuss the longitudinal method, where a group of subjects is seen repeatedly and each subject is asked on every occasion if she has yet to begin to menstruate. They believe that 'if the interval between visits is short, the precise date can usually be determined with reasonable confidence', and that 'this is the most accurate method of determining the age at menarche'. However, the optimum length of time between visits needs to be determined empirically. The disadvantages of longitudinal data are mainly financial and administrative.

However, if the time intervals between visits are long enough that the reported date is considered unreliable, then current status at each time-point yields lower and/or upper bounds between which the true age at milestone is known to fall. This approach yields the most general type of interval-censored data: examples include annual surveys recording only whether or not, at each occasion, the milestone has occurred.

### Current Status or Status Quo Data

Data on age at milestone are often collected by interview, usually by conducting a survey or census. Respondents are asked their age and whether the milestone has occurred. An affirmative answer (age at milestone < age at survey) yields left-censored data, while a negative response (age at milestone > age at survey) results in right-censored data. Therefore, this method of data collection yields only right- or left-censored data on the age at milestone but does not yield the age at milestone for any individual! Such data are termed current-status data in demography and status quo data in the medical/human biology literature (see Aw and Tye 1970; Atwood and Taube 1976).

### Advantages

A principal advantage of current-status data is that it may be readily available from administrative sources, surveys, or censuses. For example, one can study age at first marriage using age at census and current marital status (see Hajnal 1953). Of course, the analysis of differentials in age at first marriage is restricted to explanatory variables found on the census schedule. Current-status data may also be easier to collect and more reliable than data collected by other means. The burden on the respondent and the interviewer is less when current-status data are collected, since the respondent does not have to recall, and the interviewer does not have to probe for, exact dates. Thus, there should be less measurement error for current-status data than for retrospective data.

While the occurrence or non-occurrence of many milestones can be of great importance to individuals, the exact age at which the milestone occurs may be relatively unimportant to them. In this situation, one would expect an unreliable or inaccurately reported age at milestone. For example, while most people may recall accurately certain facts about their first intercourse, such as who their partner was and the location, the exact date or their exact age at first intercourse would probably be reported inaccurately by a substantial proportion of respondents.

The dates of infant-feeding transitions are of great importance to demographers in their study of infant and child mortality and of birth intervals. A study in Lansing, Michigan by Quandt (1987) found that some mothers make substantial errors in their recall of the timing of infant-feeding transitions. Three specific feeding transitions were studied: weaning, introduction of formula, and introduction of solid foods. To evaluate the accuracy of recall data, longitudinally gathered records (based on 24-hour dietary records) were compared with retrospective data collected when infants reached six months of age. All dates were converted to months of age using the child's birth date. A recall date was considered accurate if it was equal to or up to .3 months less than the recorded date for the same transition. The sample consisted of 68 mothers of first-born normal singleton births who were white high-school graduates and were considered at low risk throughout pregnancy.

While the number studied by Quandt was small, the recall period was short (not greater than six months). Of the responses, 39% of those ever weaning ($n = 27$) were inaccurate, with 12% inaccurate by more than one month. Approximately equal numbers over- and under-reported the date of weaning so that there was no systematic bias in misreporting. However, some substantial misreporting occurred, with the errors ranging from $-2.6$ months (recalling too early an age at weaning) to $+1.2$ months (recalling too late an age at weaning). Of those mothers who introduced formula, 44% ($n = 39$) gave inaccurate dates, with 42% inaccurate by at least one month. The errors ranged from $-3.9$ to $+2.5$ months. There was some evidence of systematic bias in the reporting, in that the majority recalled too early a date of introduction of formula. For the case of solid foods, 59% of mothers introducing solids ($n = 66$) reported the date inaccurately, with

25% inaccurate by at least one month. The errors ranged from − 3.0 to + 3.8 months. Here there was stronger evidence that mothers recalled too late a date.

Weaning may represent the most salient feeding transition because its importance may be perceived by the mother and thus be better remembered. The other feeding transitions may have lower degrees of salience that result in less accurate recall. While the mean ages at transition may be estimated reasonably well, the fact that some mothers make substantial errors has implications for the choice of data-collection strategies and data-analysis techniques. Quandt concludes: 'Where accurate data on feeding practices for a whole population are required and error is not known to be random, methods other than retrospective longitudinal data collection should be used. Probit analysis of cross-sectional data collected from mothers of all age infants should be preferable.' Thus Quandt favours using current-status data rather than retrospective data to study feeding transitions.

Rather than base an analysis on unreliably reported age-at-event data, many analysts besides Quandt also prefer to use reliable current-status data (Page, Lesthaeghe, and Adegbola 1977; Lesthaeghe and Page 1980; Ferry 1981; Anderson, Rodrigues, and Thome 1984). McKinlay, Jeffreys, and Thompson (1972) note that 'date of final menstruation (LMP) given by women cannot be considered reliable because of the difficulty of recall after, frequently, many years' and 'A much more reliable measure would be the menopausal status of the respondents at the time of the survey, since this can be determined on the basis of each woman's "Yes" or "No" reply to events occurring within only the previous year'.

The Demographic and Health Surveys program (Lapham and Westoff 1986) is conducting about 70 surveys around the world with an emphasis on the collection and analysis of data on major health and demographic phenomena. This program has decided to collect data on a number of maternal and child health variables on a current-status basis. For all births in the past five years, current-status data is collected for: (1) tetanus toxoid injection, (2) prenatal care, (3) assistance at delivery, (4) postpartum amenorrhoea, (5) postpartum abstinence, (6) breastfeeding duration and frequency, and (7) supplementary foods.

## Disadvantages

The use of current-status data involves a loss of information, since only an upper limit for the timing or dating of the milestone is used in the analysis rather than the reported exact timing or date of the event. The use of current-status data is also problematic when secular trends in the phenomenon studied are occurring, because secular trends are confounded with age. If these time-trends are exponential, then it is possible to estimate the time-trends as well as the age incidence using a Gompertz hazard model (Hudson 1986). Bracher and Santow (1981) criticize the use of current-status data to study age at some milestone when the milestone is a 'recurrent event' (but not when the milestone is a non-recurrent event such as first marriage or menarche). Their concern is that recurrent events such as postpartum abstinence and amenorrhoea are affected by length-bias sampling problems. In this context, the survey or census produces a length-biased sample, where the probability of selecting an individual in a particular state basically depends on the length of the birth interval or some component of it. Various sampling schemes and the sampling problems associated with recurrent events are discussed by John, Menken, and Trussell (1988). They show analytically that only one sampling scheme can recover the correct survival distribution. Consider, for example, the distribution of weaning times for infants in the population. They show that, if a sample of all births during a fixed period or sample of all births of a given parity is used, then the distribution of weaning times estimated from current-status (or retrospective-history) data is the same as the distribution of weaning times for infants in the population as a whole. Therefore, there is no problem in analysing current-status data when the sampling frame is appropriate.

## Impact of Measurement Error on Analysis

The classical methods of survival analysis implicitly assume accurate measurement of the timing or date of events. The impact of measurement error in dates has been studied by Carroll *et al.* (1978) who found that such errors caused only moderate deterioration in the 'quality' of the maximum-likelihood estimator. However, since their Monte Carlo study dealt with only a limited class of situations, the impact of measurement error in dates should still remain a serious concern for data analysts.

The effect of measurement error in dates is to bias estimators of the regression parameters. One should be concerned with both the size and direction of reporting errors. If the errors are 'random noise' unrelated to age at milestone and the explanatory variables, these reporting errors may be tolerable for the research purpose for which such data are used. If the response bias centres on zero, estimators of mean age at milestone may be unbiased. For example, Bergsten-Brucefors (1976) studied the accuracy of recalled age at menarche approximately four years after the date of menarche. She found that only 31% recalled the actual month and year, only 63% recalled within ± 3 months accuracy, and only 91% within ± 12 months accuracy. Some 11% were exactly ± 1 year mistaken about the date. However, if the responses are classified into 10 intervals of error (± 1–3, 4–6, 7–9, 10–12, over 12 months), then the errors are symmetrically distributed about zero (a formal test of symmetry yields a test statistic of 2.364, which is not significant when compared to the null chi-squared distribution with 5 degrees of freedom). Since there was no systematic bias in the reported age at menarche, an estimate of the mean age at menarche using these data is probably reasonable.

However, if systematic under- or over-reporting of age at milestone exists, then we should be worried. Quandt (1987) found some evidence of systematic bias in the reporting of the date of introduction to solid foods, in that mothers recalled too late a date rather than too early a date. McKinlay, Jeffreys, and Thompson (1972) found 'understatement of the age at the last menstrual period (LMP) by women, with increased lapse of time'.

Response bias may also be related to explanatory variables. A WHO (1981*a*; 1981*b*) cross-cultural study of menstruation found: 'In Egypt and India there was a tendency for rural women to be more accurate than urban women in the prediction and recall of menstrual events. Rural women are more affected by behavioral restrictions during menstruation, which may make them more aware of menstrual events.' Also, 'Menstrual bleeding is an important factor in the life of Egyptian peasant women, and rural mothers question pubescent daughters about the presence or absence of menstrual symptoms.' Therefore, we might expect that rural women may be able to report age at menarche more accurately than urban women. Any rural/urban differentials in age at menarche may be confounded with rural/urban differentials in recall accuracy, which are probably due to the relative salience of menstruation in the two areas. Therefore, if response bias is related to one or more explanatory variables, then differentials in age at milestone may be confounded with reporting-error differentials.

The use of current-status data versus retrospectively reported data is basically a question of the trade-off between precision and bias. We have presented a number of examples where various analysts have concluded that retrospectively reported data are unreliable. If the analyst is concerned only with an age-at-milestone response variable (and not with the influence of time-dependent covariates), we believe that, until the factors influencing the accuracy of retrospectively collected event histories and the pattern of reporting errors are studied, the more reliable current-status data should be collected and analysed.

## Parametric Regression Models for Continuous-Survival Data Adapted to Current-Status Data

For the $i^{th}$ individual, we observe whether or not the milestone has occurred before known age $a_i$ which, in general, differs between individuals. Current-status data often involve a large number of haphazardly determined censoring points (the $a_i$s) with the possibility of a large number of repeated censoring points (e.g. if age at survey or census is measured in completed months or years). Most parametric survival models can be specialized to current-status data. For example, log-logistic and log-normal AL models when specialized yield logit and probit binary regression models. By including the logarithm of $a_i$ as an explanatory variable in a binary regression model, one can fit parametric AL models to right- and left-censored survival data where the right- and left-censored indicator is taken as the response variable.

Binary regression models are of the general form

$$\text{link}\{p(z)\} = \beta_0 + \mathbf{z}'\beta_1 \tag{1}$$

where some 'link' function of the probability, $p(z)$, of 'success' has a linear regression on the explanatory variables $z$. The link can be any continuous monotone increasing function from the unit interval $(0, 1)$ to the real line. The 'natural type' of link for a statistician to use is the inverse of a cumulative distribution function (CDF) of a continuous random variable: link $F^{-1}\{p(z)\}$ where $F(\bullet)$ is a CDF. The term link was introduced by Nelder and Wedderburn (1972) in their definition of the class of generalized linear models (see also McCullagh and Nelder 1983). All the binary regression models considered are examples of generalized linear models, and the computer package GLIM 3.77 (Payne 1985) can be used to fit these models easily. Three link functions for binary data are provided as standard options in GLIM. The logit link, $\text{logit}(p) = \log\{p/(1-p)\}$, is the inverse of the CDF of the standard logistic distribution. The probit link, $\Phi^{-1}(p)$, is the inverse of the CDF of the standard normal distribution. The complementary $\log-\log$ transformation, defined as $\log\{-\log(1-p)\}$, is the inverse of the CDF of the extreme minimum-value distribution. The $\log-\log$ link, $\log\{-\log(p)\}$, is the inverse of the CDF of the extreme maximum-value distribution. The CDFs of these distributions are given in the section below on parametric accelerated-life models.

## Likelihood for Current-Status Data

For individual $i$ with vector of explanatory variables $\mathbf{x}_i$, instead of observing age at milestone $T_i$, we observe at known age $a_i$ only

$$Y_i = \begin{cases} 1 & \text{if } T_i < a_i \quad \text{(left-censored age at milestone)} \\ 0 & \text{if } T_i > a_i \quad \text{(right-censored age at milestone)} \end{cases} \qquad (2)$$

The information contained in a current-status sample of size $n$ is described by the $n$ triples $(Y_i, a_i, \mathbf{x}_i)$, where $i = 1, \ldots, n$. The likelihood is the usual Bernoulli likelihood

$$\prod_{i=1}^{n} p_i^{Y_i} (1 - p_i)^{1 - Y_i} \qquad (3)$$

where $p_i = \Pr(Y_i = 1; a_i, \mathbf{x}_i)$ is the probability that the age at milestone $T_i$ is less than $a_i$.

The likelihood equations and Fisher information matrix for distributions having a location and scale parameter are given in Nelson (1978), so that the Newton–Raphson algorithm may be used to find maximum-likelihood estimates and their covariance matrix. These equations may be easily modified to include a location parameter that depends linearly on explanatory variables.

## Parametric Proportional-Hazards (PH) Models

The usual PH model assumes that the hazard function at time $t$ for an individual with vector of explanatory variables $\mathbf{x}$ has the form

$$h(t; \mathbf{x}) = h_0(t) \, e^{\mathbf{x}'\boldsymbol{\beta}} \tag{4}$$

where $h_0(t)$ is a non-negative function of time $t$ and $\boldsymbol{\beta}$ is a column vector of unknown regression parameters. $h_0(t)$ is called the baseline hazard, and represents the hazard function for a (perhaps hypothetical) individual whose explanatory variables are all zero.

The PH model is very flexible since it specifies only that a certain relationship exists: in other words, proportionality among hazard functions. Some versions do not specify the shape of the hazard, and these are called semi- or non-parametric PH models. Parametric PH models assume that lifetimes have a known distribution, so that the baseline hazard function has a known functional form. Parametric PH models can provide a powerful alternative to the semi-parametric PH models discussed later if one can find an adequate representation of the baseline hazard. Knowledge about the shape of the hazard function is often of use in choosing a particular parametric hazard. For example, (1) constant hazard—exponential; (2) monotonic hazard—Weibull, Rayleigh, Gompertz, Makeham, Pareto, gamma, and normal; (3) bathtub-shaped; and (4) upside-down bathtub-shaped—log-normal and log-logistic.

Assuming a PH model for individual $i$, the probability that $T_i$ is less than $a_i$,

$$p_i = 1 - \exp\left\{-\int_0^{a_i} h_0(t) \exp(\mathbf{x}_i'\boldsymbol{\beta}) \, dt\right\} \tag{5}$$

$$= 1 - \exp[-\exp\{\alpha(a_i) + \mathbf{x}_i'\boldsymbol{\beta}\}]$$

where $\alpha(a_i) = \log\left\{\int_0^{a_i} h_0(t) \, dt\right\}$. Now consider the Weibull distribution where the baseline hazard

$$h_0(t) = \frac{p}{\mu}\left(\frac{t}{\mu}\right)^{p-1} \tag{6}$$

is a power function of time and both parameters are positive. For the Weibull, $\alpha(a_i) = \alpha + p \log a_i$, where $\alpha = -p \log \mu$ and (5) can be shown to equal

$$1 - \exp\{-\exp(\alpha + p \log a_i + \mathbf{x}_i'\boldsymbol{\beta})\}. \tag{7}$$

We can invert expression (7) so that

$$\log\{-\log(1 - p_i)\} = \alpha + p \log a_i + \mathbf{x}_i'\boldsymbol{\beta} \tag{8}$$

Therefore, for Weibull-distributed survival data the complementary $\log - \log$ transformation of the probability of a lifetime in the interval $(0, a_i)$ can be expressed as a linear function of $\log a_i$ and explanatory variables.

GLIM can be used to fit a Weibull PH model to current-status data by declaring a complementary $\log - \log$ link and including $\log a_i$ as a covariate. We will not present other parametric models, since we believe that the specification of the baseline hazard using splines (discussed later) is a superior model specification.

## Parametric Accelerated-Life (AL) Models

Regression effects in survival models can be modelled in terms of a time-scale change. AL models specify that the effect of explanatory variables is to alter the rate at which an individual proceeds along the time axis. This may be thought of as a time-scale change or a change in clock speed. Since the role of explanatory variables is to accelerate (or decelerate) time, this type of model is referred to as an accelerated-life model. This idea is contained in a quote from Thoreau: 'If a man does not keep pace with his companions, perhaps he hears a different drummer. Let him step to the music which he hears, however measured or far away.' For the AL model the pace across the time axis or each individual's clock speed depends on each individual's characteristics as measured by the explanatory variables.

For example, it is not unusual to hear the comment that a dog that died at age 15 died at a ripe old age for a dog. The thought underlying such a statement is that a dog dying at age 15 is equivalent to a human dying at the ripe old age of, say, 75, in the sense that the proportion of dogs surviving to age 15 equals the proportion of humans surviving to age 75. Formally, we can equate the survivor functions for dogs and humans where the survivor function $S(t) = \text{pr}(T > t)$ is the probability of surviving to time $t$ so that $S(75; \text{human}) = S(15; \text{dog})$.

The AL model may be expressed as $S(t; \mathbf{x}) = S_0(te^{\mathbf{x}'\beta})$ where $\mathbf{x}$ is a column vector of explanatory variables and $\beta$ a column vector of regression parameters. For the single explanatory variable

$$x = \begin{cases} 1 & \text{if} \quad \text{dog} \\ 0 & \text{if} \quad \text{human} \end{cases} \qquad \text{and} \quad e^\beta = 5$$

$$
\begin{aligned}
S(t; x=0) &= S(t; \text{human}) & &= S_0(t) \\
S(t; x=1) &= S(t; \text{dog}) & &= S_0(t\,e^\beta) \\
S(15; \text{dog}) &= S(15 \times 5; \text{human}) & &= S(75; \text{human})
\end{aligned}
$$

or dogs cross the time (age) axis 5 times faster than humans.

AL models are usually expressed as location-scale models for log lifetime (Kalbfleisch and Prentice 1980). The log transformation of lifetime is a natural way of ensuring that the estimated lifetimes are positive and of dealing with data skewed to the right. A location-scale model relates the distribution of a random variable $Y$ in terms of a random variable $X$ where $Y = \mu + \sigma X$. The density and survival function of $Y$ can be expressed as

$$F_Y(y; \mu, \sigma) = \frac{1}{\sigma} f_X\left(\frac{y-\mu}{\sigma}\right) \quad \text{and} \quad S_Y(y) = S_X\left(\frac{y-\mu}{\sigma}\right) \tag{9}$$

Log-linear regression models for lifetime $T$ assume that $\log T$ is related to the explanatory variables, $x_1, \ldots, x_k$ via a linear model

$$\log T = \mu_0 - x_1\beta_1 - x_2\beta_2 - \ldots - x_k\beta_k + \sigma\varepsilon \tag{10}$$

where:

$\mu_0 - x_1\beta_1 - x_2\beta_2 - \ldots - x_k\beta_k$ is a general location parameter
$\mu_0$ is the location parameter for the baseline hazard
  (when all the explanatory variables equal zero)
$\sigma$ is a constant scale parameter
$\varepsilon$ is an error term with known parametric distribution
  (that does not depend on the explanatory variables).

The minus signs occur in this specification of the AL model since the PH model is a model for risk and the AL model for lifetime, and high risk implies a short lifetime. The equivalency of these two formulations of the model follows easily. Let $W = \mu_0 + \sigma \varepsilon$ so that $\log T = -\mathbf{x}'\beta + W$ and

$$S_T(t) = \Pr(\log T > \log t) = \Pr(\log T + \mathbf{x}'\beta > \log t + \mathbf{x}'\beta)$$

$$= \Pr(W > \log t + \mathbf{x}'\beta) = \Pr(e^W > te^{\mathbf{x}'\beta}) = S_{T_0}(te^{\mathbf{x}'\beta}) \qquad (11)$$

where $T_0 = e^W$ and $T_0 = T/e^{\mathbf{x}'\beta}$.

## Parametric Distributions for AL Models

Models for lifetime $T$ are induced or specified by location-scale models for log-lifetime $T$. The error distribution is in standard form when $\mu = 0$ and $\sigma = 1$.

(1) If $\varepsilon$ is distributed as a standard normal distribution, then $T$ has a log-normal distribution, i.e. $\log T$ is $N(\mu, \sigma^2)$ with density

$$f_T(t) = \frac{1}{t(2\pi\sigma^2)^{1/2}} e^{-\frac{1}{2\sigma^2}(\log t - \mu)^2} \qquad \text{for} \quad t > 0 \qquad (12)$$

(2) If $\varepsilon$ is distributed as a standard logistic distribution, then $T$ has a log-logistic distribution. The density and CDF for the standard logistic distribution are

$$f(\varepsilon) = \exp(\varepsilon)/\{1 + \exp(\varepsilon)\}^2 \quad \text{and} \quad F(\varepsilon) = \exp(\varepsilon)/\{1 + \exp(\varepsilon)\}. \qquad (13)$$

The logistic density is similar in shape to the normal density, i.e. symmetrical about zero with slightly heavier tails than the normal density, so that the log-logistic distribution is similar in shape to the log-normal distribution.

(3) If $\varepsilon$ is distributed as a standard extreme minimum-value distribution, then $T$ has a log-extreme minimum-value distribution (better known as the Weibull). The density and CDF for the standard extreme minimum-value distribution are

$$f(\varepsilon) = \exp\{\varepsilon - \exp(\varepsilon)\} \quad \text{and} \quad F(\varepsilon) = 1 - \exp\{-\exp(\varepsilon)\} \qquad (14)$$

(4) If $\varepsilon$ is distributed as a standard extreme maximum-value distribution, then $T$ has a log-extreme maximum-value distribution. The density and CDF of the standard extreme maximum-value distribution are

$$f(\varepsilon) = \exp\{-\varepsilon \exp(-\varepsilon)\} \quad \text{and} \quad F(\varepsilon) = \exp\{-\exp(-\varepsilon)\}. \qquad (15)$$

Location and scale models with censored data can be fitted using GLIM (for details see Jorgensen 1984 or Stirling 1984). Vanderhoeft (1982) first made the observation that log-normal, log-logistic, and log-extreme minimum-value AL models could be fitted to current-status data using GLIM. Vanderhoeft showed that, if $\log T = \mu + \mathbf{x}'\beta + \sigma\varepsilon$, the probability that lifetime $T_i$ is less than $a_i$ is given by

$$p_i = F(\alpha + \delta \log a_i + \mathbf{x}'\gamma) \tag{16}$$

where $F$ is the CDF of the standard-error distribution of the log-linear model for lifetime $T$ and $\alpha = -\mu/\sigma$, $\delta = 1/\sigma$, and $\gamma = -\beta/\sigma$. Therefore, any parametric AL model that is expressed as a log-linear regression model for $\log T$ with error CDF $F$ can be fitted to current-status data using GLIM by specifying the inverse of $F$ as the link. The standard logistic, normal, extreme minimum-value, and extreme maximum-value error distributions correspond to the logit, probit, complementary $\log - \log$, and $\log - \log$ links, respectively and correspond to log-logistic, log-normal, log-extreme minimum-value (Weibull), and log-extreme maximum-value distributions for lifetime $T$.

## Tests of Distributional Shape for AL Models

The problem now is to find an error distribution that will fit the data well. The usual way of tackling this problem is to use a rich and flexible family of error (or equivalently survival) distributions that cover a wide range of distributional shapes and test that the candidate distribution gives a reasonable fit (see Prentice 1975; Farewell and Prentice 1977). Embedding competing models in a single parametric framework allows the methods of ordinary parametric inference to be used for discrimination, and leads to an assessment of each competing model relative to a more comprehensive one. However, one problem with this approach is that large amounts of data are often necessary to discriminate between distributions that, in some sense, are close, e.g. the log-normal and log-logistic. Therefore, if it is impossible to discriminate between two or more candidate distributions, it is best to use the one that is most easily interpretable, e.g. the Weibull distribution if it is one of the candidates.

For current-status data, however, the problem of testing one distributional shape versus another becomes the problem of testing one link function versus another. For example, discriminating between the log-normal and log-logistic distributions corresponds to discriminating between probit and logit links. Chambers and Cox (1967) investigated the sample sizes needed to discriminate between these two similar links, and concluded that about 1 000 observations are needed 'for even modest sensitivity'. While large sample sizes are needed to discriminate between the logit and probit links, it is often feasible to discriminate between the logit (probit), and $\log - \log$ and complementary $\log - \log$ links.

Several authors (Prentice 1976; van Monfort and Otten 1976; Copenhaver and Mielke 1977; Pregibon 1980; Aranda-Ordaz 1981, 1983; Genter 1982; Genter and Farewell 1985) have considered generalized link functions that include some of the commonly used links and allow goodness-of-fit testing for these links. Another way of testing between different links and different functional forms for the explanatory variables (e.g. age versus log age) is through the use of a Monte Carlo method called the bootstrap (see Wahrendorf, Becher, and Brown 1987; Cole and McDonald 1989). Of course, conclusions from the goodness-of-fit testing are intrinsically linked to the correct specification of the regression model.

While these all-encompassing generalized links are appealing since they allow the estimation of 'intermediate' link functions between logit (probit), log – log, and complementary log – log links, model-fitting using these generalized links and likelihood-ratio testing cannot yet be carried out easily using standard statistical packages. Genter (1982, personal communication) found that 'fitting either generalized link takes an incredible amount of computing time'. However, Genter (1982) recommends fitting the probit (logit), log – log, and complementary log – log links and comparing their likelihoods. If twice the difference of two log-likelihoods (in GLIM terminology the deviance) exceeds the appropriate percentile of the chi-squared distribution with one degree of freedom, then one can infer that the link with the smaller log-likelihood is inappropriate. This provides a conservative goodness-of-fit test compared with the likelihood-ratio test based on the full, 'all-encompassing' model.

Note that the absolute deviance cannot be used to measure the goodness of fit of a linear-logistic model to binary observations, since the deviance is a function of the fitted values only and hence cannot tell us anything about the agreement between the observed values and the fitted values (Williams 1982). This result is true exactly only for the logistic link and not for the alternative links, but for these alternative links one must still view the deviance with suspicion.

It is beyond the scope of this chapter to provide a full critique of rival parametric models. We will now turn to non-parametric survival models that we believe are superior to the parametric models for current-status data.

## Non-Parametric Regression Models for Survival Data

This section describes models that relate the distribution of lifetimes to explanatory variables without assuming a parametric model for the form of the distributions. The usual Cox PH model for continuous data is non-parametric in the sense that one does not have to specify the form of the baseline hazard in order to make inferences about the regression parameters. This is accomplished through the use of partial-likelihood methods (Cox 1972; 1975), but, unfortunately, these methods cannot be applied to current-status data. However, there are two models, one for grouped continuous data and the other for continuous data, for which conventional maximum-likelihood procedures can be used. The grouped-data model makes no assumption about the form of the underlying baseline hazard, while the second model uses splines to specify the baseline hazard in an essentially non-parametric manner.

## PH Model for Grouped Continuous Data

Since age data are often collected in the form of completed years or completed months of age or are grouped for analysis, the grouped continuous-data model is of substantial importance. The usual grouped-data version of the PH model (Kalbfleisch and Prentice 1973; Prentice and Gloeckler 1978; Pierce, Stewart, and Kopecky 1979) supposes that continuous lifetimes are grouped into a number of mutually exclusive and exhaustive intervals that partition the time or age axis. For this model, the complementary log – log transformation of the conditional probability of a lifetime ending in an interval, conditional on survival up to that interval, can be expressed as a linear function of parameters for explanatory variables (Bartlett 1978), and the number of lifetimes ending in an interval has a binomial distribution. This model is another example of a generalized linear model.

For current-status data, the complimentary log – log transformation of the probability of a lifetime ending in the interval $(0, a_i)$ can be expressed as a linear function of parameters for the time-intervals and parameters for the explanatory variables (see Equations 5–8 or Diamond, McDonald, and Shah 1986). The parameter for the time interval $(0, a_i)$ equals the logarithm of the integral of the baseline hazard from the time origin zero to $a_i$, i.e.,

$$c_i = \log \int_0^{a_i} h_0(t) \, dt \tag{17}$$

If the discrete time-points are ordered from smallest to largest so that $0 < a_1 < a_2 < \ldots < a_k$, then the $c_i$ parameters must necessarily form a non-decreasing sequence, i.e., $0 \leq c_1 \leq c_2 \leq \ldots \leq c_k$.

These inequality constraints for the parameters for each time-interval ensure that the estimated baseline survival function is non-increasing (as well as ensuring that the estimated survival function for any individual is non-increasing). Because of sampling variability, it is possible for one or more of these constraints to be violated. Order restrictions on the parameters and their violation in practice require the use of a constrained estimation procedure when fitting the model. Constrained maximum-likelihood estimates of the parameters can be found using methods described by McDonald and Diamond (1983; 1990). For the special case involving no explanatory variables, the pool-adjacent violators-algorithm can be used (Robertson, Wright, and Dykstra 1988).

Unfortunately, the computational cost of model-fitting and screening becomes prohibitive when the number of time-intervals is large (since one parameter is estimated for each time-interval) or when there are many violations of the inequality constraints. Therefore, we now turn to a discussion of whether a more complete flexible specification of the baseline hazard in terms of a few unknown parameters may reduce the computational cost of model-fitting and model-screening to a manageable size, while at the same time retaining an essentially non-parametric representation of the baseline hazard. The basic approach is to model the transformation of the baseline hazard that appears in the linear predictor part of the model with a spline. Since this approach is applicable to continuous data as well as to grouped continuous data, we will discuss this approach with continuous-data models.

### Continuous-Data Models

Splines are smooth functions that are extremely flexible in shape and are represented by a minimal number of parameters. In a real sense, splines can be used to bridge the gap between parametric and non-parametric models. The extremely rich class of shapes represented by splines can be used to specify the baseline hazard (or some function of the baseline hazard) in an essentially non-parametric manner. At the same time, the smoothness properties of splines may have the added benefit of appreciably improving our inferences for the regression parameters by increasing efficiency.

A spline is a smooth function that is defined in pieces, and the pieces are joined together in a suitably smooth fashion at join points called knots. Each piece of a spline is a low-degree polynomial. Cubic splines (splines of degree 3) are often used in practice, since they are reasonably flexible in shape and reliable algorithms are available for their calculation. A simple method for calculating cubic splines is given by Lenth (1977). The use of splines in statistics has recently been reviewed by Wegman and Wright (1983). Expository discussions on using splines in regression are given by Smith (1979; 1982). Splines have been used in survival analysis by Anderson and Senthilselvan (1980), Klotz (1982), Gilks (1983), Ciampi and Etezadi-Amoli (1985), Whittemore (1985), Bloxom (1985), Diamond, McDonald, and Shah (1986), Whittemore and Keller (1986), and Etezadi-Amoli and Ciampi (1987). By using splines, one can analyse survival data in an essentially non-parametric manner using standard maximum-likelihood techniques. For the case of current-status data, see Diamond, McDonald, and Shah (1986) for details.

### Reanalysis of English Current-Status Age at Menarche Data

Roberts, Rozner, and Swan (1971) studied differentials in age at menarche in north-east England using current-status data, and kindly provided their data for reanalysis. Girls aged 9–16 in 1967 who were living in the urban community of South Shields were interviewed at school. Five schools were included: a comprehensive ($n = 387$), a grammar ($n = 653$), a Catholic secondary ($n = 215$), a secondary modern ($n = 301$), and a junior school ($n = 98$). For each girl, the date of examination, her date of birth, and whether she had attained menarche was recorded. Of 1 654 girls interviewed, 56.5% had attained menarche. Also recorded were number of siblings, birth order, and social class. Roberts, Rozner, and Swan (1971) applied an empirical logistic transform to the proportion who had attained menarche at each age, where the girl's age to the nearest half-year was used as an explanatory variable. The family size effect was highly significant ($p < 0.005$), but no effect of social class or birth order was found after controlling for family size. Each of these factors was treated as a categorical variable. They conclude: 'Taken overall these findings ... suggest that environment (and in particular standards of nutrition and general care) is still an important determinant of age at menarche, but that today in Britain it operates through family size and no longer through accepted socio-economic categories.'

We reanalysed these data, first omitting, like the original study, the twins and fatherless children with mothers receiving National Assistance and then the 109 children without a well-defined social class (i.e. those whose father was unemployed or dead, or whose parents were separated). Unlike the original study, we further omitted all 98 cases from the junior school. This left a final sample size of 1409. Note that the omitted junior-school girls were much younger than the girls in the other schools (the oldest junior-school girl was younger than the youngest girl in each of the other schools) and only one junior-school girl had attained menarche. The exclusion of the very youngest girls who had small probabilities of attaining menarche results in the loss of little 'information' about the parameter estimates. For example, for a random sample of observations, if the probability of attaining menarche for the $i^{\text{th}}$ girl is $p_i = F(\mathbf{z}_i'\boldsymbol{\beta})$, where $\mathbf{z}_i$ is a vector of explanatory variables (including log age at survey), $\boldsymbol{\beta}$ is our vector of parameters to be estimated, and $F(\bullet)$ is the CDF of the standard logistic distribution, then it is easily shown that the Fisher information matrix is given by

$$I(\boldsymbol{\beta}) = \sum_{i=1}^{n} p_i(1 - p_i)\, z_i z_i' \tag{18}$$

Hence, if a girl's probability of attaining menarche is small, that girl's contribution to the information matrix is small. Similar results hold for other links (see e.g. Griffiths, Carter Hill, and Hope 1987).

Overall, our substantive conclusions are the same as Roberts, Rozner, and Swan (1971), but we found that the complementary log – log link fitted the data better than the logit link, both for the best model including exact age (in days) as an explanatory variable and for the best model including log-exact age (see Table 9.1). We followed Genter's (1982) recommendations and fitted the logit, probit, log – log and complementary log – log links and compared twice the difference of the log-likelihoods (deviances). If the deviances exceeded 3.84, the upper 5% point of the $\chi^2$ distribution with one degree of freedom, then one can infer that the link with the smaller log-likelihood is inappropriate. Unfortunately, since there is no all-encompassing generalized link that includes both the logit and probit as special cases, there is formally no justification for comparing the goodness-of-fit statistics for the logit and probit links. However, the observed difference would be declared significant at the 5% level with the probit providing a better fit. As is shown in Table 9.1, the complementary log – log link provides a significantly better fit (at the 5% level) for the model with log-age as an explanatory variable, but the probit proves to be the best link for the model with age as an explanatory variable. Since these two alternative models are not nested and we have not carried out a Monte Carlo comparison of goodness of fit, we have no formal basis on which to choose between them. We much prefer the model that includes log-age as an explanatory variable as our final model, since we may then interpret this model either as a PH or AL model with underlying Weibull distribution.

TABLE 9.1. *Analysis of deviances for age at menarche in South Shields.*

| | Logit | Probit | Complementary log – log | log – log | DF |
|---|---|---|---|---|---|
| Total Deviance | 1900.1 | 1900.1 | 1900.1 | 1900.1 | 1408 |
| Model A: Reduction in deviance | | | | | |
| Age in days | 632.2 | 636.1 | 632.4 | 610.4 | 1 |
| + no. of siblings | 25.9 | 26.7 | 29.2 | 26.4 | 5 |
| + social class | 3.7 | 3.9 | 4.1 | 4.6 | 4 |
| + birth order | 1.5 | 1.6 | 2.3 | 1.3 | 2 |
| Best model Age + no. of siblings | 1243.3 | 1237.5 | 1237.8 | 1256.5 | 1402 |
| Model B: Reduction in deviance | | | | | |
| Log (age) | 629.2 | 633.7 | 635.4 | 610.4 | 1 |
| + no. of siblings | 24.9 | 26.7 | 29.2 | 26.4 | 5 |
| + social class | 3.9 | 4.1 | 4.2 | 4.8 | 4 |
| + birth order | 1.5 | 1.6 | 2.2 | 1.4 | 2 |
| Best model Log (age) + no. of siblings | 1246.0 | 1239.7 | 1235.2 | 1263.2 | 1402 |

Bootstrap goodness-of-link testing was also carried out for models including log-age at survey as an explanatory variable (see Cole and McDonald 1989 for details). Using bootstrap Monte Carlo testing, we can differentiate among several pairs of links, but are unable to discriminate between the complementary log – log and probit links or between the complementary log – log and logit links. However, Genter's conservative test enabled discrimination among all links at the 5% level. We conclude that the complementary log – log link is significantly better than the other links. The parameter estimates and their standard errors for our final model with complementary log – log link are given in Table 9.2. First we interpret this model as a PH model by exponentiating the parameter estimates in order to estimate the relative risks (relative to those with no other siblings, who have a relative risk of one). The relative risks are presented in Table 9.3, along with their asymptotic 95% confidence intervals. The general pattern is of declining risks, with a relative risk of 0.9245 for one sibling, 0.7031 for two, 0.5765 for three, 0.6039 for four, and 0.5085 for five or more siblings. The relative risks for none and for one sibling are not significantly different at the 5% level.

TABLE 9.2. *Parameter estimates, standard errors, and relative risks for the complementary log − log link.*

|  | Estimate | Standard error | Relative risk |
|---|---|---|---|
| Constant | − 34.35 | 5.73 | n/a |
| Log (age) | 13.19 | 0.67 | n/a |
| No. of siblings |  |  |  |
| None | 0.00 |  | 1.00 |
| 1 | − 0.08 | 0.17 | 0.92 |
| 2 | − 0.35 | 0.17 | 0.70 |
| 3 | − 0.55 | 0.18 | 0.58 |
| 4 | − 0.50 | 0.19 | 0.60 |
| 5 + | − 0.67 | 0.18 | 0.51 |

TABLE 9.3. *Relative and asymptotic 95% confidence intervals for the model given in Table 9.2.*

| No. of siblings | Relative risk | Lower bound | Upper bound |
|---|---|---|---|
| None | 1.0000 |  |  |
| 1 | 0.9245 | 0.6680 | 1.2795 |
| 2 | 0.7031 | 0.5065 | 0.9762 |
| 3 | 0.5765 | 0.4026 | 0.8256 |
| 4 | 0.6039 | 0.4089 | 0.8919 |
| 5 + | 0.5085 | 0.3550 | 0.7283 |

Since developmental biologists would prefer the accelerated-life model interpretation, where some girls age faster than their sisters, we now interpret this model as an AL model. It is relatively easy to show that the regression coefficients for a Weibull PH and Weibull AL model are proportional, and that this constant of proportionality equals the Weibull-shape parameter $p$, i.e. $\beta_{PH} = p\,\beta_{AL}$. This relationship implies that the $p^{th}$ root of the relative risks of the PH model (where $\hat{p}$ is the coefficient of log(-age) in Table 9.2) equals the clock-speed factors of the AL model (relative to no other siblings with clock speed of one). The general pattern is of declining clock speeds, with a clock speed of 0.9941 for one sibling, 0.9736 for two, 0.9591 for three, 0.9625 for four, and 0.9500 for five or more. Hence, the clock speed for those girls with five or more siblings ticks the slowest, so they reach menarche the latest.

Note that the size of the effect estimated for the number of siblings seems much more dramatic on a relative-risk scale than on a clock-speed scale; yet these are but two different interpretations of the same model. Obviously, considerable care is needed in judging the impact of differences on a relative-risk scale versus a time-scale. Alternatively, we may estimate the median age at menarche for girls having different numbers of siblings by using Equation (8) and the estimated parameters. In general, the estimated median age at menarche increases with number of siblings. The estimated median age at menarche is 13.15 for zero siblings, 13.23 for one sibling, 13.51 for two, 13.71 for three, 13.66 for four, and 13.84 for five or more. Note, for example, that the ratio of the estimated median age at menarche for zero and five or more siblings is 13.15/13.84 = 0.95, i.e. the clock-speed factor for five or more siblings relative to zero siblings.

## Summary

Interval-censored event history data are common in demography, particularly when the data come from censuses or retrospective surveys. A particular example is current-status data, which are all either right-censored or left-censored; for example, either a child is still breast-feeding (so that the age at weaning exceeds the child's current age) or the child was weaned at a duration less than the current age. The distribution of interest can be estimated using only current-status data. This is usually undertaken using a parametric model, but, as has been demonstrated by Diamond, McDonald, and Shah (1986), a non-parametric approach can prove fruitful. This chapter has reviewed the estimation of proportional-hazards and accelerated-life models to current-status data and provided an example concerning age at menarche. In conclusion, there are many situations when current-status data are either the only data available or are to be preferred to the retrospectively reported data. In such situations, accurate estimates of a wide variety of models are relatively straightforward.

## References

Anderson, J. A., and Senthilselvan, A. (1980), 'Smooth Estimates for the Hazard Function', *Journal of the Royal Statistical Society*, ser. B, 42. 3: 322–7.

Anderson, J. E., Rodrigues, W., and Thome, A. (1984), 'Breastfeeding and Use of the Health Care System in Bahia State, Brazil: Three Multivariate Analyses', *Studies in Family Planning*, 15. 3: 127–35.

Aranda-Ordaz, F. J. (1981), 'On Two Families of Transformations to Additivity for Binary Response Data', *Biometrika*, 68. 2: 357–63.

—— (1983), 'An Extension of the Proportional Hazards Model for Grouped Data', *Biometrics*, 39. 1: 109–17.

Atwood, C. L., and Taube, A. (1976), 'Estimating Mean Time to Reach a Milestone, Using Retrospective Data', *Biometrics*, 32. 1: 159–72.

Aw, E., and Tye, C. Y. (1970), 'Age of Menarche of a Group of Singapore Girls', *Human Biology*, 42. 2: 329–36.

Bartlett, N. R. (1978), 'A Survival Model for a Wood Preservative Trial', *Biometrics*, 34. 4: 673–9.

Bergsten-Brucefors, A. (1976), 'A Note on the Accuracy of Recalled Age at Menarche', *Annals of Human Biology*, 3. 1: 71–3.

Bernard, H. R., Killworth, P., Kronenfield, D., and Sailer, L. (1984), 'The Problem of Informant Accuracy: The Validity of Retrospective Data', *Annual Review of Anthropology*, 13: 495–517.

Bloxom, B. (1985), 'A Constrained Spline Estimator of a Hazard Function', *Psychometrika*, 50. 3: 301–21.

Bracher, M., and Santow, G. (1981), 'Some Methodological Considerations in the Analysis of Current Status Data', *Population Studies*, 35. 3: 425–37.

Cannell, C. F., Kent, H. M., and Laurent, A. (1977), 'A Summary of Research Studies of Interviewing Methodology, 1959–1970', *Vital and Health Statistics*, ser. 2, No. 69, DHEW Publ. No. HRA-77-1343 (Rockville, Md.).

Carroll, G. R., Hannan, M. T., Tuma, N. B., and Warsavage, B. (1978), 'Alternative Estimation Procedures for Event-History Analysis: A Monte Carlo Study', Laboratory for Social Research, Technical Report No. 70, Stanford Univ.

Chambers, E. A., and Cox, D. R. (1967), 'Discrimination between Alternative Binary Response Models', *Biometrika*, 54. 3–4: 573–8.

Ciampi, A., and Etezadi-Amoli, J. (1985), 'A General Model for Testing the Proportional Hazards and the Accelerated Failure Time Hypotheses in the Analysis of Censored Survival Data with Covariates', *Communications in Statistics: Theory and Methods*, 14: 651–67.

Cole, M. J., and McDonald, J. W. (1989), 'Bootstrap Goodness-of-Link Testing in Generalized Linear Models', in A. Decarli, B. Francis, R. Gilchrist, and G. Seeber (eds.), *Statistical Modelling: Proceedings of GLIM89 and 4th International Workshop on Statistical Modelling* (Springer-Verlag, New York).

Copenhaver, T. W., and Mielke, P. W. (1977), 'Quantit Analysis: A Quantal Assay Refinement', *Biometrics*, 33. 1: 175–86.

Cox, D. R. (1972), 'Regression Models and Life Tables' (with discussion), *Journal of the Royal Statistical Society*, ser. B, 34. 2: 187–208.

—— (1975), 'Partial Likelihood', *Biometrika*, 62. 2: 269–76.

Damon, A., and Bajema, C. J. (1974), 'Age at Menarche: Accuracy of Recall after Thirty-Nine Years', *Human Biology*, 46. 3: 381–4.

—— Damon, S. T., Reed, R. B., and Valadian, I. (1969), 'Age at Menarche of Mothers and Daughters, with a Note on Accuracy of Recall', *Human Biology*, 41. 2: 161–75.

Diamond, I. D., McDonald, J. W., and Shah, I. H. (1986), 'Proportional Hazards Models for Current Status Data: Application to the Study of Differentials in Age at Weaning in Pakistan', *Demography*, 23. 4: 607–20.

Etezadi-Amoli, J., and Ciampi, A. (1987), 'Extended Hazard Regression for Censored Survival Data with Covariates: A Spline Approximation for the Baseline Hazard Function', *Biometrics*, 43. 1: 181–92.

Farewell, V. T., and Prentice, R. L. (1977), 'A Study of Distributional Shape in Life Testing', *Technometrics*, 19. 1: 69–76.

Ferry, B. (1981), *Breastfeeding*. WFS Comparative Studies No. 13, (International Statistical Institute, Voorburg).

Genter, F. C. (1982), 'A Generalized Regression Model for Ordinal Response Variables', Ph.D. dissertation, Univ. of Washington, Seattle.

—— and Farewell, V. T. (1985), 'Goodness-of-Link Testing in Ordinal Regression Models', *Canadian Journal of Statistics*, 13. 1: 37–44.

Gilks, W. R. (1983), 'Modelling with Age, Period and Cohort in Demography', Ph.D. dissertation, Univ. of Southampton.

Griffiths, W. E., Carter Hill, R., and Hope, P. J. (1987), 'Small Sample Properties of Probit Model Estimators', *Journal of the American Statistical Association*, 82. 399: 929–37.

Hajnal, J. (1953), 'Age at Marriage and Proportions Marrying', *Population Studies*, 7. 2: 111–36.

Hudson, H. M. (1986), 'Evaluation of Trends in Middle Ear Disease Among Australian Aborigines', *Biometrics*, 42. 1: 159–69.

John, A. M., Menken, J. A., and Trussell, J. (1988), 'Estimating the Distribution of Interval Length: Current Status and Retrospective History Data', *Population Studies*, 42. 1: 115–27.

Jorgensen, B. (1984), 'The Delta Algorithm and GLIM', *International Statistical Review*, 52. 3: 283–300.

Kalbfleisch, J. D., and Prentice, R. L. (1973), 'Marginal Likelihoods Based on Cox's Regression and Life Model', *Biometrika*, 60. 2: 267–78.

—— —— (1980), *The Statistical Analysis of Failure Time Data* (John Wiley & Sons, New York).

Klotz, J. (1982), 'Spline Smooth Estimates of Survival', in J. Crowley and R. A. Johnson (eds.), *Institute of Mathematical Statistics Lecture Notes: Special Meeting on Survival Analysis* (Institute of Mathematical Statistics, Hayward, Calif.), 14–25.

Lapham, R. J., and Westoff, C. F. (1986), 'Demographic and Health Surveys: Population and Health Information for the Late 1980s', *Population Index*, 52. 1: 28–34.

Lenth, R. V. (1977), 'Spline Regression', *American Statistician*, 31. 1: 53–4.

Lesthaeghe, R., and Page, H. (1980), 'The Post Partum Non-Susceptible Period: Development and Application of Model Schedules', *Population Studies*, 34. 1: 143–69.

McCullagh, P., and Nelder, J. A. (1983), *Generalized Linear Models* (London).

McDonald, J. W., and Diamond, I. D. (1983), 'Fitting Generalized Linear Models with Linear Inequality Parameter Constraints', *GLIM Newsletter*, 8: 29–36.

—— —— (1990), 'On the Fitting of Generalized Linear Models with Non-Negativity Parameter Constraints', *Biometrics*, 46. 1: 201–6.

McKinlay, S., Jeffreys, M., and Thompson, B. (1972), 'An Investigation of the Age at Menopause', *Journal of Biosocial Science*, 4. 2: 161–73.

MacMahon, B., and Worcester, J. (1966), *Age at Menopause, United States 1960–1962*, National Center for Health Statistics (Vital and Health Statistics Series, ser. 11: Data from the National Health Survey, No. 19, DHEW publication No. (HSM) 66–1000) (Washington, DC).

Marshall, W. A., and Tanner, J. M. (1986), 'Puberty', in F. Falkner and J. M. Tanner (eds.), *Human Growth*, ii (Plenum, New York), 171–290.

van Monfort, M. A. J., and Otten, A. (1976), 'Quantal Response Analysis: Enlargement of the Logistic Model with a Kurtosis Parameter', *Biometrische Zeitschrift*, 18: 371–80.

Moss, L., and Goldstein, H. (1985) (eds.), *The Recall Method in Social Surveys* (Heinemann, Portsmouth).

Nelder, J. A., and Wedderburn, R. W. M. (1972), 'Generalized Linear Models', *Journal of the Royal Statistical Society*, ser. A, 135. 3: 370–84.

Nelson, W. (1978), 'Life Data Analysis for Units Inspected Once for Failure (Quantal Response Data)', *IEEE Transactions on Reliability*, R-27, 274–9.

Nelson, W. (1982), *Applied Life Data Analysis* (John Wiley & Sons, New York).

Page, H., Lesthaeghe, R., and Adegbola, O. A. (1977), 'Current Status Data and Techniques of Analysis for Specially Designed Surveys', *International Population Conference, Mexico*, iii (Liège), 371–86.

Payne, C. D. (1985) (ed.), *The GLIM System Release 3.77 Manual* (Numerical Algorithms Group, Oxford).

Pierce, D. A., Stewart, W. H., and Kopecky, K. J. (1979), 'Distribution-Free Regression Analysis of Grouped Survival Data', *Biometrics*, 35. 4: 785–93.

Pregibon, D. (1980), 'Goodness of Link Tests for Generalized Linear Models', *Applied Statistics*, 29. 1: 15–24.

Prentice, R. L. (1975), 'Discrimination among Parametric Models', *Biometrika*, 62. 3: 607–14.

—— (1976), 'A Generalisation of the Probit and Logit Methods for Dose Response Curves', *Biometrics*, 32. 4: 761–8.

—— and Gloeckler, L. A. (1978), 'Regression Analysis of Grouped Survival Data with Application to Breast Cancer Data', *Biometrics*, 34. 1: 57–67.

Quandt, S. (1987), 'Material Recall Accuracy for Dates of Infant Feeding Transitions', *Human Organization*, 46. 2: 152–9.

Roberts, D. F., Rozner, L. M., and Swan, A. V. (1971), 'Age at Menarche, Physique and Environment in Industrial North East England', *Acta Paediatrica Scandinavica*, 60: 158–64.

Robertson, T., Wright, F. T., and Dykstra, R. L. (1988), *Order Restricted Statistical Inference* (John Wiley & Sons, New York).

Smith, P. L. (1979), 'Splines as a Useful and Convenient Statistical Tool', *American Statistician*, 33. 2: 57–62.

—— (1982), 'Hypothesis Testing in B-Spline Regression', *Communications in Statistics: Simulation and Computation*, 11. 2: 143–57.

Stirling, W. D. (1984), 'Iteratively Reweighted Least Squares for Models with a Linear Part', *Applied Statistics*, 33. 1: 7–17.

Vanderhoeft, C. (1982), 'Accelerated Failure Time Models: An Application to Current Status Breastfeeding Data from Pakistan', *Genus*, 38. 1: 135–57.

Wahrendorf, J., Becher, H., and Brown, C. C. (1987), 'Bootstrap Comparison of Non-Nested Generalized Linear Models: Applications in Survival Analysis and Epidemiology', *Applied Statistics*, 36. 1: 72–81.

Wegman, E. J., and Wright, I. W. (1983), 'Splines in Statistics', *Journal of the American Statistical Association*, 78. 382: 351–66.

Whittemore, A. S. (1985), 'Analyzing Cohort Mortality Data', *American Statistician*, 39. 4: 437–41.

—— and Keller, J. B. (1986), 'Survival Estimation Using Splines', *Biometrics*, 42. 3: 495–506.

WHO (World Health Organisation) (1981*a*), 'A Cross-Cultural Study of Menstruation: Implications for Contraceptive Development and Use', *Studies in Family Planning*, 12. 1: 3–16.

—— (1981*b*), 'Women's Bleeding Patterns: Ability to Recall and Predict Menstrual Events', *Studies in Family Planning*, 12. 1: 17–27.

Williams, D. A. (1982), 'The Use of the Deviance to Test Goodness of Fit of a Logistic-Linear Model to Binary Data', *GLIM Newsletter*, 6: 60–2.

# 10 A Discrete-Time Method for the Analysis of Event Histories

ELJA ARJAS, PEKKA KANGAS

In demographic longitudinal studies, time measurements in the data are mostly reported in a rounded form: a time unit is fixed, typically a month or a year, and then the interval (of unit length) during which the event in question occurred is reported. Such rounding does cause some problems, however. For example, it may result in a considerable number of ties, and the computer-time requirement can be excessive for methods such as Cox's proportional-hazards regression. A slightly different problem arises in using the Poisson regression technique with piecewise constant-baseline hazards, which requires the estimation of exposure in the various groups. To do this, the rounded time measurements are conventionally modified by applying 'actuarial methods', thus introducing an element of spurious accuracy into the data. For example, if the time-interval is a month, a single event is dated to the fifteenth day, and if there are two events, one is dated to the tenth and the other to the twentieth day of the month. If the time-intervals are short, these somewhat *ad hoc* modifications of the essentially discrete data, which are required in order to apply a continuous time-method, appear rather harmless, since the differences between the true, recorded, and modified time measurements are small. However, 'spurious accuracy' is somewhat awkward, and it is natural to look for alternatives.

The obvious alternative is to fit discrete-time models. The foundations of this approach have been discussed by Allison (1982), and recent applications include Rindfuss, Morgan, and Swicegood (1984) and Morgan, Lye, and Condran (1988). We will consider probabilities that the demographic event in question occurs to an individual during a considered time-interval. For example, suppose that the event in question is death and that the time-unit is one month. Then the life of an individual can be thought of as a sequence of 'monthly Bernoulli trials', resulting in a sequence of zeros as long as the individual stays alive, and ending with a one for the month during which the individual dies. For the data as a whole, the number of trials equals the number of person-months of exposure. Moreover, the estimated probabilities from such a model are easily converted into continuous-time intensities, relative risks, etc., if it is felt that these form a preferred way of reporting the results.

It is not difficult to accommodate modern regression techniques, involving, say, generalized linear models and time-dependent covariates, into such a discrete-time framework. The discrete time also applies in situations where the response splits into different 'types' corresponding to e.g. different causes of death, or where the event can repeat itself several times, as in employment studies. However, the following two conventions seem more or less unavoidable if the data are in a discrete-time form. First, censoring and possible other forms of controlling the risk set are always thought to happen at times which are integer multiples of the chosen time unit. Second, if the model involves time-dependent covariates, their measured values need to be interpreted as 'prevailing conditions of exposure during the time interval (of unit length) to which the corresponding response is related'. For an interesting discussion of this second aspect see Sandefur and Tuma (1987). In particular, if the occurrence of the response can change the conditions of exposure, these must be determined at the beginning of the time-interval, before the response occurs. In a sense, the discrete-time model consists of a set of short-term predictions, each made at the beginning of a unit time-interval.

Below, we use the notion of a history (mathematically, a σ-field) as a description of such conditions. Briefly, the history $H_{t-1}$ is taken to be the set of conditions prevailing during the time-interval $(t-1, t)$, and then leading to the response indexed in our discrete-time model by $t$. The exact mathematical definition of the history $H_{t-1}$ is given in the Appendix. Apart from the explicit conditioning on histories, our models below are identical to the discrete-time models discussed by Allison (1982). In fact, this chapter, and particularly the Appendix, can be seen as a contribution to the discussion concerning the legitimacy of the discrete-time model (see the section 'Problems with the Discrete Time Approach' in Allison's paper). In particular, we hope that the Appendix will straighten the apparent confusion in Allison's paper concerning the product form of the likelihood expression and independence. The product form is really a consequence of the chain multiplication rule of conditional probabilities. The computer program discussed in the section 'Computational Aspects' below, on the other hand, can be viewed as a pragmatic way to answer the practicality question raised by Allison.

We now explain the structure of the discrete-time regression model used in this chapter. For a more careful discussion of the model and its properties the reader is referred to Arjas (1986) and Arjas and Haara (1987).

Let $j = 1, 2, \ldots$ index an individual, let $t = 1, 2, \ldots$ be the discrete-time variable indicating the $t^{\text{th}}$ 'month' of the follow-up, so that $t$ corresponds to the time-interval $(t-1, t)$ in continuous time.

Denote

$$\Delta N_j(t) = \begin{cases} 1, & \text{if the demographic event occurs to } j \text{ during the } t^{\text{th}} \text{ month} \\ 0, & \text{otherwise} \end{cases} \tag{1}$$

Let $Z_j(t) = \{Z_{j,1}(t), \ldots, Z_{j,p}(t)\}$ be a known (possibly time-dependent) covariate vector for $j$. We now postulate that, given the observed 'history' $H_{t-1}$ corresponding to times 0, 1, 2, ..., $t-1$ in the follow-up, the conditional probability that the considered demographic event occurs to $j$ at $t$ (i.e. during the $t^{th}$ month) can be expressed as

$$\Pr\{\Delta N_j(t) = 1 \mid H_{t-1}\} = Y_j(t) \cdot g^{-1}\{\beta' Z_j(t)\} \tag{2}$$

where

$$Y_j(t) = \begin{cases} 1, & \text{if } j \text{ is the risk set during the } t^{th} \text{ month} \\ 0, & \text{otherwise} \end{cases} \tag{3}$$

$\beta = (\beta_1, \ldots, \beta_p)$ is a vector of model parameters, and $g^{-1}$ is the inverse of a link function in the sense of generalized linear models (McGullagh and Nelder 1983). Specifically, we shall consider the logit-link

$$g(x) = \log\{x/(1-x)\} \qquad (0 < x < 1),$$
$$g^{-1}(x) = \exp(x)/\{1 + \exp(x)\} \qquad (-\infty < x < \infty) \tag{4}$$

and the complementary $\log - \log$ link

$$g(x) = \log\{-\log(1-x)\} \qquad (0 < x < 1)$$
$$g^{-1}(x) = 1 - \exp\{-\exp(x)\} \qquad (x > 0). \tag{5}$$

Under general conditions (presented in detail in the Appendix), the likelihood corresponding to an entire follow-up data set becomes a product over $j$ and $t$ of the terms

$$\Pr\{\Delta N_j(t) = 1 \mid H_{t-1}\}^{\Delta N_j(t)} [1 - \Pr\{\Delta N_j(t) = 1 \mid H_{t-1}\}]^{1 - \Delta N_j(t)} \tag{6}$$

This likelihood function is log-concave in $\beta$, which leads to an unproblematic numerical maximum-likelihood (ML) estimation of the parameter vector. It is shown in Arjas and Haara (1987) that the 'standard asymptotic normality results' hold for the estimates when the logit-link (4) is used.

It is important to note that, should one prefer to present the results from a statistical analysis in the form of continuous time-rates (intensities) instead of probabilities, the discrete-time model will provide such estimates as well. In the case of the logit-link (4) we have

$$\Pr\{\Delta N_j(t) = 1 \mid H_{t-1}\} = \frac{Y_j(t) \cdot \exp\{\beta' Z_j(t)\}}{1 + \exp\{\beta' Z_j(t)\}}. \tag{7}$$

For most demographic events such probabilities are small, and therefore $\Pr\{\Delta N_j(t) = 1 \mid H_{t-1}\} \simeq Y_j(t) \cdot \exp\{\beta' Z_j(t)\}$ holds as an approximation. It is natural to use a constant first covariate $Z_{j1}(t) \equiv 1$ so that $\beta_1$ can be viewed as an intercept. The value of $\beta_1$ will, of course, depend on the length of the 'month', the chosen time-unit. The other $\beta$-coefficients, which have the role of relative risks modulating the baseline, tend to be quite stable towards such changes. Therefore it is quite convenient to use longer intervals for provisional model-fitting if the computing time otherwise becomes a problem.

On the other hand, postulating that $\Delta N_j(t)$ has a constant $H_{t-1}$ conditional intensity $\lambda_j(t)$, say, over the unit interval corresponding to $t$, we also have that for short intervals approximately $\Pr\{\Delta N_j(t) = 1 \mid H_{t-1}\} \simeq \lambda_j(t)$. Combining these two, we find that $\lambda_j(t) \simeq Y_j(t) \cdot \exp\{\beta' Z_j(t)\}$, i.e., the familiar multiplicative-intensity form holds as an approximation. When the complementary $\log - \log$ link is used, this relationship actually becomes exact: from (5) we obtain

$$\Pr\{\Delta N_j(t) = 1 \mid H_{t-1}\} = Y_j(t) \cdot [1 - \exp\{-\exp(\beta' Z_j(t))\}] =$$
$$1 - \exp[-Y_j(t) \cdot \exp\{\beta' Z_j(t)\}]. \tag{8}$$

But this probability equals $1 - \exp\{-\lambda_j(t)\}$ and so $\lambda_j(t) = Y_j(t) \cdot \exp\{\beta' Z_j(t)\}$ holds exactly.

## A Case Study: Third Births in Modern Sweden

In order to compare the method explained above with a more conventional one used in demography (the Poisson regression based on piecewise constant proportional-occurrence rates and on actuarial methods for adjusting the dates), we reanalysed the data on third births in modern Sweden collected by B. Hoem and J. Hoem (1987, henceforth abbreviated as H&H). Since the emphasis is on the comparison of the methods, we followed the steps taken in H&H very closely, including initially employing the same covariates. As it turns out, our numerical results are in very close agreement with those obtained in H&H. We do not

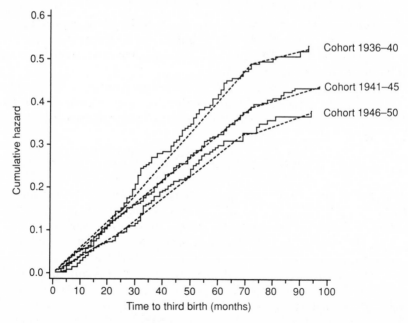

Fig. 10.1 Nelson–Aalen cumulative-hazard plot of third births (with piece-wise exponential segments cut at 24 and 72 months).

describe the data here, nor make an attempt to assess the significance of the demographic findings, but refer the reader to H&H for those.

TABLE 10.1. *Definitions of covariates.*

| | |
|---|---|
| *Interval between first two births* | $Z_{j,4}(t) = 1$ (birth interval $\leq$ 29 months) (base level: 30–53 months) $Z_{j,5}(t) = 1$ (birth interval $\geq$ 54 months) |
| *Educational level at second birth* | (base level: education 'low' or 'middle') $Z_{j,6}(t) = 1$ (education 'high') |
| *Cohort * (age at first birth) interaction* | $Z_{j,7}(t) = 1$ (cohort 1936–40, age 16–19) $Z_{j,8}(t) = 1$ (cohort 1941–5, age 16–19) $Z_{j,9}(t) = 1$ (cohort 1946–50, age 16–19) $Z_{j,10}(t) = 1$ (cohort 1936–40, age 20–5) (base level: cohort 1941–6, age 20–5) $Z_{j,11}(t) = 1$ (cohort 1946–50, age 20–5) $Z_{j,12}(t) = 1$ (cohort 1936–40, age 26–34) $Z_{j,13}(t) = 1$ (cohort 1941–5, age 26–34) $Z_{j,14}(t) = 1$ (cohort 1946–50, age 26–34) |
| *Combined employment status (% of time spent as housewife, current employment status)* | $Z_{j,15}(t) = 1$ (less than 25%, full-time) $Z_{j,16}(t) = 1$ (25–75%, full-time) $Z_{j,17}(t) = 1$ (more than 75%, full-time) (base level: less than 25%, part-time) $Z_{j,18}(t) = 1$ (25–75%, part-time) $Z_{j,19}(t) = 1$ (more than 75%, part-time) $Z_{j,20}(t) = 1$ (less than 25%, child-minder) $Z_{j,21}(t) = 1$ (25–75%, child-minder) $Z_{j,22}(t) = 1$ (more than 75%, child-minder) (base level: less than 25%, housewife[a]) $Z_{j,23}(t) = 1$ (25–75%, housewife) $Z_{j,24}(t) = 1$ (more than 75%, housewife) |

[a] In the present study, unlike in H&H, the category 'less than 25%, housewife' was combined with 'less than 25%, part-time' to form a baseline.

We started by drawing the Nelson–Aalen plots for the third births. There is one plot for each age cohort. Time $t$ is measured in months from 10 months after the second birth (Fig. 10.1). As in H&H, there was complete censoring of follow-up times exceeding 98 months. The birth rates seem approximately proportional in the cohorts, with younger cohorts having slightly lower rates. Corresponding to these 'baseline rates', we decided to split the time axis into three intervals where the levels were approximately constant: 0–24 months, 25–72 months and 73–98 months. In the model we used the following three 'baseline covariates' that are common to all individuals (we denote the indicator function by $1(\bullet)$):

$$Z_{j,1}(t) = 1$$
$$Z_{j,2}(t) = 1(t \leq 24)$$

$$Z_{j,3}(t) = 1\,(73 \leqslant t \leqslant 98). \tag{9}$$

The middle interval from 25 to 72 months is therefore directly represented by the intercept $\beta_1$ (= coefficient of $Z_{j,1}(t)$).

The remaining covariates depend on the individual. Following H&H, we initially used information of the interval between first two births (fixed covariate, 3 levels), the educational level of the mother at second birth (fixed covariate, 2 levels), a cohort $*$ (age at first birth) interaction term (fixed covariate, 9 categories), and a combined employment status covariate (time-dependent, 12 categories). Always including one of the levels/covariates in the baseline, we were thus led to the first menu of covariates shown in Table 10.1 (cf. table 3 in H&H).

The results of fitting this model ('Model 1'), by using the logit-link, are displayed in Tables 10.2 and 10.3. We also tried the complementary log – log link, but do not report the results here. The reason is that the results are so similar; typically, differences in the coefficient estimates appeared in the third significant digit. We make two rather obvious comments:

1. The column 'exp(parameter)' in Table 10.2 contains the numbers $\exp(\hat{\beta}_i)$, where $\hat{\beta}_i$ is the $i^{\text{th}}$ coordinate of the ML-estimate $\hat{\beta}$. As explained in the first section above, these numbers are approximately the same as the relative intensities in a multiplicative-intensity model. They can therefore be compared directly to the numerical results in table 3 of H&H (reproduced here in the rightmost column of Table 10.2). The agreement is very good; the differences are only a few per cent.

2. Since we have also produced (estimates of) the standard deviations and the correlations of the coefficient estimators, we can, using the asymptotic normality of the estimators, consider their statistical significance. Our first impression is that the division of the 'combined employment status' covariate into 12 response categories (of which we consider 11) is too fine to let us infer reliably the values of the individual coefficients. Only 2 of the 10 'test statistics' have an absolute value exceeding 2. This raises the question of finding another model with a more parsimonious parametrization. A second set of covariates where parameters could perhaps be saved is $Z_{j,7}(t), \ldots, Z_{j,14}(t)$, where we could consider only the cohort and age-at-first-birth 'main effects'.

From the results and discussion in H&H we concluded that those categories in the combined employment status that could be associated with changes in employment correspond to either low or high third-birth fertility, whereas those categories that correspond to a stable employment behaviour seem to have an average third-birth intensity. Thus we lumped the 3 categories corresponding to covariates $Z_{j,16}(t)$, $Z_{j,17}(t)$ and $Z_{j,19}(t)$ into a single '< 25%, full-time and > 75%, part-time' category, expecting low third-birth fertility, and the 2 categories corresponding to $Z_{j,20}(t)$ and $Z_{j,23}(t)$ into a '< 25%, child-minder and 25–75%, housewife' category, expecting high third-birth fertility. The remaining 5 original response categories were combined with the previous baseline '< 25%, part-time'

TABLE 10.2. *Third-births Model 1: deviance 5004.26 (logit-link).*

| Parameter index | Covariate name | Parameter estimate | Estim. std. dev. | Param. std. dev. | Exp. (param.) | Relative intensity in H&H |
|---|---|---|---|---|---|---|
| 1 | Constant | −5.44 | 0.17 | −31.98 | 0.0043 | |
| 2 | Indicator (time ≤ 24) | −0.32 | 0.11 | 2.98 | 0.73 | |
| 3 | Indicator (time ≥ 73) | −0.98 | 0.21 | −4.70 | 0.37 | |
| 4 | Birth interval ≤ 29 | 0.72 | 0.10 | 6.97 | 2.06 | 2.06 |
| 5 | Birth interval ≥ 54 | −0.98 | 0.22 | −4.37 | 0.37 | 0.38 |
| 6 | Education 'high' | 0.55 | 0.15 | 3.64 | 1.73 | 1.73 |
| 7 | Cohort 1936–40, age 16–19 | 0.49 | 0.25 | 1.95 | 1.62 | 1.63 |
| 8 | Cohort 1941–5, age 16–19 | 0.67 | 0.19 | 3.61 | 1.95 | 1.94 |
| 9 | Cohort 1946–50, age 16–19 | 0.52 | 0.18 | 2.82 | 1.68 | 1.68 |
| 10 | Cohort 1936–40, age 20–5 | 0.27 | 0.15 | 1.84 | 1.32 | 1.32 |
| 11 | Cohort 1946–50, age 20–5 | −0.49 | 0.16 | −3.02 | 0.61 | 0.61 |
| 12 | Cohort 1936–40, age 26–34 | −0.12 | 0.23 | −0.55 | 0.88 | 0.89 |
| 13 | Cohort 1941–5, age 26–34 | −0.52 | 0.22 | −2.35 | 0.59 | 0.60 |
| 14 | Cohort 1946–50, age 26–34 | −0.39 | 0.36 | −1.11 | 0.67 | 0.70 |
| 15 | <25%, full-time work | −0.11 | 0.21 | −0.51 | 0.90 | 0.92 |
| 16 | 25–75%, full-time work | −0.41 | 0.40 | −1.03 | 0.66 | 0.69 |
| 17 | >75%, full-time work | −0.82 | 0.72 | −1.13 | 0.44 | 0.45 |
| 18 | 25–75%, part-time work | −0.22 | 0.24 | −0.92 | 0.80 | 0.83 |
| 19 | >75%, part-time work | −1.21 | 0.52 | −2.33 | 0.30 | 0.31 |
| 20 | <25%, child-minder | 0.48 | 0.52 | 0.92 | 1.62 | 1.67 |
| 21 | 25–75%, child-minder | −0.01 | 0.41 | −0.02 | 0.99 | 1.02 |
| 22 | >75%, child-minder | −0.15 | 0.60 | −2.25 | 0.86 | 0.87 |
| 23 | 25–75%, housewife | 0.57 | 0.19 | 2.94 | 1.77 | 1.79 |
| 24 | >75%, housewife | 0.13 | 0.15 | 0.84 | 1.14 | 1.15 |

TABLE 10.3. Third-births Model 1: estimated asymptotic correlation matrix.

|    | 1 | 2 | 3 | 4 | 5 | 6 | 7 | 8 | 9 | 10 | 11 | 12 |
|----|----|----|----|----|----|----|----|----|----|----|----|----|
| 1  | 1.000 | | | | | | | | | | | |
| 2  | -0.187 | 1.000 | | | | | | | | | | |
| 3  | -0.136 | 0.170 | 1.000 | | | | | | | | | |
| 4  | -0.195 | -0.043 | -0.009 | 1.000 | | | | | | | | |
| 5  | -0.207 | -0.005 | 0.005 | 0.226 | 1.000 | | | | | | | |
| 6  | -0.341 | -0.031 | 0.026 | -0.056 | 0.063 | 1.000 | | | | | | |
| 7  | -0.163 | -0.010 | 0.001 | -0.083 | -0.035 | 0.093 | 1.000 | | | | | |
| 8  | -0.253 | -0.035 | 0.007 | -0.031 | -0.015 | 0.147 | 0.219 | 1.000 | | | | |
| 9  | -0.258 | -0.028 | 0.011 | -0.048 | -0.039 | 0.145 | 0.217 | 0.288 | 1.000 | | | |
| 10 | -0.369 | -0.003 | -0.008 | -0.026 | 0.006 | 0.100 | 0.253 | 0.331 | 0.331 | 1.000 | | |
| 11 | -0.353 | -0.010 | 0.042 | -0.089 | 0.046 | 0.038 | 0.215 | 0.289 | 0.293 | 0.362 | 1.000 | |
| 12 | -0.219 | 0.007 | -0.015 | 0.013 | 0.033 | -0.098 | 0.139 | 0.185 | 0.183 | 0.250 | 0.233 | 1.000 |
| 13 | -0.272 | -0.016 | 0.028 | -0.051 | 0.038 | -0.113 | 0.135 | 0.182 | 0.184 | 0.252 | 0.254 | 0.193 |
| 14 | -0.142 | -0.116 | 0.019 | -0.036 | 0.031 | -0.110 | 0.079 | 0.108 | 0.110 | 0.153 | 0.162 | 0.126 |
| 15 | -0.392 | 0.007 | -0.015 | -0.047 | -0.019 | -0.096 | -0.002 | -0.038 | -0.011 | -0.005 | 0.037 | -0.029 |
| 16 | -0.274 | 0.025 | -0.029 | -0.014 | 0.017 | 0.068 | 0.005 | -0.037 | -0.013 | 0.018 | 0.048 | 0.014 |
| 17 | -0.149 | 0.008 | -0.046 | 0.000 | 0.014 | 0.044 | -0.029 | -0.017 | -0.009 | 0.002 | 0.015 | 0.001 |
| 18 | -0.433 | 0.056 | -0.056 | -0.049 | 0.013 | 0.108 | 0.008 | -0.030 | -0.036 | 0.033 | 0.013 | 0.032 |
| 19 | -0.216 | 0.029 | -0.060 | -0.015 | 0.014 | 0.074 | -0.013 | -0.009 | -0.000 | 0.016 | 0.030 | 0.011 |
| 20 | -0.219 | -0.005 | -0.019 | -0.015 | 0.016 | 0.070 | 0.022 | 0.031 | -0.024 | 0.057 | 0.026 | 0.036 |
| 21 | -0.273 | 0.052 | 0.001 | -0.061 | 0.010 | 0.112 | -0.008 | -0.088 | -0.029 | 0.043 | 0.022 | 0.021 |
| 22 | -0.191 | 0.017 | 0.004 | -0.021 | -0.005 | 0.081 | 0.012 | -0.030 | -0.005 | 0.021 | 0.011 | 0.010 |
| 23 | -0.519 | -0.093 | 0.023 | -0.046 | 0.021 | 0.180 | 0.004 | -0.007 | -0.023 | 0.012 | 0.021 | 0.005 |
| 24 | -0.696 | -0.032 | 0.038 | -0.119 | 0.096 | 0.267 | -0.077 | -0.049 | -0.035 | 0.010 | 0.084 | 0.008 |
|    | 1 | 2 | 3 | 4 | 5 | 6 | 7 | 8 | 9 | 10 | 11 | 12 |

|    | 13 | 14 | 15 |
|----|----|----|----|
| 13 | 1.000 | | |
| 14 | 0.147 | 1.000 | |
| 15 | 0.052 | 0.022 | 1.000 |

TABLE 10.3. (contd.)

|    | 13 | 14 | 15 | 16 | 17 | 18 | 19 | 20 | 21 | 22 | 23 | 24 |
|----|------|------|------|------|------|------|------|------|------|------|------|------|
| 16 | 0.055 | 0.037 | 0.181 | 1.000 |       |       |       |       |       |       |       |       |
| 17 | 0.028 | 0.017 | 0.100 | 0.064 | 1.000 |       |       |       |       |       |       |       |
| 18 | 0.069 | 0.040 | 0.299 | 0.184 | 0.104 | 1000 |       |       |       |       |       |       |
| 19 | 0.035 | 0.020 | 0.138 | 0.090 | 0.052 | 0.146 | 1.000 |       |       |       |       |       |
| 20 | 0.042 | 0.013 | 0.134 | 0.084 | 0.047 | 0.141 | 0.067 | 1.000 |       |       |       |       |
| 21 | 0.029 | 0.015 | 0.175 | 0.118 | 0.065 | 0.191 | 0.092 | 0.087 | 1.000 |       |       |       |
| 22 | 0.029 | 0.019 | 0.118 | 0.078 | 0.043 | 0.127 | 0.061 | 0.059 | 0.084 | 1.000 |       |       |
| 23 | 0.055 | 0.040 | 0.362 | 0.217 | 0.121 | 0.357 | 0.168 | 0.171 | 0.223 | 0.153 | 1.000 |       |
| 24 | 0.108 | 0.075 | 0.460 | 0.290 | 0.164 | 0.471 | 0.227 | 0.221 | 0.306 | 0.203 | 0.594 | 1.000 |

category. This lumping reduced the number of parameters by 8 when compared to Model 1. Considering cohort and age at first birth only as 'main effects' reduced the number of parameters further by 4.

TABLE 10.4. *Third-births Model 2: deviance 5017.58 (logit-link).*

| Parameter index | Covariate name | Parameter estimate | Estim. std. dev. | Param./ std. dev. | Exp. (param.) |
|---|---|---|---|---|---|
| 1 | Constant | − 5.43 | 0.11 | − 48.77 | 0.0044 |
| 2 | Indicator (time ⩽ 24) | − 0.29 | 0.10 | − 2.70 | 0.75 |
| 3 | Indicator (time ⩾ 73) | − 1.02 | 0.21 | − 4.91 | 0.36 |
| 4 | Birth interval ⩽ 29 | 0.71 | 0.10 | 6.91 | 2.03 |
| 5 | Birth interval ⩾ 54 | − 1.01 | 0.22 | − 4.54 | 0.36 |
| 6 | Education 'high' | 0.48 | 0.14 | 3.46 | 1.62 |
| 7 | Cohort 1936–40 | 0.22 | 0.12 | 1.85 | 1.24 |
| 8 | Cohort 1946–50 | − 0.32 | 0.12 | − 2.63 | 0.72 |
| 9 | Age 16–19 | 0.68 | 0.12 | 5.63 | 1.98 |
| 10 | Age  26–34 | − 0.37 | 0.15 | − 2.43 | 0.69 |
| 11 | > 75%, full-time and > 75%, part-time | − 0.91 | 0.32 | − 2.81 | 0.40 |
| 12 | < 25%, child-minder and 25–75%, housewife | 0.53 | 0.15 | 3.54 | 1.69 |

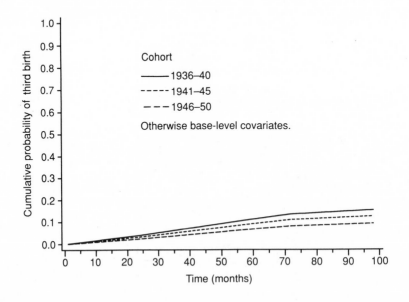

Fig. 10.2 Data on third births in Sweden: estimated birth probabilities (employment: > 75%, full-time and > 75%, part-time).

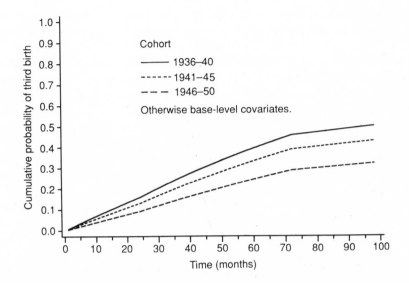

Fig. 10.3 Data on third births in Sweden: estimated birth probabilities (employment: < 25%, child-minder and 25–75%, housewife).

The results of fitting this model, called 'Model 2', are shown in Table 10.4. The increase of the deviance is 12.73, corresponding to the 12 degrees of freedom saved. We do not make an attempt to comment on how natural this reduced model is from the point of view of demography, but note that the 6 covariates that are common to Model 1 and Model 2 had very similar coefficient estimates.

It is obvious that from the estimated model we can also calculate, for any given covariate profile $\{Z_j(t), t = 1, 2, \ldots\}$, the estimated third-birth probabilities. This is done most conveniently in the form of an estimated cumulative distribution $\hat{\text{Pr}}$ (time to third birth $\leq t$), $t = 1, 2, \ldots$. We demonstrate this possibility in Figs. 10.2 and 10.3, which illustrate the estimated effects (Model 2) of cohort and employment profile (as a fixed covariate) when other covariates are at base level.

## Computational Aspects

The results presented here were produced by using a computer program that is designed to handle time-dependent covariates in an efficient manner. The idea is that the covariate vector $Z_j(t) = \{Z_{j,1}(t), \ldots, Z_{j,p}(t)\}$ is continuously updated for each subject $j$, instead of arranging all 'monthly Bernoulli experiments' into a conventional data matrix. Time-dependent covariates are updated only when their values change.

In practice this is done by dividing the covariates into three classes: fixed, preset time-dependent, and computed time-dependent. Fixed covariates are specified in the usual way as a rectangular data matrix. Preset time-dependent covariates are defined by giving their initial values and a file of update records describing the subject, the time of change, the changing covariate, and a new covariate value. Computed time-dependent covariates are used to specify functions of time and may reference fixed covariates. A typical example would be the logarithm of the time elapsed after an operation on a patient.

Output consists of the model description, time grid interval used, estimated parameter values, their asymptotic standard deviations, corresponding approximate relative risks, estimated asymptotic correlation matrix of parameters, and the deviance of the model. Predictions for given covariate combinations can be obtained as a separate step. It is also possible to output the 'Bernoulli trial' type of data into a file for further processing by SAS, BMDP, GLIM, or other statistical software to provide influence statistics. Since the number of these trials can be very large (in this data there are about 86 000 months of exposure), BMDPLR or SAS PROC CATMOD can be used to combine trials with the same covariate combination. This works well with dichotomous design-type covariates but is less useful with continuous covariates.

Model 1 (Table 10.2), with 23 covariates and an intercept, requires about 6 minutes of CPU time on an IBM 3083 EX2 under VM/SP CMS-operating system, starting from zero initial values and with a time-grid of one month. Models with fewer covariates (Table 10.4) use about 1–3 minutes of CPU. To save computer resources, a wider time-grid value of e.g. 5 months can be used to obtain good initial values of parameter estimates. In our experience a wider time-grid usually leads to nearly the same estimates (excepting, of course, the intercept $\hat{\beta}_1$ ).

The program is written entirely in standard FORTRAN 77 without using machine-dependent features (except for time and date). The current versions work under IBM VM/SP CMS and VAX VMS operating systems, but should be easily adaptable to other environments. The program consists of 23 modules with a total of about 3300 lines of code. It is extensively commented; in fact, half of the lines are comments. A short manual is provided with sample data and results. It should be noted that, even though the program is self-contained, it is designed to be used with accompanying software: for example, it has no facilities of subsetting the observations or transforming the covariates, nor does it have a command language. The specification of time-dependent covariates usually requires the help of other software. We have utilized the versatility of SAS (Statistical Analysis System) to convert this data into a suitable form.

## Appendix: Details of the Statistical Model

Let $(\Omega, F)$ be a measurable space in which the variables $Y_j(t-1)$, $\mathbf{Z}_j(t-1)$ and $\Delta N_j(t)$ are defined, and let $R(t-1) = \{ j : Y_j(t-1) = 1 \}$ be the risk set at $t$ (i.e. during interval

$[t-1, t])$. Let $F_0$ be the σ-field representing 'initial information'; usually $F_0$ is the trivial field. Then the σ-fields $F_t$ and $H_{t-1}$, $t \geq 1$, defined inductively by

$$H_{t-1} = F_{t-1} \cup \sigma[R(t-1), (\mathbf{Z}_j(t-1); \ j \in R(t-1)\}],$$

$$F_t = H_{t-1} \cup \sigma\{\Delta N_j(t); \ j \in R(t-1)\}, \tag{A1}$$

represent the experimental history registered up to time $t$, $F_t$ including and $H_{t-1}$ excluding the responses $\Delta N_j(t)$ during $(t-1, t)$.

Consider a statistical model $(P^\theta, \theta \in \Theta)$ for the observation process $[R(s-1)$, $\{\Delta N_j(s), \mathbf{Z}_j(s-1); j \in R(s-1)\}]_{s \geq 1}$ and a $P^\theta$-likelihood that corresponds to data collected up to time $t$, $t \geq 1$.

Suppose that the parameter $\theta$ can be represented in the form $\theta = (\theta_1, \theta_2)$, where $\theta_1$ is the parameter of interest and $\theta_2$ is a nuisance parameter. Typically, we think of $\theta_1$ as parametrizing the conditional distribution of the variables $\Delta N_j(s)$, conditioned on $H_{s-1}$, and of $\theta_2$ as the parameter associated with the conditional law of the variables $R(s)$ and $\mathbf{Z}_j(s)$ ($j \in R(s)$), given $F_{s-1}$. It is then a simple consequence of the chain multiplication rule of conditional probabilities that the full likelihood corresponding to the observed values $[r(s-1), \{\Delta n_j(s), \mathbf{z}_j(s-1); j \in r(s-1) \mid F_{s-1}\}$ and $s \leq t]$ can be expressed as the product of two terms, viz.

$$\prod_{s \leq t} P\theta \{R(s-1) = r(s-1), \mathbf{Z}_j(s-1) = \mathbf{z}_j(s-1); \ j \in r(s-1) \mid F_{s-1}\}$$

$$\prod_{s \leq t} P\theta(\Delta N_j(s) = \Delta n_j(s); \ j \in r(s-1) \mid H_{s-1}). \tag{A2}$$

Following Cox (1975), the second factor can be called a partial likelihood. Ordinary ML estimation of $\theta_1$, the parameter of interest, can be done by considering that factor alone provided that the following condition holds:

*Assumption 1.* (i) For each $s \geq 1$, the conditional $P^\theta$-distribution of $[R(s-1)$, $\{\mathbf{Z}_j(s-1); j \in R(s-1)\}]$, given $F_{s-1}$, does not depend on $\theta_1$. (ii) For each $s \geq 1$, the conditional $P^\theta$-distribution of $\{\Delta N_j(s); j \in R(s-1)\}$, given $H_{s-1}$, does not depend on $\theta_2$.

Of course, the validity of Assumption 1 depends on the model $(P^\theta; \theta \in \Theta)$. Actual verification of this assumption would require that the model were fully specified, including the probability law of the censoring mechanism and possible random covariates. This is usually not done explicitly. However, part (ii) of Assumption 1 becomes obvious if the censoring times and the covariates are fixed, or random but $F_0$-measurable. More generally, we can consider part (ii) to be valid if the censoring is non-informative about $\theta_1$ and the covariates are external (cf. Kalbfleisch and Prentice 1980). For internal covariates more caution is needed: if (i) is not met, also the first factor in (A2) can depend on $\theta_1$, and then using only the second factor in the maximization is a potential source of bias. Finally, it seems that part (ii) of Assumption 1 can always be met in practice by making a convenient choice of $\theta_1$, the parameter of interest.

For a continuous-time version of Assumption 1, see Arjas and Haara (1984).

Our next assumption imposes an independence condition between the individuals and simplifies, in particular, the handling of ties.

*Assumption 2.* For each $s \geq 1$, and $\theta \in \Theta$, the random variables $\{\Delta N_j(s); j \geq 1\}$ are conditionally $P^\theta$-independent given $H_{s-1}$.

This assumption is likely to hold in practice if there are no multiple responses of common cause, or if such responses can occur but the background variable causing the failure can be included as a covariate.

Under Assumptions 1 and 2 the likelihood function (A2) depends on $\theta_1$ only through the factor

$$\prod_{s \leq t} \prod_{j \in r(s-1)} P^\theta \{\Delta N_j(s) = \Delta n_j(s) \mid H_{s-1}\}. \tag{A3}$$

On the other hand, because of Assumption 1 part (ii), this expression does not depend on $\theta_2$.

It remains to specify the conditional probabilities in (A3). Our next assumption guarantees that all relevant information in $H_{s-1}$, when used as a condition for the probability of $\{\Delta N_j(s) = \Delta N_j(s)\}$, is actually contained in the $p$-vector $\mathbf{Z}_j(s-1)$ and the indicator $Y_j(s-1)$.

*Assumption 3.* For all $s \geq 1$, $j \geq 1$ and $\theta \in \Theta$, $\Delta N_j(s)$ and $H_{s-1}$ are conditionally $P^\theta$ independent given $Y_j(s-1)$ and $\mathbf{Z}_j(s-1)$.

As a last step, the conditional probabilities in (A3) are specified in Formula (2). There we also change the notation slightly, writing $\beta = (\beta_1, \ldots, \beta_p)'$ instead of $\theta_1$ and Pr instead of $P^\theta$.

# References

Allison, P. D. (1982), 'Discrete Time-Methods for the Analysis of Event Histories', in S. Leinhardt (ed.), *Social Methodology 1982* (Jossey-Bass, San Francisco), 61–98.

Arjas, E. (1986), 'Stanford Heart Transplantation Data Revisited: A Real Time Approach', in S. H. Moolgavkar and R. L. Prentice (eds.), *Modern Statistical Methods in Chronic Disease Epidemiology* (John Wiley & Sons, New York), 65–81.

—— and Haara, P. (1984), 'A Marked Point Process Approach to Censored Failure Time Data with Complicated Covariates', *Scandinavian Journal of Statistics*, 11. 4: 193–209.

—— —— (1987), 'A Logistic Regression Model for Hazard', *Scandinavian Journal of Statistics*, 14. 1: 1–18.

Cox, D. R. (1975), 'Partial Likelihood', *Biometrika*, 62. 2: 269–76.

Hoem, B., and Hoem, J. (1987), *The Impact of Female Employment on Second and Third Births in Modern Sweden*, Stockholm Research Reports in Demography No. 36, Univ. of Stockholm.

Kalbfleisch, J. D., and Prentice, R. L. (1980), *The Statistical Analysis of Failure Time Data* (John Wiley & Sons, New York).

McGullagh, P., and Nelder, J. A. (1983), *Generalized Linear Models* (Chapman & Hall, London).

Morgan, S. P., Lye, D. N., and Condran, G. A. (1988), 'Sons, Daughters and the Risk of Marital Disruption', *American Journal of Sociology*, 94. 1: 110–29.

Rindfuss, R. R., Morgan, S. P., and Swicegood, C. G. (1984), 'The Transition to Motherhood: The Intersection of Structural and Temporal Dimensions', *American Sociological Review*, 49. 3: 359–72.

Sandefur, G. D., and Tuma, N. B. (1987), 'How Data Type Affects Conclusions about Individual Mobility', *Social Science Research*, 16. 4: 301–28.

# INDEX OF NAMES

# INDEX OF SUBJECTS